MERIDIAN

Crossing Aesthetics

Werner Hamacher

& David E. Wellbery

Editors

Edited and Translated
With an Introduction
By Daniel Heller-Roazen

Stanford
University
Press

_____

Stanford
California

POTENTIALITIES

Collected Essays in Philosophy

Giorgio Agamben

Stanford University Press

Stanford, California

© 1999 by the Board of Trustees of the

Leland Stanford Junior University

Printed in the United States of America

CIP data appear at the end of the book

Contents

Editor's Note

English passages cited from French, German, Greek, Italian, or Latin editions identified in the text or notes are my own translations. Passages cited from published English translations identified in the notes are the work of those translators unless otherwise indicated. I have on occasion silently modified the quotations from these published translations.

"The Thing Itself" was published in *Di-segno: La giustizia nel discorso* (Milan: Jaca, 1984), ed. Gianfranco Dalmasso, pp. 1–12. "The Idea of Language" appeared in *aut-aut* 201 (1984), pp. 67–74. "Language and History: Linguistic Categories and Historical Categories in Benjamin's Thought" was first published in *Walter Benjamin: Tempo storia linguaggio*, ed. Lucio Belloi and Lorenzina Lotti (Roma: Riuniti, 1983), pp. 65–82. "Philosophy and Linguistics" appeared in *Annuaire philosophique* (Paris: Seuil, 1990), pp. 97–116. "Kommerell, or On Gesture" was written as an introduction to Max Kommerell, *Il poeta e l'indicibile: Saggi di letteratura tedesca*, ed. Giorgio Agamben and trans. Gino Giometti (Genova: Marietti, 1991), pp. vii–xv. "Aby Warburg and the Nameless Science" first appeared in *Prospettive Settanta*, July–September 1975, pp. 3–18; it was reprinted, with the "Postilla" published here, in *aut-aut* 199–200 (1984), pp. 51–66. "Tradition of the Immemorial" first appeared in *Il centauro* 13–14 (1985), pp. 3–12. "*Se*: Hegel's Absolute and Heidegger's *Ereignis*" was published in *aut-aut* 187–88 (1982), pp. 39–58. "Walter Benjamin and the Demonic: Happiness and Historical Redemption" was first published in *aut-aut* 189–90 (1982), pp. 143–163. "The Messiah and the Sovereign: The Problem of Law in Walter Benjamin" was given as a lecture at the Hebrew University of Jerusalem, in July 1992 and was published in

Anima e paura: Studi in onore di Michele Ranchetti (Macerata: Quodlibet, 1998), pp. 11–22. "On Potentiality" was held as a lecture in Lisbon, 1986, in the context of conference organized by the Collège international de philosophie; it appears in this volume for the first time. "The Passion of Facticity" was published in *Heidegger: Questions ouvertes, Cahiers du CIPH* (Paris: Osiris, 1988), pp. 63–84. "*Pardes*: The Writing of Potentiality" appeared in *Revue philosophique* 2 (1990), pp. 131–45. "Absolute Immanence" was published in *aut-aut* 276 (1996), pp. 39–57. "Bartleby, or On Contingency" first appeared in Giorgio Agamben and Gilles Deleuze, *Bartleby: La formula della creazione* (Macerata: Quodlibet, 1993), pp. 47–92.

D. H.-R.

POTENTIALITIES

Editor's Introduction

"To Read What Was Never Written"

Among the notes and sketches for Walter Benjamin's last work, the "Theses on the Philosophy of History," we find the following statement: "Historical method is philological method, a method that has as its foundation the book of life. 'To read what was never written,' is what Hofmannsthal calls it. The reader referred to here is the true historian."[1] Giorgio Agamben is perhaps the only contemporary thinker to have assumed as a philosophical problem the task that Benjamin, in these words, sets for historical and philological "method." What does it mean to confront history as a reader, "to read what was never written"? And what is it that "was never written" in the "book of life"? The question concerns the event that Benjamin throughout his works calls "redemption." The essays collected in this volume can be said to elaborate a philosophy of language and history adequate to the concept of this event. A single matter, truly something like the "thing itself" of which Agamben writes in his essay on Plato's Seventh Letter, animates the works gathered together here. Whether the subject is Aristotle or Spinoza, Heidegger or Benjamin, what is at issue is always a messianic moment of thinking, in which the practice of the "historian" and the practice of the "philologist," the experience of tradition and the experience of language, cannot be told apart. It is in this moment that the past is saved, not in being returned to what once existed but, instead, precisely in being transformed into something that never was: in being read, in the words of Hofmannsthal, as what was never written.

But what is it that, in the course of history, never was? What is it that, in the text of tradition, remains in some way present yet forever unwritten? Agamben's essay "Tradition of the Immemorial" (Chapter 7 in this volume) helps address the question. "Every reflection on tradition," we read at the beginning of that essay, "must begin with the assertion that before transmitting anything else, human beings must first of all transmit language to themselves. Every specific tradition, every determinate cultural patrimony, presupposes the transmission of that alone through which something like a tradition is possible." The statement concerns linguistic signification and historical transmission alike, since the presupposition at issue is common to both. The fact of the transmission of language or, more simply, *that there is language*, is what every communication must have always presupposed, for without it there would be neither transmission nor signification; and it is this fact, Agamben argues, that cannot be communicated in the form of a particular statement or series of statements. Actual utterances, after all, are possible only where speech has already begun, and the very affirmation of the existence of language— "there is language"—only renders explicit what is, in effect, implied by the fact of its own utterance.

That language must already have taken place for linguistic acts to be performed is not a fact without relation to forms of actual communication. The presuppositional structure of language is clearly registered first of all in the classical form of linguistic signification, the predicative assertion. According to Aristotle's canonical definition of the statement as a "saying something about something" (*legein ti kata tinos*),[2] what is said in the proposition is necessarily divided into a first "something" and a second "something," and the proposition appears as a meaningful statement only on condition that the first "something," the subject, already be given. The distinction between the predicate and its subject thus has the form of a presupposition, and it is precisely this presupposition that renders predication possible. Were a thing not already manifest in language, it could not be qualified in any way through the form of attribution; were the identity of a first "something" not presupposed in the form of an absolutely simple and indefinable subject, or *hypokeimenon*, the predication of a second "something" (*legein kat' hypokeimenou*) could not be accomplished. "To speak of a being," Agamben thus writes in "Tradition of the Immemorial," "human language supposes and distances what it brings to light, in the very act in which it brings it to light."

The necessary logical division of the proposition into a presupposed subject and an attributed predicate has its correlate, in the field of linguistic elements, in the traditional philosophical distinction between name and discourse. All discourse (*logos*), according to a doctrine that Agamben finds expressed as early as Antisthenes, necessarily presupposes the existence of names (*onomata*), which, precisely because they found the possibility of all articulated speech, can themselves have no definition. Varro, in his *De lingua latina*, places a thesis of this kind at the foundation of his study of language when, following the linguists of the Stoa, he distinguishes a moment of pure naming (*impositio, quemadmodum vocabula rebus essent imposita*) from that of actual discourse;[3] and Jean-Claude Milner, who writes in his *Introduction à une science du langage* that "linguistic entities are of two kinds," "terms" and syntactical "positions," can be said to reinstate the Sophist's distinction at the heart of contemporary linguistics.[4] In each case, Agamben argues, the name appears as the cipher of the event of language that must always already be presupposed in actual signification. "*Discourse,*" we read in "Tradition of the Immemorial," "*cannot say what is named by the name. . . .* Names certainly enter into propositions, but what is said in propositions can be said only thanks to the presupposition of names." It is this fundamental difference between names and discourse that appears in Wittgenstein's determination of names as "simple signs" (*Urzeichen*)[5] and, most clearly, in his position of a radical disjunction between naming and assertion: "I can only *name* objects," we read in the *Tractatus*.[6] "Signs represent them. I can only speak *of* them. I cannot *assert* them. A proposition can only say *how* a thing is, not *what* it is."[7]

Strictly speaking, however, it is not only the subject of the judgment and the name that have the peculiar characteristic of constituting logical and linguistic elements that are, in some sense, unsayable in language. *Any* linguistic term, insofar as it expresses an object, cannot itself be expressed. This is the principle that Agamben, referring to an episode in *Through the Looking-Glass*[8] in his essay on Derrida ("Pardes," Chapter 13 in this volume), calls "the White Knight's theorem" and expresses in the following Carrollian formula: "The name of the name is not a name." Agamben explains the theorem by means of the medieval distinction between an *intentio prima*, a sign signifying an object, and an *intentio secunda*, a sign signifying an *intentio prima*, another sign. The crux of the matter lies in how one understands the nature of an *intentio secunda*: "What does it mean," Agamben asks, "to signify a sign, to intend an *intentio*?" The difficulty here is that whenever one sign signifies another sign, it signifies the second sign not as a mere signifier, an *intentio*, but only as a signified, an *intentum*. It is thus possible for one word to refer to another word, but only insofar as the second word is referred to as an object, an acoustically or graphically determined entity (the *suppositio materialis* of medieval logic); the word insofar as it is a *nomen nominans*, and not a *nomen nominatum*, necessarily escapes the possibility of nomination. Agamben notes in "*Pardes*" that the "logicians' expedients to avoid the consequences of this radical anonymity of the name are destined to fail," as in the case of Rudolf Carnap's project to resolve the paradox by means of quotation marks, which K. Reach proved to be unsuccessful.[9] In natural language, at least, it is simply not possible for one linguistic term to signify another without the second as a result losing its character of being a linguistic term and appearing as a mere object.

It is this impossibility that Agamben, in "Pardes," finds clearly formulated in Frege's statement that "the concept 'horse' is not a concept,"[10] in Wittgenstein's thesis that "*we* cannot express through language what expresses *itself* in language,"[11] and in Milner's axiom that "the linguistic term has no proper name."[12] Perhaps closest to Agamben is Heidegger's discussion in *On the Way to Language* of "the word for the word" (*das Wort für das Wort*), which "is to be found nowhere."[13] What is essential, for Agamben, is that the "anonymity" of language at stake in each case acquires its full sense only when referred to the presuppositional structure of language. The linguistic element cannot be said as such, Agamben explains, for the simple reason that what is at issue in it—the making manifest of something in language—is always presupposed in everything said; the intention to signify always exceeds the possibility of itself being signified precisely because it always already anticipates and renders possible signification in general. Only because they always presuppose the fact that there is language are statements necessarily incapable of saying the event of language, of naming the word's power to name; only because language, as actual discourse, always presupposes itself as having taken place can language not say itself. Preceding and exceeding every proposition is not something unsayable and ineffable but, rather, an event presupposed in every utterance, a *factum linguae* to which all actual speech incessantly, necessarily bears witness.

In his one French aphorism, Paul Celan remarks: "Poetry no longer imposes itself; it exposes itself" (*La poésie ne s'impose plus, elle s'expose*).[14] It could be said that Agamben attempts to accomplish in philosophy a movement close to the one Celan, in these words, ascribes to poetry: to conceive of the event of language in the form not of its presupposition but of its *exposition*. "Exposed," the taking place of language no longer appears as an event accomplished *in ille tempore*, once and for all, before the commencement of actual speech acts. It emerges, rather, as a dimension immanent in every utterance. Here Agamben, having followed the presuppositional structure of language to its limit, displaces the question into an altogether novel region, in which what is most philosophically radical in his thought comes fully to light: *the problem of the mode of existence of language*. The aporia, or, literally, "lack of way," inherent in any attempt to grasp the essence of language is thus resolved, as Agamben writes in "*Pardes*," into a *euporia*, a felicitous way, and a new question is posed: in what sense does language exist in all actual transmission, and in what sense does all transmission communicate the fact that there is language? It is at this point that Agamben's work fully inherits the task set by Benjamin when he called for thought to experience an "involuntary memory" of something "never seen before,"[15] and thereby to "read" in all transmission "what was never written."

II

The ways in which figures in the history of philosophy consider the problem of the existence of language remain, to a large extent, to be investigated. Agamben's essay "The Thing Itself," which opens this collection, suggests that a point of departure can be found in Plato's Seventh Letter. Here Agamben considers the philosophical excursus at the center of the Platonic epistle, in which the philosopher recounts how he attempted to show Dionysius, the tyrant of Syracuse, the essence of philosophy and the "whole thing" (*pan to pragma*) with which it is concerned. Plato writes to the friends and family of his follower Dion:

> This, then, was what I said to Dionysius on that occasion. I did not, however, expound the matter fully, nor did Dionysius ask me to do so. . . . There does not exist, nor will there ever exist, any treatise of mine dealing with this thing. For it does not at all admit of verbal expression like other disciplines [*mathēmata*], but, after having dwelt for a long time close to the thing itself

[*peri to pragma auto*] and in communion with it, it is suddenly brought to birth in the soul, as light that is kindled by a leaping spark; and then it nourishes itself.[16]

In the passage that he describes as a "story and wandering" (*mythos kai planos*),[17] Plato repeats the "true argument" (*logos alēthes*) that he has "frequently stated . . . in the past." "Each being," he explains, "has three things which are the necessary means by which knowledge of that being is acquired; the knowledge itself is a fourth thing; and as a fifth one must posit the thing itself, which is knowable and truly is. First of these comes the name [*onoma*]; second, the definition [*logos*]; third, the image [*eidōlon*]; fourth, the knowledge [*epistēmē*]."[18] In Plato's example of the circle, the name is thus the word "circle"; the definition, "that which is everywhere equidistant from the extremities to the center"; the image, the drawn circle; and the knowledge, the intellection or opinion of the circle. It is evident that the fourth term listed by Plato, *epistēmē*, can be located without too much difficulty in a modern conception of knowledge. Agamben, moreover, notes that the first three terms have precise equivalents in contemporary doctrines of linguistic signification: the Platonic "name" corresponds to what Saussurian linguistics calls the signifier; "definition," to signified or virtual reference (what Frege termed *Sinn*); and "image," to designation or actual reference (Fregean *Bedeutung*). Like the Ideas, which Socrates found upon "seek[ing] refuge in the *logoi*,"[19] the "thing itself" is thus first of all situated with respect to language and the knowledge it allows. Plato even warns that if the soul does not seize hold of the first four terms by which a thing is known in language, it "will never be able to participate perfectly in knowledge of the fifth."[20]

The "thing itself," Agamben writes in the opening essay of this volume, "therefore has its essential place in language, even if language is certainly not adequate to it, on account, Plato says, of what is weak in it. One could say, with an apparent paradox, that the thing itself, while in some way transcending language, is nevertheless possible only in language and by virtue of language: precisely the thing of language." In this light, Agamben rereads the passage in which Plato defines the final term of knowledge: "Each being has three things which are the necessary means by which knowledge of that being is acquired; the knowledge itself is a fourth thing; and as a fifth one must posit the thing itself, which is knowable and truly is." Here the Platonic text seems to suggest that the fifth term is to be referred to the object of the first four, such that the "thing itself" appears (in accordance with a common conception of the Platonic Idea) as a mere duplicate of the thing, indistinguishable from the being with which the excursus begins in stating that "each being has three things which are the necessary means by which knowledge of that being is acquired." Such a reading is certainly sanctioned by the Greek text reproduced in modern editions; yet Agamben notes that this text differs in one crucial instance from the manuscripts on which it is based. Where John Burnet's and Joseph Souilhé's versions print *pempton d'auto tithenai dei ho dē gnōston te kai alēthes estin,* "and as a fifth one must posit the thing itself, which is knowable and truly is," the two original sources instead read *pempton d'auto tithenai di'ho dē gnōston te kai alēthes estin,* "[one must] posit the fifth, by which [each being] is knowable and truly is."[21] With a correction that concerns only a few letters, Agamben thus restores the Platonic phrase to its earlier form, and the "thing itself" emerges not as an obscure object presupposed for knowledge but, rather, as the very medium "through which" beings are known in language.

The philological adjustment proposed by Agamben, however, does not dismiss as simply erroneous the form in which Plato's text is commonly reproduced. In a sense, the twelfth-century scribe who, in a marginal annotation, emended the phrase at issue (suggesting *dei ho* instead of *di'ho*) was perfectly justified. He was "most likely concerned," Agamben writes in "The Thing Itself," "with the risk that knowability itself—the Idea— would be, in turn, presupposed and substantialized as *another thing,* as a duplicate of the thing before or beyond the thing." Hence his correction, which has the force of referring the "thing itself" back to the same thing in question in knowledge and language. That "through which" knowledge of beings is possible, after all, is not itself a particular being; yet neither is it simply identical to the beings whose apprehension it renders possible. "The thing itself," Agamben makes clear, "is not a thing; it is the very sayability, the very openness at issue in language, which, in language, we always presuppose and forget, perhaps because it is at bottom its own oblivion and abandonment." It is the Idea in the sense in which Agamben defines it in *The Coming Community* when he writes that "the Idea of a thing is the thing *itself*," that in which a thing "exhibits its pure dwelling in language":[22] the being-manifest of a thing in language, which, "neither presupposed nor presupposable" (*anypothetos*),[23] exists as the "thing itself" in everything that can be uttered and known.

Despite its centrality in Plato's philosophy, the "thing itself" soon dis-

appears from classical Greek accounts of the structure of linguistic signification. Agamben notes that in the Aristotelian treatise on the nature of
the proposition, precise correlates can be found to the first four terms of
which Plato writes in the Seventh Letter. At the beginning of *De interpretatione*, we read:

> What is in the voice [*ta en tēi phōnēi*] is the sign of affections in the soul [*en
> tēi psychēi*]; what is written [*ta graphomena*] is the sign of what is in the voice.
> And just as letters are not the same for all men, so it is with voices. But that of
> which they are signs, that is, affections in the soul, are the same for all; and
> the things [*pragmata*] of which the affections are semblances [*homoiōmata*]
> are also the same for all men.[24]

Aristotle's tripartite division between "what is in the voice," "affections in
the soul," and "things" corresponds to the threefold Platonic distinction
between name and definition, which are "in voices" (*en phōnais*); knowledge and opinion, which are "in souls" (*en psychais*); and the sensible object (*en sōmatōn skhēmasin*).[25] Yet nothing remains in this account of the
Platonic "thing itself." "In Aristotle," Agamben observes, "the thing itself
is expelled from *hermēneia*, the linguistic process of signification." In its
place *De interpretatione* introduces "what is written" (*ta graphomena*) and
its constitutive element, the letter (*gramma*).

The significance of Aristotle's substitution of writing for the "thing itself" cannot be overestimated, both for the philosophical economy of *De
interpretatione* and for the history of the theory of language. In Aristotle's
treatise, Agamben writes in "The Thing Itself," the letter constitutes the
"final interpreter, beyond which no *hermēneia* is possible: the limit of all
interpretation." The Aristotelian text refers the voice to the affections of
the soul, which are in turn referred to things; yet the final intelligibility
of the voice itself is assured by the letter. This much is also indicated by
the very beginning of the passage in question, which takes as its subject
not the mere voice but rather "what is *in* the voice" (*ta en tēi phōnēi*).
Agamben notes that according to a tradition of interpretation that originates in ancient grammatical commentaries on *De interpretatione*, what
is said to be "in" the voice is nothing other than the voice's capacity to be
written and, therefore, "articulated." In the terms of Augustine's *De dialectica*, which are also those of the Stoic analysis of language, the Aristotelian treatise can be said to begin not with the voice as such but rather
with "the smallest part of the voice that is articulated" (*pars minima vocis*

articolatae; *hē phōnē enarthos amerēs*), with the "voice insofar as it can be comprehended by letters" (*quae comprendi litteris potest*).[26] Despite appearances, Agamben observes, the "letter" thus does not merely occupy the status of a sign, alongside "voices" and the "affections in the soul"; rather, it constitutes the very "element of the voice" (*stoikheion tēs phōnēs*), without which vocal sounds would not be intelligible.[27] In Aristotle, the "letter" is what every "signifying sound" always already implies; it is the cipher that there has been "writing" in the soul and that language has already taken place.

It is in this sense that the "letter," in *De interpretatione*, truly replaces what Plato's Seventh Letter had called the "thing itself." In its own way, each concept denotes the fact that things are manifest and can be known in language, and that language therefore exists. It is here, however, that the Aristotelian *gramma* must be distinguished from the Platonic *to pragma auto*. Plato's "thing itself" denotes that part of a thing that renders it "knowable" (*gnōston*) in language; and in doing so, the "thing itself" conversely indicates the existence of language insofar as language is present in anything known. Plato's "thing itself," in short, is a term for the point at which language, in exposing itself as such, shows itself fully in everything that can be known. In Aristotle's *De interpretatione*, by contrast, the "letter" bears witness to the event of language by indicating it as already having taken place; the writing in the voice with which the Aristotelian treatise begins marks the event of language as an original "articulation" always presupposed in speech. "The *gramma*," Agamben writes in "The Thing Itself," "is thus the form of presupposition itself and nothing else." In this way, the Aristotelian account of language eliminates the "thing itself" and, along with it, the Platonic attempt to conceive of the integral exposition of language. In its place, Aristotle sets forth his doctrine of the "letter," in which writing takes the form of the original and insuperable presupposition of all signification.

III

It is only with the logic and linguistic theory of the Stoa that a being close to the Platonic "thing itself" is placed at the center of the Western reflection on language. The Stoics gave the name "expressible" (*lekton*) to a linguistic entity that they distinguished from both the sign or signifier (*sēmeion*) and its actual referent (*tygkhanon*). The "expressible," Émile

Bréhier tells us in his reconstruction of the Stoic doctrine of the incorporeal, "was something so novel that an interpreter of Aristotle such as Ammonius has the greatest difficulty in situating it with respect to peripatetic
classifications."[28] The Aristotelian theory of signification, as we have seen,
conceives of words as signifying thoughts (*noēmata*) and thoughts as signifying things (*pragmata*). But the Stoics, Ammonius reports with some
perplexity, "propose another term, an intermediary between thought and
the thing, which they call *lekton*, the expressible."[29] It is in the form of
this "intermediary" being that the Platonic "thing itself" survives in the
history of Western logic and philosophy of language.

For the philosophers of the Stoa, the "expressible" differs from both
the signifier and its objective referent in that while the latter two constitute actual bodies, the *lekton* does not. Instead, it has the status of an "incorporeal" (*asōmaton*);[30] it is not a real determination of a body, but simply expresses the modification undergone by a body in being transformed
into the matter of a statement. In a letter that constitutes a *locus classicus*
for medieval Stoicism, Seneca clearly explains the status of the incorporeal *lekton*.[31] "What I see and understand with my eyes and soul is
a body," he writes to Lucillus. "But when I say, 'Cato walks,' I affirm that
what I say is not a body; rather it is an *enuntiativum* said of a body,
which some call *effatum*, some *enuntiatum*, and others *dictum*."[32] The expressible is thus not a thing but rather a thing insofar as it has entered
into speech and thought: as Sextus Empiricus writes, summarizing the
Stoic doctrine in terms strikingly reminiscent of the Platonic "thing itself," the expressible (in this case the term is *sēmainomenon*)[33] is "the
thing itself indicated or revealed by sound, which we apprehend as subsisting together with our thought" (*de to auto to pragma to hyp' autēs
dēloumenon kai hou hēmeis men antilambanometha tēi hemeterai paryphis-
tamenou dianoiai*).[34] In the expressible, the "thing itself" thus appears as
nothing other than the thing insofar as it can be uttered and, in this way,
understood.[35]

But what does it mean for a thing to be "expressible," for a thing to exist in the mode of something that can be said? Almost fifteen centuries
after the beginnings of the Stoa, the question of the mode of Being of
what exists in language alone was again placed at the center of the reflection on language and signification. Twelfth-century logicians identify a
specific entity in every utterance, an entity that, in accordance with the
Latin translations of the Greek term *lekton*,[36] they call *dictum*, *dicibile*, or

enuntiabile, "the sayable."[37] As in the philosophy of the ancient Stoa, the attribute denoted by the "sayable" of the early terminists in no way concerns a real determination of the matters referred to in speech. The anonymous authors of the *Ars Burana*, composed around 1200,[38] are so conscious of the incorporeal status of the "sayable" that they define the *enuntiabile* in insisting that, though it is said of things and is therefore a category, it is nevertheless irreducible to the different categories of Being distinguished by Aristotle. Far from being a "category" through which a real state of Being can be determined, they write, the *enuntiabile* paradoxically constitutes a category that is not truly a category, a specific category to which they give the term "extracategory" (*extrapredicamentale*). In the third part of the *Ars*, under the heading "The Sayable" (*De dicto sive enuntiabile*), we read:

> If you ask what kind of thing it is, whether it is a substance or an accident, it must be said that the sayable [*enuntiabile*], like the predicable, is neither substance nor accident nor any kind of other category. For it has its own mode of existence [*Suum enim habet modum per se existendi*]. And it is said to be *extracategorial* [*extrapredicamentale*], not, of course, in that it is not of any category, but in that it is not of any of the ten categories identified by Aristotle. Such is the case with this category, which can be called *the category of the sayable* [*predicamentum enuntiabile*].[39]

Rarely in the history of philosophy has the specific quality of "being said" been identified with such clarity. The mode of Being that the *Ars Burana* grasps as "the category of the sayable," however, is never entirely absent from the theory of the proposition and its signification. Historians of philosophy have noted its presence in Peter Abelard's logic in the concept of *dictum propositionis*.[40] In later medieval philosophy, the "extracategorial" being of the twelfth-century philosophers is most fully considered in the "thing" (*ens, res, aliquid*) that Gregory of Rimini, a little more than a century after the *Ars Burana*, called *complexe significabile*: the total signification of a sentence, insofar as it is as such irreducible either to the linguistic terms in the sentence or to any actual objects to which they refer.[41]

In modern philosophy, it is such an entity that Alexius von Meinong attempts to conceive in his theory of the contents of ideas, to which he gives the name of "objectives." Meinong defines a being as "objective" insofar as it is merely intended in a mental representation; and he argues that the existence of such a being is implied by the form of any thought as such. "Whether I have a representation [*Vorstellung*] of a church steeple or a mountain peak, a feeling or a desire, a relation of diversity or causality or any other thing whatsoever," Meinong writes,

> I am in each case having a representation. . . . On the other hand, representations, insofar as they are ideas of distinct objects, cannot be altogether alike; however we may conceive the relation of the idea to its object, diversity of object must in some way go back to diversity of representation. That element, therefore, in which representations of different objects differ, in spite of their agreement in the act, may be properly called the content of the representation.[42]

Thought contents, or "objectives," thus appear as "objects of a higher order," independent of existing objects, yet built upon them (for example, an "objective" is such a thing as "that the circus manager is sitting down," or "that Sven is the tallest trapeze artist," or "that your act is trickier than mine"). Although not constituting real entities, such contents of representation, Meinong tells us, are still not nothing; while relations, numbers, and matters of fact, for instance, cannot in Meinong's terms be said "to exist" (*existieren*), they can nevertheless be said to "subsist" (*bestehen*). Hence the Austrian philosopher's apparently paradoxical thesis, which Russell sought to refute,[43] according to which "there are objects concerning which it is the case that there are no such objects" (*es gibt Gegenstände, von denen es gilt, daß es dergleichen Gegenstände nicht gibt*).[44] According to Meinong, "objectives" thus exist only insofar as they are implied in speech and thought, as mere *intentionalia* and *entia rationis*, in a mode of Being to which he gives the name *Außersein*, "extra-Being."

Like the *lekton* of the Stoics and the *enuntiabile* of the medievals, Meinong's subsisting "objectives" simply denote the "thing itself" that is always in question in speech: the fact that something appears in language and that language itself, in this appearance, takes place. Both the "sayable category" and the "objective" are concepts that intend the existence of language; they are each attempts to conceive of the sense of the specific Being at issue in the fact "that language *is*." In this sense, the philosophical registration of the "thing itself" necessarily leads to a further question. Once the existence of language is identified as what is at issue in all speech and knowledge, how can one conceive of the precise way in which it exists? The hesitation with which the forms of the "expressible" are positively characterized in the history of philosophy bears witness to the difficulty of the question. Having identified Being with bodies, the Stoics were forced to withdraw all ontological consistency from the incorporeal *lekton*. In the same way, the logicians of the *Ars Burana* define the *enuntiabile* as a category literally "outside" the categories of Being (*predicamentum extrapredicamentale*); and, with a perfectly analogous gesture, Meinong assigns his "objectives" to the ontologically indifferent state of what is literally "outside Being" (*außer Sein*). When Deleuze defines the event, with reference to the doctrine of the expressible, as "*aliquid*, at once extra-Being [or outside-Being: *extra-être*] and insistence, that minimum of Being that is characteristic of insistences,"[45] he simply repeats the original Stoic subtraction of the incorporeal from the field of Being. The sense of the difference between Being and the expressible, to be sure, is clear: the "thing itself" is not an extant thing, and the *lekton* refers not to a particular being but to the event of language itself. If the sayable, however, is not to appear as something simply ineffable and thus be transformed anew into an unthinkable presupposition of language, the question must be posed: how is it possible to conceive the mode of existence of the "thing itself," to consider the nature of the event of language? How is the fact that there is language, in other words, not to appear as the Stoic incorporeal appeared to Proclus, "a thing without consistency and on the edge of non-Being" (*amenēnon kai eggista tou mē ontos*)?[46]

Agamben's treatment of the question can be said to follow from what is inscribed in the grammatical form of the terms that, throughout the history of philosophy, denote the "thing itself" at issue in language. *Lekton, dicibile, enuntiabile, significabile* are all verbal adjectives; they all, in other words, express a capacity. But what does it mean for language to exist as *capable* of expression, as express*ible*, or, to use the term with which Benjamin reformulates the concept of the Stoic *lekton*, as communic*able* (*mitteil*bar)?[47] In every case, the "thing itself" exists in the mode of possibility, and the problem of the existence of language necessarily leads to the problem of the existence of potentiality. Agamben's recent work takes precisely this implication as its point of departure in formulating its most original philosophical project: *to conceive of the existence of language as the existence of potentiality*. If language, however, exists in the form in which potentiality exists, then the reflection on language must first of all be a reflection on the mode of existence of potentiality; if linguistic Being is, as Agamben argues, simply potential Being, then the study of the nature of language must take the form of a study of what it means "to be capable."

That there is language—in the form of linguistic signification and the transmission of tradition alike—simply indicates the fact that there exists such a thing as potentiality. It is in this sense that the first two parts of this book, "Language" and "History," lead to the final ones, "Potentiality" and "Contingency"; and it is in this context that Agamben's writings on *dynamis* and *potentia* acquire their true sense.

IV

The concept of potentiality has become so familiar to us that we must often struggle to comprehend the difficulties Aristotle encountered when, in his metaphysics and physics, he first created the concept and distinguished it from actuality. Any attempt to examine the status of potentiality must confront a specific aporia: the fact that, by definition, a potentiality is a possibility that exists. Unlike mere possibilities, which can be considered from a purely logical standpoint, potentialities or capacities present themselves above all as things that exist but that, at the same time, do not exist as actual things; they are present, yet they do not appear in the form of present things. What is at issue in the concept of potentiality is nothing less than a mode of existence that is irreducible to actuality. As such, potentiality and the nature of its presence become problems of the greatest importance in developing a coherent metaphysics and articulating the many ways in which "Being is said." But the existence of such a thing as potentiality is also necessarily at issue in every consideration of "faculties," "capacities," and even the sense of the simple expression "to be able." In "On Potentiality" (Chapter 11 in this volume), Agamben thus begins his study of the problem of potentiality with a purely lexical question: "Following Wittgenstein's suggestion, according to which philosophical problems become clearer if they are formulated as questions concerning the meaning of words, I could state the subject of my work as an attempt to understand the meaning of the verb 'can' [*potere*]. What do I mean when I say: 'I can, I cannot'?"

Every reference to a "capacity" implies a reference to something that exists in the state of potentiality. Aristotle's treatment of the nature of the soul's faculty of sensation in *De anima* is exemplary here:

> There is an aporia as to why there is no sensation of the senses themselves. Why is it that, in the absence of external objects, the senses do not give any sensation, although they contain fire, earth, water, and the other elements of

which there is sensation? This happens because sensibility [the faculty of sensation: *to aisthētikon*] is not actual but only potential [*ouk estin en energeiai, alla dynamei monon*]. This is why it does not give sensation, just as the combustible does not burn by itself, without a principle of combustion; otherwise it would burn itself and would not need any actual fire [*tou entelekheia pyros ontos*].[48]

Aristotle's argument concerning the faculty of sensation is all the more striking if one considers that, as Agamben notes in "On Potentiality," the word by which Aristotle denotes "sensation," *aisthēsis*, belongs to a class of Greek words (ending in -*sis*) signifying activity. In Aristotle, "sensation" distinguishes itself as a faculty of the soul precisely in that it does not itself give sensation. Were sensation actual and not "only potential," sensation would immediately sense itself, and the soul could in no way be said to be capable of sensation. Aristotle's "sensation" is in a certain sense closer, Agamben therefore writes, to a "lack of sensation," an *anaisthēsis*, than to any *aisthēsis* in the traditional sense. What is at issue in the soul's faculty is necessarily something that, in a real sense, does not exist; and for the soul to have a faculty can consequently only be for the soul to have something that is actually lacking, "to have," as Agamben writes, "a privation."

The existence of this non-Being constitutes the true subject of Aristotle's analysis of potentiality. In the *Physics* (193 b 19–20) we read that "privation [*sterēsis*] is like a face, a form [*eidos*]," and in his treatment of the problem of potentiality in *Metaphysics*, Book Theta, Aristotle undertakes to conceive of the mode of existence of potentiality precisely in order to assure the consistency of this "form" or "face." In what way, Aristotle asks, can something that is not actual exist and, in existing, even condition and render possible what is actual? Here Aristotle's argument is directed against the Megarians, who hold that potentiality exists only in act and in this way abolish the autonomous existence of what is potential. According to the Megarians, the kithara player, for example, can be said to be capable of his art only in the moment in which he actually plays his kithara (*energei monon dynasthai*); at all other times he cannot in any way be said to possess the potential to set his art and his craft, his *tekhnē*, into effect. It is clear that the Megarians simply eliminate the autonomous existence of such a thing as potentiality, for if potentiality exists only in act, it cannot be distinguished from actuality. But how is potentiality then to exist, if not as a form of actuality?

The answer Aristotle gives to this question in *Metaphysics*, Book Theta, is subtle. "All potentiality," he argues, "is impotentiality of the same [potentiality] and with respect to the same [potentiality]" (*tou autou kai kata to auto pasa dynamis adynamiai*) (1046 a 32). And a little later, we read: "what is potential can both be and not be, for the same is potential both to be and not to be" (*to ara dynaton einai endekhetai kai einai kai mē einai*) (1050 b 10). As presented by Aristotle, the notion of potentiality thus constitutively requires that every potential to be (or do) be "at the same time" a potential not to be (or do), and that every potentiality (*dynamis*) therefore be an impotentiality (*adynamia*). After all, if potentiality were always only potential to be (or do), everything potential would always already have been actualized; all potentiality would always already have passed over into actuality, and potentiality would never exist as such. "The 'potential not to,'" Agamben thus writes in "Bartleby, or On Contingency" (Chapter 15 in this volume), "is the cardinal secret of the Aristotelian doctrine of potentiality, which transforms every potentiality in itself into an impotentiality." Something can be capable of something else only because it is originally capable of its own incapacity, and it is precisely the relation to an incapacity that, according to Agamben, constitutes the essence of all potentiality: "in its originary structure," he states in "On Potentiality," "*dynamis*, potentiality, maintains itself in relation to its own privation, its own *sterēsis*, its own non-Being. . . . To be potential means: to be one's own lack, *to be in relation to one's own incapacity*."

If all potentiality, however, is originally impotentiality, if to be capable is first of all to be capable of an incapacity, then how is it possible to conceive of the passage from potentiality to actuality? Agamben's analysis of the problem of potentiality leads to a reconsideration of the relation between actuality and potentiality and, ultimately, to a point at which the two cannot rigorously be distinguished. Here Agamben takes as his point of departure what is perhaps Aristotle's most enigmatic definition of potentiality: "A thing is said to be potential if, when the act of which it is said to be potential is realized, there will be nothing impotential" (*Metaphysics*, 1047 a 24–26). "Usually," Agamben comments, "this sentence is interpreted as if Aristotle had wanted to say, 'What is possible (or potential) is that with respect to which nothing is impossible (or impotential). If there is no impossibility, then there is possibility.' Aristotle would then have uttered a banality or a tautology." But another reading is possible. If the "impotentiality" (*adynamia*) of which Aristotle speaks in this passage is referred to the impotentiality that, as we have seen, necessarily belongs to all potentiality, the sense of Aristotle's affirmation changes greatly. Agamben writes, "What Aristotle then says is: 'if a potential to not-be originally belongs to all potentiality, then there is truly potentiality only where the potential to not-be does not lag behind actuality but passes fully into it *as such*.'" The potential not to be (or do), Agamben suggests, is not effaced in the passage into actuality; on the contrary, actuality is itself nothing other than the full realization of the potential not to be (or do), the point at which, as Aristotle writes, "there will be nothing impotential" (*ouden estai adynaton*).

Far from stating that "what is potential is what is not impotential," Aristotle's definition of potentiality therefore concerns the precise condition in which potentiality realizes itself. Agamben's *Homo Sacer: Sovereign Power and Bare Life*, which treats the problem of constituting and constituted power with reference to Aristotle's doctrine of potentiality, offers a further clarification of the matter. "What is potential can pass over into actuality only at the point at which it sets aside its own potential not to be (its *adynamia*)," Agamben writes, discussing the Aristotelian definition of potentiality. "To set im-potentiality aside," he continues, "is not to destroy it but, on the contrary, to fulfill it, to turn potentiality back upon itself in order to give itself to itself."[49] In this light, the passage to actuality appears not as a destruction or elimination of potentiality but, rather, as the very conservation of potentiality as such. Agamben finds such a concept of the passage to actuality in the text of the second book of *De anima*, where Aristotle discusses the nature of "suffering" or "undergoing" (*paskhein*):

> To suffer is not a simple term. In one sense it is a certain destruction through the opposite principle, and in another sense the preservation [*sōtēria*, salvation] of what is in potentiality by what is in actuality and what is similar to it. . . . For he who possesses science [in potentiality] becomes someone who contemplates in actuality, and either this is not an alteration—since here there is the gift of the self to itself and to actuality [*epidosis eis auto*]—or this is an alteration of a different kind.[50]

In this passage, actuality is presented as the "preservation" and "salvation" of potentiality, and the very distinction between potentiality and actuality is, consequently, profoundly complicated. If all potentiality is originally impotentiality, and if actuality is the conservation of potentiality itself, then it follows that actuality is nothing other than a potentiality to the second degree, a potentiality that, in Aristotle's phrase, "is the gift of the self to itself." At this point, actuality reveals itself to be simply a potential not to be (or do) turned back upon itself, capable of *not* not being and, in this way, of granting the existence of what is actual. This is why Agamben writes, in an important passage in *Homo Sacer*, that "potentiality and actuality are simply the two faces of the sovereign self-grounding of Being," and that "at the limit, pure potentiality and pure actuality are indistinguishable."[51] Here Agamben's analysis of the existence of potentiality steps beyond itself to propose a new account, not merely of potentiality but of the genesis of actuality and the *pathē tou ontos* as such. The apparent modal distinction articulated in Aristotle's concept of *dynamis* and *energeia* then appears in a different light, and Agamben's treatment of potentiality gives way to a reconsideration of the origin of the modal categories in their totality. Agamben can thus be said to carry out, in its general ontological implications, Heidegger's project to conceive of "the quiet power of the possible" (*die stille Kraft des Möglichen*) as "not the *possibile* of a merely represented *possibilitas*, nor *potentia* as the *essentia* of an *actus* of *existentia*, but rather [as] Being itself."[52] For in the movement of the "gift of the self to itself," potentiality and actuality, what is capable and what is actual, what is possible and what is real, can no longer strictly be distinguished: Being itself, in its very actuality, appears as essentially and irreducibly potential. The metaphysical and logical consequences of this fundamental reorganization of the modal categories are significant, and it is to them that we must now turn.

V

If the "thing itself" in question in language exists in the mode of potentiality, then it follows that language must originally have the form not of actual signification but of the mere capacity to signify. And if all potentiality, as Aristotle writes, is necessarily "impotential with respect to that of which it is said to be potential," the potential to signify constitutive of language is necessarily always also a potential not to signify. The "expressible," in other words, must be capable of expressing nothing and, in this way, of assuring the autonomy of its own existence with respect to all actual expression. Were it otherwise, particular things would always already have been signified in language; language, as pure potentiality, would not exist as such. Only because it can say nothing is language truly "sayable," and only in displacing speech from the register of affirmation and negation does language therefore announce itself in its pure potential to signify.

For Agamben, the exemplary literary figure of this announcement of the potentiality of language is Herman Melville's Bartleby, the scrivener who answers every demand that he write with the simple phrase, "I would prefer not to." "As a scribe who has stopped writing," Agamben states in "Bartleby, or On Contingency," "Bartleby is the extreme figure of the Nothing from which all creation derives; and, at the same time, he constitutes the most implacable vindication of this Nothing as pure, absolute potentiality." Deleuze, in his essay "Bartleby, or the Formula," notes Philippe Jaworski's observation that in simply stating "I would prefer not to," Bartleby neither refuses nor accepts.[53] Developing this insight, Deleuze writes that Bartleby's "formula is devastating because it impetuously eliminates both the preferable and anything that is not preferred," producing a "zone of indiscernibility or indetermination between some nonpreferred activities and a preferable activity."[54] To this Agamben therefore adds that the zone of indistinction constituted by Bartleby's reply is equally one between the potential to be (or do) and the potential not to be (or do), a zone in which language, emancipated from both position and negation, abstains from referring to anything as such. This much, Agamben argues, is inscribed in Bartleby's repeated statement, "I would prefer not to." "The final 'to' that ends Bartleby's phrase," Agamben observes,

> has an anaphoric character, for it does not refer directly to a segment of reality but, rather, to a preceding term from which it draws its only meaning. But here it is as if this anaphora were absolutized to the point of losing all reference, now turning, so to speak, back toward the phrase itself—an absolute anaphora, spinning on itself, no longer referring either to a real object or to an anaphorized term: *I would prefer not to prefer not to.*

"In the history of Western culture," Agamben continues, "there is only one formula that hovers so decidedly between affirmation and negation, acceptance and rejection, giving and taking." The formula at issue appears in a work that, Agamben states, "was familiar to every cultured man of the nineteenth century: Diogenes Laertius's *Lives of Eminent Philosophers*." The formula is *ou mallon*, "no more than," which, Agamben notes, was the "technical term with which the Skeptics denoted their most characteristic experience: *epokhē*, suspension." Diogenes Laertius writes: "The

Skeptics use this expression neither positively [*thetikōs*] nor negatively [*anairetikōs*], as when they refute an argument by saying: 'Scylla exists no more than [*ou mallon*] a chimera.'"[55] In his *Outlines of Pyrrhonism*, Sextus Empiricus further clarifies the nature of the Skeptics' phrase: "The most important thing," he states, "is that in uttering this expression, the Skeptic says the phenomenon and announces the affect without any opinion [*apaggellei to pathos adoxastōs*]."[56] "*Aggellō* and *apaggellō*," Agamben writes, discussing this passage in "Bartleby, or On Contingency,"

> are verbs that express the function of the *aggelos*, the messenger, who simply carries a message without adding anything, or who performatively announces an event (*polemon apaggellein* means "to declare war"). The Skeptic does not simply oppose aphasia to *phasis*, silence to discourse; rather, he displaces language from the register of the proposition, which predicates something of something (*legein ti kata tinos*), to that of the announcement, which predicates nothing of nothing.

What is suspended in the *epokhē* of the Skeptics, therefore, is first of all the actuality of linguistic signification. And the formula that articulates this suspension, "no more than," like Bartleby's "I would prefer not to," marks the point at which language retreats from actual predication into a mode in which it appears as purely potential, capable of expression precisely by virtue of actually saying nothing. "Announcing the pathos without opinion," language then announces itself in its own capacity to present the pathos "with opinion"; it expresses itself, in its pure potentiality, as expressible.

Agamben argues that an analysis of the potentiality of language therefore leads to a solution, or more precisely, to a dissolution of the aporia of self-reference. "The name can be named and language can be brought to speech," we read in "Pardes," Agamben's essay on Derrida, which bears the significant subtitle, "The Writing of Potentiality,"

> because self-reference is displaced onto the level of potentiality; what is intended is neither the word as object nor the word insofar as it *actually* denotes a thing but, rather, a pure potential to signify (and not to signify). . . . But this is no longer meaning's self-reference, a sign's signification of itself; instead, it is the materialization of a potentiality, the materialization of its own possibility.

Hence the significance, for Agamben, of those parts of language whose connotative value can be determined only on the basis of their relation to an event of language: the first- and second-person personal pronouns, according to Émile Benveniste, which "exist as virtual signs, actualized in the instance of discourse";[57] or, in Roman Jakobson's terms, "shifters," markers of deixis ("here," "there," "now") whose sense rests wholly on the discursive context in which they are invoked.[58] At issue in each case are parts of speech that, in themselves, bear no meaning; they are capable of functioning in discourse only because they suspend their own incapacity to signify and, in this way, refer to an actual event of language.

Language, however, does not exist as pure potentiality in indexicals and pronouns alone, and such statements as Bartleby's "I would prefer not to" and the Skeptic's "no more than" are not the only expressions of the expressible essence of language. We have seen that Agamben's analysis of potentiality leads to the recognition that actuality is nothing other than the self-suspension of potentiality, the mode in which Being can *not* not be. The same must be said of the potentiality constitutive of language: like all potentiality, it is not effaced but rather fulfilled and completed in the passage to actuality. Actual, accomplished reference is therefore not the elimination of the purely expressible dimension of language; instead, it is the form in which the potentiality of language, capable of *not* not referring, passes wholly into actuality in referring to something as such. Every utterance, every word is, in this sense, a mode in which the "thing itself" exists; every enunciation, of any kind, is simply a manner in which the potentiality of language resolves itself, as such, into actuality. Here Agamben can be said to develop fully what is already implicit in the Platonic nomination of the Idea, by which the anaphora "itself" (*auto*) is simply added to a thing's name to arrive at the Idea of the thing (the "Idea of the Good," for instance, has the literal form of "the good itself," *auto to agathon*). It suffices to add "itself" to any thing's name, Plato seems to say, for it to step forth as an Idea. And this "saving of phenomena" (*ta phainomena sōzein*) is possible, Agamben leads us to think, because every utterance is in essence nothing other than the irreparable exposition of the "thing itself," the very taking place of language as the potentiality for expression.

VI

It is now possible to clarify the sense in which the essays collected in this volume can, as a whole, be said to respond to Benjamin's injunction "to read what was never written." Agamben suggests that "what was never written" in the course of all communication, linguistic and historical, is the fact that there is language; and he shows that this fact is "never written" in the precise sense that it can only enter into "writing" and the *gramma* in the form of a presupposition. Yet this fact can, nevertheless, be "read": exposed, it can be comprehended in its existence as potentiality. "To read what was never written" is in this sense to bring to light, in what is said and thought, the "thing itself" by which anything is expressible; it is to return everything that has ever been said to the event of its taking place in its pure potential to be said (or not to be said). In this *apokatastasis pantōn* of speech, language is, in Benjamin's terms, "redeemed": it "stands in the Idea," as we read in the preface to *The Origin of the German Tragic Drama*, "and becomes what it was not."[59] Brought back to the dimension of its pure potentiality, speech then has, quite literally, nothing to say: in the "death" of every discrete intention to signify,[60] in the elimination of "all outwardly-directed communication,"[61] language, becoming wholly and purely expressible, reveals itself as essentially expressionless.

In the present collection, the concept of this integral redemption of language is perhaps most clearly articulated in Agamben's essay on Max Kommerell (Chapter 5). Here Agamben, following Kommerell, defines "gesture" as that dimension of language that is not exhausted in any communication of meaning and that, in this way, marks the point at which language appears in its mere capacity to communicate.[62] In an implicit gloss on Benjamin's statement that "criticism is the mortification of works,"[63] Agamben writes that "criticism is the reduction of works to the sphere of pure gesture." He continues:

> This sphere lies beyond psychology and, in a certain sense, beyond all interpretation. . . . Consigned to their supreme gesture, works live on, like creatures bathed in the light of the Last Day, surviving the ruin of their formal garment and their conceptual meaning. They find themselves in the situation of those *commedia dell'arte* figures Kommerell loved so dearly; Harlequin, Pantaloon, Columbine, and the Captain, emancipated from written texts and fully defined roles, oscillate forever between reality and virtuality, life and art, the singular and the generic. In the comedy that criticism substitutes for literary history, the *Recherche* or the *Commedia* ceases to be the established text that the critic must investigate and then consign, intact and inalterable, to tradition. They are instead the gestures that, in those wondrous texts, exhibit

only a gigantic lack of memory, only a "gag" destined to hide an incurable speechlessness.

Reduced to its speechless capacity for speech, the object of Agamben's criticism is, at last, saved. It is nothing other than its own potentiality for expression, and what it shows is simply the existence of language: that there exists a medium in which communication takes place, and that what is communicated in this medium is not one thing or another but, first of all, communicability itself. It is here that the thought articulated in these essays opens onto the terrain of political philosophy that Agamben considers in his most recent works. For if politics concerns itself, as Agamben writes, "not with a *state*, but with an *event* of language," if politics has to do "not with one grammar or another, but with a *factum loquendi* as such,"[64] then to interrogate this *factum*—"to read what was never written"—is also to reflect on what it means to be "the political animal," as Aristotle said, precisely in being "the animal that has language." And to examine the pure existence of language, freed from the form of any presupposition, is to consider a community inconceivable according to any representable condition of belonging: a "coming community," without identity, defined by nothing other than its existence in language as irreducible, absolute potentiality.

PART ONE

Language

§ 1   The Thing Itself

For Jacques Derrida
and in memory of Giorgio Pasquali

The expression "the thing itself," *to pragma auto*, appears at the beginning of the so-called philosophical digression of Plato's Seventh Letter, a text whose importance for the history of Western philosophy has yet to be fully established. After Richard Bentley had come to suspect the entire Platonic corpus of letters of being fraudulent, and Christoph Meiners (in 1783) and subsequently Karsten and Friedrich Ast declared them to be inauthentic, Plato's letters—which until then had always been considered a central part of the philosopher's work—were slowly expelled from philosophical historiography, precisely when it was most fervent and active. When philological opinion began to change in our century, and more and more critics asserted the authenticity of Plato's letters (the letter that interests us is by now generally considered to be genuine), philosophers and scholars had to break the hundred-year-old quarantine of the Platonic epistles if they wanted to study them at all. What had been lost in the meantime was the living connection between text and philosophical tradition, with the result that the philosophical excursus contained in the Seventh Letter appeared as an arduous, solitary fragment resisting any attempt at comprehension. Naturally, it was also transformed by its long isolation into something rich and strange, which could be considered with a freshness probably unattainable in regard to any other Platonic text.

The scenario of the letter is well known: the seventy-five-year-old Plato tells Dion's friends of his encounters with Dionysius and the dramatic failure of the latter's Sicilian political projects. In the passage that interests us here, Plato recounts the story of his third stay in Sicily. Once again on the island because of the tyrant's persistent invitations, he decided to put Dionysius to the test concerning his professed desire to become a philosopher. "Now there is a method," Plato writes, "of testing such matters which is not ignoble but really suitable in the case of tyrants, and especially such as are crammed with borrowed doctrines; and this was certainly what had happened to Dionysius, as I perceived as soon as I arrived."[1] Men such as these, he continues, should be immediately shown the whole thing (*pan to pragma*) and the nature and number of its difficulties. If the listener is truly equal to "the thing," he will then think that he has heard the tale of a wonderful life, which must be led without delay and to which he must devote himself at all costs. On the other hand, those who are not truly philosophers and have only an outer glow of philosophy, like those whose skin is tanned by the sun, will see the difficulty of "the thing" and think it too hard or even impossible, convincing themselves that they already know enough and need nothing more. "This, then," Plato writes,

> was what I said to Dionysius on that occasion. I did not, however, expound the matter fully, nor did Dionysius ask me to do so; for he claimed that he himself knew many of the most important doctrines and was sufficiently informed owing to the versions he had heard from his other teachers. And I am even told that he himself subsequently wrote a treatise on the subjects in which I instructed him, composing it as though it were something of his own invention and quite different from what he had heard; but of all this I know nothing. I know indeed that certain others have written about these same subjects; but what manner of men they are not even they themselves know. But thus much I can certainly declare concerning all these writers, or prospective writers, who claim to know the subjects with which I concern myself [*peri ōn egō spoudazō*], whether as hearers of mine or of other teachers, or from their own discoveries; it is impossible, in my judgment at least, that these men should understand anything about this subject. (Epistle VII, 341 a 7–c 4; pp. 529–31)

It is at this point that Plato uses the expression *to pragma auto*, the thing itself—a formulation that remained so determining as an expression of the cause of thinking and the task of philosophy that it appeared again almost two thousand years later, like a watchword passed on from Kant to Hegel, and then to Husserl and Heidegger: "There does not exist, nor will there ever exist, any treatise of mine dealing with this thing. For it does not at all admit of verbal expression like other disciplines [*mathēmata*], but, after one has dwelt for a long time close to the thing itself [*peri to pragma auto*] and in communion with it, it is suddenly brought to birth in the soul, as light that is kindled by a leaping spark; and then it nourishes itself [*auto heauto ēdē trefei*]" (341 c 4–d 2; p. 531).

This passage has been cited countless times as proof of esoteric inter- pretations of Plato and as irrefutable documentation for the existence of Plato's unwritten doctrines. According to these readings, the dialogues transmitted by our culture for centuries as a venerable legacy would not address what Plato was seriously concerned with, which would have been reserved for a purely oral tradition! This is not the place to take a posi- tion on this problem, which is surely an important one. We shall instead seek to consider the nature of the "thing itself" of which Plato speaks and which Dionysius wrongly thought he understood. What is *the thing of thinking*?

An answer to this question can follow only from an attentive reading of the next passage, which Plato defines as a "story and wandering" (*mythos kai planos*) (344 d 3; p. 541) and also as a "certain true argument, which . . . although I have frequently stated it in the past, also seems to be in need of repetition at the present time" (342 a 3–7; p. 533). Any thought that wants to grasp its "thing" must thus always reckon with in- terpreting this "extravagant story." Let us then attempt to read it. "Each being," Plato writes,

> has three things which are the necessary means by which knowledge of that being is acquired; the knowledge itself is a fourth thing; and as a fifth one must posit the thing itself, which is knowable and truly is. First of these comes the name [*onoma*]; second, the definition [*logos*]; third, the image [*eidōlon*]; fourth, the knowledge. If you wish, then, to understand what I am now saying, take a single example and learn from it what applies to all. There is something called a circle [*kyklos estin ti legomenon*], which has for its name the word we have just mentioned; and, second, it has a definition, composed of names and verbs; for "that which is everywhere equidistant from the ex- tremities to the center" will be the definition of that object which has for its name "round" and "spherical" and "circle." And in the third place there is that object which is portrayed and obliterated, which is shaped with a lathe and falls into decay. But none of these affections is suffered by the circle itself [*au- tos ho kyklos*, which here is the example of the thing itself], to which all these others are related, for it is different from them. The fourth is knowledge and intelligence and true opinion regarding these objects; and all this must be conceived as a single thing, which exists neither in voices [*en phōnais*] nor in

corporeal figures [*en sōmatōn skhēmasin*], but in souls [*en psychais*]. Hence it is clear that it differs both from the nature of the circle itself and from the three previously mentioned. Of those four, intelligence is closest in kinship and similarity to the fifth; the others are further removed. The same is equally true of the straight figure and the sphere, color, and the good and the fair and the just, and of all bodies, whether made or naturally produced (such as fire and water and all such substances), all living creatures, and ethos in the soul and all creations [*poiēmata*] and passions [*pathēmata*]. For if someone does not grasp the first four for each thing, he will never be able to participate perfectly in knowledge of the fifth. Moreover, the first four things express the quality [*ti poion ti*] of each being no less than its real essence, on account of the weakness of language [*dia to tōn logōn asthenes*]. This is why no man of intelligence will ever venture to entrust his thoughts to language, especially if the language is unalterable, like language written with letters. (342 a 8–343 a 3; pp. 533–35)

Let us pause for a moment to catch our breath. In the face of this extraordinary excursus, which constitutes the final and most explicit presentation of the theory of the Ideas, we can measure the damage done to philosophical historiography by the nineteenth century's claim of the Platonic epistles' falsity. It is not my intention to climb that impervious massif. But it is certainly possible to seek to establish a first trail, to determine the difficulty of the climb, and to situate it with respect to the surrounding landscape.

One remark that we can make (and that has already been made by, among others, Pasquali) concerns the status of unsayability that the Seventh Letter, according to the esoteric reading of Plato, would ascribe to the thing itself. This status must be tempered by the fact that from the context it is clear that the thing itself is not something that absolutely transcends language and has nothing to do with it. Plato states in the most explicit fashion that "if the first four [which, we recall, include name and *logos*] are not grasped" it will never be possible fully to know the fifth. In another important passage in the letter, Plato writes that the knowledge of the thing itself suddenly emerges in "rubbing together names, definitions, visions and sense-perceptions, proving them in benevolent proofs and discussions without envy" (344 b 4–7; p. 541).

These unequivocal statements are, moreover, perfectly coherent with the very close relation between the Ideas and language that is suggested by the Platonic dialogues. When in the *Phaedo* Socrates presents the genesis of the Ideas, he says, "it seemed to me necessary to seek refuge in the *logoi*, to find the truth of beings in them" (99 e 4–6). Elsewhere, he presents the hatred of language as the worst of evils (*Phaedo*, 89 d 2) and the disappearance of language as the loss of philosophy itself (*Sophist*, 260 a 6–7); in the *Parmenides*, the Ideas are defined as "what can be apprehended to the greatest degree by means of *logos*" (153 e 3). And does not Aristotle, in his historical reconstruction of Plato's thought at the beginning of the *Metaphysics*, state that the theory of Ideas was born from a *skepsis en tois logois*, a search in language (987 b 33)?

The thing itself therefore has its essential place in language, even if language is certainly not adequate to it, on account, Plato says, of what is weak in language. One could say, with an apparent paradox, that the thing itself, while in some way transcending language, is nevertheless possible only in language and by virtue of language: precisely the thing of language. When Plato says that what he is concerned with is in no way sayable *like other mathēmata*, it is therefore necessary to place the accent on the last three words: it is not sayable in the same way as other disciplines, but it is not for that reason simply unsayable. As Plato does not tire of repeating (341 e 1–5), the reasons why it is inadvisable to entrust the thing itself to writing are ethical and not merely logical. Platonic mysticism—if such a mysticism exists—is, like all authentic mysticism, profoundly implicated in the *logoi*.

Now that we have made these preliminary observations, let us closely examine the list contained in the digression. The identification of the first four members does not pose any great difficulties: name, defining discourse, image (which indicates the sensible object), and, finally, the knowledge achieved through them. Name (*onoma*) is, in modern terms, which are those of Stoic logic, the "signifier"; *logos* is the "signified" or virtual reference; "image" is denotation or actual reference.

These terms are familiar to us, though it should not be forgotten that it is only with Plato and the Sophists that we see the beginning of the very reflection on language that will later lead to the precise logico-grammatical constructions of the Stoa and the Hellenistic schools. As in book 10 of the *Laws* or the last part of the *Sophist*, here in the Seventh Letter Plato presents a theory of linguistic signification in its relation to knowledge. The difficulty naturally begins with the fifth term, which introduces a new element into the theory of signification as we know it. Let us reread the passage: "Each being has three things which are the necessary means by which knowledge of that being is acquired; the knowledge itself is a fourth thing; and as a fifth one must posit the thing itself, which is knowable and truly is." By "fifth" it seems that we should understand the same being with which the excursus begins in saying that "each being has three things." The thing itself would then simply be the thing that is the object of knowledge, and we would thus have found proof for the interpretation of Platonism (which appeared as early as Aristotle) that sees the Idea as a kind of useless duplicate of the thing. Moreover, the list then appears as circular, since what is listed as fifth is what is in truth the first to be named, as the very presupposition from which the whole excursus follows.

Perhaps here we can be aided by philological attention to details, in which, as it has been said, the good God likes to hide himself. At this point the Greek text to be found in modern editions (in Burnet's version, which was in some respects exemplary for all following editions, but also in Souilhé's more recent text) reads: *pempton d'auto tithenai dei ho dē gnōston te kai alēthes estin,* "and as a fifth one must posit the thing itself, which is knowable and truly is." But the two principal codices on which both scholars base their editions, that is, the *Parisinus graecus* of 1807 and the *Vaticanus graecus* I, contain a slightly different text, which instead of *dei ho* ("one must . . . which") has *di'ho* ("by which"). If we restore the text of the codices by writing *di'ho*, the translation becomes, "[one must] posit the fifth, by which [each being] is knowable and truly is."[2]

In the margin of this text, a twelfth-century hand had noted *dei ho* as an emendation, and modern editors based their text on this variant. But the codex that Marsilio Ficino had before him for his Latin translation of the works of Plato still respected the text of *di'ho*, for Ficino's translation reads as follows: *quintum vero oportet ipsum ponere quo quid est cognoscibile, id est quod agnosci potest, atque vere existit.*

What then changes, what is the significance of this restoration of the original text? Essentially that the thing itself is no longer simply the being in its obscurity, as an object presupposed by language and the epistemological process; rather, it is *auto di'ho gnōston estin,* that *by which* the object is known, *its own knowability and truth.* Even if it is inexact, the marginal variant followed by modern editors is not erroneous. The scribe who introduced it (and we have reason to think it was not an inexpert scribe) was most likely concerned with the risk that knowability itself—the Idea—would be, in turn, presupposed and substantialized as *another thing,* as a duplicate of the thing before or beyond the thing. The thing itself—hence the term *auto* as the technical designation of the Idea—is not another thing but the thing *itself*; not, however, as supposed by the name and the *logos*, as an obscure real presupposition (a *hypokeimenon*), but rather in the very medium of its knowability, in the pure light of its self-manifestation and announcement to consciousness.

The "weakness" of *logos* therefore consists precisely in the fact that it is not capable of bringing this very knowability and sameness to expression; it must transform the knowability of beings that is at issue in it into a pre-supposition (as a hypo-thesis in the etymological sense of the word, as *that which is placed beneath*).

This is the sense of the distinction between *on* and *poion*, between Being and its qualification, which Plato insists on several times in the epistle (342 e 3; 343 b 8–c 1). Language—our language—is necessarily pre-suppositional and objectifying, in the sense that in taking place it necessarily decomposes the thing itself, which is announced in it and in it alone, into a being *about which one speaks* and a *poion*, a quality and a determination *that one says of it*. Language sup-poses and hides what it brings to light, in the very act in which it brings it to light. According to the definition contained in Aristotle (which is also implicit both in *Sophist*, 262 e 6–7, and in the modern distinction between sense and reference), language is thus always *legein ti kata tinos*, saying something-on-something; it is therefore always pre-sup-positional and objectifying language. Presupposition is the form of linguistic signification: speaking *kat' hypokeimenou*, speaking about a subject.

The warning that Plato entrusts to the Idea is therefore that *sayability itself remains unsaid in what is said and in that about which something is said, that knowability itself is lost in what is known and in that about which something is known.*

The specific problem that is at issue in the letter, and that is necessarily the problem of every human discourse that wants to make a subject out of what is not a subject, is therefore: how is it possible to speak without sup-posing, without hypo-thesizing and subjectifying that about which one speaks? How is it thus possible *legein kat'auto*, to speak not by means of a presupposition but absolutely? And since the field of names is, for the Greeks, that which is essentially said *kat' auto*, can language give reasons (*logon didonai*) for what it names, can it *say* what the name has named?

Even the earliest commentators understood that something like a contradiction is implicit in this problem. We possess a gloss of a late Platonic scholiast that says more or less the following: "Why is it that in the *Phaedrus* the master gives little value to writing and yet, in having written, in some way holds his own work to be valuable? In this too," the scholiast says, "he wanted to follow the truth. Just as the divinity wanted to create both invisible things and things that fall under our gaze, so he also wanted to leave some things unwritten and others things written." This question certainly holds for the Seventh Letter as well, in which Plato, writing of what concerns him most and what cannot be written about, seems to challenge the weakness of the *logos* and in a sense to betray himself. And it is certainly not a vain jest that, in another letter, he ends by rejecting the authorship of the dialogues circulating under his name, stating that they are the work of "a Socrates become fair and young."[3] Here the paradox of Plato's written works momentarily flashes up before us: in a letter that the moderns have often taken to be apocryphal, he declares his dialogues to be inauthentic, attributing them to an impossible author, Socrates, who is dead and has been buried for many years. The character *about which* the text speaks now takes the place of the author in the dialogues in which he appears. The earliest and sharpest critics, such as Demetrius and Dionysius, observe that Plato's style, which is limpid in the earlier dialogues, becomes darker, swollen (*zofos*) and paratactic (*eperriptai allēlois ta kōla aph' eterō heteron*, "the phrases are hurled one upon the other," Demetrius writes) when he confronts the subjects dearest to him.

By a curious coincidence, the weakness of language that is called into question by the father of Western metaphysics seems to prophesy from a distance of two thousand years the difficulty implicit in the metaphysical character of our language, which so burdens the writing of the late Heidegger. But in Plato the weakness of the *logos* does not found a mystical status of the Idea; on the contrary, it renders possible the coming to speech of speech, for the sake of helping speech (*logōi boēthein*), which in the *Phaedrus* (278 c 6) is described as the authentic task of philosophical presentation. Here the risk is that the nonthematizability that is at issue in the thing itself will be in turn thematized and presupposed once again in the form of a *legein ti kata tinos*, a speaking about that about which it is not possible to speak. The thing itself is not a simple hypostasis of the name, something ineffable that must remain unsaid and hence sheltered, as a name, in the language of men. Such a conception, which is implicitly refuted at the end of the *Theatetus*, still necessarily hypothesizes and sup-poses the thing itself. The thing itself is not a *quid* that might be sought as an extreme hypothesis beyond all hypotheses, as a final and absolute subject beyond all subjects, horribly or beautifully unreachable in its obscurity. We can, in truth, conceive of such a nonlinguistic thing only in language, through the idea of a language without relation to things. It is a chimera in the Spinozian sense of the term, that is, a purely verbal being. The thing itself is not a thing; it is the very sayability, the very openness at issue in language, which, in language, we always presuppose and forget, perhaps because it is at bottom its own oblivion and abandonment. In the words of the *Phaedo* (76 d 8), it is what we are always disclosing in speaking, what we are always saying and communicating, and that of which we nevertheless are always losing sight. The presuppositional structure of language is the very structure of tradition; we presuppose, pass on, and thereby—according to the double sense of the word *traditio*—betray the thing itself in language, so that language may speak about something (*kata tinos*). The effacement of the thing itself is the sole foundation on which it is possible for something like a tradition to be constituted.

The task of philosophical presentation is to come with speech to help speech, so that, in speech, speech itself does not remain presupposed but instead comes to speech. At this point, the presuppositional power of language touches its limit and its end; language says presuppositions as presuppositions and, in this way, reaches the unpresupposable and unpresupposed principle (*arkhē anypothetos*) that, as such, constitutes authentic human community and communication. As Plato writes in a decisive passage of a dialogue that presents more than mere affinities with the "extravagant myth" of the Seventh Letter:

> Understand then that by the other section of the intelligible I mean what language itself [*auto ho logos*] touches by the power of dialogue, hypothesizing not by principles [*archai*] but truly by hypotheses, underpinnings, footings, and springboards, so that it reaches the principle of all things, touching it, and, once again holding to the things near it, returns toward the end, being concerned not with the sensible, but with the Ideas, through the Ideas, toward the Ideas, so that it may end with the Ideas.[4]

I realize that I may have gone beyond the task that I set myself; I may be guilty, in some way, of precisely the human folly against which the myth of the Seventh Letter warns us (344 d 1–2): the folly of carelessly consigning one's own thoughts about the thing itself to writing. It is therefore appropriate that I end here, to turn more cautiously to the preliminary historiographical matter that I raised earlier.

We have seen that the digression of the Seventh Letter contains a treatment of the Idea in its relation to language. The determination of the thing itself is, indeed, carried out in close relation with a theory of linguistic signification, one that may constitute the first organic exposition of the material, if in an extremely abbreviated form. If this is true, we should then be able to follow its traces in the Greek reflection on language that immediately follows it. One instantly thinks of the text that, for centuries, determined all reflection on language in the ancient world, Aristotle's *De interpretatione*. Here Aristotle presents the process of linguistic signification in a way apparently without relation to the Platonic digression. "What is in the voice [*ta en tēi phōnēi*]," he writes,

> is the sign of affections in the soul [*en tēi psychēi*]; what is written [*ta graphomena*] is the sign of what is in the voice. And just as letters are not the same for all men, so it is with voices. But that of which they are signs, that is, affections in the soul, are the same for all; and the things [*pragmata*] of which the affections are semblances [*homoiōmata*] are also the same for all men.[5]

A more attentive examination, however, shows precise correspondences with the text of the Platonic excursus. The tripartite division by which Aristotle articulates the movement of signification (*en tēi phōnēi, en tēi psychēi, pragmata*) textually recalls the Platonic distinction between what is *en phōnais* (name and *logos*), what is *en psychais* (knowledge and opinion) and what is *en sōmatōn skhēmasin* (sensible object) (Epistle VII, 342 c 6). In view of these affinities with the Platonic epistle, the disappearance of the thing itself in *De interpretatione* is all the more noticeable. In Aristotle, the thing itself is expelled from *hermēneia*, the linguistic process of signification. When, later, it momentarily returns in the philosophy of language (as in Stoic logic), it will be so estranged from the original Platonic intention as to be practically unrecognizable.

Aristotle's *hermēneia* is therefore defined in opposition to the Platonic list, of which it constitutes both a repetition and a refutation. The decisive proof of this polemical distinction is precisely the appearance in the Aristotelian text of *grammata*, letters. Even ancient commentators wondered about the apparently incongruous appearance of a fourth interpreter alongside the other three (voices, concepts, things). If one keeps in mind that the Platonic excursus aimed to show precisely the impossibility of writing the thing itself and generally the unreliability, for thought, of every written discourse, the marked difference between the two texts is even more evident.

Expelling the thing itself from his theory of signification, Aristotle absolves writing of its weakness. In the place of the thing itself, in the *Categories* there appears *protē ousia*, first substance, which Aristotle defines as that which is said neither about a subject (*kat' hypokeimenou*, by means of a presupposition) nor in a subject. What does this definition mean? First substance is not said on the basis of a presupposition; it does not have presuppositions, because it is itself the absolute presupposition on which all discourse and knowledge are founded. It alone—as name—can be said *kat' auto*, by itself; it alone—not being in a subject—clearly shows itself. But in itself, as *individuum*, it is ineffable (*individuum ineffabile*, according to the formulation of medieval Aristotelianism) and cannot enter into the linguistic signification that it founds, except by abandoning its status as deixis and becoming universal predication. The "what," *ti*, that was at issue in the name is subsumed into discourse as a *kata tinos*, "that about which" something is said. They—both the *what* and the *about which*—are therefore the *same thing*, which can be grasped as *to ti ēn einai*, the Being-the-what-that-was. In this logico-temporal process, the Platonic *thing itself* is removed and conserved or, rather, conserved only in being removed: e-liminated.

This is why the *gramma* appears in *De interpretatione*. An attentive examination shows that in the hermeneutic circle of *De interpretatione*, the letter, as the interpreter of the voice, does not itself need any other interpreter. It is the final interpreter, beyond which no *hermēneia* is possible: the limit of all interpretation. This is why ancient grammarians, in analyzing *De interpretatione*, said that the letter, which is the sign of the voice, is also *stoikheion tēs phōnēs*, that is, its element. Insofar as it is the *element of that of which it is a sign*, it has the privileged status of being an *index sui*, self-demonstration; like *protē ousia*, of which it constitutes the linguistic cipher, it shows itself, but only insofar as it *was* in the voice, that is, insofar as it always already belongs to the past.

The *gramma* is thus the form of presupposition itself and nothing else. As such, it occupies a central place in all mysticism, and as such, it also has a decisive relevance in our time, which is much more Aristotelian and mystical than is usually believed. In this sense—and only in this sense—Aristotle, and not Plato, is the founder of Western mysticism, and this is why Neoplatonism could formulate the accord between Plato and Aristotle that lay at the basis of its school.

Insofar as language bears within it the ontological structure of presupposition, thought can immediately become writing, without having to reckon with the thing itself and without betraying its own presupposition. Indeed, the philosopher is the scribe of thought and, through thought, of the thing and Being. The late Byzantine lexicon that goes under the name of *Suda* contains, under the entry "Aristotle," the following definition: *Aristotelēs tes physeōs grammateus ēn ton kalamon apobrekhōn eis noun*, "Aristotle was the scribe of nature who dipped his pen in thought."

Many centuries later, Hölderlin unexpectedly cited this phrase from *Suda* at a decisive point in his annotations (*Anmerkungen*) to his translation of Sophocles, namely, in his attempt to explain the sense and nature of *Darstellung*, tragic presentation. The citation, however, contains an amendment, which Hölderlinian philology, despite its diligence, has not been able to explain. Hölderlin writes: *tēs physeōs grammateus ēn ton kalamon apobrekhōn eunoun* (instead of *eis noun*): "he was the scribe of nature who dipped his benevolent pen." Here there is no more dipping of the pen in thought; the pen—that simple material instrument of human writing—is alone, armed solely with its benevolence in the face of its task. To restore the thing itself to its place in language and, at the same time, to restore the difficulty of writing, the place of writing in the poetic task of composition: this is the task of the coming philosophy.

§ 2 The Idea of Language

Whoever has been raised or has simply lived in a Christian or Jewish environment has some familiarity with the word *revelation*. This familiarity, however, does not imply a capacity to define the word's meaning. I would like to begin my reflections with an attempt to define this term. I am convinced that its correct definition is not irrelevant to the subject of philosophical discourse, which, it has been said, may speak of everything on condition of first speaking of the fact that it does so. The constant trait that characterizes every conception of revelation is its heterogeneity with respect to reason. This is not simply to say—even if the Church Fathers often insisted on this point—that the content of revelation must necessarily appear ridiculous to reason. The difference at issue here is more radical, and it concerns the plane on which revelation is situated as well as the precise structure of revelation itself.

If the content of a revelation were something, however absurd, that human reason and language could still say and know with their own strength (for example, that "pink donkeys sing in the sky of Venus"), this would not be revelation. What revelation allows us to know must, therefore, be something not only that we could not know without revelation but also that conditions the very possibility of knowledge in general.

It is this radical difference of the plane of revelation that Christian theologians express by saying that the sole content of revelation is Christ himself, that is, the Word of God, and that Jewish theologians affirm in stating that God's revelation is his name. When St. Paul wanted to explain to the Colossians the sense of the economy of divine revelation, he wrote: "Even the mystery which hath been hid from ages and from generations . . . now is made manifest" (Col. 1:26). The word "mystery" (*to mysterion*) in this phrase is placed in apposition to "the word of God" (*ton logon tou theou*), which ends the previous verse ("Whereof I am made a minister, according to the dispensation of God which is given to me for you, to fulfill the word of God"). The mystery that was hidden and that is now made manifest concerns not this or that worldly or otherworldly event but, simply, the word of God.

If the theological tradition has therefore always understood revelation as something that human reason cannot know on its own, this can only mean the following: the content of revelation is not a truth that can be expressed in the form of linguistic propositions about a being (even about a supreme being) but is, instead, a truth that concerns language itself, the very fact that language (and therefore knowledge) exists. The meaning of revelation is that humans can reveal beings through language but cannot reveal language itself. In other words: humans see the world through language but do not see language. This invisibility of the revealer in what is revealed is the word of God; it is revelation.

This is why theologians say that the revelation of God is also His concealment, or to put it differently, that God reveals himself in the word as incomprehensible. It is a matter not simply of a negative determination or a defect in knowledge but of an essential determination of divine revelation, which one theologian expressed in the following terms: "supreme visibility in the deepest darkness," and "revelation of an unknowable." Once again, this can only mean that what is revealed here is not an object concerning which there would be much to know, if it were not for the lack of adequate instruments of knowledge. Instead what is revealed here is unveiling itself, the very fact that there is openness to a world and knowledge.

From this perspective, the construction of Trinitarian theology appears as the most rigorous and coherent way to consider the paradox of the word's primordial status, which the prologue to the Gospel of John expresses in stating, *en arkhē ēn ho logos*, "In the beginning was the Word." The Trinitarian movement of God that has become familiar to us through the Nicene Creed ("Credo in unum dominum . . . ," "I believe in one Lord . . . ") says nothing about worldly reality; it has no ontic content. Instead, it registers the new experience of the word that Christianity brought to the world. To use Wittgenstein's terms, it says nothing about *how* the world is, but rather reveals *that* the world is, that language exists. The word that is absolutely in the beginning, that is therefore the absolute presupposition, presupposes nothing if not itself; it has nothing before itself that can explain it or reveal it in turn (*there is no word for the word*); its Trinitarian structure is nothing other than the movement of its own self-revelation. And this revelation of the word, this presupposition of nothing, which is the sole presupposition, is God: "and the Word was God."

The proper sense of revelation is therefore that all human speech and knowledge has at its root and foundation an openness that infinitely transcends it. But at the same time, this openness concerns only language itself, its possibility and its existence. As the great Jewish theologian and neo-Kantian philosopher Hermann Cohen said, the meaning of revelation is that God reveals himself not *in* something but *to* something, and that his revelation is therefore nothing other than *die Schöpfung der Vernunft*, the creation of reason. Revelation does not mean this or that statement about the world, nor does it indicate something that could be said through language; it concerns the fact that the word, that language, exists.

But what is the meaning of a statement such as "language exists"?

It is from this perspective that we must examine the *locus classicus* of the problem of the relation of reason and revelation, namely, Anselm's ontological argument. For, as was immediately objected to Anselm, it is not true that the simple utterance of the word "God," "that of which one cannot think anything greater" (*quod maius cogitari nequit*), necessarily implies the existence of God. But there is a being whose nomination implies its existence, and that being is language. The fact that I speak and that someone listens implies the existence of nothing—other than language. *Language is what must necessarily presuppose itself.* What the ontological argument proves is therefore that the speech of human beings and existence of rational animals necessarily imply the divine word, in the sense that they presuppose the signifying function and openness to revelation (only in this sense does the ontological argument prove the existence of God—only, that is, if God is the name of the preexistence of language, or his dwelling in the *arkhē*). But this openness, contrary to what Anselm thought, does not belong to the domain of signifying discourse; it is not a proposition that bears meaning but rather a pure event of language before or beyond all particular meaning. From this perspective, it is worth rereading the objection that a great and misunderstood logician, Gaunilo, raises against Anselm's argument. Anselm argues that to utter the word "God" is, for whoever understands the word, necessarily to imply God's own existence. But Gaunilo opposes Anselm's argument with the experience of an idiot or a barbarian who, in the face of signifying discourse, certainly understands that there is an event of language—that, as Gaunilo says, there is a *vox*, a human voice—but cannot in any way grasp the meaning of the statement. Such an idiot or barbarian, Gaunilo writes, considers

> not so much the voice itself, which is something somehow true, that is, the sound of the syllables and letters, as the signification of the voice that is heard; not, however, as it is conceived by him who knows what is usually signified by that voice, but rather as it is conceived by him who does not know its signification and thinks only according to the movement of the soul, which seeks to represent the signification of the voice that is perceived.

No longer the experience of mere sound and *not yet* the experience of a meaning, this "thought of the voice alone" (*cogitatio secundum vocem solam*) opens thinking to an originary logical dimension that, indicating the pure taking place of language without any determinate event of meaning, shows that there is still a possibility of thought beyond meaningful propositions. The most original logical dimension at issue in revelation is therefore not that of meaningful speech but rather that of a voice that, without signifying anything, signifies signification itself. (It is in this sense that we should understand those thinkers, such as Roscelin, who were said to have discovered "the meaning of the voice" and who stated that universal essences were only *flatus vocis*. Here *flatus vocis* is not mere sound but, rather, in the sense which we have seen, voice as pure indication of an event of language. And this voice coincides with the most universal dimension of meaning, Being.) This gift of the voice by language is God, the divine word. The name of God, that is, the name that names language, is therefore a word without meaning.

In the terms of contemporary logic, we can then say that the sense of revelation is that if there is a metalanguage, it is not a meaningful discourse but rather a pure, insignificant voice. That there is language is as certain as it is incomprehensible, and this incomprehensibility and this certainty constitute faith and revelation.

The principal difficulty inherent in philosophical presentation concerns this very order of problems. Philosophy considers not merely what is revealed through language, but also the revelation of language itself. A philosophical presentation is thus one that, regardless of what it speaks about, must also take into account the fact that it speaks of it; it must first of all say language itself. (Hence the essential proximity—but also the distance—between philosophy and theology, a proximity that is at least as ancient as Aristotle's definition of first philosophy as *theologikē*).

This can also be expressed by saying that philosophy is not a vision of the world but a vision of language; and contemporary thought, indeed, has followed this path all too zealously. Here a difficulty arises, however, from the fact that—as is implicit in Gaunilo's definition of the voice— what is at issue in a philosophical presentation cannot be simply a discourse that has language as its subject, a metalanguage that speaks of language. The voice says nothing; instead, it shows itself, precisely like logical form according to Wittgenstein. It therefore cannot become the subject of discourse. Philosophy can only lead thought to the limit of the voice; it cannot say the voice (or, at least, so it seems).

Contemporary thought has become resolutely conscious that a final and absolute metalanguage does not exist and that every construction of a metalanguage is caught in an infinite regress. Yet the paradox of pure philosophical intention is precisely that of a discourse that must speak of language, exposing its limits without making use of a metalanguage. Philosophy thus encounters what constituted the essential content of revelation, *logos en arkhē*: the fact that the word is essentially in the beginning, that language is the absolute presupposition (or as Mallarmé once wrote, the word is a principle that develops through the negation of all principles). And it is with this dwelling of the word in the beginning that philosophy and logic must always reckon, if they are to be conscious of their task.

If there is one point of agreement among contemporary philosophies, it is precisely their recognition of this presupposition. Hermeneutics thus founds itself on this irreducible priority of the signifying function, stating—according to the citation from Friedrich Schleiermacher that opens *Truth and Method*—that "in hermeneutics there is only one presupposition: language," or interpreting, as does Karl-Otto Apel, the concept of "language game" in Wittgenstein as a transcendental condition of all knowledge. For hermeneutics, this a priori is the absolute presupposition, which can be reconstructed and rendered explicit but not transcended. In accordance with these principles, hermeneutics is capable of nothing other than positing a horizon of infinite tradition and interpretation whose final meaning and foundation must remain unsaid. It can question itself on how understanding takes place, but that there is understanding is what, remaining unthought, renders all understanding possible. "In taking place," Hans-Georg Gadamer writes, "every act of speech also renders present the unsaid to which it refers, as an answer and a recollection." (It is therefore possible to understand how hermeneutics, while referring to Hegel and Heidegger, leaves unexamined precisely those aspects of their thought that involve absolute knowledge and the end of history, on the one hand, and *Ereignis* and the end of the history of Being, on the other.)

In this sense, hermeneutics is opposed—though not as radically as it might seem—to those discourses, like science and ideology, that more or less consciously presuppose the preexistence of the signifying function and, nevertheless, repress this presupposition and leave it in force in its productivity and nullifying power. And, in truth, it is difficult to see how hermeneutics could convince these discourses to renounce their position, at least insofar as they have become nihilistically conscious of their own lack of foundation. But if the foundation is unsayable and irreducible, if it always already anticipates speaking beings, throwing them into history and epochal destiny, then a thought that records and shelters this presupposition seems ethically equivalent to one that fully experiences the violence and bottomlessness of its own destiny.

It is hardly an accident, therefore, that an authoritative current of contemporary French thought posits language in the beginning and yet conceives of this dwelling in the *arkhē* according to the negative structure of writing and the *gramma*. There is no voice for language; rather, language is always already trace and infinite self-transcendence. In other words: language, which is in the beginning, is the nullification and deferral of itself, and the signifier is nothing other than the irreducible cipher of this ungroundedness.

It is legitimate to ask oneself if the recognition of the presupposition of language that characterizes contemporary thought truly exhausts the task of philosophy. It could be said that here thought believes that its task consists simply in recognizing what constituted the most proper content of faith and revelation: the dwelling of the *logos* in the beginning. What theology proclaimed to be incomprehensible to reason is now recognized by reason as its presupposition. All comprehension is grounded in the incomprehensible.

But does such a thought not obscure precisely what should be the philosophical task par excellence, that is, the elimination and "absolution" of presuppositions? Was philosophy not perhaps the discourse that wanted to free itself of all presuppositions, even the most universal presupposition, which is expressed in the formula "there is language"? Is philosophy not concerned precisely with comprehending the incomprehensible? The fact that current philosophy has abandoned this task may constitute its fundamental difficulty, condemning the handmaiden to a marriage with its theological master, even as the difficulty of faith coincides with its acceptance by reason. The abolition of the boundaries between faith and reason also marks their *crisis*, that is, their reciprocal judgment.

Contemporary thought has approached a limit beyond which a new epochal-religious unveiling of the word no longer seems possible. The primordial character of the word is now completely revealed, and no new figure of the divine, no new historical destiny can lift itself out of language. At the point where it shows itself to be absolutely in the beginning, language also reveals its absolute anonymity. There is no name for the name, and there is no metalanguage, not even in the form of an insignificant voice. If God was the name of language, "God is dead" can only mean that there is no longer a name for language. The fulfilled revelation of language is a word completely abandoned by God. And human beings are thrown into language without having a voice or a divine word to guarantee them a possibility of escape from the infinite play of meaningful propositions. Thus we finally find ourselves alone with our words; for the first time we are truly alone with language, abandoned without any final foundation. This is the Copernican revolution that the thought of our time inherits from nihilism: we are the first human beings who have become completely conscious of language. For the first time, what preceding generations called God, Being, spirit, unconscious appear to us as what they are: names for language. This is why for us, any philosophy, any religion, or any knowledge that has not become conscious of this turn belongs irrevocably to the past. The veils that theology, ontology, and psychology cast over the human have now fallen away, and we can return them to their proper place in language. We now look without veils upon language, which, having breathed out all divinity and all unsayability, is now wholly revealed, absolutely in the beginning. Like a poet who finally sees the face of his Muse, philosophy now stands face to face with language (this is why—because "Muse" names the most originary experience of language—Plato can say that philosophy is the "supreme music").

Nihilism experiences this very abandonment of the word by God. But it interprets the extreme revelation of language in the sense that there is nothing to reveal, that the truth of language is that it unveils the Nothing of all things. The absence of a metalanguage thus appears as the negative form of the presupposition, and the Nothing as the final veil, the final name of language.

If, at this point, we take up Wittgenstein's image of the fly imprisoned in the glass, we can say that contemporary thought has finally recognized the inevitability, for the fly, of the glass in which it is imprisoned. The preexistence and anonymity of the signifying function constitute the insuperable presupposition that always already anticipates speaking beings. Human beings are condemned to understand each other in language. But, once again, what is left aside is precisely the original project assigned to this image: the possibility that the fly might leave the glass.

The task of philosophy is therefore to be assumed exactly at the point at which contemporary thought seems to abandon it. If it is true that the fly must begin by seeing the glass in which it is enclosed, what can such a vision mean? What does it mean to see and to expose the limits of language? (For the fly, the glass is not a *thing* but rather *that through which* it sees things.) Can there be a discourse that, without being a metalanguage or sinking into the unsayable, says language itself and exposes its limits?

An ancient tradition of thought formulates this possibility as a theory of Ideas. Contrary to the interpretation that sees in it the unsayable foundation of a metalanguage, at the basis of the theory of Ideas lies a full acceptance of the anonymity of language and the homonymy that governs its field (it is in this sense that one should understand Plato's insistence on the homonymy between Ideas and things, as well as the Socratic rejection of the hatred of language). Yet precisely the finitude and polysemy of human language becomes the path opened for the "dialectical voyage" of thought. If every human word always presupposed another word, if the presuppositional power of language knew no limits, then there would truly be no possible experience of the limits of language. On the other hand, a perfect language purged of all homonymy and composed solely of univocal signs would be a language absolutely without Ideas.

The Idea is fully contained in the play between the anonymity and the homonymy of language. *The Idea neither is and has a name nor is not and does not have a name.* The Idea is not a word (a metalanguage), nor is it a vision of an object outside language (there is no such object, no such unsayable thing); it is a *vision of language itself.* Language, which for human beings mediates all things and all knowledge, is itself immediate. Nothing immediate can be reached by speaking beings—nothing, that is, except language itself, mediation itself. For human beings, such an *immediate mediation* constitutes the sole possibility of reaching a principle freed of every presupposition, including self-presupposition. Such an *immediate mediation* alone, in other words, allows human beings to reach that *arkhē anypothetos*, that "unpresupposed principle" that Plato, in the *Republic*, presents as the *telos*, fulfillment and end of *autos ho logos*, language itself: the "thing itself" and essential matter of human beings.

There can be no true human community on the basis of a presupposition—be it a nation, a language, or even the a priori of communication of which hermeneutics speaks. What unites human beings among themselves is not a nature, a voice, or a common imprisonment in signifying language; it is the vision of language itself and, therefore, the experience of language's limits, its *end*. A true community can only be a community that is not presupposed. Pure philosophical presentation, therefore, cannot merely be the presentation of ideas about language or the world; instead, it must above all be the presentation of *the Idea of language.*

§ 3 Language and History:
Linguistic and Historical Categories
in Benjamin's Thought

Among the preparatory notes to Walter Benjamin's "Theses on the Philosophy of History," we find the following passage, which is repeated in several versions:

> The messianic world is the world of total and integral actuality. In it alone is there universal history. What goes by the name of universal history today can only be a kind of Esperanto. Nothing can correspond to it as long as the confusion originating in the Tower of Babel is not smoothed out. It presupposes the language into which every text of a living or dead language must be wholly translated. Or, rather, it itself is this language. Not, though, as written, but as festively celebrated. This celebration is purified of every ceremony; it knows no celebratory songs. Its language is the idea of prose itself, which is understood by all humans just as the language of birds is understood by those born on Sunday.[1]

The comparison suggested in this passage between language and history, linguistic categories and historical categories, may seem surprising at first glance. The history of redeemed humanity, Benjamin says, is the only universal history; but the history of redeemed humanity is one with its language. Universal history presupposes or, rather, *is* the universal language that puts an end to the Babelic confusion of tongues. The figure of this language of redeemed humanity is, however, a language that is not written but joyously celebrated. It is the idea of prose, the "freed prose," as we read in one variant, "which has broken the chains of writing"[2] and is therefore understood by all humans just as the language of birds, according to a popular Christian legend concerning the supernatural powers of "children born on Sunday," is understood by such *Sonntagskinder*.

In the pages that follow, I suggest a reading of this text, in which Benjamin expressed one of his deepest intentions in an exemplary gesture.

The approximation between historical categories and linguistic categories that is at issue here is not as unusual as it may appear to us today. It was familiar to medieval thought through a formulation that is perhaps even more extreme: "history," we read in Isidore of Seville's *Etymologies*, "pertains to grammar" (*haec disciplina [scil. historia] ad grammaticam pertinet*).[3] In the Augustinian text in which Isidore's sentence found its authority, this pertinence is explained by the fact that every historical transmission necessarily refers to the domain of the "letter." Having considered what he calls the "infancy of grammar" (*quaedam grammaticae infantia*), from the invention of alphabetic characters to the identification of parts of speech, Augustine continues:

> Grammar might have ended there. But since its very name indicated letters, which in Latin is the root of "literature," it so happened that anything memorable consigned to letters [*litteris mandaretur*] necessarily pertained to it. This discipline was thus associated with history, which is one by name but infinite in material, diverse, more full of cares than joy or truth, and a serious affair that is more the business of grammarians than of historians.[4]

If history is presented here, in the gloomy light familiar to us, as "a serious affair that is more the business of grammarians than of historians," it is because Augustine, with an acute comprehension of the nature of language, understands that the science of language includes not only grammar in the strict sense (the synchronic analysis of linguistic structures) but also the "infinite" dimension of historical transmission (*litteris mandaretur*). For Augustine, the letter, the *gramma*, is thus first of all a historical element. In what sense?

Augustine's conception of the matter has its foundation in the Stoic theory of language, which was still expressed, for example, in Varro's great treatise on the Latin language. This theory clearly distinguishes two planes in language: the level of names (or of pure nomination, *impositio, quaemadmodum vocabula rebus essent imposita*) and the level of discourse, which is derived from it as "a river from its source."[5]

Since humans can receive names—which always precede them—only through transmission, the access to this fundamental dimension of language is mediated and conditioned by history. Speaking beings do not invent names, and names do not emerge from speaking beings as from animal voices. Instead, Varro says, names reach humans *in descending*, that is, through historical transmission. Names can only be given and passed on; the act of speech is the object of an *ars* and therefore susceptible to a technical and rational science. It does not matter here whether names are conceived as a divine gift or a human invention; what is important is that in every case their origin escapes the speaker.

This decomposition of the plane of language into the two hierarchically distinct levels of names and actual speech constitutes an intuition so lasting and central that we can still find it in perfectly analogous terms in Wittgenstein's *Tractatus logico-philosophicus*. Here names are defined as "simple signs" (*Urzeichen*) whose meaning must already have been explained for us to understand them.[6] With propositions, Wittgenstein says, we understand each other without any further explanations. (It is worth reflecting on this character of human access to language, which is such that every act of speech presupposes the level of names, which can be reached only historically, through a "thus it is said" that is in fact a "thus it was said.")

It is this primordial historical foundation of language, which resists all purely technical and rational penetration, that Dante, in a passage of the *Convivio*, presents in an astronomical image as the "shadow" of language. Here Dante compares grammar to the moon's heaven, on account of "the shadow in [that heaven], which is nothing but the rarity of its substance in which the rays of the sun cannot terminate and be reflected back as in its other parts."[7] For Dante, grammar too possesses this property, "for because of its infinitude the rays of reason are not terminated, especially insofar as words are concerned."[8]

Reason cannot reach the origin of names (*li vocaboli*) and cannot master them because, as we have seen, they reach reason only though history, *in descending*. This infinite "descent" of names is history. Language thus always anticipates the original place of speaking beings, retreating toward the past and the future of an infinite descent, such that thinking can never find an end to it. And this is the incurable "shadow" of grammar, the darkness that originally inheres in language and that—in the necessary coincidence of history and grammar—founds the historical condition of human beings. History is the cipher of the shadow that denies human beings direct access to the level of names; *history is the place of names.* The transparency of language—the ungroundedness of every act of speech—founds both theology and history. As long as human beings cannot reach the origin of language, there will be the transmission of names. And as long as there is the transmission of names, there will be history and destiny.

In this light, the coincidence between language and history stated in Benjamin's text no longer seems surprising. The historical condition of human beings is inseparable from their condition as speaking beings; it is inscribed in the very mode of their access to language, which is originally marked by a fracture. But how does Benjamin understand this cohesion of language and history, linguistic categories and historical categories? In a text of 1916, entitled "The Meaning of Language in the German Mourning-Play and in Tragedy," he expressed it in a striking, abbreviated form: "in human language," we read there, "history is born together with meaning."[9] And yet in this text, the cohesion of language and history is not total. It coincides, indeed, with a fracture in language itself, that is, with the fall of language (*Wort*) from the "pure life of feeling" (*reines Gefühlsleben*), in which it is "the pure sound of feeling," into the domain of meaning (*Bedeutung*). "Along the course of this path [away from pure sound]," Benjamin writes, "nature sees herself betrayed by language, and this immense inhibition of feeling becomes mourning."[10] History and meaning are thus produced together, but they follow a condition of language that is, so to speak, prehistoric, in which language exists in a "pure life of feeling" without meaning.

In the essay "On Language as Such and the Language of Men" (1916), the decomposition of language into two levels is clearly articulated by a mythologeme founded on the exegesis of the Bible. Here, as in medieval thought, the original level of language is that of names, which is exemplified in the Genesis account by Adamic naming. What Benjamin defines here as "pure language" (*reine Sprache*) or the language of names (*Namensprache*), however, is in no way what we, according to a more and more common conception, understand as language—that is, meaningful speech as the means of a communication that transmits a message from one subject to another. Such a conception of language is expressly rejected by Benjamin as a "bourgeois notion of language" whose "inconsistency and vacuity" he intends to show. The pure language of names, by contrast, appears as an example of a notion of language "that knows no means, no object, and no addressee of communication." The name, as "the innermost nature of language itself," is that "*through which* nothing is communicated, and *in which* language communicates itself absolutely. In naming the mental entity that communicates itself is *language.*" This is why Benjamin can define the name as "the language of language (if the genitive refers to the relationship not of a means but of a medium)."[11]

The status of this Adamic language is therefore that of speech that does not communicate anything other than itself and in which spiritual essence and linguistic essence thus coincide. Such a language does not have a content and does not communicate objects through meanings; instead, it is perfectly transparent to itself: "There is no such thing as a content of language; as communication, language communicates a spiritual entity, that is, a communicability pure and simple." This is why the problem of the unsayable (as a "conflict . . . between what is expressed and expressible and what is inexpressible and unexpressed"), which is characteristic of human language, cannot exist in pure language.[12] Here the philosophy of language has its point of contact with religion in the concept of revelation, which does not admit the concept of the unsayable.

The original sin for which humans are driven out of Paradise is, first of all, the fall of language from being a language of insignificant and perfectly transparent names to signifying speech as the means of an external communication: "The word must communicate *something* (other than itself). That is really the Fall of language-spirit. . . . In stepping outside the pure language of names, man makes a language into a means (that is, a knowledge inappropriate to him), and therefore also, in one part at any rate, a *mere* sign; and this later results in the plurality of languages."[13]

It is this fallen condition of language, which is confirmed by the Babelic confusion of tongues, that Benjamin's 1921 essay "The Task of the Translator" presents from the perspective of its messianic redemption. Here the multiplicity of historical languages is grasped in its movement toward the pure language that the 1916 essay "On Language as Such and the Language of Men" presented as their Edenic origin. Pure language now appears as what every language, in its own way, means [*vuole dire*].[14] "All suprahistorical kinship of languages," Benjamin writes, "rests in the intention underlying each language as a whole—an intention, however, which no single language can attain by itself but which is realized only by the totality of their intentions supplementing each other: pure language."[15] What is meant in language lies in every single language in expectation of flowering, from the harmony of all languages, into the one language that Benjamin defines as "the messianic end of their history." Just as history tends toward its messianic fulfillment, so linguistic movement as a whole tends toward "a final, conclusive, decisive stage of all linguistic creation."[16] The task of the philosopher, like that of the translator, is to "describe" and "intimate" this single true language, which seeks to "show itself" and "constitute itself" in the becoming of languages. And at the end of the essay, this pure language is described in the decisive figure of an "expressionless word" freed from the weight and extraneousness of meaning:

> To relieve it of this [meaning], to turn the symbolizing into the symbolized, to regain pure language fully formed in the linguistic flux, is the tremendous and only capacity of translation. In this pure language—which no longer means anything [*nichts mehr meint*] and no longer expresses anything [*nichts mehr ausdrückt*] but, as expressionless and creative word, that which is meant in all languages—all communication, all sense, and all intention finally encounter a stratum in which they are destined to be extinguished.[17]

How are we to understand this "expressionless word," this pure language in which all communication and all meaning are extinguished? How are we to think—since this and nothing less is the task given to thinking at this point—of a word that no longer means anything, that is no longer destined to the historical transmission of a meaning? And in what sense can this word—which has necessarily extinguished the Babelic confusion of languages—furnish us with the model of the universal language of redeemed humanity, "which is understood by all humans just as the language of birds is understood by those born on Sunday"? In other words, how can human beings simply speak and comprehend speech without the mediation of meaning?

All historical languages, Benjamin writes, mean pure language. It is what is meant (*das Gemeinte*) in every language, what every language means to say. On the other hand, however, it itself does not mean anything; it does not want to say anything, and all meaning and intention come to a halt in it. We may thus say that *all languages mean to say the word that does not mean anything*.

Let us seek to consider this paradox fully. Benjamin writes, "all suprahistorical kinship of languages rests in the intention underlying each language as a whole—an intention, however, which no single language can attain by itself but which is realized only by the totality of their intentions supplementing each other."[18] What remains unsayable and unsaid in every language is therefore precisely what every language means and wants to say: pure language, the expressionless word. And the fact that what is meant is permanently unsaid founds and sustains the signifying tension of languages in their historical becoming. The level of the language of names—whose difference from discourse, as we have seen, inaugurates the cohesion of language and history—is what is meant in all languages, what all languages transmit without ever being able to express. It is thus (and this is how we may now interpret the biblical myth of the loss of Edenic language) what destines the multiplicity of languages to their historical movement. They signify and have meaning because they mean to say something; but what they mean to say—pure language—remains unsaid in them.

The relationship between the multiplicity of historical languages and their single meaning is thus dialectical: to say what they mean, languages would have to cease to mean it, that is, transmit it. But this is exactly what they cannot do without abolishing themselves, for this can be accomplished only by the totality of linguistic meanings, that is, their messianic fulfillment. This is why Benjamin writes that "an instant and final rather than a temporary and provisional solution of this foreignness remains out of the reach of mankind; at any rate, it eludes any direct attempt."[19] This does not mean that we are confronted here by an infinite dialectic. Indirectly, this task is possible and real (as Benjamin writes for religion, which "ripens the hidden seed into a higher development of language").[20] The universal and expressionless language "constitutes" itself and "shows" itself in the historical becoming of languages. Its constitution, however, definitively extinguishes all linguistic meaning, eliminating the unsayable that destined it to historical transmission and signification. Insofar as pure language is the only language that does not mean anything but simply speaks, it is also the only language that accomplishes the "crystalline elimination of the unsayable in language" that Benjamin evoked in a letter to Martin Buber in July 1916. It is truly "the language of language," which saves the meaning of all languages and in whose transparency language finally says itself.

Now that we have distinguished the physiognomic characteristics of pure language, however paradoxical they may be, let us return to the passage from which we began and ask: how are we to represent its reality as the universal language of redeemed humanity?

We may begin by imagining this language in accordance with a hypothesis that Benjamin explicitly excludes, that is, as a kind of Esperanto. It certainly did not escape Benjamin that a messianic intention lies at the basis of Esperanto and is expressed in its very name. (In a preparatory note to the "Theses on the Philosophy of History," Benjamin writes: "Universal history in the contemporary sense is always only a kind of Esperanto. It gives expression to the hopes of humankind just as well as universal language does.")[21] The term "Esperanto" means "he who hopes," and it is the pseudonym under which the Polish Jewish physician Ludwig Zamenhof published his *Lingvo internacia* in 1887, presenting the foundations of a universal language to which the author entrusted his hopes for a lasting and universal understanding among peoples. That he represented his language in a messianic sense (that is, to use Benjamin's words, as the "language in which every text of a living or dead language must be wholly translated") is shown by his tenacious translation work, which culminated in the translation of the Old Testament into Esperanto, published in 1926 (that is, at the same time that Franz Rosenzweig and Buber were preparing their German translation of the Bible).

How is Esperanto formed? It is based on the 4,013 (principally neo-Latin) roots deduced from Indo-European, which form substantives through the addition of the suffix -o, adjectives through the suffix -a, and verbal infinitives through the suffix -i. Thus from *skrib*, which signifies writing, one has *skribo* (writer), *skriba* (written), and *skribi* (to write). Esperanto thus consists in a regularization and extreme grammatical simplification of the structure of historical languages, which leaves intact the fundamental conception of language as a system of signs transmitting meanings. A limit is set on the plurality of languages in the sense not of their messianic fulfillment and transfiguration but of an in-finite conservation of their signification and meaning. It takes only an instant to realize that what is excluded from Esperanto is precisely the messianic fulfillment of which Benjamin wrote. Esperanto is a language of infinite meaning that can never find fulfillment. A conception of universal history with Esperanto as its model could only be a summary organization of the essential elements of all particular histories. But such a compendium would not be the world of an integral actuality freed from all writing; it would, instead, be writing consigned to infinite transmission.

Another interpretation against which Benjamin explicitly warns his readers is that of conceiving universal language (or universal history) as an "Ideal" in the sense of an infinite task traversing all historical becoming. The expressionless word, in this sense, would be an infinite task that could never be accomplished as such and toward which the historical experience of speaking humanity would be directed. Today such a conception of language and history (which is only falsely termed religious) is maintained by a philosophical current that, having emerged out of an interpretation of Heidegger's thought, has gained a position of notable importance in contemporary academic parlance through its marriage with the Anglo-Saxon analytic tradition.

According to this conception, "every word, as the event of a moment, carries with it the unsaid, to which it is related by responding and summoning. . . . All human speaking is finite in such a way that there is laid up within it an infinity of meaning to be explicated and laid out."[22] This infinity of sense is what all perception of speech must be attentive to: authentic interpretation is interpretation that, in sheltering the openness of the infinite historical community of messages, situates everything said within the historical unsaid that is destined to infinite interpretation. From this perspective, an interpreter who does not want to shelter the infinity of tradition appears, in Hans-Georg Gadamer's words, as "a dog to whom one tries to point something out, but who bites the pointing hand, instead of looking in the direction indicated." Benjamin explicitly warns against such a perspective when, in a single gesture, he criticizes both the Social-Democratic transformation of the Marxian idea of a classless society (which for him was a genuinely messianic idea) into an infinite task and neo-Kantianism's analogous transformation of the Kantian Idea into an Ideal. Just as the classless society becomes what founds and guides all historical development without ever being attained in experience, so hermeneutics transforms ideal language into the unsayable foundation that, without ever itself coming to speech, destines the infinite movement of all language. For Benjamin, on the other hand, "the classless society is not the final end of historical progress, but rather its often failed and finally accomplished interruption."[23]

For Benjamin, the true hermeneutics of a text is the opposite of the one proposed by contemporary hermeneutics. If the interpreter looks toward the unsaid and the infinity of sense, for Benjamin the purpose of doing so is certainly not to preserve them but rather to put an end to them. Like the dog in Gadamer's example, he obstinately bites the hand of the historical instant so that it may cease pointing beyond itself in an infinite reference. Authentic criticism is the fulfillment and mortification of the work. Exposing the Idea in the work, criticism reduces the work to a torso; it dazzles the work, it *says* the work.

The mystical foundation of this conception of language and history clearly appears in another theory, which might also claim to offer a legitimate interpretation of Benjamin's thought. We refer here to the ancient Cabalistic theory of language, which has found its most authoritative presentation in our time in the work of Gershom Scholem. According to this theory, the foundation of every human language is the name of God. This name, however, has no proper meaning, nor can it itself be uttered; it is simply constituted by the twenty-two letters of the alphabet from whose combination all human languages derive.

"For the Kabbalists," Scholem writes,

> this name has no "meaning" in the traditional understanding of the term. It has no concrete signification. The meaninglessness of the name of God indicates its situation in the very central point of the revelation, at the basis of which it lies. Behind every revelation of a meaning in language . . . there exists this element which projects over and beyond meaning, but which in the first instance enables meaning to be given. It is this element which endows every other form of meaning, though it has no meaning itself. What we learn from creation and revelation, the word of God, is infinitely liable to interpretation, and it is reflected in our own language. Its radiation of sounds, which we catch, are not so much communications as appeals. That which has meaning—sense and form—is not this word itself, but the tradition behind this word, its communication and reflection in time.[24]

With this mystical conception of the relationship between the "literal" name of God and human language, we enter into a horizon of thought that was certainly familiar to Benjamin and that has been secularized in our time through the theory of the supremacy of the letter or *gramma* (as the originary negative foundation of language), which, starting with Derrida, appears in innumerable forms in contemporary French thought. Yet once again, Benjamin's text excludes the possibility of such an interpretation. While the mystical and in-significant character of the name of God is, in the Cabala as in grammatology, tied to its being constituted by pure letters, Benjamin explicitly states that the language of redeemed humanity has "burst the chains of writing" and is a language that "is not writ-

ten, but festively celebrated." Here Benjamin opposes the Cabala's writing of what was never said with a "reading of what was never written." If
the letters that compose the unpronounceable name of God are what destines human language to historical transmission and infinite interpretation, we may then say that universal language represents the definitive
cancellation and resolution of these letters, the definitive and absolute utterance of God's name in speech. (This much also accords with the intention that Benjamin once expressed by likening his own relationship to
theology to that of a blotting pad to ink: "It is soaked through with it.
But if it were up to the blotting pad, there would be no more ink.")

Having excluded these three hypotheses, we have delineated certain
features of pure language, if only negatively. But we have certainly not
presented its full figure. That what is at issue here was, for Benjamin,
something like the supreme problem of thought is shown by the fact that
in the "Epistemological-Critical Preface" to the *Origin of the German
Tragic Drama* he ties the pure language of Adamic names to the Platonic
theory of Ideas. "The Idea," we read there,

> is something linguistic [*ein Sprachliches*]; it is that element of the symbolic in
> the essence of any word. In empirical perception, in which words have be-
> come fragmented, they possess, in addition to their more or less hidden, sym-
> bolic aspect, an obvious, profane meaning. It is the task of the philosopher to
> restore, by presentation, the primacy of the symbolic character of the word,
> in which the Idea is given self-consciousness, and that is the opposite of all
> outwardly-directly communication. . . . In philosophical contemplation, the
> Idea is released from the heart of reality as the word, reclaiming its name-
> giving power.[25]

And it is precisely the pure power of nomination, which is "not lost in the
cognitive meaning," that in the immediately following passage constitutes
Adam, alongside Plato, as the true father of philosophy.

At this point, the comprehension of the status of names becomes as essential—and as aporetic—as the comprehension of the status of the Ideas
in Plato's *Parmenides* (those Ideas that, Plato says, were born precisely out
of an inquiry into *logoi*, words). Do names, like Ideas with respect to phenomena, exist as real things in themselves, separate (*khōris*) with respect
to existing words? Is there a separation (*khōrismos*) between the language
of names and human language? Once again, it is precisely the capacity to

think of this relation that will decide whether the language of names and universal language are to be conceived as an unattainable origin and infinite task, or whether instead the actual construction of this relation and this region constitutes the true task of the philosopher and the translator, the historian and the critic, and, in the final analysis, the ethical engagement of every speaking being.

In the "Epistemological-Critical Preface," the exposition of the Idea in phenomena is inseparable from the salvation of phenomena in the Idea: the two penetrate each other in a single gesture. The exposition of phenomena, Benjamin writes, is at the same time that of the Ideas; what is unique in phenomena is saved in the Ideas alone. This unity, however, implies a dialectic in which origin and end are identified and transformed. The origin here indicates not origination (*Entstehung*) but rather something like Goethe's *Urphänomen*, an "original phenomenon" in which "there takes place . . . a determination of the form in which an Idea will constantly confront the historical world, until it is revealed fulfilled, in the totality of its history."[26] At the same time, here the end is no longer simple cessation but, first of all, totality ("in the science of philosophy the concept of Being is not satisfied by the phenomenon until it has consummated all its history"). In the Idea, the phenomenon is fulfilled, "it becomes what it was not—totality." This is why the power of the Idea does not lie in the sphere of facts, "but refers to their pre-history and post-history," to their origin and their fulfilled totality.[27]

As origin, the language of names is therefore not an initial chronological point, just as the messianic end of languages, the universal language of redeemed humanity, is not a simple chronological cessation. Together they constitute the two faces of the single *Idea of language*, which the 1916 essay "On Language as Such and the Language of Men" and the 1921 essay on the task of the translator presented as divided.

If we now return to the text that was our starting point, we will understand the sense in which Benjamin writes that the universal language of redeemed humanity, which is one with its history, is "the idea of prose itself, which is understood by all humans just as the language of birds is understood by those born on Sunday." With an intuition whose audacity and coherence must be considered, Benjamin thus holds that the universal language at issue here can only be the Idea of language, that is, not an *Ideal* (in the neo-Kantian sense) but the very *Platonic Idea* that saves and in itself fulfills all languages, and that an enigmatic Aristotelian fragment describes as "a kind of mean between prose and poetry." For Benjamin, however, it coincides with the Idea of prose itself, in the sense in which Benjamin develops the concept of the prosaic nucleus of every linguistic formulation in his thesis on the romantic concept of criticism.

One of Paul Valéry's observations in an article in the *Encyclopédie française* struck Benjamin so forcefully that he transcribed it in one of his notebooks while working on his "Storyteller" essay. It reads: "the essence of prose is to perish, that is, to be comprehended, to be dissolved, destroyed without residue, wholly substituted by an image or impulse." Insofar as it has reached perfect transparency to itself, insofar as it now says and understands only itself, speech restored to the Idea is immediately dispersed; it is "pure history"—history without grammar or transmission, which knows neither past nor repetition, resting solely in its own *never having been*. It is what is continually said and what continually takes place in every language not as an unsayable presupposition but as what, in never having been, sustains the life of language. The Idea of language is language that no longer presupposes any other language; it is the language that, having eliminated all of its presuppositions and names and no longer having anything to say, now simply speaks.

In the perfect transparency of language in which there is no more distinction between the level of names and the level of signifying speech, between what is meant and what is said, it truly seems that languages—and with them all human culture—reach their messianic end. But what ends here is only a determinate conception of language and a determinate conception of culture: the conception to which we are accustomed, which founds all historical becoming and transmission on the incurable division between the thing to be transmitted and the act of transmission, names and discourse, thereby securing the infinity and continuity of the historical (and linguistic) process.

Benjamin criticized this conception without reservation when he wrote that the past must be saved not so much from oblivion or scorn as from "a determinate mode of its transmission," and that "the way in which it is valued as 'heritage' is more insidious than its disappearance could ever be." Or, to cite another statement: "[The history of culture] may well increase the burden of the treasures that are piled up on humanity's back. But it does not give humankind the strength to shake them off, so as to get its hands on them."[28]

Here, instead, humanity has truly taken its "treasures" in its hands: its language and its history, its language-history, we could say. The division of the plane of language, which simultaneously grounded the inextricable intertwining of language and history and guaranteed their asymptotic noncoincidence, now disappears and gives way to a perfect identity of language and history, praxis and speech.

This is why universal history has no past to transmit, being instead a world of "integral actuality."

Here language disappears as an autonomous category; it is possible neither to make any distinct image of it nor to imprison it in any writing. Human beings no longer write their language; they celebrate it as a holiday without rites, and they understand each other "just as those born on Sunday understand the language of birds."

§ 4 Philosophy and Linguistics

To undertake a philosophical review of a work of linguistics poses a problem of legitimization. The history of the relations between philosophy and the science of language (taking this term in the large sense, such that it includes the *technē grammatikē* of the ancients and the *grammatica* of the medievals) is so rich in exchanges, crossings, and accidents that any attempt to distinguish the two with precision appears both necessary and impossible. Not only does the ancient tradition attribute to Plato and Aristotle the origin of grammar, but further, from the beginning, logical categories and grammatical categories have been so tightly interlaced that they appear inseparable. The Stoics, whose linguistic theory had such decisive importance for the history of the study of language, thus considered *phōnē* (in the grammatical sense of *phōnē enarthros*, "articulated voice") as the *arkhē* and foundation of dialectics. And in Aristotle's *Categories* it was already impossible to understand what was indicated by the concept of *legomena kata mēdemian symplokēn* without taking into account the necessarily grammatical part of speech (*meros tou logou*) that it implies. In the same treatise, moreover, the determination of pure Being (*protē ousia*) is inseparable from the meaning of the deictic pronoun and the proper name, in accordance with a parallelism that characterizes the entire history of ontology (it suffices to think of the importance of the pronoun and the proper name, and more generally of grammatical categories, in the treatment of the problem of supreme Being in medieval theology, or of the impossibility of distinguishing between logic and grammar in a Scholastic treatise *de modis significandi*).

The project proposed by Heidegger in a crucial passage of *Being and Time*—"to liberate grammar from logic"—cannot, therefore, be easily accomplished. Language would have to be simultaneously liberated from grammar (a program formulated, more or less consciously and according to different modalities, throughout the history of Western thought). And this would presuppose a critique of the interpretation of language implicit in the most elementary grammatical categories: the concepts of articulation (*arthron*), letter (*gramma*), and part of speech. Such is the significance of these categories, which the Greeks already clearly defined in their reflection on language and which, strictly speaking, are neither logical nor grammatical but rather what renders possible every logic, every grammar, and perhaps even every *epistēmē* in general.

II

Forms of thought find their first exteriorization in man's language, where they are so to speak deposited. . . . One finds the intervention of language in everything that becomes his interiority, in his representation in general, in everything that he makes his own. Everything with which he forms his language and by which he expresses himself in language contains a more or less concealed, mixed or explicit category. Thus he naturally thinks according to his logic; or, rather, his logic constitutes his very nature. But if one wanted to oppose nature in general to the spiritual, as something belonging to the physical world, one would have to say that logic constitutes the supernatural, penetrating into all of man's attitudes toward nature, his feelings, intuitions, desires, needs, impulses; and one would have to say that man is what humanizes them.

This passage from the preface to the second edition of Hegel's *Science of Logic* clearly expresses one of the enduring subjects of the philosophical tradition: the intertwining of thought and language and the task it implies for thinking. In our time, this task was decisively reformulated in a different way by Alexandre Kojève when he defined philosophy as the discourse "that can speak of everything, on the condition that it also speak of the fact that it does so." If this definition is correct, the so-called "linguistic turn" by which contemporary philosophy and its interest in language (in the large sense) have been defined risks stating merely a trivial truth. The fact is that the term "language," to take up Aristotle's phrase, "is said in many ways," and only an elucidation of what philosophy and linguistics respectively understand by this term can lead to a useful consideration of their relationship. That there is an interlacement between philosophy and the study of language does not necessarily mean that philosophy and linguistics have the same object. Heidegger's observations that "the Being of the being that linguistics takes for its object remains hidden" and that philosophical reflection, for its part, should give up "the philosophy of language" to ask itself above all "what mode of Being should be attributed to language" (in other words, if language has the mode of Being of a worldly object or not)—these observations have lost none of their currency today. As something "said in many ways" (*pollakhōs legomenon*), the very concept of language is caught in a vague homonymy and often remains imprecise, both in the field of linguistics and in that of philosophical research.

III

Milner's book presents itself as an "introduction to the science of language." It is the work of a linguist who is also a thinker of great originality. While his two recent books (*L'amour de la langue* and *Les noms indistincts*) are among the most important contemporary French contributions to the study of language, references to them are rare. This is perhaps because Milner's enterprise, as he describes it in his *Introduction*, aims at being "resolutely scientific," in the sense that it undertakes to examine and maintain "the hypothesis according to which linguistics is a science, just as a natural science may be a science."[1]

It is not by accident that this introduction to "a" science of language appears at a time when the glorious season of linguistics seems a thing of the past. With the exhaustion of the project of comparative grammar and the decline of the no less brilliant, if perhaps less significant, project of generative grammar, linguistics today is no longer the "foremost" human science, as it was clearly thought to be only two decades ago. The prestige of the human sciences in general is now in a period of decline. The project of a "general science of the human," which reached its apex at the end of the 1960s, dissolved with the political project of the same years. The severe prose of the world of the 1980s tolerates only positive sciences and, alongside them, a philosophy that is more and more oblivious of its destination.

One could think that a book such as this *Introduction*, which wishes to be wholly consecrated to the foundation of a positive science of language, could not help clarify the relationship between philosophy and language. But precisely the contrary is the case, for in more than one point Milner's *Introduction* contributes decisively to the clarification of the concept of language and its homonyms. This review cannot, of course, take account of the book in its entirety (a task to which only a linguist would be adequate); it will, instead, concentrate on some of the points to which we have already alluded. In discussing them, I propose to show how this book, while maintaining itself inside the science of language, allows for a precise determination of the relationship between philosophy and linguistics as well as their respective tasks.

IV

A first point is to be found in Part I of the book, which is devoted to the epistemological status of language and concerns the identification of the very object of the science of language. While Milner does not mean "to propose a theory of knowledge" (p. 23), it would be difficult to find a work of epistemology that contained such a clear and original presentation of the concept of Galilean science. According to Milner, the mathematization characteristic of Galilean science has as its basis not (as is usually thought) quantification but "literalization," by which Milner means that "one uses symbols that can and must be taken completely literally, without regard to what they may designate," and that "one uses these symbols solely in accordance with their own rules." "The possibility of full communication . . . rests on the fact that, once the rules for the use of the letters are learned, everyone will use them in the same way" (p. 24). Literalization therefore implies "the irreducible difference between restriction and the substance of restricted beings." "What is then taken from mathematics is the dimension of restriction, which applies to beings whose objective reference (substance) can certainly be determined, but does not have to be when one uses restraint itself. It then follows that one can use beings without 'seeing' what they designate, and one then correctly speaks of blind use" (pp. 91–92).

Immediately afterward, Milner lists a series of "primitive facts" that

function as irreducible limits, which linguistics must confront and beyond which it cannot venture. In the first place there is the *factum loquendi*, whose sole content is the existence of language, the fact that there
are speaking beings:

> The usual name for this brute fact is *language*. One may note that it presup-
> poses only one thing: that there are speaking beings. In this sense, to speak of
> language is simply to speak of the fact that speaking beings exist. Neverthe-
> less, to speak of this fact in an interesting manner, it will be necessary to call
> the existence of speaking beings into question. But this is precisely what lin-
> guistics cannot do; for linguistics, this existence can be neither deduced nor
> explained in general. It is thus possible to understand the sense in which lin-
> guistics does not have language as its object: language is its axiom.
>
> This does not at all mean that one cannot consider this existence in itself,
> questioning its conditions of possibility. It is only that one then finds a ques-
> tion of the following kind: "Why is there language rather than no language
> at all?" And this is a properly metaphysical question. (p. 41)

The second "primitive fact," which must be clearly distinguished from
the first, is the *factum linguae*:

> It suffices to establish that beings speak to conclude that language exists. The
> question as to the properties of what they say is not pertinent at this level.
> Linguistics cannot remain here; it must therefore admit more than the single,
> massive existence of language. Linguistics admits that speaking beings speak
> *languages*.
>
> To say that the effectuations of language are languages is to suppose at least
> that the set of linguistic productions merits being designated by a common
> name. It is, moreover, to suppose that they are distributed, like the different
> realms of nature, in classes and subclasses, each class generally corresponding
> to what one calls a species in nature. It is, finally, to suppose that one can say
> what a particular *language* is. Briefly, it is supposed (1) that one can distin-
> guish a language from nonlanguage and (2) that one can distinguish one lan-
> guage from another language. It is therefore necessary to reason in terms of
> properties; one must, in other words, distinguish the properties of a language
> from the properties of nonlanguage and the properties of one language from
> those of another language. (p. 43)

This implies not only that languages are diverse while belonging to a
homogeneous class (what Milner calls the *factum linguarum*), but also
and above all that languages are describable in terms of properties. Mil-

ner calls this fact the *factum grammaticae*, and for him it is the constitutive and characteristic fact of linguistics.

The clarity of this definition makes it the only one to untangle the ambiguity inherent in the term "language" and to distinguish with precision the object of philosophy from the object of linguistics. If the object of linguistics is language (understood as shorthand for the *factum linguae*, the *factum linguarum*, and the *factum grammaticae*), philosophy is instead concerned with the *factum loquendi*, which linguistics must simply presuppose. Philosophy is the attempt to *expose* this presupposition, to become conscious of the meaning of the fact that human beings speak. It is possible to see how it is the *factum grammaticae* that marks the difference between philosophy and linguistics: philosophy is concerned with the pure existence of language, independent of its real properties (transcendental properties, which belong to philosophical reflection, do not go beyond the field of pure existence), while linguistics is concerned with language insofar as it is describable in terms of real properties, insofar as it has (or, rather, is) a grammar.

Hence the exclusion from philosophy of speculations on the origin of language, which traditionally belong to the patrimony of the philosophy of language. As Milner observes, hypotheses on the origin of language are nothing other than "the fictional form of the limit between 'language does not exist' and 'language exists,' insofar as this limit is presented as a passage. What is supposed to appear in this fictional passage are essential and defining properties: those properties without which one cannot say that there is language" (p. 42). Philosophy's attempts to identify the real properties defining the essence of language are doomed to failure precisely because they illegitimately step beyond their own boundaries into the territory of science. For philosophy, there is not and there cannot be an *essence* of language (or, consequently, a philosophical grammar), since the task of philosophy is exhausted in the presentation of the existence of language. Here one encounters the boundary separating the field of *epistēmē* from that of first philosophy. In its relation to language, philosophy can only remain faithful to its originary vocation as the science of pure existence. If science in the strict sense is the discipline that knows the properties of beings (or of beings insofar as they possesses real, describable properties), philosophy (as first philosophy) is the science that contemplates beings insofar as they exist (*on hē on, on haplōs*), that is, independent of their real properties.

V

But the relationship between philosophy and language (and hence between philosophy and linguistics) is in fact more complex. In the face of an *epistēmē*, philosophy can only assert its proper vocation as a science of pure existence through a particular experience of language. The pure existence (without any properties other than transcendental ones) that constitutes the sole object of philosophy is something to which philosophy has no access other than through reflection on the *factum loquendi* and the construction of an experience in which this *factum* is thematically at issue. Only the *experience of the pure existence of language allows thought to consider the pure existence of the world.*

Hence—from Plato to Wittgenstein—the striking relation of philosophy to language, which is one of both defiance and disavowal, "philology" and "misology." Hence also the proximity of and distance between philosophy and the science of language. Both refer back to the same place, whose existence one discipline must contemplate and the other presuppose for the establishment of grammatical categories. Both lack particular instruments and firm ground for the realization of their goals; both must experience language without having at their disposal (as do the other sciences with respect to their objects) any external observation post. One could thus say of philosophy what Milner says of linguistics—that it is "an experimental science without an observation post" (p. 128), a science that has the example as its proper mode of experimentation. The questions that philosophy poses (like the fictions it sometimes employs) do not demand any information as their answer (nor do they have any narrative value). They hold, instead, as examples, in the sense in which Milner defines examples for linguistics.[2] Despite the refinement of its logical technique, philosophy, like linguistics, must ultimately keep to natural language. If linguistics, according to Milner's phrase, is a *scientia infima*—which "gives itself the most minimal object conceivable" and of which it is true that "whatever a theory's degree of mathematical formalization, the final instance will always be a proposition stated in natural language" (p. 130)—it is from a still more minimal place, namely from the pure existence of language, that philosophy must depart.

Do the two sciences, at once so close and so far apart with respect to their object, touch at any point? Is there a place in linguistics in which the existence of language can be said to emerge as such?

VI

A place of this kind can be found in the third chapter of the second part of Milner's book, which is called "Restricted Theory of Terms." These forty pages constitute an exemplary analysis of one of the most complex parts of linguistic theory (one of its fundamental claims about this field is, as Milner states, that if "positions" concern syntax, "linguistic entities" can be said to be "of two kinds: terms and positions," p. 409).

From its beginnings, the Greek reflection on language assigned a fundamental place to the distinction between *onoma* (name or term) and *logos* (speech or proposition). According to a tradition that originated with the Stoa, the event of nomination (*appellatio, nominum impositio*) is conceptually and genetically distinct from actual discourse. In Antisthenes, this grammatical distinction is linked to the problem of the unsayability of pure existence, in the sense that primal and simple elements can have no defining discourse but only names. A proposition cannot *say* what the name has named (as Wittgenstein would write in proposition 3.221 of his *Tractatus*: "I can only *name* objects. . . . I can only speak *of* them. I cannot *assert them*").

In the *Categories*, Aristotle distinguishes the deictic pronoun and the proper name, which signify a pure existence (*protē ousia*), from other names, which always designate qualities. And Plato, who uses the anaphora *auto* to designate the Idea, does not allow language any possibility of directly designating pure existence without properties (hence the *asthenia* of the *logoi* in the philosophical excursus of the Seventh Letter).

Another philosophical problem is tied to the domain of names (and hence to the theory of terms), namely, the problem of self-reference (of the name of the name). This problem has given birth to a series of paradoxes, the most famous being what one could call "the White Knight's paradox," referring to an episode in *Through the Looking-Glass*. Can the name of an object be itself named without thereby losing its character as a name and becoming a named object? Is it, in other words, possible for a name to refer to itself in its existence as a name (*nomen nominans* and not *nomen nominatum*)? In proposition 4.126 of his *Tractatus*, Wittgenstein implicitly gives a negative answer to the question. Carnap, by contrast, maintained that a name can perfectly well be named, by means of the use of quotation marks; but Reach refuted him in a famous article.[3]

Once again, Milner's precise awareness of the problems at issue allows him to order complex material. He does so in a mere ten theorems, with a clarity unparalleled in the history of linguistics. To begin with, he abandons the "contextual principle" (usually attributed to Frege) according to which it is not possible to determine the properties of a linguistic term without reference to its discursive context. The first theorem of the "Restricted Theory of Terms" thus reads as follows: "It is possible to establish the properties of a term without reference to its use" (for example, in recognizing its lexical sense, which constitutes the fundamental principle of dictionaries). But what is a linguistic term considered in itself? What is the *onoma* of Greek linguistic theory?

According to Milner, a term is nothing other than the set of its distinctive properties, which Milner defines by the three traits: (1) belonging to a category; (2) phonological form; (3) lexical meaning (or virtual reference). None of these three properties (not even phonological form, which we are used to identifying with the term itself, as when we say, for example, "*cat* is a one-syllable word") in itself constitutes a linguistic term. And if, in this sense, linguistic individuals are not substantial realities but only "packets of properties" (p. 330), it will not be possible to name a term other than by an indirect procedure:

> The procedure is well known: it is the operation of quotation by which one says *table* to designate the linguistic individual, *table*. . . . Let us be more precise: what designates the linguistic individual *table* is in fact the phonological concatenation t^a^b^l^e. It goes without saying that in using the phonological concatenation t^a^b^l^e, we mean the lexeme *table* with all its lexical properties: its meaning, its categorial belonging, and, of course, its phonological form. In other words, one uses one of its identifying properties to take down in shorthand the set of identifying properties that constitute the individual. (pp. 330–31)

The problem is that of linguistic entities and their names. Here Milner takes his point of departure from Saul Kripke's thesis on the proper name, according to which the proper name is not shorthand for a series of identifying properties:

> Let us recall his demonstration: the mere fact that on the basis of the proper name *Aristotle* and a predicate P, one can construct a proposition such as "Aristotle is P" and its counterfactual "Aristotle is not-P," proves that the proper name *Aristotle* is not shorthand for a packet of identifying predicates. It is thus crucial that if the proposition "Aristotle liked cats" is held to be fac-

tual, "Aristotle did not like cats" be held to be counterfactual. Let us consider the terms of a language: a proposition such as "*table* does not have the phonological form of *table*" is clearly a contradiction *in adjecto* and not a counterfactual. The same holds, despite appearances, for propositions such as "*table* is not a noun" or even "in French, *table* is not feminine." (p. 331)

Kripke's thesis therefore cannot apply to linguistic terms, and Milner can then state a new theorem: "The linguistic term has no proper name" (p. 332). With this theorem, whose importance cannot be overestimated, Milner introduces into linguistics the principle of the impossibility of metalanguage, which is a fact without precedent in the history of linguistics. It is precisely by means of the anonymity and insubstantiality of linguistic Being that philosophy was able to conceive of something like pure existence, that is, a singularity without real properties. If the linguistic term were not anonymous, if we always already had names for the name, we would always already encounter things with their real properties; there would never be a point at which our power of naming (or of the attribution of properties) would come to a halt. This stopping point cannot be constituted by a nonlinguistic being, since language can name everything, its naming power knowing no limits (the nonlinguistic, in this sense, is nothing other than a presupposition of language). But language cannot name itself as naming; the only thing for which names are truly lacking is the name. It is this anonymity of the name that in Plato allows for the appearance of the Idea (which is designated not by another name but simply by means of the syntagma name-*auto*, the Idea of a thing thus having the form of "the thing itself," *to pragma auto*). It is only because the term *rose* is anonymous, because *rose* is not the name of the name *rose*, that in uttering "a rose" I can make *l'absente de tous bouquets*, that is, the rose itself, appear. And it is only the anonymity of linguistic Being that gives meaning to the metaphysical thesis according to which existence is not a real property, or, in other words, the position of the transcendental. If one considers the matter, the fact that "being" (*ens*) is not a real predicate, that it—like the other transcendental predicates (*unum, verum, bonum,* etc.)—belongs to all predication without thereby adding any real property to it, can only mean that predicated Being is not itself namable, as is implicit in Milner's theorem. Being said is, in this sense, the archi-transcendental that allows for the possibility of all predication; but precisely for this reason it cannot apply to the name. Milner's theorem is in reality also a theorem concerning the transcendental; neither the name of the name nor the named name are names, and what maintains itself in relation to this anonymity of the name is pure existence. (Here one recognizes Heidegger's central thesis on language: Being can emerge only where the word is lacking, but the word is lacking only at the point at which one wants to say it.)

VII

Another point at which the existence of language as such seems to emerge within linguistics is the problem of the predisposition to language and its innateness (a thesis maintained in particular by the school of Cambridge). Milner very clearly illustrates the difficulties and contradictions to which this thesis inevitably gives rise.[4] The claim that "language is innate" cannot concern individual languages, which are wholly acquired by individuals according to the linguistic environment in which they find themselves; it can only concern language in general. But what does it mean to speak of a predisposition to "language in general"?

> Let us recall that no one can suppose that a speaking being speaks French innately. Those who reason in terms of innateness suppose only the following: a speaking being speaks innately, and "to speak" is "to be capable of speaking a language in general." And this is language. Of course, it has been maintained that this "disposition to language" is not empty (and that, in other words, language has properties). But the content of this disposition is a disposition to *any* language or *any* type of language. If the disposition to language is not empty, then it is necessary that there exist properties common to many languages, if not all. Consequently, the supposition of a disposition to language necessarily meets up with the question of universal grammar. (p. 227)

Yet the expressions "language in general" and "universal grammar" risk being meaningless:

> Language can only ever be observed in a particular language. In anthropology, it always appears possible to separate clearly and sufficiently the innate part of behavior from its acquired part. In linguistics, this point of departure is never simple; more precisely, it concerns theory and not observation. Let us suppose that it can be shown that in all languages, certain properties can

be found, which in each of them are always combined with particular properties. Theoretical reflection must certainly give a distinct representation of the universal and the particular, but observation only ever encounters a state in which the two are combined. (p. 232)

This disposition to language in general (or to any language) is, in truth, something like the famous *tabula rasa* of the potential intellect of Aristotelian philosophy, which is itself not an actual intelligible but is nevertheless capable of being any intelligible whatsoever. What is to be found in all these general notions, while remaining unthought, is nothing other than the *factum loquendi*, the pure existence of language grasped as a universal linguistic essence. The innateness of language in general in the form of a universal grammar is, in short, only a shadow of this *factum loquendi* with which the science of language cannot reckon. That there is language, that human beings speak, is not a real property that could be determined as a universal grammar in which all languages would participate. Here we can observe the mechanism by which Aristotelian *protē ousia*, which is pure singular existence, becomes the *sub-stantia* underlying all categories. Thought that seeks to grasp the *factum loquendi*, language as pure existence without properties, is always about to become a kind of grammar.

It does not come as a surprise, then, that the different projects that, throughout the history of Western culture, sought to construct a pure experience of the existence of language (that is, of language without real properties) often ended by being substantialized in the form of a (more or less universal) grammar. At the beginning of Romance culture—at the basis of the project of Provençal love poetry and in Dante—there lay the attempt (which is philosophical and not simply poetic) to grasp the pure existence of language by means of the figure of a woman who was held to be the supreme love object and through whom the mother tongue was explicitly opposed to grammar. However one understands the properties that Dante assigned to his "vulgar" language (illustriousness, nobility, etc.), they are certainly not grammatical properties; they seem, instead, to constitute an equivalent to the *transcendentia* of medieval logic, being just as empty of real content as they are. But it is also thus that both Provençal lyric poetry and Dante, in historical circumstances that cannot be examined here, ultimately led to the construction of a grammar. Provençal poetry ended with the *Lays d'amors*, that is, with a monumental grammar of the Provençal language, in which the laws of language were assimilated to the rules of love; and Dante's project of an "illustrious vernacular" ended, albeit at the price of betrayal and contradiction, in the attempt to construct the grammar of a national language.

When, on the other hand, these projects appeared in Western culture in an authentically philosophical form (examples in our century can be found in both Benjamin's "pure language" and the late Heidegger's *die Sage*), what is at issue each time is not the phantasm of a universal language (or grammar) but an experience whose object is the *factum loquendi*, the pure existence of language.

One could make analogous observations (though the register would be different) regarding the science of language. The different attempts to construct a universal language or grammar (from the *lingua matrix* of seventeenth-century philology, to the universal language and the *characteristica* that interested Leibniz, to certain aspects of the reconstruction of Indo-European) register the need to take account in some way of the *factum loquendi* but end up simply showing language's excess with respect to science.

But how, then, is it possible to bear witness legitimately, through knowledge, to the pure existence of language?

VIII

The preceding observations should give an idea of the complexity of the relationship of philosophy and linguistics insofar as it is implicitly shown by Milner's *Introduction*. As a *scientia infima*, linguistics certainly has the fundamental position attributed to it by medieval classifications, which placed grammar first among the seven disciplines of the School. If language is the condition of all learning, grammar—which renders a science of language possible—is the science that conditions all others. And it is easy to see that a science in the modern sense is possible only if language possesses certain recognizable properties; if language were without such properties, or if they had not remained the same, no knowledge would be possible. But there is more to be said. It is only because linguistics presupposes the *factum loquendi*, presupposes the existence of language, that other sciences can presuppose the existence of something that, in turn, underlies the objects whose properties they describe. Pure existence corresponds to the pure existence of language, and to contemplate one is to contemplate the other. The "literalization" effected by grammar—"literalization" in the sense we have seen, insofar as it implies the irreducible difference between restriction and the substance of restricted beings—then constitutes the fundamental literalization determining all others. In this sense, it is surely significant that the grammarians of antiquity held as the principle of their knowledge not the pure voice but the "written voice," *phōnē engrammatos, vox quae scribi potest.* The principle of the science of language (and hence of every *epistēmē*) is grammaticalization, the literalization of the voice. What is at issue in this literalization is the existence of language as presupposition, the transformation of the *factum loquendi* into a presupposition that must remain unthought.

How, we must then ask ourselves, is the science of language itself marked by the existence of language as the presupposition at issue in literalization? In his preceding books (not only in *L'amour de la langue* but also in *De la syntaxe à l'interprétation*), Milner brought to light the points at which something in language exceeds language as an object of knowledge, whether it be in the theory of the subject of enunciation or in the grammar of insults.

If there is something in the *Introduction* that bears the trace or scar of this presupposition and excess, it is the theme of contingency, which traverses the whole book. In Milner's conception, Galilean (or literalized) science is destined to contingency. What clearly distinguishes it from classical science is that its object could have been otherwise than it is; the properties that belong to it are certain and constant but not necessary. The disorder that contingency introduces into the world is nevertheless balanced by a principle that is more or less present in all knowledge and that was clearly formulated by Aristotle. This principle, which is usually called the "principle of conditioned necessity," states that if all potentiality is potentiality of a thing and its contrary, and if every being could have been different, nevertheless, in the instant in which it actually is, it cannot be otherwise. As Milner wrote in a text on Lacan, "in the instant of a flash, each point of each referent of each proposition of science appears as if it could be infinitely different, from an infinite number of viewpoints; in the final instant, the letter fixes it as it is and as incapable of being otherwise."[5] It follows that contingency is contained in a barrier that always necessarily inscribes its expression in the form of a past: something *could have been* otherwise than it is. This temporal articulation in fact conditions Western science's entire representation of possibility (and this is as true of linguistics as of all other disciplines).

This said, is it possible to grasp contingency otherwise than as "something that could have been"? Is it possible, in other words, to call into question the principle of conditioned necessity, to attest to the very *existence* of potentiality, the actuality of contingency? Is it possible, in short, to attempt to say what seems impossible to say, that is: that something *is* otherwise than it is?

This appears to be precisely the task of coming philosophy: to redefine the entire domain of categories and modality so as to consider no longer the *presupposition* of Being and potentiality, but their *exposition*. This is the direction in which Milner's most recent work seems to move. And if there is a linguist today who is capable of grasping language's point of excess with respect to science (as Saussure and Benveniste did in their time), it is surely the author of this *Introduction*.

§ 5 Kommerell, or On Gesture

I

Criticism has three levels: philologico-hermeneutic, physiognomic, and gestic. Of these three levels, which can be described as three concentric spheres, the first is dedicated to the work's interpretation; the second situates the work (in both historical and natural orders); the third resolves the work's intention into a gesture (or into a constellation of gestures). It can be said that every authentic critic moves through all three fields, pausing in each of them according to his own temperament. The work of Max Kommerell—certainly the greatest German critic of the twentieth century after Benjamin, and perhaps the last great personality between the wars who still remains to be discovered—is almost wholly inscribed in the third field, where supreme talents are rarest (among the critics of the twentieth century, other than Benjamin, only Jacques Rivière, Félix Fénéon, and Gianfranco Contini truly belong to this category).

What is a gesture? It suffices to glance through Kommerell's essay on Heinrich von Kleist to register the centrality and complexity of the subject of gesture in Kommerell's thought, as well as the decisiveness with which he always leads the author's intention back to this sphere. Gesture is not an absolutely nonlinguistic element but, rather, something closely tied to language. It is first of all a forceful presence in language itself, one that is older and more originary than conceptual expression. Kommerell defines linguistic gesture (*Sprachgebärde*) as the stratum of language that is not exhausted in communication and that captures language, so to speak, in its solitary moments. "The sense of these gestures," he writes with reference to lyric poetry, is not exhausted in communication. However compelling it may be for an Other, gesture never exists only for him; indeed, only insofar as it also exists for itself can it be compelling for the Other. Even a face that is never witnessed has its mimicry; and it is very much a question as to which gestures leave an imprint on its physical appearance, those through which he makes himself understood with others or, instead, those imposed on him by solitude and inner dialogue. A face often seems to tell us the history of solitary moments.[1]

Thus Kommerell can write that "speech is originary gesture [*Urgebärde*], from which all individual gestures derive," and that poetic verse is essentially gesture: "Language is both conceptual and mimetic. The first element dominates in prose, the second in verse. Prose is above all the understanding of a concept; beyond prose and more decisively than prose, verse is expressive gesture."[2] If this is true, if speech is originary gesture, then what is at issue in gesture is not so much a prelinguistic content as, so to speak, the other side of language, the muteness inherent in humankind's very capacity for language, its *speechless* dwelling in language. And the more human beings have language, the stronger the unsayable weighs them down, to the point that in the poet, the speaking being with the most words, "the making of references and signs is worn out, and something harsh is born—violence toward speech."[3]

In Kommerell's essay on Kleist, this state of speechlessness in language appears on three levels: the enigma (*Rätsel*), in which the more the speaker tries to express himself in words, the more he makes himself incomprehensible (as happens to the characters of Kleist's drama); the secret (*Geheimnis*), which remains unsaid in the enigma and is nothing other than the Being of human beings insofar as they live in the truth of language; and the mystery (*Mysterium*), which is the mimed performance of the secret. And in the end the poet appears as him who "remained without words in speech, dying for the truth of the sign."[4]

Precisely for this reason—insofar, that is, as gesture, having to express Being in language itself, strictly speaking has nothing to express and nothing to say other than what is said in language—gesture is always the gesture of being at a loss in language; it is always a "gag" in the literal sense of the word, which indicates first of all something put in someone's mouth to keep him from speaking and, then, the actor's improvisation to make up for an impossibility of speaking. But there is a gesture that felicitously establishes itself in this emptiness of language and, without filling it, makes it into humankind's most proper dwelling. Confusion turns to dance, and "gag" to mystery.

In his book on Jean Paul, which for some readers is his masterpiece, Kommerell delineates this dialectic of gesture in his own terms:

> The beginning is a feeling of the "I" that, in every possible gesture and espe-
> cially in each of its own gestures, experiences something false, a deformation
> of the inside with respect to which all faithful presentation seems a curse
> against the spirit. It is a feeling in which the "I," looking at itself in the mir-
> ror, discerns a pamphlet stuck to it, even incorporated into it, and, looking
> outside, laments himself, amazed to see in the face of his fellow men the full-
> ness of comical masks. . . . The disjunction between appearance and essence
> lies at the basis of both the sublime and the comical; the small sign of the cor-
> poreal points to the indescribable.[5]

Kommerell opposes Jean Paul's gesture to Goethe's gesture, which shelters the enigma of his characters in a symbol:

> Very rarely and in fact only for the enchanting excess of his two girlish
> demons, Goethe allows himself the exception of a gesture that belongs to
> them alone. It is a gesture that is repeated and that somehow contains the per-
> son; it is the person's symbol. The assistant describes the manner in which
> Ottilie refuses to do something that is demanded of her and that she cannot
> do: "Her hands held up in the air, she presses her palms together and lowers
> them to her breast, leaning forward only a little bit and looking at whoever
> is demanding something of her in such a way that he gladly renounces any-
> thing he might have wanted of her." In a similar way, it is said that Mignon
> puts her left hand on her chest and her right hand on her forehead, bowing
> deeply. With such simple means, Goethe masters a nature that lies at the edge
> of the human. But his gestures, unlike Jean Paul's, are not obtrusive; they are
> restrained, and they shelter in themselves the enigma of the figure.[6]

Beyond this order of gestures, which Kommerell defines as "gestures of the soul," lies a higher sphere, which he calls pure gesture:

> Beyond the gestures of the soul and the gestures of nature there is a third
> sphere, which one may call pure gestures. Its temporality is the eternity of
> Jean Paul's dreams. These dreams, dreamt in a superhuman sleep of the
> brightest wakefulness, are fragments of an other world in the soul of Jean
> Paul. Worldly wisdom, piety and art are indistinguishable in this world, and
> their essence is not relation, as in the Romantic dream, but the soul itself,
> which burns in its own adventure without any earthly fuel. The sonorous and

luminous vibrations of these dreams refer to the biography of the poet, just as physiological colors, which the eye produces on its own, refer to externally perceived colors. The linguistic forms in which the soul expresses itself . . . are the pure possibility of speaking itself, and, when placed together with the gestures of the soul and the gestures of nature, they show their supernatural origin. These "pure gestures" have given up all claim to reality. . . . Consumed in themselves, the soul paints itself with its own luminous shades.[7]

These are the gestures of which Kommerell writes at the end of his essay on Kleist, stating that "a new beauty begins, one that is similar to the beauty of the gestures of an animal, to soft and threatening gestures."[8] They call to mind the redeemed world, whose uncertain gestures Benjamin, in the same years, discerned in Kafka's "Oklahoma Nature Theater":

> One of the most significant functions of this theater is to dissolve happenings into their gestic components. . . . Kafka's entire work constitutes a code of gestures which surely had no definite symbolic meaning for the author from the outset; rather, the author tried to derive such a meaning from them in ever-changing contexts and experimental groupings. The theater is the logical place for such groupings.[9]

Criticism is the reduction of works to the sphere of pure gesture. This sphere lies beyond psychology and, in a certain sense, beyond all interpretation. It opens not onto literary history or a theory of genres but onto a stage such as the Oklahoma theater or Calderón's *Great Theater of the World* (Kommerell dedicated his last critical works to Calderón in *Beiträge zu einem deutschen Calderón*). Consigned to their supreme gesture, works live on, like creatures bathed in the light of the Last Day, surviving the ruin of their formal garment and their conceptual meaning. They find themselves in the situation of those *Commedia dell'arte* figures Kommerell loved so dearly; Harlequin, Pantaloon, Columbine, and the Captain, emancipated from written texts and fully defined roles, oscillate forever between reality and virtuality, life and art, the singular and the generic. In the comedy that criticism substitutes for literary history, the *Recherche* or the *Commedia* ceases to be the established text that the critic must investigate and then consign, intact and inalterable, to tradition. They are instead the gestures that, in those wondrous texts, exhibit only a gigantic lack of memory, only a "gag" destined to hide an incurable speechlessness.

II

"In San Gimignano my hands were flayed by the thorns of a rose bush in George's garden that was in surprisingly beautiful, partial bloom."[10] The book to which Benjamin cryptically refers in this letter of July 27, 1929, to his friend Scholem is *Der Dichter als Führer in der deutschen Klassik*, the first work of the twenty-six-year-old Max Kommerell. I do not have the first edition (1928) before me, but in accordance with the characteristic typography of Bondi, the publishing house of the Stefan George circle, it should have borne the seal of the swastika, a hooked cross, slightly different from the one that was to become the symbol of Hitler's Germany a few years later. That early swastika marked the *Werke der Wissenschaft aus dem Kreise der Blätter für die Kunst*, a publishing house that had already brought out, among other works, Gundolf's essays on Goethe and George, Bertram's book on Nietzsche, and *Herrschaft und Dienst* by Wolters, who had been Kommerell's teacher in Marburg. Kommerell's intimate participation in George's circle and subsequent break with it (which is something similar to Benjamin's early break with Gustav Wyneken) mark Kommerell's youth in a decisive fashion.

If one wanted to characterize the physiognomy of the George circle in one salient trait, one could say that it sought to exorcise its own inner anguish through a ritual. What is decisive in George is the contrast between the prophetic lucidity of his diagnosis of his own time and the esoteric bearing that he derived from it. Perhaps nowhere else is this diagnosis expressed so radically as in the verse with which George summarizes the precept to which the poet must adhere: "There can be no thing where the word is lacking."[11] The extent to which George could not bear the experience of this emptiness can be clearly seen in one of the dreams that the poet transcribed in *Works and Days*. Here George is confronted by a head hanging in his room, and he desperately tries to make it speak, forcibly moving its lips with his fingers.[12] It can be said that the entire work of the George circle consists in the anguished attempt to speak at the point at which a word (and hence a thing) is no longer possible. Where the word and the thing are lacking, the George circle establishes a ritual of imminence.

The sense of George's "secret Germany" is precisely that of preparing the way for what, nevertheless, was bound to happen: the regeneration of the German people. In this way, George betrays his own precept and—if only in the form of expectation—posits a thing where a name is no longer possible. At times Heidegger also engages in this evocation of an imminence, though he understood perfectly that the thing for which the word is lacking is nothing other than the word itself. But prophecy can never establish itself in the form of expectation, even and above all if the former refers to language; prophecy is legitimate only as an interruption of existing words (and things). This is why history has taken revenge on George's secret Germany, condemning it, in Benjamin's words, to being in the final analysis only the "arsenal of the official Germany, in which the helmet hangs beside the magic hood."[13] And a second time, in the failure of the heroic assassination attempt on Hitler with which Claus von Stauffenberg, together with one of Kommerell's closest friends in the George circle, tried to buy back German honor.

With his acute sensitivity to false gestures, Kommerell broke with George at the end of 1930, on the occasion of the publication of Wolters's book *Stefan George und die Blätter für die Kunst*, which inaugurates the hagiography of George. Kommerell severely denounced the "liturgical pathos" that here intruded into poetry, together with a lack of rigor in "the spiritual sphere." "Between simple magic—be it ecclesiastical or theatrical—and Philistinism dressed up as spirit," he stated, "there are some profound differences as to means, but none as to quality."[14] In response to Kommerell's objection that Wolters's book did not answer to the truth, the master wrote, "what is at issue there is not the truth, but the State" ("the State" was, not by chance, the term with which the adepts referred to the George circle). The only remaining possibility was rupture. But the association had been too close for the break not to produce a victim; unable to decide between friend and master, on February 25, 1931, Hans Anton, a George disciple involved in a passionate relationship with Kommerell, took his own life.

The pall that this suicide cast upon Kommerell's youth perhaps explains the omission that marks the limit of his work: this great critic never wrote about any of his contemporaries. For Kommerell (who was unfamiliar with none of the great European cultural traditions), not only do Kafka, Proust, and Robert Walser seem never to have existed, but even the slightest reference to contemporaneity is lacking in his writings. In this ascesis, which is surely not accidental, one can discern the final reflection of the blindness to the present for which Benjamin reproved the George circle when he wrote, "Today is the bull whose blood must fill the ditch, so that the spirits of the dead may appear at its edge."[15]

III

At the end of his book on Jean Paul, Kommerell speaks of modern man as a man who has lost his gestures. The age of Jean Paul is the age in which the bourgeoisie, which in Goethe still seemed to possess its symbols, fell victim to interiority:

> Both Jean Paul's humor and the philosophy of German Idealism derive from this situation of the bourgeoisie, in which forms of life have lost their intimacy and simplicity, and the inane pettiness of all exteriority isolates interiority. Goethe and Jean Paul are both writers of the bourgeoisie . . . , but in Goethe the bourgeoisie is still a class [*Stand*]; in Jean Paul it is only in disorder [*Mißstand*]. As long as "external" life can still be seen as beautiful or, to the degree that it has a melody, can still be heard as beautiful, the spirit is not unconditionally free to reject it. . . . Fully liberated spirit is a consequence of the bourgeoisie that has lost its gestures.[16]

But an epoch that has lost its gestures is, by the same token, obsessed by them; for men from whom all authenticity has been taken, gesture becomes destiny. And the more gestures lost their ease under the pressure of unknown powers, the more life became indecipherable. And once the simplest and most everyday gestures had become as foreign as the gesticulations of marionettes, humanity—whose very bodily existence had already become sacred to the degree that it had made itself impenetrable—was ready for the massacre.

In modern culture, Nietzsche marks the apex of this polar tension toward the effacement of gestures and transfiguration into destiny. For the eternal return is intelligible only as a gesture (and hence solely as theater) in which potentiality and actuality, authenticity and mannerism, contingency and necessity have become indistinguishable. *Thus Spake Zarathustra* is the ballet of a humanity that has lost its gestures. And when the age became aware of its loss (too late!) it began its hasty attempt to recuperate its lost gestures *in extremis*. Isadora and Diaghilev's ballets, Proust's novel, Rilke and Pascoli's great *Jugendstil* poetry, and, finally, in the most exemplary fashion, silent film—all these trace the magic circle in which humanity tried to evoke for the last time what it was soon to lose irretrievably. And in the same years, Aby Warburg began his research, which truly had gesture at its center (and which only the myopia of psychologizing art history could define as a "science of the image"), gesture as the crystal of historical memory and gesture in its petrifaction as destiny, which artists strenuously (and, according to Warburg, almost madly) attempted to grasp through dynamic polarities.

Kommerell may well be the thinker who best knew how to read this impulse of the epoch toward a liberation and absolutization of gesture. In his essay "Poetry in Free Verse and the God of Poets," he looks to poetry to consider what modern poets, from Hölderlin to Rilke, search for in the angel, the half-god, the marionette, and the animal. And he finds that what is at issue is not a namable substance but, rather, a figure of annihilated human existence, its "negative outline" and, at the same time, its self-transcendence not toward a beyond but in "the intimacy of living here and now," in a profane mystery whose sole object is existence itself. And perhaps nowhere else does he succeed so clearly in expressing the final intention of his writing as in his essay on *Wilhelm Meister*, in which, as has been noted,[17] he makes the most explicit confession of which he is capable:

> Indeed, the path that Wilhelm Meister follows is, in its worldliness, a path of initiation. He is initiated into life itself. . . . Initiation must be distinguished from both teaching and doctrine. It is both less and more. . . . And if it is life that initiates, it does not do so thanks to holy institutions but, precisely, outside them. If the state could still teach, if society could still educate and the Church could still sanctify . . . then life would not be able to initiate. This is life, purely worldly, purely earthly, purely contingent—and precisely this life initiates. For life has been given a power that is otherwise exercised only in sacred domains. Now life is the sacred domain, the only one that remains. And into what does it initiate? Not into its meaning, only into itself. Into something that, in its incarnation in beauty, pain, and enigmas, constantly borders on meaning without ever uttering it and while remaining unnamable. Life thus has a secret; indeed, life is a secret. After every single realization, however compelling, after every single disenchantment, however terrible, life returns to its secret. And if in the old novels of Christian Baroque, the series of individual disillusionments ended with the irrevocable, irreparable disillusionment of man about the world and about himself, here all disillusionments lead only to this point, where life itself remains secret and where its charm grows on account of its having kept not its promise but, instead, far more than it promised. Perhaps one should not call life holy, for we are accustomed to tie the concept of holiness to a determinate religious or, more recently, ethical domain. No: the fact that life is assigned this force of initiation gives rise to something new, a mystery of the everyday and the worldly that is this poet's possession.[18]

In this text, the man who in the George circle had known the sacred pathos of the sect and who, through that circle, had been initiated into the myth of the poet as "guide" and "model of a community of creative people"[19] frees himself of his youthful initiation, seeing in poetry only the self-initiation of life to itself. But precisely in this idea of a wholly profane mystery in which human beings, liberating themselves from all sacredness, communicate to each other their lack of secrets as their most proper gesture, Kommerell's criticism reaches the political dimension that seems obstinately lacking from his work. For politics is the sphere of the full, absolute gesturality of human beings, and it has no name other than its Greek pseudonym, which is barely uttered here: philosophy.

PART TWO

History

§ 6 Aby Warburg and the Nameless Science

This essay seeks to situate a discipline that, in contrast to many others, exists but has no name. Since Aby Warburg was its creator,[1] only an attentive analysis of his thought can furnish the point of view from which a critical assessment of it will be possible. And only on the basis of such an assessment will we be able to ask if this "unnamed discipline" can be given a name, and if the names that have until now been given to it are legitimate.

The essence of Warburg's teaching and method—an essence embodied in the Library for the Science of Culture, which later became the Warburg Institute[2]—is usually presented as a rejection of the stylistico-formal method dominant in art history at the end of the nineteenth century. On the basis of a study of literary sources and an examination of cultural tradition, Warburg is understood to have displaced the focal point of research from the study of styles and aesthetic judgment to the programmatic and iconographic aspects of the artwork. The breath of fresh air that Warburg's approach to the work of art brought to the stagnant waters of aesthetic formalism is shown by the growing success of the studies inspired by his method. These studies have acquired such a vast public, outside as well as within academic circles, that it has been possible to speak of a "popular" image of the Warburg Institute. Yet this growth in the fame of the institute has been accompanied by an increasing obliteration of the figure of the institute's founder and his original project. The edition of Warburg's writings and unpublished fragments that was proposed long ago, for example, still remains to be published.[3]

The conception of Warburg's method summarized above reflects an attitude toward the artwork that undoubtedly belonged to Aby Warburg. In 1889, while he was at the University of Strasbourg preparing his thesis on Botticelli's *Birth of Venus* and *Spring*, he realized that any attempt to comprehend the mind of a Renaissance painter was futile as long as the problem was confronted from a purely formal point of view.[4] For his whole life he kept his "honest repugnance" for "aestheticizing art history"[5] and merely formal considerations of the image. But, for Warburg, this attitude originated neither from a purely erudite and antiquarian approach to the problem of the artwork nor from indifference to the artwork's formal qualities. Warburg's obsessive, almost pious attention to the force of images proves, if proof is necessary, that he was all too sensitive to "formal values." A concept such as *Pathosformel*, which designates an indissoluble intertwining of an emotional charge and an iconographic formula in which it is impossible to distinguish between form and content, suffices to demonstrate that Warburg's thought cannot in any sense be interpreted in terms of such inauthentic oppositions as those between form and content and between the history of styles and the history of culture. What is unique and significant about Warburg's method as a scholar is not so much that he adopts a new way of writing art history as that he always directs his research toward the overcoming of the borders of art history. It is as if Warburg were interested in this discipline solely to place within it the seed that would cause it to explode. The "good God" who, according to the famous phrase, "hides in the details" was for Warburg not the guardian spirit of art history but the dark demon of an unnamed science whose contours we are only today beginning to glimpse.

II

In 1923, while he was in Ludwig Binswanger's mental hospital in Kreuzlingen during the period of mental illness that kept him far from his library for six years, Warburg asked his physicians if they would discharge him if he cured himself by delivering a lecture to the clinic's patients. Unexpectedly, he drew the subject for his lecture, the serpent rituals of the North American native peoples,[6] from an experience that he had had thirty years before and that must therefore have left a deep impression in his memory. In 1895, during a trip to North America taken when he was almost thirty years old, Warburg had spent several months among the

Pueblo and Navaho peoples of New Mexico. His encounter with Native American culture (to which he was introduced by Cyrus Adler, Frank Hamilton Cushing, James Mooney, and Franz Boas) definitively distanced him from the idea of art history as a specialized discipline, thereby confirming his views on a subject he had considered for a long time while studying in Bonn with Hermann Usener and Karl Lamprecht.

Usener (whom Pasquali once defined as "the philologist who was the richest in ideas among the great Germans of the second half of the nineteenth century")[7] had drawn Warburg's attention to an Italian scholar, Tito Vignoli. In his *Myth and Science*, Vignoli had argued for an approach to the study of the problems of man that combined anthropology, ethnology, mythology, psychology, and biology.[8] Warburg heavily underlined the passages in Vignoli's book that contain statements on this subject. During his stay in America, Warburg's youthful interest in Vignoli's position became a resolute decision. Indeed, one can say that the entire work of Warburg the "art historian," including the famous library that he began to put together in 1886,[9] is meaningful only if understood as a unified effort, across and beyond art history, directed toward a broader science for which he could not find a definite name but on whose configuration he tenaciously labored until his death. In the notes for the Kreuzlingen lecture on serpent rituals, Warburg thus defines the goal of his library as a "collection of documents referring to the psychology of human expression."[10]

In the same notes, he reaffirms his aversion to a formal approach to the image, which, Warburg writes, cannot grasp the image's biological necessity as a product "between religion and artistic production."[11] This position of the image between religion and art is important for the delimitation of the horizon of Warburg's research. The object of that research is more the image than the artwork, and this is what sets Warburg's work resolutely outside the borders of aesthetics. In the conclusion to his lecture of 1912, "Italian Art and International Astrology in Palazzo Schifanoia in Ferrara," Warburg had already called for a "methodological amplification of the thematic and geographical borders" of art history:

> Overly limiting developmental categories have until now hindered art history from making its material available to the "historical psychology of human expression" that has yet to be written. Because of its excessively materialistic or excessively mystical tenor, our young discipline denies itself the panoramic view of world history. Groping, it seeks to find its own theory of evolution

between the schematisms of political history and the doctrines of genius. By the method of my interpretation of the frescoes in the Palazzo Schifanoia in Ferrara, I hope to have shown that an iconological analysis, which, in refusing to submit to petty territorial restrictions, shies away neither from recognizing that antiquity, the Middle Ages, and the modern age are in fact one interrelated epoch, nor from examining the works of the freest as well as the most applied art as equally valid documents of expression—that this method, by applying itself to the illumination of a single darkness, sheds light on the great universal evolutionary processes in their context. I was less interested in neat solutions than in formulating a new problem. I would like to put it to you in the following terms: "To what extent are we to view the onset of a stylistic shift in the representation of the human figure in Italian art as an internationally conditioned process of disengagement from the surviving pictorial conceptions of the pagan culture of the eastern Mediterranean peoples?" Our enthusiastic wonderment at the inconceivable achievement of artistic genius can only be strengthened by the recognition that genius is both a blessing and conscious transformatory energy. The great new style that the artistic genius of Italy bequeathed to us was rooted in the social will to recover Greek humanism from the shell of medieval, Oriental-Latin "practice." With this will toward the restitution of antiquity, the "good European" began his struggle for enlightenment in the age of the international migration of images that we refer to—a little too mystically—as the age of the Renaissance.[12]

It is important to note that these observations are contained in the lecture in which Warburg presents one of his most famous iconographic discoveries, that is, his identification of the subject of the middle strip of frescos in the Palazzo Schifanoia on the basis of the figures described in Abu Ma'shar's *Introductorium maius*. In Warburg's hands, iconography is never an end in itself (one can also say of him what Karl Kraus said of the artist, namely, that he was able to transform a solution into an enigma). Warburg's use of iconography always transcends the mere identification of a subject and its sources; from the perspective of what he once defined as "a diagnosis of Western man," he aims to configure a problem that is both historical and ethical. The transfiguration of iconographic method in Warburg's hands thus closely recalls Leo Spitzer's transformation of lexicographic method into "historical semantics," in which the history of a word becomes both the history of a culture and the configuration of its specific vital problem. To understand how Warburg understood the study of the tradition of images, one may also think of the revolution in paleography brought about by Ludwig Traube, whom Warburg called "the

Great Master of our Order" and who always knew how to draw decisive discoveries for the history of culture from errors of copyists and influences in calligraphy.[13]

The theme of the "posthumous life"[14] of pagan culture that defines a main line of Warburg's thought makes sense only within this broader horizon, in which the stylistic and formal solutions at times adopted by artists appear as ethical decisions of individuals and epochs regarding the inheritance of the past. Only from this perspective does the interpretation of a historical problem also show itself as a "diagnosis of Western man" in his battle to overcome his own contradictions and to find his vital dwelling place between the old and the new.

If Warburg could present the problem of the *Nachleben des Heidentums*, the "posthumous life of paganism," as the supreme subject of his scholarly research,[15] this is because he had already understood, with a surprising anthropological intuition, that "transmission and survival" is the central problem of a "warm" society such as the West, insofar as it is so obsessed with history as to want to make it into the driving force of its own development.[16] Once again, Warburg's method and concepts are clarified if one compares them to the ideas that led Spitzer, in his research into semantic history, to accentuate the simultaneously "conservative" and "progressive" character of our cultural tradition, in which apparently great changes are always in some way connected to the legacy of the past (as is shown by the striking continuity of the semantic patrimony of modern European languages, which is essentially Graeco-Roman-Judaeo-Christian).

From this perspective, from which culture is always seen as a process of *Nachleben*, that is, transmission, reception, and polarization, it also becomes comprehensible why Warburg ultimately concentrated all his attention on the problem of symbols and their life in social memory.

Ernst Gombrich has shown the influence exerted on Warburg by the theories of Hering's student Richard Semon, whose book *Mneme* Warburg bought in 1908. According to Gombrich, Semon holds that

> memory is not a property of consciousness but the one quality that distinguishes living from dead matter. It is the capacity to react to an event over a period of time; that is, a form of preserving and transmitting energy not known to the physical world. Any event affecting living matter leaves a trace which Semon calls an "*engram*." The potential energy conserved in this "engram" may, under suitable conditions, be reactivated and discharged—we

then say the organism acts in a specific way because it *remembers* the previous event.[17]

The symbol and the image play the same role for Warburg as the "engram" plays in Semon's conception of the individual's nervous system; they are the crystallization of an energetic charge and an emotional experience that survive as an inheritance transmitted by social memory and that, like electricity condensed in a Leydan jar, become effective only through contact with the "selective will" of a particular period. This is why Warburg often speaks of symbols as "dynamograms" that are transmitted to artists in a state of great tension, but that are not polarized in their active or passive, positive or negative energetic charge; their polarization, which occurs through an encounter with a new epoch and its vital needs, can then bring about a complete transformation of meaning.[18] For Warburg, the attitude of artists toward images inherited from tradition was therefore conceivable in terms neither of aesthetic choice nor of neutral reception; rather, for him it is a matter of a confrontation—which is lethal or vitalizing, depending on the situation—with the tremendous energies stored in images, which in themselves had the potential either to make man regress into sterile subjection or to direct him on his path toward salvation and knowledge. For Warburg, this was true not only for artists who, like Dürer, polarized and humanized the superstitious fear of Saturn in the emblem of intellectual contemplation,[19] but also for historians and scholars, whom Warburg conceives of as extremely sensitive seismographs responding to distant earthquakes, or as "necromancers" who consciously evoke the specters threatening them.[20]

For Warburg, the symbol thus belongs to an intermediary domain between consciousness and primitive reactions, and it bears in itself the possibilities of both regression and higher knowledge. It is a *Zwischenraum*, an "interval," a kind of no-man's-land at the center of the human. And just as the creation and enjoyment of art require the fusion of two psychic attitudes that exclude each other ("a passionate surrender of the self leading to a complete identification with the present—and a cool and detached serenity which belongs to the categorizing contemplation of things"), so the "nameless science" sought by Warburg is, as one reads in a note of 1929, an "iconology of the interval," or a "psychology of the oscillation between the positing of causes as images and as signs."[21] Warburg clearly presents this "intermediary" status of the symbol (and its capacity, if mastered, to "heal" and direct the human mind) in a note that dates from the period of the Kreuzlingen lecture, during which he was undergoing and telling others about his recovery:

> All mankind is eternally and at all times schizophrenic. Ontogenetically, however, we may perhaps describe one type of response to memory images as prior and primitive, though it continues on the sidelines. At the later stage the memory no longer arouses an immediate, purposeful reflex movement—be it one of a combative or a religious character—but the memory images are now consciously stored in pictures and signs. Between these two stages we find a treatment of the impression that may be described as the symbolic mode of thought.[22]

Only from this perspective is it possible to appreciate the sense and importance of the project to which Warburg devoted the last years of his life, and for which he chose the name that he also wanted as the motto for his library (which can still be read today upon entering the library of the Warburg Institute): Mnemosyne. Gertrud Bing once described this project as a figurative atlas depicting the history of visual expression in the Mediterranean area. Warburg was probably guided in his choice of this striking model by his own difficulty with writing; but he was probably led above all by his determination to find a form that, beyond the traditional types and modes of art criticism and history, would finally be adequate to the "nameless science" he had in mind.

When he died, in October 1929, Warburg had not completed his "Mnemosyne" project. There remain some forty black canvases to which Warburg attached approximately one thousand photographs in which it is possible to recognize his favorite iconographic themes, but whose material expands almost infinitely, to the point of including an advertisement for a steamship company and photographs of a golf player as well as of the meeting of Mussolini and the Pope. But "Mnemosyne" is something more than an organic orchestration of the motifs that guided Warburg's research over the years. Warburg once enigmatically defined "Mnemosyne" as "a ghost story for truly adult people." If one considers the function that he assigned to the image as the organ of social memory and the "engram" of a culture's spiritual tensions, one can understand what he meant: his "atlas" was a kind of gigantic condenser that gathered together all the energetic currents that had animated and continued to animate Europe's memory, taking form in its "ghosts." The name "Mnemosyne" finds its true justification here. The atlas that bears this title recalls the mnemotechnical theater built in the sixteenth century by Giulio Camillo, which so stunned his contemporaries as an absolutely novel wonder.[23] Its creator sought to enclose in it "the nature of all things that can be expressed in speech," such that whoever entered into the wondrous building would immediately grasp the knowledge contained in it. Warburg's "Mnemosyne" is such a mnemotechnical and initiatory atlas of Western culture. Gazing upon it, the "good European" (as he liked to call himself, using Nietzsche's expression) would become conscious of the problematic nature of his own cultural tradition, perhaps succeeding thereby in "educating himself" and in healing his own schizophrenia.

"Mnemosyne," like many other of Warburg's works, including his library, may certainly appear to some as a mnemotechnic system for private use, by which Aby Warburg, scholar and psychopath, sought to resolve his personal psychological conflicts. And this is without a doubt the case. But it is a sign of Warburg's greatness as an individual that not only his idiosyncrasies but even the remedies he found to master them correspond to the secret needs of the spirit of the age.

III

Today, philological and historical disciplines consider it a methodological given that the epistemological process that is proper to them is necessarily caught in a circle. The discovery of this circle as the foundation of all hermeneutics goes back to Schleiermacher and his intuition that in philology "the part can be understood only by means of the whole and every explanation of the part presupposes the understanding of the whole."[24] But this circle is in no sense a vicious one. On the contrary, it is itself the foundation of the rigor and rationality of the social sciences and humanities. For a science that wants to remain faithful to its own law, what is essential is not to leave this "circle of understanding," which would be impossible, but to "stay within it in the right way."[25] By virtue of the knowledge acquired at every step, the passage from the part to the whole and back again never returns to the same point; at every step, it necessarily broadens its radius, discovering a higher perspective that opens a new circle. The curve representing the hermeneutic circle is not a circumference, as has often been repeated, but a spiral that continually broadens its turns.

The science that recommended looking for "the good God" in the details perfectly illustrates the fecundity of a correct position in one's own hermeneutic circle. The spiraling movement toward an ever greater broadening of horizons can be followed in an exemplary fashion in the two central themes of Warburg's research: that of the "nymph" and that of the Renaissance revival of astrology.

In his dissertation on Botticelli's *Spring* and *Birth of Venus*, Warburg used literary sources to identify Botticelli's moving female figure as a "nymph." Warburg argued that this figure constituted a new iconographic type, one that makes it possible both to clarify the subject of Botticelli's paintings and to demonstrate "how Botticelli was settling accounts with the ideas that his epoch had of the ancients."[26] But in showing that the artists of the fifteenth century relied on a classical *Pathosformel* every time they sought to portray an intensified external movement, Warburg simultaneously revealed the Dionysian polarity of classical art. In the wake of Nietzsche, Warburg was the first to affirm this polarity in the domain of art history, which in his time was still dominated by Johann Joachim Winckelmann's model. In a still broader circle, the appearance of the nymph thus becomes the sign of a profound spiritual conflict in Renaissance culture, in which the rediscovery of the orgiastic charge of classical *Pathosformeln* had to be skillfully reconciled with Christianity in a delicate balance that is perfectly exemplified in the personality of the Florentine Francesco Sassetti, whom Warburg analyzes in a famous essay. And in the greatest circle of the hermeneutic spiral, the "nymph" becomes the cipher of a perennial polarity in Western culture, insofar as Warburg likens her to the dark, resting figure that Renaissance artists took from Greek representations of a river god. In one of his densest diary entries, Warburg considers this polarity, which afflicts the West with a kind of tragic schizophrenia: "Sometimes it looks to me as if, in my role as a psycho-historian, I tried to diagnose the schizophrenia of Western civilization from its images in an autobiographical reflex. The ecstatic 'Nympha' (manic) on the one side and the mourning river-god (depressive) on the other."[27]

An analogous progressive broadening of the hermeneutic spiral can also be observed in Warburg's treatment of the theme of astrological images. The narrower, properly iconographic circle coincides with the analysis of the subject of the frescos in the Palazzo Schifanoia in Ferrara, which Warburg, as we have noted, recognized as figures from Abu Ma'shar's *Intro-*

ductorium maius. In the history of culture, however, this becomes the discovery of the rebirth of astrology in humanistic culture from the fourteenth century onwards and therefore of the ambiguity of Renaissance culture, which Warburg was the first to perceive in an epoch in which the Renaissance still appeared as an age of enlightenment in contrast to the darkness of the Middle Ages. In the final lines traced by the spiral, the appearance of the images and rivers of demonic antiquity at the very start of modernity becomes the symptom of a conflict at the origin of our civilization, which cannot master its own bipolar tension. As Warburg explained, introducing an exhibit of astrological images to the German Oriental Studies Conference in 1926, those images show "beyond all doubt that European culture is the result of conflicting tendencies, of a process in which—as far as these astrological attempts at orientation are concerned—we must seek neither friends nor enemies, but rather symptoms of a movement of pendular oscillation between the two distinct poles of magico-religious practice and mathematical contemplation."[28]

Warburg's hermeneutic circle can thus be figured as a spiral that moves across three main levels: the first is that of iconography and the history of art; the second is that of the history of culture; and the third and broadest level is that of the "nameless science" to which Warburg dedicated his life and that aims to diagnose Western man through a consideration of his phantasms. The circle that revealed the good God hidden in the details was not a vicious circle, even in the Nietzschean sense of a *circolus vitiosus deus.*

IV

If we now wish to ask ourselves, following our initial project, if the "unnamed science" whose lineaments we have examined in Warburg's thought can indeed receive a name, we must first of all observe that none of the terms that he used over the course of his life ("history of culture," "psychology of human expression," "history of the psyche," "iconology of the interval") seems to have fully satisfied him. The most authoritative post-Warburgian attempt to name this science is certainly that of Erwin Panofsky, who in his own research gives the name "iconology" (as opposed to "iconography") to the deepest possible approach to images. The fortune of this term (which, as we have seen, was already used by Warburg) has been so vast that today it is used to refer not only to Panofsky's works but to all research that presents itself in the tradition of Warburg's work. But even a summary analysis suffices to show how distant the goals Panofsky assigns to iconology are from what Warburg had in mind for his science of the "interval."

It is well known that Panofsky distinguishes three moments in the interpretation of a work, moments that, so to speak, correspond to three strata of meaning. The first stratum, which is that of the "natural or primary subject," corresponds to pre-iconographic description; the second, which is that of the "secondary or conventional subject, constitutive of the world of *images*, of *stories*, and of *allegories*," corresponds to iconographic analysis. The third stratum, the deepest, is that of the "intrinsic meaning or content, constitutive of *symbolic values*." "The discovery and interpretation of these 'symbolical' values . . . is the object of what we may call 'iconology' as opposed to 'iconography.'"[29] But if we try to specify the nature of these "symbolic values," we see that Panofsky oscillates between considering them as "documents of the unitary sense of the conception of the world" and considering their interpretation as "symptoms" of an artistic personality. In his essay "The Neo-Platonic Movement and Michelangelo," he thus seems to understand artistic symbols as "symptomatic of the very essence of Michelangelo's personality."[30] The notion of symbol, which Warburg took from Renaissance emblematics and religious psychology, thus risks being led back to the domain of traditional aesthetics, which essentially considered the work of art as the expression of the creative personality of the artist. The absence of a broader theoretical perspective in which to situate "symbolic values" thus makes it extremely difficult to widen the hermeneutic circle beyond art history and aesthetics (which is not to say that Panofsky did not often succeed brilliantly within their borders).[31]

As to Warburg, he would never have considered the essence of an artist's personality as the deepest content of an image. As the intermediary zone between consciousness and primitive identification, symbols did not appear to him as significant insofar (or only insofar) as they made possible the reconstruction of a personality or a vision of the world. For Warburg, the significance of images instead lay in the fact that, being strictly speaking neither conscious nor unconscious, they constituted the ideal terrain for a unitary approach to culture, one capable of overcoming the opposition between *history*, as the study of "conscious expressions," and *anthropology*, as the study of "unconscious conditions," which Lévi-

Strauss identified twenty years later as the central problem in the relations between these two disciplines.[32]

I could have mentioned anthropology more often in the course of this essay. And it is certainly true that the point of view from which Warburg examined phenomena coincides strikingly with that of anthropological sciences. The least unfaithful way to characterize Warburg's "nameless science" may well be to insert it into the project of a future "anthropology of Western culture" in which philology, ethnology, and history would converge with an "iconology of the interval," a study of the *Zwischenraum* in which the incessant symbolic work of social memory is carried out. There is no need to underline the urgency of such a science for an epoch that, sooner or later, will have to become fully conscious of what Valéry noted thirty years ago when he wrote, "the age of the finite world has begun."[33] Only this science would allow Western man, once he has moved beyond the limits of his own ethnocentrism, to arrive at the liberating knowledge of a "diagnosis of humanity" that would heal it of its tragic schizophrenia.

It was in the service of this science, which after almost a century of anthropological studies is unfortunately still at its beginnings, that Warburg, "in his erudite, somewhat complicated way,"[34] carried out his research, which must not in any sense be neglected. His works allow his name to be inscribed alongside those of Mauss, Sapir, Spitzer, Kerényi, Usener, Dumézil, Benveniste, and many—but not very many—others. And it is likely that such a science will have to remain nameless as long as its activity has not penetrated so deeply into our culture as to overcome the fatal divisions and false hierarchies separating not only the human sciences from one another but also artworks from the *studia humaniora* and literary creation from science.

Perhaps the fracture that in our culture divides poetry and philosophy, art and science, the word that "sings" and the word that "remembers," is nothing other than one aspect of the very schizophrenia of Western culture that Warburg recognized in the polarity of the ecstatic nymph and the melancholic river god. We will be truly faithful to Warburg's teaching if we learn to see the contemplative gaze of the god in the nymph's dancing gesture and if we succeed in understanding that the word that sings also remembers and the one that remembers also sings. The science that will then take hold of the liberating knowledge of the human will truly deserve to be called by the Greek name of *Mnemosyne*.

Postilla (1983)

This essay was written in 1975, after a year of lively work in the Warburg Institute Library. It was conceived as the first of a series of portraits dedicated to exemplary personalities, each of which was to represent a human science. Other than the essay on Warburg, only the one on Émile Benveniste and linguistics was begun, although it was never finished.

With seven years of distance, the project of a general science of the human that is formulated in this essay strikes the author as one that is still valid, but that certainly cannot be pursued in the same terms. By the end of the 1970s, moreover, anthropology and the human sciences had already entered into a period of disenchantment that in itself probably rendered this project obsolete. (The fact that this project was, at times, proposed again in various ways as a generic scientific ideal only testifies to the superficiality with which historical and political problems are often resolved in academic circles.)

The itinerary of linguistics that in Benveniste's generation had already exhausted the grand nineteenth-century project of comparative grammar can serve as an example here. While Benveniste's *Indo-European Language and Society* brought comparative grammar to a limit point at which the very epistemological categories of the historical disciplines seemed to waver, Benveniste's theory of enunciation carried the science of language into the traditional territory of philosophy. In both cases, this coincided with a movement by which science (which includes linguistics, the so-called "pilot science" of the human sciences) was forced to confront a limit, which, in being recognized, seemed to allow for the delimitation of a field on which it would be possible to construct a general science of the human freed from the vagueness of interdisciplinarity. This is not the place to investigate the reasons why this did not happen. It remains the case that what took place instead was, in the rear guard, an academic enlargement of the field of semiology (to pre-Benvenistian and even pre-Saussurian perspectives) and, in the avant-garde, a massive turn toward Chomskian formalized linguistics, which is still proving fruitful today, although its epistemological horizon hardly seems to admit of something like a general science of the human.

To return to Warburg, whom I had, perhaps antiphrastically, invoked to represent art history, what continues to appear as relevant in his work is the decisive gesture with which he withdraws the artwork (and also the image) from the study of the artist's consciousness and unconscious structures. Here, once again, it is possible to draw analogies with Benveniste. While phonology (and, in its wake, Lévi-Straussian anthropology) turned to the study of unconscious structures, Benveniste's theory of enunciation, treating the problem of the subject and the passage from language (*lingua*) to speech (*parola*), opened linguistics to a field that could not be properly defined through the conscious/unconscious opposition. At the same time, Benveniste's research in comparative linguistics, which culminates in his *Indo-European Language and Society*, presented a number of findings that could not be easily understood through oppositions such as diachrony/synchrony and history/structure. In Warburg, precisely what might have appeared as an unconscious structure par excellence—the image—instead showed itself to be a decisively historical element, the very place of human cognitive activity in its vital confrontation with the past. What thus came to light, however, was neither a kind of diachrony nor a kind of synchrony but, rather, the point at which a human subject was produced in the rupture of this opposition.

In this context, the problem that must be immediately posed to Warburg's thought is a genuinely philosophical one: the status of the image and, in particular, the relation between image and speech, imagination and rule, which in Kant had already produced the aporetic situation of the transcendental imagination. The greatest lesson of Warburg's teaching may well be that the image is the place in which the subject strips itself of the mythical, psychosomatic character given to it, in the presence of an equally mythical object, by a theory of knowledge that is in truth simply disguised metaphysics. Only then does the subject rediscover its original and—in the etymological sense of the word—speculative purity. In this sense, Warburg's "nymph" is neither an external object nor an intrapsychical entity but instead the most limpid figure of the historical subject itself. In the same way, for Warburg the "Mnemosyne" atlas (which struck Warburg's successors as banal and full of capricious idiocies) was not an iconographical repertory but something like a mirror of Narcissus. For those who do not perceive it as such, it seems useless or, what is worse, an embarrassing private concern of the master, like his all-too-commonly discussed mental illness. How can one not see, instead, that what attracted Warburg in this conscious and dangerous play of mental alienation was precisely the possibility of grasping something like pure historical matter, something perfectly analogous to what Indo-European phonology offered Saussure's secret illness?

It is superfluous to recall that neither iconology nor the psychology of art has always been faithful to these demands. If we are to look for the most fruitful outcome of Warburg's legacy, perhaps, as W. Kemp has suggested, we should look to heterodox research, such as Benjamin's studies of the dialectical image. It continues to be imperative, in the meantime, that Warburg's unpublished papers in the London Institute appear in print.

§ 7 Tradition of the Immemorial

I

Every reflection on tradition must begin with the assertion that before transmitting anything else, human beings must first of all transmit language to themselves. Every specific tradition, every determinate cultural patrimony, presupposes the transmission of that alone through which something like a tradition is possible. *But what do humans transmit in transmitting language to themselves? What is the meaning of the transmission of language, independent of what is transmitted in language?* Far from being of no importance for thinking, these questions have constituted the subject of philosophy from its inception. Philosophy concerns itself with what is at issue not in this or that meaningful statement but in the very fact that human beings speak, that there is language and opening to sense, beyond, before, or, rather, *in* every determinate event of signification. What has always already been transmitted in every tradition, the *archi-traditum* and the *primum* of every tradition, is the thing of thinking.

א According to his report, you say that you have not had a sufficient demonstration of the doctrine concerning the nature of the First. I must therefore expound it to you, but in riddles, so that if this letter ends up at the bottom of the ocean or at the end of the earth, whoever reads it will not understand it. The matter stands as follows: all beings stand around the king of everything, and everything exists for his sake. And he is the cause of everything that is beautiful. The second things stand around the second; the third things stand around the third. The human soul strives to learn what all these things are, looking to things similar to them, but it is not fully satisfied with any one of them. There is nothing similar to the king and the things I have told you about. "But what," the soul then asks, "is it?" And this question, O son of Dionysius and Doris, is the cause of all troubles, of the labor pains suffered by the soul. And unless the soul frees itself of them, it will never be able to reach the truth.[1]

II

What do these considerations imply for the constitutive structure of all human tradition? What must be transmitted is not a *thing*, however eminent it might be; nor is it a truth that could be formulated in propositions or articles of faith. It is, instead, the very unconcealment (*a-lētheia*), the very opening in which something like a tradition is possible. But how is it possible to transmit an unconcealment; how can there be tradition not simply of a *traditum* but of openness itself, transmissibility itself? It is clear that this transmissibility cannot be thematized as a First *inside* tradition, nor can it become the content of one or more propositions among others, in any hierarchical order. Implicit in every act of transmission, it must remain unfinished and, at the same time, unthematized.

The tradition of transmissibility is therefore immemorially contained in every specific tradition, and this immemorial legacy, this transmission of unconcealment, constitutes human language as such. It is the closed fist that, according to Kafka's image, is inscribed in the coat of arms of every tradition, announcing its fulfillment. Yet this means that the structure of language must be such that in all discourse, language can transmit—and betray, according the double sense of the Latin *tradere*, "to transmit"—the unconcealment that it *is*, leaving it concealed in what it brings to light.

א Memory: disposition of the soul, which keeps watch over the unconcealment within it. (Plato, *Definitions*, 414 a 8)

III

This is why from its inception, philosophy, which seeks to give an account of this double structure of tradition and human language, has presented knowledge as caught in a dialectic of memory and oblivion, unconcealment and concealment, *alētheia* and *lēthē*. In its Platonic definition, the task of memory is not to shelter this or that truth, this or that remembrance, but to keep watch over the soul's very openness, its own unconcealment. The anamnestic structure of consciousness refers not to a chronological past or to ontic preeminence but, rather, to the very structure of truth. Being incapable of grasping itself and transmitting itself without becoming a remembered thing, this structure can preserve itself only by remaining immemorial in memory, by betraying itself, as Idea, in giving itself to sight—that is, in giving itself not as a teaching (*didaskalia*) but as a divine mission (*theia moira*). In modern terms: as historico-epochal opening.

Truth is thus not the tradition of either an esoteric or a public doctrine, as is maintained by the false determination of a tradition still dominant today. Truth is, rather, a memory that, in its very taking place, forgets itself and destines itself, as both historical opening and chronothesis. This is why anamnesis is constituted in the *Meno* as a memory of "the time in which man was not yet man." What must be grasped and transmitted is what is absolutely nonsubjective: oblivion as such.

> ℵ Because the full essence of truth contains the non-essence and above all holds sway as concealing, philosophy as a questioning into this truth is intrinsically discordant. Philosophical thinking is gentle releasement that does not renounce the concealment of being as a whole. Philosophical thinking is especially the stern and resolute openness that does not disrupt the concealing but entreats its unbroken essence into the open region of understanding and thus into its own truth.[2]

IV

This double structure of language and tradition lay at the center of the Greek reflection on *logos* from its beginnings. When Plato, in the Seventh Letter, presents the plane of language as governed by the irremediable difference between *on* and *poion*, Being and quality, what he seeks to bring to light is the necessarily fractured structure of linguistic signification as a specific weakness (*to tōn logōn asthenes*, Epistle VII, 343 a 1) of human communication, which thought must in some way master. Human language is necessarily pre-sup-positional and thematizing in the sense that in taking place, it decomposes the thing itself (*to pragma auto*) that is at issue in it and in it alone into a being *about which something is said* and a *poion*, a quality or determination *that is said of it*. To speak of a being, human language supposes and distances what it brings to light, in the very act in which it brings it to light. Language is thus, according to Aristotle's definition (*De anima*, 430 b 26, which was already implicit in Plato's *Sophist*, 262 e 6–7), *legein ti kata tinos*, a "saying something about something." It is therefore always presuppositional and objectifying, in that it always supposes that the being *about which* it speaks is already open and has already taken place. Presupposition is, indeed, the very form of linguistic signification—speaking *kat' hypokeimenou*, about a subject, on the basis of a presupposition. (The principle Plato seeks is, instead, a non-presupposed principle, an *arkhē anypothetos* [*Republic* 511 b 6]).

א Since there are two things, Being and quality, while the soul seeks to know the essence and not quality, each of the four [i.e., name, definition, image, and knowledge] offers the soul in speech and in facts what it does not seek.[3]

א Thought finds the double; it divides it until it arrives at a simple term that can no longer be analyzed. It continues as long as it can, dividing it to the bottom [*bathos*]. The bottom of all things is matter; this is why all matter is dark, why language is light, and why thought is language. And thought, seeing language in every thing, judges that what lies beneath is a darkness beneath the light, just as the eye, being of a luminous nature, looks toward light and luminous colors and says that what lies beneath colors is dark and material.[4]

V

This double structure of signification has its correlate in the fracture between name (*onoma*) and defining discourse (*logos*) that traverses all of language and that the Greeks considered so important as to attribute its discovery to Plato himself. In truth, it was Antisthenes who first insisted on the radical asymmetry between these two levels of language, stating that simple and primal substances can have names but no *logos*.

The plane of discourse is always already anticipated by the hermeneutics of Being implicit in names, for which language cannot give reasons (*logon didonai*) in propositions. According to this conception, what is unsayable is not what language does not at all bear witness to but, rather, what language can only name. *Discourse cannot say what is named by the name.* What is named by the name is transmitted and abandoned in discourse, as untransmittable and unsayable. The name is thus the linguistic cipher of presupposition, of what discourse cannot *say* but can only *presuppose* in signification. Names certainly enter into propositions, but what is said in propositions can be said only thanks to the presupposition of names.

> א Primal elements . . . do not have *logos*. Each alone by itself can only be named; discourse can add nothing to it, neither that it is nor that it is not, for that would be to add to it existence or non-existence, whereas if we are to speak of it itself we must add nothing to it. . . . [Primal elements] can only be named, for they have only a name.[5]

> א I can only *name* objects. Signs represent them. I can only speak *of* them. I cannot *assert them*. A proposition can only say *how* a thing is, not *what* it is.[6]

VI

In Aristotle's thought, the double structure of linguistic presupposition is identified with the logico-metaphysical structure of knowledge, whose foundation it articulates. The Being that the name indeterminately grasps as one is what the *logos* necessarily presents according to the plurality of *ti kata tinos*. This is why, in Aristotle, the question of the foundation (of Being as *arkhē*) has the following form: "why, through what does something belong to (or is something said of) something else?" (*zēteitai de to dia ti aei houtōs; dia ti allo allōi tini hyparkhei*; "the foundation is always sought thus: why does something belong to [does something lie beneath as the principle of] something?" [*Metaphysics*, 1041 a 10]). Truth, the originary unconcealment in which each being shows itself, is thus separated from beings and presupposed as the foundation of meaningful discourse, the foundation of the fact that something is predicated of something. As foundation, it is what always already was (*to ti ēn einai*) knowable and known. Knowledge of it, however, cannot in itself be formulated, either in the mind or in propositions; it can only be "touched" (*thigein*) by the intellect (*nous*) and uttered in the name. This arche-past, this ineffable Being that has already been, thus becomes the *dia ti, that through the presupposing of which* something can be known and said of something. In remaining ineffable, it thus guarantees that discourse has a meaning, that it is founded, and that it *speaks about something* (that it speaks by means of a *hypokeimenon*, a pre-supposition). Insofar as it is presupposed in discourse, the foundation is *hypokeimenon*, subject and matter, that is, the potentiality (*dynamis*) of *logos*; insofar as it is noetically known in its truth, it is, instead, *telos*, event and fulfillment of what always already was.

(The duality of *Grund* and *Bewegung* by which Hegel articulates his logic of grounding is implicit in this presupposition of the foundation.)

> א All assertion [*phasis*] is something-about-something and, as affirmation, is either true or false. But this is not so with thinking. The thinking of what is according to what was [*ho tou ti esti kata to ti ēn einai*] is true, and yet it is not something-about-something.[7]

VII

Let us analyze the mechanism of presupposition and foundation in Aristotle more closely. In Book Gamma of the *Metaphysics*, it is articulated through the distinction between *hen sēmainein* (signifying one) and *kath'henos sēmainein* (signifying about one). The entire demonstration by refutation of the principle of noncontradiction rests on the assumption that there is necessarily a point at which language no longer signifies *about something*, but rather *signifies something*. For Aristotle, this limit point is the nonhypothetical principle (which we always carry with us in knowledge) on which he founds the "strongest of principles," the principle of noncontradiction and, along with it, the very possibility of meaningful discourse. *Only because there is a point at which language signifies-one is it possible to signify about that one, uttering meaningful statements.* The nonhypothetical principle is the foundation, that alone *through the presupposing of which* there can be knowledge and *logos*; it is possible to speak and to state propositions about a subject (*kath' hypokeimenou*) because what is thus presupposed is the fundamental intentionality of language, its signifying-and-touching-one. (What was the weakness of *logos* for Plato becomes for Aristotle the strength of *logos*. The Platonic constitution of truth, unlike the Aristotelian, never comes to a halt at a presupposition.)

> א The foundation cannot be said on the basis of a presupposition. Otherwise there would be a foundation of the foundation. The foundation is presupposed, and it appears to be anterior to what is predicated.[8]

> א Every truth that is not itself a first principle must be demonstrated by means of some truth that is a first principle. Therefore, in any inquiry, it is a prerequisite to have a full understanding of the principle that, under analysis, we see to guarantee the certainty of all the other propositions that are deduced from it.[9]

VIII

It is this presuppositional structure of language and reflection that Hegel develops in the duality of "ground" (*Grund*) and "condition" (*Bedingung*) in the chapter of the *Science of Logic* devoted to the problem of the "ground" or "foundation." The condition is the immediate, that "to which the ground refers as essential presupposition." It is thus what language always presupposes in the name for the sake of the relation it establishes: "the non-relational, to which relation, in which the non-relation is condition, is extrinsic." The ground, on the other hand, is "the relation or form by which the determinate existence of the condition is merely material." In the name, the pure, nonrelational, and immediate Being of something is thus presupposed; then it is assumed that this non-relational enters into the relation of predication in the form of a subject. The task of the dialectic of grounding is to show how condition and ground are not two independent realities but, rather, "the two sides of the whole" that "each presuppose the other" and whose truth is to be found in the reciprocal overcoming constitutive of the "tautological movement of the thing to itself." This is why it is not at all possible to oppose presupposition and ground, which, in isolation, exhibit only their essential negativity. The tradition of truth has the threefold form of presupposition, ground, and their unity in the thing itself. (This unity of name [the Father], *logos* [the Son], and their *spiritual* relation is the speculative content of the doctrine of the Trinity.)

> ℵ The rose in potentiality, the rose in actuality, and the rose in potentiality and actuality are not other and different. . . . Thus I see the one and threefold rose thanks to the one and threefold principle. But I thus see the principle shining in everything, as there is no principle that is not one and threefold. . . . Hence when I see God not presupposing his principle, when I see God presupposing his principle, and when I see God emerging from both, I do not see three gods but the unity of divinity in the trinity.[10]

IX

Let us now once again ask: how can there be a tradition of truth? How is it possible to transmit not a thing but an unconcealment? What do human beings transmit in transmitting language to themselves? It is certain that the mechanism of presupposition and foundation has, in our time, entered a lasting crisis. Hegel was the last thinker who, through the movement of dialectical negativity, sought to assure the historical self-movement of truth (the fulfillment of which he also announced). And it is surely not an accident that the thinker who posed the question of the ground and its nullity more forcefully than any other in our century is also the one who most vigorously posed the problem of tradition and its destruction. *Today we find ourselves more and more thrown before the originary unconcealment of truth. We can neither transmit nor master this unconcealment, which, as a dark presupposition, is abandoned in the tradition to which it destines us.* The absence of a foundation for truth—that is, the radical crisis of the presupposition—is itself thought according to the form of the presupposition. (This is the structure of trace and originary writing in which our age has remained imprisoned. Truth is written—that is, it always remains presupposed and, at the same time, deferred in its very taking place.)

When Neoplatonism, at the end of the ancient world, undertook its summation of pagan philosophy in the form of a synthesis between Platonism and Aristotelianism, it was forced to rethink the problem of the foundation as an absolutization of the presupposition and its transcendence. Plato's *arkhē anypothetos*, his nonpresupposed and nonpresupposable principle, thus assumed the status of the ineffability and incomprehensibility of the Neoplatonic One, which gives itself only in an infinite flight from itself to itself. In the words of the last *diadoch* of pagan philosophy, it is a pure, incomprehensible plane, or in the words of Proclus, the Unparticipated at the foundation of all participation:

א All that is unparticipated constitutes the participated out of itself. All hypostases are linked by an upward tension to existences not participated. The unparticipated, having the *logos* of unity (being, that is, its own and not another's, and being separated from the participated) generates what can be participated. For either it must remain fixed in sterility and isolation, and so must lack a place of honour; or else it will give something of itself, such that the receiver becomes a participant and the given subsists by participation. Everything that is participated, becoming a property of that by which it is participated, is secondary to that which in all is equally present and has filled them all out of its own being. That which is in one is not in the others; that which is present to all alike, that it may illuminate all, is not in any one, but is prior to them. For either it is in all, or in one out of all, or prior to all. But a principle which was in all would be divided amongst all, and would itself require a further principle to unify the divided; and further, all the particulars would no longer participate in the same principle, but this in one and that in another, through the diremption of its unity. And if it be in one out of all, it will be a property no longer of all but of one. If, then, it is both common to all that can participate and identical for all, it must be prior to all: such is the Unparticipated.[11]

ℵ Perhaps the absolutely ineffable is so ineffable that one cannot even say of it that it is ineffable. As to the One, it is ineffable in the sense that it cannot be grasped by a definition and a name, or a distinction such as that between the knowable and the knowing. It must be conceived as a kind of threshing floor, a light, smooth glowing in which no point can be distinguished from any other.[12]

X

Have we moved even one step beyond this unparticipated threshing floor, where "no point can be distinguished from any other" and in which we nevertheless find both destiny and sending? Do we experience the principle of all things as anything other than an Unparticipated that destines and historically produces us as *parts*, im-parting us in its incessant participation? Are we truly capable of conceiving the generic and universal essence of human being and its community without presuppositions? Are we capable of thinking of the tradition of truth and language as anything other than an unfounded and yet destining presupposition?

The historico-social experience of our time is that of an *original partition*, an *Ur-teilung*, that has no appropriation to accomplish, a sending that has no message, a destiny that does not originate in any foundation. Of the three categories by which Carl Schmitt articulates the political— "taking" (*Nehmen*), "dividing" (*Teilen*), and "pastoring" (*Weiden*)—*Teilen* is the one that is fundamental here. We are united only through our common participation in an Unparticipated; we are anticipated by a presupposition, but one without an origin; we are divided, without any inheritance. *This is why everything we can take is always already divided,* and why the community that binds us—or, rather, the community into which we are thrown—cannot be a community of something into which we are appropriated and from which we are subsequently separated. Community is from the beginning a community *of parts and parties.* (The domination and simultaneous devastation of the form of the party, its *destitution of every foundation*, has its root in this epochal situation.)

It is this epochal situation that has been most rigorously considered in France by Jean-Luc Nancy and Maurice Blanchot as "inoperative community" and "unavowable community," and it is the constitution of this very figure of presupposition that, in Italy, Massimo Cacciari has sought in the mystical tradition. Our time thus registers the demand for a community without presuppositions; yet without realizing it, it simultaneously maintains the empty form of presupposition beyond all foundations—presupposition of nothing, pure destination. Damascius's "light and smooth" threshing floor, or Proclus's Unparticipated principle. This is the root of our discomfort and, at the same time, our only hope.

> א Sie sich nicht fassen können
> Einander, die zusammenlebten
> Im Gedächnis.
>
> (They cannot grasp one another who
> lived together in remembrance.)[13]

א It is not enough to say that there is an undecidable in discourse. It does not suffice to decide the fate, structure, or power of discourse. Today the undecidable is to be found everywhere as an answer, one which one would like to substitute for the old answers to this or that truth, or to Truth. . . . The signs of the decomposition, dislocation, and dismemberment of the system—that is, of the entire architectonics and history of the West—which, for example, are called . . . "text," "signifier," "lack," "derivation," "trace," etc., have been converted into values; they have thus been erected as truths and hypostatized as substances.[14]

XI

In 1795, Hölderlin composed a brief note in which it seemed to him that he had "made a step beyond the Kantian borders." The text, which bears the name "Judgment and Being," poses the problem of "absolute Being" (*Sein schlechthin*), which cannot in any way be the presupposition of a division. Being that is expressed reflectively in identity (A = A or, in Hölderlin's terms, *Ich bin Ich*) is not absolute Being but, according to Hölderlin, Being as the necessary presupposition of the division of subject and object. This division, which is judgment (*Urtheil*) as originary partition (*Ur-theilung*), contains a presupposition of a whole, of which subject and object are parts. ("In the concept of separation, there already lies the concept of the reciprocity of object and subject and the necessary presupposition of a whole of which object and subject form the parts. 'I am I' is the most fitting example of this concept of originary division [*Ur-theilung*].")[15]

Absolute Being-one is therefore not to be mistaken for the self-identical Being of reflection, which, as the form of self-consciousness, always already implies the possibility of division. ("How can I say: 'I!' Without self-consciousness? Yet how is self-consciousness possible? In opposing myself to myself, separating myself from myself, yet in recognizing myself as the same in the opposed regardless of this separation.")[16]

Hölderlin's attempt to grasp undivided Being, which cannot be presupposed in division, is very close here to the central concern of the *Philosophical Notes* of his friend Isaak von Sinclair, which seeks to consider precisely "the unposited" (*athesis*) without falling into the form of presuppositional reflection:

> ℵ As soon as one wants to know and posit *theos* (athetic unity, essence), it is transformed into an "I" (into Fichte's absolute "I"). Insofar as one reflects on its highest essence and posits it, one separates it and, after separating it, gives it back its character of non-separation by means of unification, such that Being is so to speak presupposed in separation: *id est* the imperfect concept. *Hen kai pan.*[17]

> ℵ Reflection has made nature manifold through the "I," for it opposed it to the unity of the "I." But reflection said only that if a manifold was outside the "I," originary division [*Urteilung*] was possible. It was certainly outside the "I"; but it was not outside reflection. For if we supposed it to be outside reflection, we would simply have deferred, and not explained, the problem of its genesis, which led us thus far. For one would always ask how the manifold in reflection derives from the manifold outside reflection. By hypothesizing this reality of the manifold, we would have only paid attention to a transcendental demand of reflection, which always requires grounding, even outside its limits. Transcendental reflection imagines there to be, beyond the reciprocal acts of subject and object, an activity of the subject that is independent of it, the "I" as substance—yet here there is an impossibility of thinking [*Denkunmöglichkeit*].[18]

VII

It may be that modern thought has not truly reckoned with the "impossibility of thinking" implicit in Sinclair's text. What, indeed, does it mean to think the One in language without presupposing its destining partition? To think, in other words, a principle not presupposed in becoming, the nonlinguistic not presupposed in the linguistic, the name not presupposed in discourse? To think the groundlessness and emptiness of language and its representations without any negativity? At issue here is whether the form of representation and reflection can still be maintained beyond representation and reflection, as contemporary thought, in its somnambulant nihilism, seems determined to maintain; or whether a realm is not instead opened here for a task and a decision of an entirely different kind. The fulfillment of the form of presupposition and the decline of the power of representation imply a poetic task and an ethical decision.

Only on the basis of this decision and this task is it possible to understand the sense in which the "Oldest Program for a System of German Idealism" founds the possibility of an overcoming of the State on the appearance of an ethics that would abandon the "philosophy of the letter" for the sake of an art of poetry (*Dichtkunst*)—an *ars dictaminis*, literally an "art of dictation," restored to its original dignity.

Are we capable today of no longer being philosophers of the letter (*Buchstabenphilosophen*), without thereby becoming either philosophers of the voice or mere enthusiasts? Are we capable of reckoning with the poetic presentation of the vocation that, as a nonpresupposed principle, emerges only where no voice calls us? Only then would tradition cease to be the remission and betrayal of an unsayable transmission, affirming itself truly as *Über-lieferung*, self-liberation and self-offering: *hen diapheron heautōi*, "one transporting itself," without vocation and without destiny. Tradition would then have truly for-*given* what cannot, in any sense, be presupposed.

ℵ Among men, one has to make sure with every thing that it is some thing, that is, that it is recognizable in the medium [*moyen*] of its appearance, that the way in which it is delimited can be determined and thought.[19]

ℵ La poésie ne s'impose plus, elle s'expose.

(Poetry no longer imposes itself; it exposes itself.)[20]

§ 8 *Se*: Hegel's Absolute and Heidegger's *Ereignis*

Sergio Solmi in memoriam
. . . accustomed
to an unexplained duty . . .

I

The reflections that follow consider the structure and meaning of the Indo-European theme *se* (*swe*). The pertinence of this theme to philosophical discourse is so little in question that it can be said to determine the fundamental philosophical problem itself, the Absolute. The Latin verb *solvo*, from which the adjective "absolute" is derived, can be analyzed as *se-luo* and indicates the work of loosening, freeing (*luo*) that leads (or leads back) something to its own *se*.

II

In Indo-European languages, the group of the reflexive *se* (Greek *he*, Latin *se*, Sanskrit *sva-*) indicates what is proper (cf. the Latin *suus*) and exists autonomously. *Se* has this semantic value in the sense of what is proper to a group, as in the Latin *suesco*, "to accustom oneself," *consuetudo*, "habit," and *sodalis*, "companion"; the Greek *hethos* (and *ēthos*), "custom, habit, dwelling place"; the Sanskrit *svadhá*, "character, habit"; and the Gothic *sidus* (cf. the German *Sitte*), "custom," as well as in the sense of what stands by itself, separated, as in *solus*, "alone," and *secedo*, "to separate." It is semantically and etymologically linked to the Greek *idios*, "proper" (hence *idioomai*, "I appropriate," and *idiōtēs*, "private citizen"); it is also related to the Greek *heauton* (*he* + *auton*), "itself" (contracted as *hauton*), as well as to the English "self," the German *sich* and *selbst* and the Italian *sé* and *si*. Insofar as it contains both a relation that unites and a relation that separates, the proper—that which characterizes every thing as a *se*—is therefore not something simple.

א The terms *absolute* and *absolutely* correspond to the Greek expression *kath' heauto*, "according to it itself." For the Greek philosophers, to consider something *kath' heauto* is to consider it absolutely, that is, according to what is proper to it, according to its own *se* (*he-auton*).

III

The fact that the term *Ereignis*, "event," with which Heidegger designates the supreme problem of his thought after *Being and Time*, can be semantically linked to this sphere is shown by the (etymologically arbitrary) relation Heidegger suggests between *Ereignis* and both the verb *eignen*, "to appropriate," and the adjective *eigen*, "proper" or "own." Insofar as it indicates an appropriation, a being proper, *Ereignis* is not far from the meaning of *se* and, with reference to it, can be grasped in the sense of ab-*so*-lution.

א Heidegger himself links the problem of *Ereignis* to that of *Selbst*, the "same." Semantically (but not etymologically), *eigen* is to *Selbst* as *idios* is to *he*. The established etymology of *Ereignis* (to which Heidegger also makes reference) relates it to the ancient Germanic term *ouga*, "eye": *ereignen* < *ir-ougen*, "to place before one's eyes." *Eigen* instead derives from another stem, **aig*, which signifies possession.

IV

The idea that *se* is not something simple is contained in one of the most ancient testimonies to Western philosophy's consideration of the proper. This testimony (Heraclitus, Diels fragment 119) reads as follows:

ēthos anthropōi daimōn.

The usual translation of this fragment is "for man, character is the demon." But *ēthos* ("character") originally indicates what is proper in the sense of "dwelling place, habit." As for the term *daimōn*, it neither simply indicates a divine figure nor merely refers to the one who determines destiny. Considered according to its etymological root (which refers it to the verb *daiomai*, "to divide, lacerate"), *daimōn* means "the lacerator, he who divides and fractures." (In Aeschylus, *Agamemnon*, ll. 1472–73 the *daimōn*, "lacerator of the heart" [*kardiodēkton*] is crouched as a wild beast over the body of the dead man.) Only insofar as it is what divides can the *daimōn* also be what assigns a fate and what destines (*daiomai* first means "to divide," then "to assign"; the same semantic development can be found in a word that is derived from the same root: *dēmos*, "people," which originally means "division of a territory," "assigned part"). Once restored to its etymological origin, Heraclitus's fragment then reads: "For man, *ēthos*, the dwelling in the 'self' that is what is most proper and habitual for him, is what lacerates and divides, the principle and place of a fracture." Man is such that, to be *himself*, he must necessarily divide himself.

ℵ A phrase that is surprisingly similar to Heraclitus's fragment and that, indeed, almost seems to be its literal translation can be found in one of Hölderlin's hemistics (in a version of the last strophe of *Brod und Wein*): *Ihn zehret die Heimat*, "the homeland lacerates it [sc., the spirit]." In Schelling, the dwelling in the absolute is compared to the "purity of the terrible blade, which man cannot approach unless he possesses the same purity." And Hegel's thought of the Absolute conceives the same dwelling in division.

V

Let us continue our reflections on the sphere of meaning of **se*. Grammarians tell us that it is a reflexive form; in other words, it indicates a movement of re-flexion, a departure from the self and a return to the self, like a ray of light reflected in a mirror. But who is reflected here, and how is this reflection achieved? Grammarians observe (and this fact is worth pausing to consider, despite its apparent obviousness) that the pronoun "self" is lacking in the nominative form (cf. the Greek *hou, hoi, he*; the Latin *sui, sibi, se*; the German *seiner* and *sich*; hence also *heautou, heautoi, heauton*). Insofar as it indicates a relation with itself, a re-flection, **se* necessarily implies a reference to a grammatical subject (or at least another pronoun or name); it is never employed by itself, nor can it be employed as a grammatical subject. The indication of the "proper," as reflection, therefore cannot have the form of a nominative; it can only appear in an "oblique" case.

The linguistic meaning of this "defect" of *se can be best understood if it is placed in relation to the essential character of the Indo-European word (to which J. Lohmann called attention in an important text, finding it in the verbal structure of the ontological difference), according to which it appears as fractured ("flexed") into a theme and endings. Ancient grammatical thought interpreted inflection as a *ptōsis*, a "fall" (in Latin, *casus, declinatio*) of the name in the occurrence of discourse. And in this sense, it opposed the nominative (the ancients do not clearly distinguish a theme and tend to identify it with the nominative as the case of the grammatical subject) to the other cases (even if the Stoics defined the nominative as *orthē ptōsis, casus rectus*, and therefore as a form of the "fall," albeit a special kind with respect to *plagiai ptōseis, casus obliqui*).

The possibility of a *reflection*, that is, of a relation of speech to itself, is in a certain sense already implicit in the inflected structure of Indo-European speech. But precisely for this reason, the reference of a word to itself, the indication of the proper, is not separable from an *oblique* course in which what reflects never has the same form as what is reflected.

Hence the apparent paradox according to which if to think something according to its *se (kath' heauto)* is to think it absolutely, beyond its ties to other words and independently of its inflection in the occurrence of discourse, *se nevertheless cannot be thought *kath' heauto*. (This is only an apparent paradox, since modern philosophy is precisely the attempt to show what it means to think *se, to think it *absolutely* and as *subject*.)

VI

The relation of one thing to itself, its being proper to itself, can also be expressed in Indo-European languages through the repetition of the same term in two different cases, the nominative and the genitive. In Aristotle, the expression of absolute thought (*hē de noēsis hē kath' heautēn*) thus has the form of the following proposition:

estin hē noēsis noēseōs noēsis. (*Metaphysics*, 1074 b 35)

(thought is the thought of thought.) .

(Aristotle's proposition is thus a phrase in which, in addition to the definite article and the verb "to be," there is only one word, which is repeated in two inflections.) The genitive is the case that indicates a predication of belonging, a being-proper (hence the term *genitive, genikos*, which expresses belonging to a family, and a *genos*; Varro also calls the genitive *patrius*). But it does so only on the condition of distinguishing between a being-proper characteristic of a logical subject (subjective genitive: *patentia animi = animus patitur*) and a being-proper characteristic of a logical object (objective genitive: *patientia doloris = pati dolorem*).

In the Aristotelian phrase cited above, the distinction between the two forms of genitive necessarily disappears; in the being-proper of thought to itself there is no more distinction between the thinking of the subject and the thought that is its object. This gives the proposition a circular structure and, at the same time, opens it to the risk of an infinite flight. Radicalizing this structure, which is implicit in thought's reference to itself, the Neoplatonists conceive of the Absolute as a "flight of One toward One" (*phygē monon pros monon*); but, at the same time, they conceive the One (or the self itself), subject-object of the flight, as beyond Being and thought (*epekeina tēs ousias, epekeina ti nou*). The relation of a self to itself is beyond Being and thought; in other words, *se, *ēthos*, the dwelling place, is without Being and thought, and only on the condition of thus remaining alone in itself does it escape demonic fracture. If *se tries to think itself, even in the authentic form of a thinking of itself, it is immediately affected (Plotinus says "speckled," *poikilon*) by division and multiplicity.

א In medieval theology, the problem of *se appears as the problem of the coincidence of essence and existence in God. It is stated in the following formula: *Deus est suum esse* (or *essentia*), "God is His own Being (or essence)." What confronts thinking in this definition (and what modern thought has never ceased to think) is precisely the enigma of *suum*, "own." The coincidence of essence and existence (being Being) signifies *suum esse*, being one's *own* Being. Spinoza's "cause of itself," *causa sui* (in this case too the genitive *sui* is both subjective and objective), as *quod in se est et per se concipitur*, is a consideration of this very problem.

VII

Given the fact that the reflexive belongs to the category of the pronoun, a presentation of the sphere of meaning of *se necessarily seems to imply a clarification of the sphere of meaning of the personal pronoun. In linguistics, the personal pronoun is classified as a "shifter," that is, as a term whose meaning can be grasped only with reference to the event of discourse in which it is contained and which indicates the speaker. "I" denotes no lexical entity; it has no reality and consistency outside its relation to actual discourse. "I" is the one who produces the *present* event of speech containing the shifter "I" (as Hegel says concerning Kant, "*I* is not a concept, but a mere *consciousness* that *accompanies every concept*").

Hence the impossibility to which one is necessarily led every time one tries to grasp the meaning of the "I" as something substantial: insofar as it is identifiable only though its pure reference to the event of actual speech, "I" necessarily has a *temporal* and *negative* structure; it is always transcendent with respect to all of its psychophysical individuations and, moreover, incapable of referring to itself without once again falling into an event of speech.

What, then, happens if we want to grasp the "I" in its propriety, in its dwelling place, in its pure reference to itself? If we want, that is, to grasp the "I" as *se, as ab-so-lute? This is Hegel's problem ("but surely it is ridiculous to call this nature of self-consciousness, namely, that the 'I' thinks itself, that the 'I' cannot be thought without its being the 'I' that thinks, an *inconvenience*").[1]

א In philosophy, the displacement of reflection from the "I" to the third person and the Absolute (*Es, Es selbst*) corresponds to the attempt to absolve the subject of its necessary relation to the event of speech, that is, to grasp the *se of the "I," what is proper to the subject independent of its "fall" into the event of speech. Or, better, to grasp the very movement of pure temporality and pure Being, beyond what is temporalized and said in actual discourse.

VIII

Hegel's determination of the Absolute is characterized by its appearance as "result," as being "only at the end what it truly is." The proper, *se, is for humans the principle and place of a fracture; according to Hegel, this is the point of departure of philosophy, "the source [*der Quell*] of the need of philosophy."[2] Philosophy must therefore absolve the proper of division, leading *se back to *se, thinking *se *absolutely*. Yet if *se is not simple, but always already implies demonic division (if it is itself *daimōn*), then to think *se absolutely—*kath' heauto*, according to itself—cannot be simply to think it beyond all relation and division. As is already implicit in its origins as a past participle, the Absolute is not something immobile or nonrelational that is equal to itself outside of time, an abyss without movement and difference (or, as Hegel also says, the pure name that has not yet entered propositions). Since *se contains difference in itself as "internal difference" (*innerer Unterschied*), to think the Absolute is to think what, through a process of absolution, has been led back to its *se; it is, in other words, to conceive of what has *become equal to itself in its being other*. Human being, insofar as it is an "I," a speaking subject, is such that to be itself, it must have come back to itself, having found itself in the Other.

IX

The proper of thought is therefore not the mere name (*blosser Name*) that remains in itself but the name that leaves itself to be uttered and "declined" in propositions. And precisely in this becoming other it becomes equal to itself, finally returning to itself (it is, in other words, Hegel's "concept"). We may say that in the Absolute, Hegel thinks the fundamental character of Indo-European languages—the "internal fracture" of speech into theme and endings—that Lohmann recognized as the linguistic mark of the ontological difference. But Hegel—and this is what is proper to him—regards this fracture as absolute, thus understanding Being as equal to itself in its being other and conceiving of fracture in its unity as the phenomenon (*Erscheinung*) of the Absolute. This—the absolute concept—is not something that is given in its truth at the beginning; it *becomes* what it *is*, and therefore only at the end is it what it truly is. *Hegel thus conceives of declension itself as the movement of the Absolute.*

In this sense, the Hegelian notion of the dialectical process is a presentation of the particular character of the reflexive form *se, namely, its lack of nominative form (which the grammarians considered to be obvious, but which only reveals its true significance in German Idealism). To clarify the matter, let us now posit the two figures of the name (inflection) and of *se (reflection):

                    ROS -a   . . . .
                         -ae   sui
                         -am   sibi
                         -a   se
                         -ae
                         -arum
                         -is
                         -as

The interpretation of the word according to *se (the absolute word) implies that the name, as presupposition of the movement of declension, is sublated (*aufgehoben*) and that it occurs as concept only at the end of the dialectical process of inflection. There is no name that first is meaningful and then falls into inflection and discourse; rather, the name, as concept, occurs in its truth only at the end of its re-flexion. Only at the end is the rose, which dances in the cross of its declensions, truly what it is: itself. This is why Hegel defines the movement of the Absolute as the "circle that returns into itself, the circle that presupposes its beginning and reaches it only at the end":[3]

In the preface to the *Phenomenology of Spirit*, Hegel himself speaks of the movement of the Absolute as the movement of a name that is only a "meaningless sound" (*sinnloser Laut*) in the beginning but that achieves its meaning as it passes into a proposition (*Übergang . . . zu einem Satze*). Only judgment, the concrete event of discourse, says what the name is, granting it meaning (*erst das Prädikat sagt, was er ist, ist seine Erfüllung und seine Bedeutung*). An empty beginning thus becomes, in the end, actual knowledge (*der leere Anfang wird nur in diesem Ende ein wirkliches Wissen*).

X

This circular character of the Absolute determines its essential relation to temporality. Insofar as the Absolute always implies a process and a becoming, an alienation and a return, it cannot be something nontemporal, an eternity *before* time, but is necessarily temporal and historical (or, in linguistic terms, it appears not as a *name* but as *discourse*). And yet, as *result* it cannot simply be identified with an infinite course of time; it must necessarily fulfill time, *ending it*. Since the Absolute becomes equal to itself in its being other, and since division is posited in it as its appearance

(*Erscheinung*)—this was the "task of philosophy" (*die Aufgabe der Philoso-phie*)[4]—this "appearance," that is, the historical and temporal becoming of "figures," has now been achieved and has become totality. Spirit can grasp itself as absolute only *at the end of time*. Eternity is not something *before* time but is, in essence, *fulfilled* time (*erfüllte Zeit*), *finished* history. Hegel states this clearly at the end of the *Phenomenology*: "Spirit neces-sarily appears in Time, and it appears in Time just so long as it has not *grasped* its pure Notion, i.e., until it has annulled time. . . . Until Spirit has completed itself *in itself*, until it has completed itself as world-Spirit, it cannot reach its consummation as *self-conscious* Spirit."[5]

Hence the essential orientation of the Absolute toward the past, its ap-pearance in the figure of totality and remembrance. Contrary to an an-cient tradition of thought that considers the present as the privileged di-mension of temporality, Hegel regards the past as the figure of fulfilled time, time that has returned to itself. It is, however, a question of a past that has abolished its essential relation to the present and the future, a "perfect" past (*teleios*, to use the term with which Stoic grammarians char-acterize one of the forms of the conjugation of the verb), in which no his-torical destination remains to be realized. "The past," Hegel writes in the text in which he most fully considered the movement (*Bewegung*) of time,

> is this time that has returned onto itself; the One Time [*Ehemals*] is a self-identity to itself [*Sichselbstgleichheit*], but it is a self-identity to itself that orig-inates in this sublation [of the present and the future]; it is a synthetic, com-pleted self-identity to itself, the dimension of the totality of time, which has in itself sublated the first two dimensions. . . . The past that has thus sublated its relation to the Now and to the Once [*Einst*] and is therefore no longer it-self One Time [*Ehemals*], this real time is the paralyzed unrest of the absolute concept, time that in its totality has become absolutely other. From the de-termination of the infinite, whose representation is time, the past has passed over into its opposite, the determination of self-identity to itself; and in this way, in this self-identity to itself whose moments now stand in front of each other, it is space."[6]

In the "paralyzed unrest" of the absolute concept, what is ultimately achieved is simply what has happened. What is fulfilled is only the past, and what human spirit must recognize as proper at the point at which it extinguishes time is its having-been, its history, which now confronts it as if gathered into a space: a "picture gallery" (*Galerie von Bildern*). The end thus spirals back to the beginning.

Only at this point, at the end of time, in the absolute knowledge in which all the figures of spirit are fulfilled (*hat also der Geist die Bewegung seines Gestaltens beschlossen*),[7] is it possible for a critique of Hegel's thought to formulate decisive questions that are truly adequate to the task. What does it mean for history to be finished, for spirit to have *withdrawn into itself* (*Insichgehen*)?[8] Are we even capable of conceiving such a fulfillment and such a journey? Does such finishing mean a simple cessation, after which there comes nothing? Or does it mean—according to an equally legitimate interpretation—an infinite, eternal "circle of circles" (*ein Kreis von Kreisen*)?[9] What happens, in any case, to what has "gone into itself" and, having sunk into its "night," is now *absolved*, fulfilled? What happens to the *perfect* past? What happens to its "figures"? It is certainly over, definitively dispersed (here, as in the mysteries, "to go into oneself" is to die, to abandon existence, *sein Dasein verlässt*),[10] and "consigned" to timeless memory. But does Hegel himself not speak of an "existence now reborn" (*aus dem Wissen neugeborene*)?[11] And how are we to conceive of a *timeless* past and memory that no longer refer to a present and to a future? A total memory that is always present to itself and that therefore has nothing to remember?

The answers we give to these questions will determine the form and sense that Hegelianism will have for us. They will decide whether Hegel's thought will survive in the form of an innocuous historiographical memory that gathers and contemplates historical becoming while infinitely repeating and enlarging its dialectical circles, or, alternatively, in the form of a dejected—but ultimately useless—wisdom by which man understands and is himself only in his death. At the same time, they will decide whether Hegel's thought will appear to us as what it is—one of the supreme attempts of philosophy to think its own supreme thought, humankind's entry into its *se*, into its being without a nominative, which constitutes its dwelling and its *ēthos*: its *so*litude and its con*su*etude, its *se*paration but also its *so*lidarity.

א Hence the legitimacy of every thought that, like Marx's, interrogates in Hegel's philosophy precisely the moment of the end of history, thus considering humanity's state once it has left the "Reign of necessity" to enter into its proper condition in the "Reign of freedom." The suggestion has been made—and this is certainly possible—that once humanity has returned to itself, it may no longer have a human form and thus appear as the fulfilled animality of *homo sapiens*. The suggestion has also been made—and this is equally possible—that with the supremacy of the Absolute's orientation toward the past, the fulfilled figure of the human may instead have the form of a book that forever gathers and recapitulates in its pages all the historical figures of humanity, such a book being a volume published by Goebhard of Bamberg in April 1807 under the title *Die Phänomenologie des Geistes* (*The Phenomenology of Spirit*). This— *but not only this*—is certainly possible.

XI

The Absolute appears equally problematic if we try to consider it in its linguistic aspect, as absolute speech or fulfilled discourse. For what is a truly *fulfilled* discourse that has exhausted all its historical figures and has returned to itself, if not a dead language? What happens when human speech, which has left itself to be uttered in the infinite multiplicity of events of discourse, ultimately returns to itself? In the last chapter of the *Science of Logic*, Hegel states:

> Logic exhibits the self-movement of the absolute Idea only as the original *word* [*das ursprüngliche Wort*], which is an *outwardizing* or *utterance* [*Äusserung*], but an utterance that in being has immediately vanished again as something outer; the Idea is, therefore, only in this self-determination of *apprehending itself*; it is in *pure thought*, in which difference is not yet *otherness*, but is and remains perfectly transparent to itself.[12]

How are we to conceive such an "original word," which is dispersed as soon as it is uttered? Has it not once again become a *sinnloser Laut*, a meaningless sound? Are we capable of fully considering all the implications of Hegel's statement that in the end the Idea "deposes" itself and lets itself go free (*sich frei entlässt*), having the form of the pure "externality of space and time"?[13] Is Hegel's "original word" an animal voice—like the singing of birds and the braying of donkeys—which man utters immediately? Or rather, as is also possible, is it a *glossolalia* (in the sense of 1 Cor. 14), a word whose meaning has been forgotten, an immemorial human word that has exhausted all its possibilities of meaning and now, fully transparent, lies fulfilled, that is, untouched and in-conceivable in the "night" of its *se*?

Or is what is at issue here a language that, while remaining human and alive, dwells in itself—a language no longer destined to grammatical and historical transmission, a language that, as the universal and novel language of redeemed humanity, coincides without residue with human activity and praxis?

א In his 1930–31 lectures on the *Phenomenology of Spirit*, Heidegger, underlining the character of the movement of the Absolute, distinguished an *absolving* element in *absolute* knowledge and defined the essence of the Absolute as "infinite absolving."

Many years later, Henry Corbin took up Heidegger's observations in the realm of religious phenomenology, reformulating the distinction in more explicit terms. "The *absolutum*," Corbin writes, "presupposes an *absolvens*, which absolves it from non-Being and concealment." It is this *absolvens* that, from a religious point of view, founds the necessity and legitimacy of angelology: "The Angel is the *absconditum* that is absolved of its concealment. This shows the necessity of the Angel, since to claim to do without the Angel is to confuse the absolving (*absolvens*) with the absolved (*absolutum*)." According to Corbin, this confusion constitutes the error of metaphysics (in its Hegelian form and, above all, in the form of orthodox Christian theology): "This is why metaphysical idolatry hides itself under the cover of the aspiration for the absolute. This idolatry does not consist in the construction of the relative as absolute, but in the construction of the absolute as absolving."

Hegel's thought of the Absolute is in fact not at odds with such a formulation. For Hegel, too, the Absolute, originating in a past participle, needs an absolution that ultimately allows it to be only at the end what it truly is. Absolution consists in "positing the fracture in the Absolute as its appearance [*Erscheinung*]," in recognizing the phenomenon *of the* Absolute. The difference between the two positions may consist in the fact that, in Hegel, the speculative proposition states that "the Absolute is absolving," whereas for Corbin it inversely affirms that "the absolving is the Absolute." In both cases, what is decisive is that in absolute knowledge, the absolved is no longer concealed in its figures, the phenomenon being fulfilled (*saved*, according to the Platonic *ta phainomena sōzein*). Here we enter into a region in which God and Angel necessarily become indistinct and in which theology and angelology can no longer be distinguished. At this point, the decisive questions become: *What happens to the phenomenon* (the Angel, the absolving)? *What happens to the Absolute* (God)?

As to the first question: at the point at which the revelation of the absolute is accomplished, the phenomenon shows itself insofar as it is no longer a phenomenon but rather a fulfilled figure (that is, no longer as figure of . . .).

As to the second question: at the point at which the *Absconditum*, having been absolved and led back to its **se*, exhausts its figures, it shows itself as *without figure*. Only if the two sides (the Without Figure and the Fulfilled Figure) are thought together in their reciprocal appropriation can there be **se* itself, the frontal vision of God. As long as we remain in only one of these two aspects, there can be only the repetition of one of the figures of the negative foundation of the metaphysical tradition, but no fulfillment. In the first case, the phenomenon subsists as the absolute appearance of nihilism; in the second, the Without Figure remains hidden in the shadows of mystical darkness.

XII

Heidegger often compares the thought of *Ereignis* to Hegel's Absolute. This comparison—which is certainly the sign of a proximity that, for Heidegger himself, constitutes a problem—always has the form of a differentiation that aims to minimize the common traits between the two notions. In his 1936 course on Schelling, Heidegger wrote that *Ereignis* "is not identical to the Absolute, nor is it its antithesis, in the sense in which finitude is opposed to infinity. With *Ereignis*, on the contrary, Being itself is experienced as such; it is not posited as a being, let alone as an unconditioned and supreme being." "Time and Being" (1962) contains a more explicit passage on the proximity and difference between Hegel's Absolute and *Ereignis*. "Starting with the lecture in which it is shown that Being is appropriated [*eignet*] in *Ereignis*," Heidegger states,

> one might be tempted to compare *Ereignis* as the ultimate and the highest with Hegel's Absolute. But back behind the illusion of identity one would then have to ask: for Hegel, how is man related to the Absolute? And: what is the manner of relation of man to *Ereignis*? Then one would see an unbridgeable difference. Since for Hegel man is the place of the Absolute's coming-to-itself, that coming-to-itself leads to the overcoming [*Aufhebung*] of man's finitude. For Heidegger, in contrast, it is precisely finitude that comes to view—not only man's finitude, but the finitude of *Ereignis* itself.[14]

In *Ereignis* as in the Absolute, what is at issue is the access to a kind of propriety (*eigen*). Here, too, the entry of thinking into the proper, into **se* and into the simplicity of *idios* and *ēthos*, is paradoxically the most difficult matter to consider. Here too, this matter appears as "the coming of what has been" (*die Ankunft des Gewesenen*).[15] In "Time and Being," *Ereignis* is defined as the reciprocal appropriation, the co-belonging (*das Zusammengehören*) of time and being,[16] while in *Identity and Difference* Being and man are led back to their propriety.[17]

In each case, the decisive element in the characterization of *Ereignis* with respect to the Hegelian Absolute is finitude. As early as the lectures on the *Phenomenology of Spirit* of 1930–31, Heidegger identified the essence of the Absolute as "in-finite absolving" (*un-endliche Absolvenz*), and the lecture "Time and Being" confirms this interpretation of Hegelianism in the sense of a sublation (*Aufhebung*) of the finitude of man. Yet we have seen that precisely with respect to the Absolute, the sense in which it is possible to speak of infinity remains problematic as long as one does not also introduce the subject of the end of history. Only a clarification of what Heidegger understands here by "finitude" will allow us, therefore, to measure the distance—or the proximity—between *Ereignis* and the Absolute.

Now, it is Heidegger himself who, at the end of "Time and Being," specifies the precise sense of this finitude:

> The finitude of *Ereignis*, of Being, of the fourfold [*Geviert*] hinted at during the seminar, is different from the finitude spoken of in the book [by Heidegger] on Kant, in that it is no longer thought in terms of the relation to infinity, but rather as finitude in itself: finitude, end, limit, the Proper—being at home in the Proper. The new concept of finitude is thought in this manner—that is, in terms of *Ereignis* itself, in terms of the concept of propriety.[18]

What is decisive in this passage as well is the idea of an end, an achievement, a *final* dwelling in the proper. The thought that considers finitude *in itself*, with no more reference to the in-finite, is the thought of the *finite* as such, that is, of the *end of the history of Being*:

> If *Ereignis* is not a new formation [*Prägung*] of Being in the history of Being, but if it is rather the case that Being belongs to *Ereignis* and is reabsorbed in it (in whatever manner), then the history of Being is at an end [*zu Ende*] for thinking *in Ereignis*, that is, for the thinking which enters into *Ereignis*—in

that Being, which lies in sending—is no longer what is to be thought explicitly. Thinking then stands in and before That [*Jenem*] which has sent the various forms of epochal Being. This, however, what sends as *Ereignis*, is itself unhistorical, or more precisely without destiny [*ungeschichtlich, besser geschicklos*].

Metaphysics is the history of the formations of Being, that is, viewed from *Ereignis*, of the history of the self-withdrawal of what is sending in favor of the destinies, given in sending, of an actual letting-presence of what is present. Metaphysics is the oblivion of Being, and that means the history of the concealment and withdrawal of that which gives Being. The entry of thinking into *Ereignis* is thus equivalent to the end of this withdrawal's history. The oblivion of Being "supersedes" [*"hebt" sich "auf"*] itself in the awakening into *Ereignis*.

But the concealment which belongs to metaphysics as its limit must belong to *Ereignis* itself. That means that the withdrawal which characterized metaphysics in the form of the oblivion of Being now shows itself as the dimension of concealment itself. But now this concealment does not conceal itself. Rather, the attention of thinking is concerned with it.

With the entry of thinking into *Ereignis*, its own way of concealment proper to it also arrives. *Ereignis* is in itself *expropriation* [*Ent-eignis*]. This word contains in a manner commensurate with *Ereignis* the early Greek *lēthē* in the sense of concealing.

Thus the lack of destiny of *Ereignis* does not mean that it has no "e-motion" [*Bewegtheit*]. Rather, it means that the manner of movement most proper to *Ereignis*—turning toward us in withdrawal—first shows itself as what is to be thought.

This means that the history of Being as what is to be thought is at an end.[19]

Any true understanding of *Ereignis* must fully consider this passage, just as any thinking capable of confronting Hegel must risk an interpretation of the last pages of the *Science of Logic*. For what can be the sense of a destination that no longer withdraws from what it destines, a concealment that no longer conceals itself, but rather shows itself to thought as such? And what does it mean that withdrawal, which "characterized metaphysics in the figure of the oblivion of Being," now shows itself as the "dimension of concealment itself"? What does it mean for *Ereignis* to be *Enteignis*? What does it mean to think concealment (*lēthē*) as such? What can it mean, if not that what appeared in metaphysics as the oblivion of Being (in the sense of an objective genitive: man forgets Being) now shows itself as what it is, that is, as the pure and absolute self-forgetting of Being? We cannot speak of there being something (Being) that subsequently forgets itself and conceals itself (we cannot speak of a name that withdraws, destining itself in events of speech). Rather, what takes place is simply a movement of concealment without anything being hidden or anything hiding, without anything being veiled or anything veiling—pure *self-destining without destiny*, simple abandonment of the self to itself.

This can only mean that "the history of Being is finished," that *Ereignis* is the place of the "farewell from Being and time";[20] Being no longer destines anything, having exhausted its figures (the figures of *its* oblivion) and revealing itself as pure destining without destiny and figure. But, *at the same time*, this pure destining without destiny appears as the Proper of man, in which "man and Being reach each other in their nature" (*Menschen und Sein einander in ihrem Wesen erreichen*).[21] That (*Jenes*) in which and before which thinking stands at the end, as "what has destined the different figures of epochal Being," is therefore not something that can be said to *be* even in the form of a "there is," an *es gibt*. In *Es gibt Sein, es gibt Zeit*—literally "it gives Being, it gives time"—the *Es*, the "it," in itself and in its propriety, denotes nothing that exists and is namable. What thinking must confront here is no longer tradition or history—destiny—but, rather, *destining* itself (the hermeneutic interpretation of Heidegger thus reaches its limit). But this destining—the Proper—is pure abandonment of the self to what has neither propriety nor destiny; it is pure ac-customing [*as-sue-fazione*][22] and habit. As Heidegger writes at the end of his 1930–31 course on the *Phenomenology of Spirit*, offering the most radical formulation of his distance from Hegel: "Can and should man as transition [*Übergang*] try to leap away from himself in order to leave himself behind as finite? Or is his essence not abandonment [*Verlassenheit*] itself, in which alone what can be possessed becomes a possession?"[23]

The most proper, *ēthos*, *se* of humankind—of the living being without nature and identity—is therefore the *daimōn* itself, the pure, undestined movement of assigning oneself a fate and a destiny, absolute self-transmitting without transmission. But this abandonment of the self to itself is precisely what destines humankind to tradition and to history, remaining concealed, the ungrounded at the ground of every ground, the nameless that, as unsaid and untransmissible, transmits itself in every name and every historical transmission.

XIII

Let us now seek to consider *Ereignis* with respect to language, as ac-customed speech led back to its "self." How can there be a language in which des-tining is no longer withdrawn from what is destined, if not in the form of a language in which saying is no longer hidden in what is said, in which the pure language of names no longer decays into concrete events of speech? And yet this would not be a language that remained present to itself in silence, a theme that never succeeds in being declined in its "cases." Rather, Heidegger says, what reveals itself in language is conceal-ment as such, pure destining without destiny; what comes to language is neither merely speech nor a pure, unspoken name, but rather the very dif-ference between language and speech, the pure—and in itself untrans-missible—movement by which saying comes to speech (*die Be-wegung der Sage zur Sprache*).[24]

In *Identity and Difference*, Heidegger formulates the difference between his thought and Hegel's philosophy with respect to the matter (*Sache*) of thinking. He writes: "For Hegel, the matter of thinking is thought [*Gedanke*] as the absolute concept. For us, formulated in a preliminary fashion, the matter of thinking is difference *as* difference."[25] Hegel thus strives to think the becoming equal to itself of speech, in its enunciation in the totality of events of discourse; he attempts to consider the word as wholly com-prehended, con-ceived: as absolute concept. Heidegger, in-stead, wants to think the difference between saying (*Sage*) and speech (*Sprache*) in itself; he thus searches for an experience of language that ex-periences the *Es* ("it") that destines itself to speech while itself remaining without destiny, the transmitting that, in every event of speech and every transmission, remains untransmissible. This is the Proper, *se, which never becomes a nominative and which is therefore nameless: not the ab-solute concept, Being that has become equal to itself in being-other, but rather difference *itself*, led back to itself. Once again, the thought of the Absolute and the thought of *Ereignis* show their essential proximity and, at the same time, their divergence. We may say that for Hegel, the un-sayable is always already said, as having-been, in every discourse (*omnis locutio ineffabile fatur*). For Heidegger, by contrast, the unsayable is pre-cisely what remains unsaid in human speech but can be experienced *in human speech* as such (*im Namenlosen zu existieren*, "to exist in the name-less").[26] And yet precisely for this reason, insofar as all human language is necessarily historical and destined,[27] only by un-speaking (*Ent-sprechen*) and by risking silence can human beings correspond to difference (*im Nichtsagen nennen, erschweigen*).

א This impossibility of grasping the *Es* itself in the propositions *Es gibt Zeit* and *Es gibt Sein* becomes transparent if one recalls that the impersonal pronoun *es* is originally a genitive (the genitive of *er*, hence *es ist Zeit, ich bin's zufrieden*, etc.). Over time, the genitive *es* in expressions of this kind ceased to be perceived as such and became equivalent to a nominative in linguistic use. An analogous process lies at the origin of the Italian impersonal pronoun *si* (in the phrase "it is said," *si dice*, or in *si fa*), which represents a dative or an accusative (the Latin *sibi, se*). A pronoun that, as genitive, indicates a predication of belonging, the being proper of something to something else, becomes a subject in a verbal syntagma that therefore appears as impersonal. If *es* is a genitive and not a nominative, it is possible to understand why Heidegger, attempting to consider the *es* of *es gibt Zeit, es gibt Sein*, was obliged to grasp it as an *Ereignis*, as an appropriation and an ac-customing. In *Ereignis*, time and Being belong to each other; they appropriate each other. But to whom and to what? As *es* and as genitive, *Ereignis* does not exist and does not give itself; like the Italian *si*, *es* does not exist as a lexical entity.

The thought that wants to think the Proper (like the thought that wants to think **se*) cannot lead to any lexical entity or existing thing. Insofar as it is itself what destines, the Proper, the *ēthos* of humankind, remains unnamed in philosophy. Unnamed, it is thus without destiny: an *untransmissible transmission*.

XIV

With Hegel and Heidegger, the tradition of philosophy has therefore truly reached its *end*. As was announced in the most explicit fashion, what was at issue here was precisely a "closing of figures"[28] and a "destruction of tradition."[29] Tradition, which covered over what was destined in figures, now shows itself for what it is: an untransmissible transmission that transmits nothing but itself. Philosophy, that is, the tradition of thought that posited wonder as its *arkhē*, has now gone back beyond its *arkhē* to dwell in its *ēthos*, thinking only its **se*. In tradition, this—the dwelling of humankind and its most proper ground—remains pure destining without destiny, an unsayable transmission. This means that man, the speaking being, is ungrounded and grounds himself by sinking into his own abyss; it means that man, as ungrounded, incessantly repeats his own ungroundedness, abandoning himself to himself. *Se is abandoned (*verlassen*) to tradition as untransmissible, and only in this negative fashion is it grounded in itself (*in sich selbst gegründete Bewegung derselben*).[30] It is the mystery of the origins that humanity transmits as its proper and negative ground.

Nevertheless, precisely insofar as the revelation of this abandonment of *se constitutes the extreme outcome of Hegel's and Heidegger's attempts to think the most proper, any thought that wants to be adequate to this outcome and confront it cannot infinitely repeat its essential gesture. And yet today, thinking, whether in the form of hermeneutics, a philosophy of difference, or negative thought, presents as a solution the pure and simple repetition of the fundamental metaphysical problem: that transmission transmits nothing (if not itself), that difference is anterior to identity, that the ground is an abyss. The end of tradition, which was the supreme outcome of the thought of the Absolute and *Ereignis*, thus becomes an in-finity; the absence of destiny and ground is thus transformed into an in-finite destiny and ground. Both Hegel and Heidegger, by contrast, clearly insisted that for thought to register the abandonment of *se in tradition was necessarily for it *at the same time* to consider the end of the history of Being and its epochal figures. This was the sense of the word "Absolute," and this was the sense of "Appropriation." To regard the trace as origin, to regard transmitting without transmission and difference as difference, can only mean that traces are canceled and that transmission is finished—that is, that historical destinies have ended, that humankind is definitively in its *ēthos*, and that its knowledge is *absolute*. The grounding of man as human—that is, philosophy, the thought of *se—is achieved. The ungroundedness of man is now proper, that is, absolved from all negativity and all having-been, all nature and all destiny. And it is this appropriation, this absolution, this *ethical* dwelling in *se that must be attentively considered, with Hegel and beyond Hegel, with Heidegger and beyond Heidegger, if what appears as the overcoming of metaphysics is not to be a falling back inside metaphysics and its in-finite repetition.

If metaphysics thinks *se as what, remaining unsaid and untransmitted, destines man to history and transmission, how are we to consider a *se that does not even destine itself as untransmitted, a dwelling of man in his *se that *has never been* and that has therefore never been transmitted in a historical *figure*? How, that is, are we to understand human speech that no longer destines itself in transmission and grammar, that with respect to its *se truly has nothing more to say (even negatively, leaving it unsaid in what is said)? Would such speech necessarily fall into silence and preserve the unsayable having-been that destined it to language? Or would such speech instead simply be the speech of humankind, the "illustrious vernacular" [*volgare illustre*] of a redeemed humanity that, having definitively exhausted its destiny, is one with its praxis and its history? Of a humanity that, having fulfilled its past, is now truly *prose* (that is, *pro-versa, pro-verted*, turned forward)? Now, when all destiny is at an end and all epochal figures—grammars—of Being are exhausted, do we not witness the beginning of the true universal history of a humanity that has finally dissolved the secret of its own, "proper" identity?

This simple figure of *fulfilled* humanity—which is to say, *human* humanity—would therefore be what is left to say for speech that has *nothing* to say; it would be what is left to do for praxis that has *nothing* to do. In the words of Bacchylides, such speech and such praxis would truly have found the doors of the unsaid, having consumed the unsayable transmission:

> heteros ek heterou sophos
> to te palai to te nyn.
> arrētōn epeōn pylas
> exeurein.
>
> (The other from the other [is] wise
> the once [is] the now.
> To find
> the doors of unsaid words.)

א That man—the animal who has language—is as such the ungrounded, that his only foundation is in his own action, his own giving himself grounds, is a truth so ancient that it lies at the basis of humanity's most ancient religious practice: sacrifice. However one interprets the sacrificial function, in every case what is essential is that the activity of human community is grounded in another one of its activities—that, as we learn from etymology, all *facere* is *sacrum facere*. At the center of sacrifice simply lies a determinate *activity* that is as such separated and excluded, becoming *sacer* and hence invested with a series of ritual prohibitions and prescriptions. Once it is marked with sacredness, an activity is not, however, simply excluded; rather, it is henceforth accessible only through certain persons and determinate rules. It thus furnishes society and its unfounded legislation with the fiction of a beginning; what is excluded from a community is in truth what founds the whole life of community, being taken up by a community as an immemorial past. Every beginning [*inizio*] is, in truth, initiation; every *conditum* is an *ab-sconditum*.

This is why the sacred is necessarily an ambiguous and circular notion (in Latin, *sacer* means "abject, ignominious" and, at the same time, "august, reserved to the gods"; "sacred" is the attribute both of the law and of whoever violates it: *qui legem violavit, sacer esto*). Whoever has violated the law is excluded from the community; such a person is thus remitted and abandoned to himself and can as such be killed without the executioner's committing a crime. As Festus writes in *De verborum significatione*, "The sacred man is the one whom the people have judged on account of a crime. It is not permitted to sacrifice this man, yet he who kills him will not be condemned for homicide" (*At homo sacer is est, quem populus iudicavit ob maleficium; neque fas est eum immolari, sed qui occidit, parricidi non damnatur*).

The ungroundedness of all human praxis is concealed in the abandonment to itself of an activity (a *sacrum facere*) that founds every lawful activity; it is what, remaining unsayable (*arrēton*) and untransmittable in every human activity, destines man to community and transmission.

It is certainly not a casual or insignificant fact that, in sacrifice as we know it, this activity is generally a killing, the destruction of a human life. Yet this killing in itself explains nothing and is itself even in need of explanation (like Karl Meuli's explanation, recently invoked by Walter Burkert, in which sacrifice is related to the hunting rites of prehistorical humanity). It is not because life and death are the most sacred things that sacrifice contains killing; on the contrary, life and death became the most sacred things because sacrifices contained killing. (In this sense, nothing explains the difference between antiquity and the modern world better than the fact that for the first, the destruction of human life was sacred, whereas for the second what is sacred is life itself). It is the very ungroundedness of human activity (which the sacrificial mythologeme wants to remedy) that constitutes the violent (that is, according to the meaning that this word has in Latin, as *contra naturam*) character of sacrifice. Insofar as it is not naturally grounded, all human activity must posit its ground by itself and is, according to the sacrificial mythologeme, violent. And it is this *sacred* violence (that is, violence that is abandoned to itself) that sacrifice assumes in order to repeat and regularize in its own structure.

This is why a *fulfilled* foundation of humanity in itself necessarily implies the definitive elimination of the sacrificial mythologeme along with the ideas of nature and culture that are grounded in it. The sacralization of life also derives from sacrifice. From this point of view, it does nothing other than abandon bare natural life to its own violence and its own foreignness, in order then to ground all cultural rules and social praxis in it. (In the same way, human speech is grounded in animal speech, on whose exclusion language is constructed insofar as it is transmitted as articulated voice.)

Se, the proper of man, is not something unsayable, something *sacer* that must remain unsaid in all human speech and praxis. Nor is it, according to the pathos of contemporary nihilism, a Nothing whose nullity grounds the arbitrariness and violence of social activity. Rather, *se—ēthos*—is the social praxis itself that, in the end, becomes transparent to itself.

§ 9 Walter Benjamin and the Demonic: Happiness and Historical Redemption

I

"Walter Benjamin and His Angel" is the title of an essay published in 1972 in which Gershom Scholem proposes a remarkable reading of a brief and exemplary prose work by Benjamin, "Agesilaus Santander." In this important interpretation, Scholem argues that the apparent luminosity of the figure of the angel—which, as has often been noted, has particular significance in Benjamin's thought—hides the dark, demonic traits of "Angelus Satanas." This unexpected metamorphosis casts a melancholic light on the entire horizon of Benjamin's reflections on the philosophy of history, in which the angel plays its properly redemptive role.

In entitling my essay "Walter Benjamin and the Demonic," I intend to complete and, in a certain sense, also rectify the interpretation offered by the scholar of Jerusalem, seeking to leave Benjamin's text open to another possible reading. The aim of my essay, nevertheless, is not to revise Scholem's interpretation. Rather, it seeks to trace the fundamental (and for now provisional) lines of Benjamin's ethics. Here the word "ethics" is intended in the sense it had when it made its appearance in the Greek philosophical schools as a "doctrine of happiness." For the Greeks, the link between the demonic (*daimonion*) and happiness was evident in the very term with which they designated happiness, *eudaimonia*. In the text that is at issue here, moreover, Benjamin ties the figure of the angel precisely to an idea of happiness, which he states in the following terms: "He wants happiness: the conflict in which lies the ecstasy of the unique, new, as yet unlived with that bliss of the 'once more,' the having again, the lived."[1]

It is this double figure of happiness, which Benjamin elsewhere characterizes through the opposition of the hymn and the elegy,[2] that I will seek to delineate. If we keep in mind that, in the Second Thesis of Benjamin's "Theses on the Philosophy of History," happiness (*Glück*) and redemption (*Erlösung*) are inseparable, we may argue that the presentation of Benjamin's theories of happiness can proceed only by means of a clarification of Benjamin's ideas on the philosophy of history, which have at their very center the concept of redemption.

II

The leading theme of the reading Scholem gives of Benjamin's text is the deciphering of the "secret name" Agesilaus Santander as an anagram for *der Angelus Satanas*. This ingenious hypothesis, formulated by a scholar with incomparable experience in the Cabalistic tradition, can be neither rejected nor confirmed in itself. Every hermeneutic conjecture of this kind has above all a divinatory character and, as such, cannot be verified *in itself*. As an eminent philologist once wrote, citing a phrase of Heidegger's, when one is confronted with a hermeneutic circle, what is important is not to leave it but to stay within it in the right way. What can, however, be verified in a hypothesis is whether its construction is necessary, that is, whether it economically explains the text without leaving unresolved the most problematic aspects and contradicting what we already know of the author's thought. Now, the anagrammatic decryption of the Satanic name behind the apparently anodyne name of Agesilaus Santander is so determining for the reading Scholem gives of the whole fragment that before he formulates the decryption in Part Four, Scholem has already projected its disquieting shadow on the image of the angel. On page 211 we thus read: "at that time," that is, in the period immediately following Benjamin's acquisition of Klee's *Angelus Novus*, "Benjamin did not yet connect any Satanic-Luciferian thoughts with the picture." One page later, the foreshadowing is repeated in analogous terms: "The angel, not yet sunk in melancholy as he was later to be . . . " By page 213, the "Luciferian element" in Benjamin's meditations on Klee's painting is treated as a given. This element, indeed, indicates the picture's non-Jewish origin: "The Luciferian element, however, entered Benjamin's meditations on Klee's picture not directly from the Jewish tradition, but rather from the occupation with Baudelaire that fascinated him for so

many years. The Luciferian element of the beauty of the Satanic, stem-
ming from this side of Benjamin's interests, comes out often enough in
his writings and notes" (p. 213). Even if the adjective "Satanic" actually
appears in the texts that Scholem cites at this point, nevertheless one
should note that it is in no way tied to the figure of the angel. And as to
the Baudelairean origin of the Luciferian elements in Benjamin's thought,
we should not forget that in a letter to Theodor Adorno, Benjamin wrote,
"I will let my Christian Baudelaire be taken into heaven by nothing but
Jewish angels."[3] That this statement is to be taken literally is suggested by
the fact that Benjamin immediately added that these angels let Baudelaire
fall "shortly before his entrance into Glory," where "Glory" is the technical term *Kabod*, which designates the manifestation of divine presence in
Jewish mysticism.

At the end of the passage that we have cited, Scholem has already fully
anticipated his Luciferian reading of "Agesilaus Santander" without having demonstrated its validity with any precise textual reference: "The anthropomorphous nature of Klee's angel, now changing into the Luciferian, is no longer present when one (perhaps two) years later he [Ben-
jamin] wrote the piece concerning us here" (p. 214).

By the time Scholem announces his anagrammatic hypothesis in the
following chapter, Benjamin's entire text has already been immersed in a
demonic light, and a Luciferian element is present in its every detail. If
Benjamin writes that the angel—it is worth remembering that in this text
Benjamin always speaks only of an angel—"sent his feminine form after
the masculine one reproduced in the picture by way of the longest, most
fatal detour, even though both happened to be, without knowing it, most
intimately adjacent to each other" (p. 207), this is interpreted in the sense
that "the angel, in this a genuine Satanas, wanted to destroy Benjamin"
(p. 221). Here Scholem takes no notice of the fact that this association of
the feminine element with the Satanic element is in no way implied by
Benjamin's text; indeed, his interpretation goes so far as to affirm that
Benjamin discerned a Satanic element in the very two figures (Jula Cohn
and Asja Lacis, according to Scholem) that he most dearly loved.

III

Only at this point does Scholem briefly pause to consider the one trait
in Benjamin's text that authorizes his interpretation of the Satanic sense

of the figure of the angel. "The Satanic character of the angel," Scholem states, "is emphasized by the metaphor of his claws and knife-sharp wings, which could find support in the depiction of Klee's picture. No angel, but only Satan, possesses claws and talons, as is, for example, expressed in the widespread notion that on the Sabbath witches kiss the clawed hands of Satan" (pp. 222–23).

Here we must first make an iconological correction. The statement that "no angel, but only Satan, possesses claws and talons" is not exact. There is no doubt that, according to a widespread iconographic tradition, Satan has claws (among other animal deformities). But the figuration of Satan that is at issue in such cases has lost every angelic connotation; it is simply the frightening, diabolical figure familiar to us through innumerable iconographic (above all, Christian) variations. The images to which Scholem refers present Satan in a purely diabolical role and often represent sabbat witches kissing his hands (or, more often, a different and shameful part of the body, as in the rite of *osculum infame*).

In the European iconographic tradition, there is only one figure that brings together purely angelic characteristics and the demonic trait of claws. This figure, however, is not Satan but Eros, Love. According to a descriptive model that we find for the first time in Plutarch (who attributes "fangs and claws" to Eros), but that is well documented in certain infrequent but exemplary iconographic appearances, Love is represented as a winged (and often feminine) angelic figure with claws. Love appears as such both in Giotto's allegory of chastity and in the fresco in the castle of Sabbionara (according to the model of what Erwin Panofsky supposed to be a "base and mythographic Cupid"), as well as in the two figures of angels with claws flanking the mysterious winged feminine figure in the *Lovers as Idolators* at the Louvre, attributed to the Maestro of San Martino.[4]

Benjamin's figure of the angel with claws and wings can therefore lead us only into the domain of Eros, that is, not a demon in the Judeo-Christian sense, but a *daimōn* in the Greek sense (in Plato, Eros appears as the demon par excellence). This is all the more probable if one considers the fact that Benjamin was aware of this specific iconographic type and, in particular, of Giotto's allegory. In his *Origin of the German Tragic Drama*, Benjamin speaks of the "representation of Cupid by Giotto, 'as a demon of wantonness with a bat's wings and claws.'"[5]

A passage from Benjamin's notes to his essay on Karl Kraus proves be-

yond the shadow of a doubt that for Benjamin, the angel is in no sense
to be considered a Satanic figure: "One must already have measured the
poverty of Herr Keuner with Bertolt Brecht and glimpsed the clawed feet
[*Krallenfüße*] of Klee's Angelus Novus—that angel-thief who would rather
free humans by taking from them than make them happy by giving to
them."[6] (In the definitive version of the essay, the detail of the clawed feet
has been removed along with the reference to Brecht; one reads only that
"One must have . . . seen Klee's *New Angel*, who preferred to free men by
taking from them, rather than make them happy by giving to them, to
understand a humanity that proves itself by destruction.")[7] The claws of
Angelus Novus (in Klee's painting, the angel's feet certainly bring to mind
a bird of prey) do not, therefore, have a Satanic meaning; instead, they
characterize the destructive—and simultaneously liberating—power of
the angel.

We have now established a correspondence between the clawed angel
of "Agesilaus Santander" and the liberating angel who, at the end of the
essay on Kraus, celebrates his victory over the demon "at the point where
origin and destruction meet." But what then disappears is precisely the
support of the one textual element that seemed to suggest the secret Luciferian nature of the angel in "Agesilaus Santander." This does not mean
that Scholem's interpretation is erroneous but, rather, that there is all the
more reason to measure its validity only on the basis of its capacity to explain economically the most problematic aspects of Benjamin's text.

IV

Scholem's interpretation, however, is insufficient on just this matter.
We have already cited the passage in which Benjamin speaks of a feminine figure of the angel in addition to the male figure of the painting.
Scholem's interpretation offers no substantial clarification of these two
figures of the angel (which, Benjamin says, were once united). It is certainly possible that on the biographical level, the "feminine figure" refers
here to Jula Cohn (a possibility not precluded by one of Benjamin's letters, discovered since the composition of Scholem's essay, that shows he
was referring to a woman whom he knew at Ibiza and who has not yet
been identified). But the claim that the angel is linked to a Satanic element is unconvincing on the biographical level and, most importantly, in
no way clarifies the *double* figure of the angel that is at issue on the tex-

tual level. In the Jewish tradition, moreover, the feminine figuration of the "other part" par excellence is Lilith, that is, a figure altogether distinct from Satan.

Nevertheless, the tradition of Jewish mysticism could have furnished material for extremely interesting comparisons precisely here. Those who have in some way studied Jewish mysticism—in particular those who have read the magnificent books that Scholem dedicated to its resurrection—are familiar with the representation of the Shechinah as the feminine moment of divinity and of divine presence in the world. In a passage of the *Zohar* that is particularly significant for us, the Shechinah is identified with the saving angel of Genesis 14:16 and characterized as both male and female. Let us read this passage, which I cite in the version offered by Scholem in his book *On the Mystical Shape of the Godhead*:

> This is the angel who is sometimes male and sometimes female. For when he channels blessings to the world, he is male and is called male; just as the male bestows [fecundating] blessings upon the female, so does he bestow blessings upon the world. But when his relationship to the world is that of judgment [i.e., when he manifests himself in his restrictive power as judge], then he is called female. Just as female is pregnant with the embryo, so is he pregnant with judgment, and is then called female.[8]

From this perspective, the feminine figure of the angel in "Agesilaus Santander" not only does not appear as a Satanic apparition but could even be seen as a figure of the Shechinah in its judging role, while the male figure would be the other, benevolent face of the same saving angel.[9] Insofar as the Shechinah designates the sphere of redemption, which in the Cabala is the proper dimension of happiness, the Cabalists call the Shechinah (in terms that recall the last lines of "Agesilaus Santander") "the eternal present," or the "return," since everything that had its beginning in it must ultimately return to it.[10]

V

Scholem invokes another important Jewish parallel (which is in fact not only Jewish) when he notes the "conception of Jewish tradition of the personal angel of each human being who represents the latter's secret self and whose name nevertheless remains hidden from him" (*On Jews*, p. 213) and when he writes further on, "in the phantasmagoria of his imagination, the picture of the *Angelus Novus* becomes for Benjamin a picture of his angel as the occult reality of his self" (p. 229). The last part of Scholem's study ties the figure of the angel in "Agesilaus Santander" to the angel of history in the Ninth Thesis of the "Theses on the Philosophy of History." "Here," Scholem writes, "Benjamin's personal angel, who stands between past and future and causes him to journey back 'whence I came,' has turned into the angel of history, in a new interpretation of Klee's picture" (p. 232). Yet the same melancholic light that the decipherment of the angel's Satanic name casts on "Agesilaus Santander" now bathes the angel of history of the "Theses." This angel, according to Scholem, "is, then, basically a melancholy figure, wrecked by the immanence of history. . . . It is a matter of dispute whether one can speak here—as I am rather inclined to do—of a melancholy, indeed desperate, view of history" (pp. 234–35). Benjamin would thus have wanted "to divide up the function of the Messiah as crystallized by the view of history of Judaism: into that of the angel who must fail in his task, and that of the Messiah who can accomplish it" (p. 235).

This interpretation is clearly at odds with Benjamin's own text, which ties the figure of the angel precisely to the idea of happiness. The angel, we read in the passage that we have already cited, "wants happiness: the conflict in which lies the ecstasy of the unique, new, as yet unlived with that bliss of the 'once more,' the having again, the lived" (p. 208). Moreover, if Benjamin's angel is "a melancholy figure, wrecked by the immanence of history," why is it said of him in "Agesilaus Santander" that on his return he "he takes a new human being along with him" (p. 208)? It is even more significant that Scholem's interpretation contrasts with another text by Benjamin that is particularly important for the problem of interest to us here. We refer to the "Theologico-Political Fragment," which Scholem dates to around 1920–21 and which Adorno instead attributes to the last years of Benjamin's life. In this text, the messianic order is certainly distinguished from that of happiness, but it is the order of happiness—and not the messianic order—that has the function of a guiding idea for the profane-historical order. Precisely because the Messiah fulfills every historical event, Benjamin says, nothing historical can claim to refer to the messianic, since the reign of God is not goal but end. Hence the rejection of the political sense of theocracy; but hence too the statement that the profane order must be founded on the idea of happiness (this, Benjamin writes, is why the relation of the order of happiness to the messianic order is one of the essential theoretical problems of the philosophy of history). The profane-historical order of happiness is in no way opposed to the messianic order; instead, the one makes the occurrence of the other possible. "For in happiness," Benjamin writes,

> all that is earthly seeks its downfall, and only in good fortune is its downfall destined to find it. . . . To the spiritual *restitutio in integrum*, which introduces immortality, corresponds a worldly restitution that leads to the eternity of downfall, and the rhythm of this eternally transient worldly existence, transient in its totality, in its spatial but also in its temporal totality, the rhythm of messianic nature, is happiness. For nature is messianic by reason of its eternal and total passing away. To strive after such passing, even for those stages of man that are nature, is the task of world politics, whose method must be called nihilism.[11]

If it is true that one must identify the angel who wants happiness in "Agesilaus Santander" with the angel of history in the Ninth Thesis, then this angel cannot be the melancholic and Luciferian figure of a shipwreck. Rather, he must be a bright figure who, in the strict solidarity of happiness and historical redemption, establishes the very relation of the profane order to the messianic that Benjamin identified as one of the essential problems of the philosophy of history.

VI

In order to find elements for a further clarification of Benjamin's text, we must now therefore turn with greater attention to the image of the personal angel briefly evoked by Scholem. Here we find ourselves before an extremely rich and yet coherent tradition, which is present not only in Judaism but also (as *idios daimōn*) in Neoplatonic mysticism, late-ancient hermeticism, gnosticism, and early Christianity, and which also has precise counterparts in Iranian and Muslim angelology. Scholem dedicated an exemplary essay to this tradition, which he entitled "Tselem: The Concept of the Astral Body";[12] but decisive material is also furnished by the works of Henry Corbin, the great scholar of Iranian and Arabic mysticism (as well as the first French translator of Heidegger). Here we will seek to delineate in brief the essential physiognomic traits of this doctrine.

In the first place we find a fusion of the ancient pagan and Neoplatonic motif of the *idios daimōn* of every man with the Jewish motif of the celestial image, *demuth* or *zelem*, in whose image each man is created. The Cabalists interpret the passage of Genesis 1:27, according to which "God created man in his own *zelem*, in the *zelem* of God created he him" (which the Vulgate translates as *creavit deus hominem ad imaginem suum: ad imaginem dei creavit illum*), in the sense that the second *zelem* designates the originary angelic form (and, later, astral body) in the image of which each man is created. Thus we read in the *Zohar*:

> When a man begins to consecrate himself before intercourse with his wife with a sacred intention, a holy spirit is aroused above him, composed of both male and female. And the Holy One, blessed be He, directs an emissary who is in charge of human embryos, and assigns to him this particular spirit, and indicates to him the place to which it should be entrusted. This is the meaning of "The night said, a man-child has been conceived" (Job 3:3). "The night said" to this particular emissary, "a man-child has been conceived" by so-and-so. And the Holy One, blessed be He, then gives this spirit all the commands that He wishes to give, and they have already explained this. Then the spirit descends together with the image [*tselem*], the one in whose likeness [*diyokna*] [the spirit] existed above. With this image [man] grows; with this image he moves through the world. This is meaning of "Surely man walks with an image" (Ps. 39:7). While this image is with him, man survives in the world. . . . A man's days exist through the image, and are dependent on it.[13]

The angel-*zelem* therefore constitutes a kind of alter ego, a celestial double and originary image in which each man existed in heaven and which also accompanies man on earth (this is also the case in the Neoplatonic doctrine of *idios daimōn*, which, in Iamblichus's words, "exists as a paradigm before the soul descends into generation"). From our point of view, what is important is the link between this theme, which concerns, so to speak, the prehistory and preexistence of man, and prophetic and redemptive motifs, which concern the destiny and salvation of man—or, in other words, his history and posthistory. According to a doctrine that can be found in both Cabalistic texts and hermetic writings, the vision of one's own angel coincides with prophetic ecstasy and supreme knowledge. In a Cabalistic anthology that dates from the end of the thirteenth century (*Shushan Sodoth*), prophecy appears as a sudden vision of one's own double: "The complete secret of prophecy . . . consists in the fact that the prophet suddenly sees the form of his self standing before him, and he forgets his own self and ignores it . . . and that form speaks with him and tells him the future."[14] In another Cabalistic text (Isaac Cohen, c. 1270), prophetic experience is described as a metamorphosis of man into his own angel: "In the prophet and seer, all kinds of potencies become weakened and change from form to form, until he enwraps himself in the potency of the form that appears to him, and then his potency is changed into the form of an angel."[15]

This vision of one's own angelic self concerns not only prophetic knowledge. According to a tradition found in Gnostic, Manichaean, Jewish, and Iranian texts, it constitutes the supreme soteriological and messianic experience. In the Arabic treatise *Picatrix*, which exerted considerable influence on Renaissance hermeticism, the angel appears as a form of an extraordinarily beautiful figure who, when questioned by the philosopher about its proper identity, answers: "I am your perfect nature." A Mandaean text describes the redemptive encounter with the angel in the following terms: "I go to meet my image, and my image comes to meet me; it embraces me and pulls me close when I leave prison." And in the "Song of the Pearl" in the *Acts of Thomas*, the prince who returns at the end to his Western homeland rediscovers his image as a bright garment: "the garment suddenly appeared before me as a mirror of myself. I saw it entirely in me, and I was entirely in it; for we were two, separated the one from the other, and yet we were one, similar in form."[16]

In this regard it is also worth noting the Iranian theme of Daênâ. Daênâ is the angel who confronts every man after death in the form of a young woman appearing as both every man's archetypal image and the result of the actions he committed on earth. In the figure of Daênâ, origin and redemption as well as the doctrine of creation and the doctrine of salvation are thus joined in the idea of a new birth on the last day, a birth in which the generator and the generated are identified and produce each other. "The generation of Daênâ through and in the human soul as the soul's action," Corbin writes,

> is at the same time the generation of the soul in and through the angel Daênâ. . . . There remains the idea of an eschatological sacred marriage accomplished *in novissimo die*, the mystery of a new birth in which a being is generated in the image of a celestial double. . . . These themes are to be found every time the fracture of a primordial celestial-terrestrial couple states the mystery of the origin. The restoration of its bi-unity, its *duality*, is then suggested as the rule for an interior ethics confirmed precisely by the encounter and eschatological recognition of man and his angel.[17]

In this horizon it is possible to understand how the *zelem*-angel is also charged with a messianic meaning in Jewish mysticism, where it appears

as the astral body assumed by the soul at the moment of death, in its return to Paradise. In the figure of the angel, the origin truly appears as
constructed by its history; prophetic experience and messianic experience
are identified. It is evident that such a figure could have exerted great
force on a thinker such as Benjamin, who appropriated Kraus's motto,
"origin is the goal."

It is in this complex background that we must situate both the epi-
phany of the angel described in "Agesilaus Santander" and the angelic figure of the Ninth Thesis. In this context, the encounter with the angel appears not as a Satanic illusion or melancholic allegory of a shipwreck but,
on the contrary, as the cipher by which Benjamin registered what was for
him humankind's most difficult historical task and most perfect experience of happiness. At this point we can abandon the figure of the angel
and turn to the true goal of this chapter, the presentation of Benjamin's
concepts of happiness and the philosophy of history. For according to an
intention that deeply characterizes Benjamin's thought, only where the
esoteric and the everyday, the mystical and the profane, theological categories and materialistic categories are wholly identified can knowledge
truly be adequate to its tasks.

VII

Before I begin this presentation, however, I must briefly pause to consider a text in which it is truly possible to say that Benjamin drew from
the history not of angelology but of demonology. I refer to the essay on
Karl Kraus, one of whose sections bears the title "Demon." The demonic
figure at issue here is a point of convergence for a number of motifs—
from the Socratic *daimonion* to its resurrection in Goethe and to Ludwig
Bachofen's idea of a pre-ethical state of humanity—that had already appeared many times in Benjamin's work.

In an early text (from 1916), the demonic light that would shine on
Karl Kraus in the 1931 essay instead illuminates the face of Socrates. Benjamin speaks of the "demonic indistinction" of sexual concepts and spiritual concepts that characterizes Socratic discourse. In the 1919 essay "Fate
and Character," Benjamin speaks of the "demonic stage of human existence when legal statutes determined not only men's relationships but also
their relation to the gods" and of "demonic fate," which is overcome in
tragedy, where "the head of genius lifted itself for the first time from the

mist of guilt."[18] In the 1921 essay "Critique of Violence," the dominant trait of the demonic sphere is ambiguity, and this ambiguity is also the mark of law. In Benjamin's great study of 1921–22 on *Elective Affinities*, Goethe's particular concept of the "demonic" (that is, an "inconceivable" and "frightening reality" that is neither divine nor human, neither angelic nor diabolic) appears as the mark of mythic humanity and its anguish in the face of death; and this concept is submitted to a critique that finds in it the cipher of Goethe's ethical insufficiency.

In all these texts, the concept of the demonic refers to a prehistorical state of human community dominated by law and guilt, along with a state that is both prereligious and pre-ethical. Here Benjamin probably took as his point of departure Konrad Theodor Preuss's idea of pre-animism as the prereligious phase of humanity. He most likely also drew on Bachofen's theories of the chthonic-neutonic moment and the ethereal promiscuity symbolized by the swamp (a symbol that returns several times in Benjamin's work, noticeably in the essay on Kafka).

All these motifs are clearly present in the essay on Kraus, published ten years later. The dark background in which Kraus's image appears is neither the contemporary world nor the ethical world but rather, we read, the "pre-historic world or the world of the demon." Furthermore, "nothing is understood about this man until it has been perceived that, of necessity and without exception, everything . . . falls within the sphere of justice."[19] Yet precisely at this point Benjamin introduces a peculiar trait that (while not among those listed by Scholem as Jewish elements in his friend's thought) can only originate in Jewish demonology. The solidarity of spirit and sex is defined on the one hand as the spirit's maxim and on the other as onanism: "spirit and sex move in this sphere with a solidarity whose law is ambiguity."[20] A little later Benjamin says that the demon comes into the world "as a hybrid of spirit and sex." In his preparatory notes, this trait of onanism is explicitly affirmed, and in a sketch Benjamin opposes it to Platonic love insofar as it is the identity of body and language, pleasure and the spirit's maxim.[21]

What is the origin of the demon's attribute of onanism, and in what sense can Benjamin say that the demon comes into the world as a hybrid of spirit and sex? These questions can be answered by Jewish demonology. According to the talmudic tradition, demons are pure spirits who, having been created by God on Friday evening at dusk, could no longer receive bodies, for the Sabbath had already begun. From then onwards, demons have insistently attempted to procure themselves bodies and therefore seek out men, trying to induce them to perform sexual acts without a female partner, so as to make a body with unused human semen.

Here the demon is truly a hybrid of pure spirit and pure sex, and it is clear why he can be associated with onanism. Developing these ideas, later Cabalists wrote that when a man dies, all the children he illegitimately fathered with demons in the course of his life appear and participate in a funereal lament:

> For all those spirits that have built their bodies from a drop of his seed regard him as their father. And so, especially on the day of his burial, he must suffer punishment; for while he is being carried to the grave, they swarm around him like bees, crying: "You are our father," and they complain and lament behind his bier, because they have lost their home and are now being tormented along with the other demons which hover [bodiless] in the air.[22]

The figure of the demon in Benjamin's essay on Kraus thus originates in this dark demonic phantasmagoria as well as in the realm of prehistoric humanity. Yet in a striking movement, these spectral traits now become positive. Here the swarm of unborn spirits who, according to Jewish demonology, raise their cries of lamentation and accusation before the coffin of the dead, is transformed into Kraus's implacable "demonic" figure, who confronts humanity with the cry of "the eternally renewed, the uninterrupted lament."[23]

In the face of the lies of the false, dominant humanism, the demon is the cipher of a guilty humanity that denounces its own guilt to the point of accusing the very legal order to which it belongs. It does so not in the name of redeemed humanity and liberated nature but in the name, Benjamin says, "of an archaic nature without history, in its pristine, primeval state." "His idea of freedom," he writes, "is not removed from the realm of guilt that he has traversed from pole to pole: from spirit to sexuality."[24]

This is the reason—the only reason—why the demon must be overcome in the end. The one who carries him to his grave is not a new man but an inhuman being—a new angel. "Neither purity nor sacrifice," Benjamin states, "mastered the demon; but where origin and destruction come together, his rule is over."[25] In his preparatory notes, Benjamin clarifies this concept in the following manner: "Transfiguration, as the state of the creature in the origin, and destruction, as the power of justice, now master the demon."[26] The new angel, who makes his appearance at the point at which origin and destruction meet, is therefore a destructive figure whom the claws of "Agesilaus Santander" suit well. Yet he is not a demonic figure but rather "the messenger of a more real humanism."[27]

We are now at last in a position to examine the categories of the philosophy of history that we wished to investigate.

VIII

Benjamin describes the link between happiness and redemption in the Second Thesis of the "Theses on the Philosophy of History":

> Reflection shows us that our image of happiness is thoroughly colored by the time to which the course of our own existence has assigned us. The kind of happiness that could arouse envy in us exists only in the air we have breathed, among people we could have talked to, women who could have given themselves to us. In other words, our image of happiness is indissolubly bound up with the image of redemption. The same applies to our view of the past, which is the concern of history. The past carries with it a temporal index by which it is referred to redemption. There is a secret agreement between past generations and the present one. Our coming was expected on earth. Like every generation that preceded us, we have been endowed with a *weak* messianic power, a power to which the past has a claim.[28]

In this passage, the concept of happiness is inextricably linked to the concept of redemption, which has the past as its object. There can be no happiness that has not reckoned with this task, which the thesis presents as a "secret agreement" between the past generations and our own. In these statements, which situate the central problem of happiness in relation to the past, there is a profound and decisive intuition that we also find both in the angel's gaze, which is directed toward the past, and in Benjamin's reflections on historical consciousness. But what does Benjamin mean here by redemption, *Erlösung*? What does it mean to redeem the past?

An answer can be found in the next thesis, in which we read, "only a redeemed humanity receives the fullness of its past." This means, Benjamin adds, that "only for a redeemed humanity has its past become citable in all its moments. Each moment it has lived becomes a *citation à l'ordre du jour*—and that day is Judgment Day."[29]

When it is truly redeemed and truly saved, humanity is therefore in possession of its past. But for humanity to be in possession of it, Benjamin says, is for it to be able to cite it. How are we to understand "citation" here?

The elements for an answer can be found in the brief theory of citation that Benjamin presents in the last part of his Kraus essay. Here citation appears as an eminently destructive procedure whose task is "not to shelter, but to purify, to rip out of context, to destroy." Its destructive force, however, is that of justice; to the very degree to which citation tears speech from its context, destroying it, it also returns it to its origin. This is why Benjamin writes that in citation, origin and destruction merge and (in the passage cited above) that what masters the demon are "transfiguration, as the state of the creature in the origin" and "destruction, as the power of justice."

If we apply this theory of citation to the possibility of citing the past in each of its moments, a possibility that constitutes the defining characteristic of redeemed humanity, then historical redemption appears as inseparable from the capacity to tear the past from its context, destroying it, in order to return it, transfigured, to its origin. Here we have an image of redemption that is certainly not consolatory; indeed, in this light it is comprehensible that Benjamin, in a note to the "Theses," speaks of a "liberation of the destructive forces that are contained in the thought of redemption."[30]

The return to the origin that is at issue here thus in no way signifies the reconstruction of something as it once was, the reintegration of something into an origin understood as a real and eternal figure of its truth. Such a task is precisely that of the historical consciousness Benjamin attributes to historicism, which is the principle target of the "Theses." "Historicism," he writes, "gives the 'eternal' image of the past; historical materialism supplies a unique experience with the past."[31] Benjamin's criticism of historicism and its representation of continuous and homogenous time (which Benjamin opposes to a messianic interruption of becoming) has been analyzed and repeated countless times, to the point of becoming a commonplace. Yet interpreters have not dared to draw the extreme consequences implied by the unique experience of the past that is at issue here. Only occasionally have they posed the simple question, "What happens to the redeemed past?" The temptation to bend Benjamin's categories in the direction of a historiographical practice was great, and Benjamin's thought has all too often been assimilated to the domi-

nant doctrine that conceives of the task of history writing as the recuper-
ation of alternative heredities that must then be consigned to cultural tradition. The idea that is presupposed in this practice is that the tradition of
the oppressed classes is, in its goals and in its structures, altogether analogous to the tradition of the ruling classes (whose heir it would be); the
oppressed class, according to this theory, would differ from the ruling
classes only with respect to its content.

According to Benjamin, by contrast—and the radicality of his thought
lies here—to redeem the past is not to restore its true dignity, to transmit
it anew as an inheritance for future generations. He argues against this
idea so clearly as to leave no doubts: "In authentic history writing," we
read, "the destructive impulse is just as strong as the saving impulse. From
what can something be redeemed? Not so much from the disrepute or
discredit in which it is held as from a determined mode of its transmission. The way in which it is valued as 'heritage' is more insidious than its
disappearance could ever be."[32] For Benjamin, what is at issue is an interruption of tradition in which the past is fulfilled and thereby brought
to its end once and for all. For humanity as for the individual human, to
redeem the past is to put an end to it, to cast upon it a gaze that fulfills
it. "Redemption," we read in a note to the essay on Kafka, "is not a com-
pensation for existence, but rather its only way out."[33] In the essay on Ed-
uard Fuchs we find the following lines: "[The history of culture] may well
increase the burden of the treasures that are piled up on humanity's back.
But it does not give humankind the strength to shake them off, so as to
get its hands on them."[34]

Benjamin therefore has in mind a relation to the past that would both
shake off the past and bring it into the hands of humanity, which
amounts to a very unusual way of conceiving of the problem of tradition.
Here tradition does not aim to perpetuate and repeat the past but to lead
it to its decline in a context in which past and present, content of transmission and act of transmission, what is unique and what is repeatable
are wholly identified. In a letter to Scholem, Benjamin once formulated
this problem with reference to Kafka in the paradoxical terms of "tradition falling ill";[35] Kafka, he wrote, renounced the truth to be transmitted
for the sake of not renouncing its transmissibility. Here the two Jewish
categories of Halakhah (which designates the law in itself, truth insofar
as it is separated from all narration) and Aggadah (that is, truth in its
transmissibility) are played off against each other such that each abolishes

the other (in the letter cited above, Benjamin says that Kafka's stories do not simply lie at the feet of doctrine as Aggadah lies beneath Halakhah, but rather "unexpectedly raise a mighty paw against it").[36] And at the end of his essay on Kafka, Benjamin expresses this particular relationship with the past and the idea of culture that follows from it in the figure of "students without writing": Bucephalus the horse, who has survived his mythical rider, and Sancho Panza, who has succeeded in distracting his knight and forcing him to walk in front of him. "Whether it is a man or a horse," Benjamin concludes, "is no longer so important, if only the burden is removed from the back."[37]

Those who see the angel of history in Benjamin's Ninth Thesis as a melancholic figure would therefore most likely be horrified to witness what would happen if the angel, instead of being driven forward by the winds of progress, paused to accomplish his work. Here Benjamin's intention is not very different from the one Marx expressed in a phrase that exerted a profound influence on Benjamin. In the introduction to the *Critique of Hegel's Philosophy of Right*, considering the fact that in the course of history every event tends to be represented as a comedy, Marx asks: "Why does history take this course?" Marx answers: "So that humanity may happily separate itself from its past."

From this perspective, Benjamin's theory of happiness once again shows its coherence with his philosophy of history. In the "Theologico-Political Fragment," the idea of happiness appears precisely as what allows the historical order to reach its own fulfillment. The worldly *restitutio in integrum*, which is properly historical redemption and which is determined as the task of world politics, "corresponds to a worldly restitution that leads to the eternity of downfall, and the rhythm of this eternally transient worldly existence, transient in its totality, in its spatial but also in its temporal totality, the rhythm of messianic nature, is happiness."[38]

IX

If these reflections leave no doubt as to the radicality and destructive forces implicit in Benjamin's idea of redemption, this is nevertheless not to say that we are confronted here by a pure and simple liquidation of the past. (The two metaphors of the origin show their difference here, "redemption" being a final, absolving payment and "liquidation" being a transformation into available funds.)

Today we are confronted by two forms of historical consciousness. On the one hand, there is the form of consciousness that understands all human work (and the past) as an origin destined to an infinite process of transmission that preserves its intangible and mythic singularity. And on the other hand, there is the form of consciousness that, as the inverted specular image of the first form of consciousness, irresponsibly liquidates and flattens out the singularity of the origin by forever multiplying copies and simulacra. These two attitudes are only apparently opposed; in reality, they are merely the two faces of a cultural tradition in which the content of transmission and transmission itself are so irreparably fractured that it can only ever repeat the origin infinitely or annul it in simulacra. In each case, the origin itself can be neither fulfilled nor mastered. The idea of origin contains both singularity and reproducibility, and as long as one of the two remains in force, every intention to overcome both is doomed to fail.

In Louis Auguste Blanqui's and Nietzsche's idea of the eternal return, Benjamin (perhaps unjustly) sees precisely the cipher of this "bewitched image of history," in which humanity tries to hold together "the two antinomical principles of happiness—that is, that of eternity and of the one-more-time."[39] According to Benjamin, humanity thereby succeeds only in inflicting upon itself *die Strafe des Nachsitzens*, that is, the punishment given to schoolchildren that consists in having to copy out the same text countless times. But it is worth emphasizing that Benjamin discerns the revolutionary value that is implicit in the image of the eternal return insofar as it exasperates mythic repetition to the point of finally bringing it to a halt. "The thought of the eternal return," he writes, "breaks the ring of the eternal return in the very moment in which it confirms it."[40] "It represents unconditional submission," Benjamin states, "but at the same time the most terrible accusation against a society that has reflected this image of the cosmos as a projection of itself onto the heavens."[41]

At this point the dialectic of the singular and the repeatable to which Benjamin entrusts his philosophy of history and his ethics must necessarily reckon with the categories of origin, Idea, and phenomenon that he develops in the "Epistemological-Critical Preface" to *The Origin of the German Tragic Drama*. The redemption of the past, moreover, must be compared to the Platonic salvation of phenomena that is at issue in that text. The more one analyzes Benjamin's thought, the more it appears—contrary to a common impression—to be animated by a rigorously systematic intention (as Benjamin once wrote of another philosopher usually thought to be fragmentary, Friedrich Schlegel).

Here Benjamin conceives of origin not as a logical category but as a historical one:

> Origin [*Ursprung*], although an entirely historical category, has, nevertheless, nothing to do with genesis [*Entstehung*]. The term origin is not intended to describe the process by which the existent came into being, but rather to describe that which emerges from the process of becoming and disappearance. Origin is an eddy in the stream of becoming, and in its current it swallows the material involved in the process of genesis. That which is original is never revealed in the naked and manifest existence of the factual; its rhythm is apparent only to a dual insight. On the one hand it needs to be recognized as a process of restoration and re-establishment, but, on the other hand, and precisely because of this, as something imperfect and incomplete. There takes place in every original phenomenon a determination of the form in which an idea will constantly confront the historical world, until it is revealed fully, in the totality of its history. Origin is not, therefore, discovered by the examination of actual findings, but it is related to their history and their subsequent development. The principles of philosophical contemplation are recorded in the dialectic which is inherent in origin. This dialectic shows singularity and repetition to be conditioned by one another in all essentials. The category of the origin is not, as Cohen holds, a purely logical one, but a historical one.[42]

Let us pause to consider the idea of origin that Benjamin presents in this passage, which is far closer to Goethe's concept of *Urphänomen* than to the idea of origin to which we are accustomed. It cannot be apprehended as an event established on the level of facts, but at the same time it does not appear as a mythic archetype. Instead, Benjamin says that it acts as a vortex in the stream of becoming and that it manifests itself only through a double structure of restoration and incompleteness. In the origin, in other words, there is a dialectic that reveals every "original phenomenon" to be a reciprocal conditioning of *Einmaligkeit*, "onceness," we might say, and repetition. What is at play in every original phenomenon, Benjamin says, is the "figure in which an Idea confronts [*auseinandersetzt*] the historical world, until it is completed in the totality of its history." Here the theory of the origin shows its ties to the theory of Ideas presented in Benjamin's preface.

What is essential for this theory is the intention by which the exposition of the Ideas and the salvation of the phenomena are simultaneous and merge in a single gesture. An *Auseinandersetzung*, a reciprocal position of the Idea and the historical totality of phenomena, is accomplished in this gesture. "In the science of philosophy," Benjamin writes, "the concept of Being" at issue in the Idea "is not satisfied by the phenomenon until it has consumed all its history."[43] In this consummation, the phenomenon does not remain what it was (that is, a singularity); rather, it "becomes what it was not—totality."[44] Here we find the same interpenetrating of "transfiguration, as the creature's form in the origin" and "destruction, as the power of justice" that we already discerned as one of the characteristics of historical redemption. To save phenomena in the Idea (to expose the Idea in phenomena) is to show them in their historical consummation, as a fulfilled totality. To show this in the work of art is the task of criticism. In historical knowledge it is the task of prophecy. This is why Benjamin writes, "criticism and prophecy must be the two categories that meet in the salvation of the past."[45] And just as in the artwork, in which the exposition of the Idea that saves the work corresponds to the "mortification" by which the "multiplicity of the work is extinguished," so, in the redemption of the past, transfiguration in the origin coincides with the power of destructive justice, which consumes the historical totality of phenomena.

X

If we now return to the image of the angel with which this chapter began, we can find in it more than casual analogies with the ideas of origin and redemption that we have just delineated.

We have seen that the angel is the originary image in the likeness of which man is created and, at the same time, the consummation of the historical totality of existence that is accomplished on the last day, such that in its figure origin and end coincide. Likewise, the reduction to the origin that takes place in redemption is also the consummation of historical totality. The fact that Benjamin often writes that this redemption takes place in a "dialectical image" does not distance us from angelology but, on the contrary, leads us to its very center. In its essence, the dialectical image "flashes." It is the "involuntary memory of redeemed humanity."[46] "The past can be seized only as an image which flashes up at the instant when it can be recognized and is no longer seen again," we read in the Fifth Thesis.[47] This is why the redemption that it accomplishes can be grasped "always only as losing itself in the unredeemable."[48]

Does this mean that redemption fails and that nothing is truly saved?

Not exactly. What cannot be saved is what was, the past as such. But what
is saved is what never was, something new. This is the sense of the "transfiguration" that takes place in the origin. In the "Epistemological-Critical
Preface," Benjamin states this explicitly: the phenomenon that is saved in
the Idea "becomes what it was not—totality." In a note that bears the title
"The Dialectical Image" ("Das dialektische Bild"), the method of historical knowledge is stated in this phrase: "to read what was never written."[49]
Just as, in the end, the angel that comes to meet man is not an original
image but the image that we ourselves have formed by our own actions,
so in historical redemption what happens in the end is what never took
place. This is what is saved.

It is now possible to comprehend why the angel in "Agesilaus Santander" has no hope "on the way of the return home": what he brings
with him is "a new man."

Benjamin expresses this profound angelological meaning of the dialectical image in a passage that bears the title "From a Short Speech on Proust
Given on My Fortieth Birthday." Concerning involuntary memory, he
writes:

> Its images do not come unsummoned; rather, it is a matter of images that we
> have never seen before remembering. This is clearest in the case of images in
> which we see ourselves as we do in dreams. We stand before ourselves just as
> we once stood in an originary past [*Urvergangenheit*] that we never saw. And
> precisely the most important images—those developed in the darkroom of
> the lived moment—are what we see. One could say that our deepest mo-
> ments, like some cigarette packs, are given to us together with a little image,
> a little photo of ourselves. And the "whole life" that is said to pass before the
> eyes of the person who is dying or whose life is threatened is composed of
> precisely these little images. They present a rapid succession, like those pre-
> cursors of cinematography, the little booklets in which, as children, we could
> admire a boxer, a swimmer, or a tennis player in action.[50]

In the paradoxical figure of this memory, which remembers what was
never seen, the redemption of the past is accomplished.

There is also a similar image for happiness. For a dialectic and a polarity also inhere in happiness. It can assume "the figure of the hymn or of
the elegy." In the first case, the height of beatitude is the unsatisfied, the
new; in the second, it is the eternal repetition of the origin. But this dialectic is also fulfilled in a new birth, whose luminous figure Benjamin

sketched in a prose work probably composed in the same period in which he wrote "Agesilaus Santander." The text bears the title "After the Achievement" ("Nach der Vollendung"):

> The origin of the great work has often been considered through the image of birth. This is a dialectical image; it embraces the process from two sides. The first has to do with creative conception and concerns the feminine element in genius. The feminine is exhausted in creation. It gives life to the work and then dies away. What dies in the master alongside the achieved creation is that part of him in which the creation was conceived. But this achievement of the work—and this leads to the other side of the process—is nothing dead. It cannot be reached from the outside; refinements and improvements do not force it. It is achieved on the inside of the work itself. And here, too, one can speak of a birth. In its achievement, creation gives birth anew to the creator. Not in its feminine element, in which it was conceived, but in its masculine element. Animated, the creator overtakes nature: he owes this existence, which the creator first conceived from the dark depth of the maternal womb, to a brighter realm. The creator's homeland is not where he was born; rather, he comes into the world where his homeland is. He is the first-born male of the work that he once conceived.[51]

At this point, in which generator and generated, memory and hope, elegy and hymn, onceness and repetition exchange parts, happiness is achieved. What happens here—new angel or new man—is what never happened. But this—what has *never happened*—is the historical and wholly actual homeland of humanity.

§ 10 The Messiah and the Sovereign: The Problem of Law in Walter Benjamin

I

In the Eighth Thesis in his "Theses on the Philosophy of History," Benjamin writes: "The tradition of the oppressed teaches us that the 'state of exception' in which we live is the rule. We must arrive at a concept of history that corresponds to this fact. Then we will have the production of a *real* state of exception before us as a task."[1] In another fragment, which the editors of Benjamin's *Collected Writings* (*Gesammelte Schriften*) published among the notes to the "Theses," Benjamin uses a similar concept to characterize messianic time:

> The apocryphal saying of a Gospel, "Wherever I encounter someone, I will pronounce judgment on him," casts a particular light on Judgment Day [*den jüngsten Tag*]. It recalls Kafka's fragment: the Day of Judgment is a summary judgment [*Standrecht*]. But it also adds something: according to this saying, the Day of Judgment is not different from others. In any case, this Gospel saying furnishes the criterion for the concept of the present that the historian makes his own. Every instant is the instant of judgment on certain moments that precede it.[2]

In these two passages, Benjamin establishes a relation between the concept of messianic time, which constitutes the theoretical nucleus of the "Theses," and a juridical category that belongs to the sphere of public law. Messianic time has the form of a state of exception (*Ausnahmezustand*) and summary judgment (*Standrecht*), that is, judgment pronounced in the state of exception.

It is this relation that the present chapter proposes to investigate. Such an investigation should be taken as a contribution to the history of the difficult relationship between philosophy and law that Leo Strauss sought to delineate throughout his works. Here it is not a matter of a problem of political philosophy in the strict sense but of a crucial issue that involves the very existence of philosophy in its relationship to the entire codified text of tradition, whether it be Islamic *shari'a*, Jewish Halakhah, or Christian dogma. *Philosophy is always already constitutively related to the law, and every philosophical work is always, quite literally, a decision on this relationship.*

II

In Benjamin's Eighth Thesis, the term *Ausnahmezustand* ("state of exception") appears in quotation marks, as if it originated in another context or another one of Benjamin's works. It is, indeed, a citation in both senses. It originated in Carl Schmitt's *Political Theology* (1922) and the theory of sovereignty that Benjamin had already commented on and developed in his failed *Habilitationsschrift* on the origin of the Baroque German mourning play. Even the term *Standrecht* ("summary judgment") can be found in Schmitt, for example in his 1931 essay, "Die Wendung zum totalen Staat."

In Schmitt's words, "Sovereign is he who decides on the state of exception," that is, the person or the power that, when declaring a state of emergency or martial law, may legitimately suspend the validity of law. The paradox implicit in this definition (which we may refer to as the paradox of sovereignty) consists in the fact that the sovereign, having the legitimate power to suspend the law, finds himself at the same time outside and inside the juridical order. Schmitt's specification that the sovereign is "*at the same time* outside and inside the juridical order" (emphasis added) is not insignificant: the sovereign *legally* places himself outside the law. This means that the paradox can also be formulated this way: "the law is outside itself," or: "I, the sovereign, who am outside the law, declare that there is nothing outside the law [*che non c'è un fuori legge*]." This is why Schmitt defines sovereignty as a "limit concept" of legal theory, and why he shows its structure through the theory of the exception.

What is an exception? The exception is a kind of exclusion. It is an individual case that is excluded from the general rule. But what properly characterizes the exception is that what is excluded in it is not, for this reason, simply without relation to the rule. On the contrary, the rule maintains itself in relation to the exception in the form of suspension. *The rule applies to the exception in no longer applying, in withdrawing from it.* The state of exception is therefore not the chaos that precedes legal order but the situation resulting from its suspension. In this sense the exception is not simply excluded but is rather truly "taken outside," as is implied by the word's etymological root (*ex-capere*). Developing a suggestion of Jean-Luc Nancy's, we shall give the name *ban* (from the Old Germanic term indicating both exclusion from the community and the power of the sovereign) to this original legal structure, through which law preserves itself even in its own suspension, applying to what it has excluded and *abandoned*, that is, banned. In this sense, the ban is the fundamental structure of the law, which expresses its sovereign character, its power to include by excluding. This is why Schmitt can say: "The exception is more interesting than the regular case. The latter proves nothing; the exception proves everything. The exception does not only confirm the rule; the rule as such lives off the exception alone [*die Regel lebt überhaupt nur von der Ausnahme*]."[3]

III

It is this last sentence that Benjamin both cites and falsifies in the Eighth Thesis. Instead of "the rule as such lives off the exception alone," he writes: "the 'state of exception' in which we live is the rule." What must be grasped here is the sense of this conscious alteration. In defining the messianic kingdom with the terms of Schmitt's theory of sovereignty, Benjamin appears to establish a parallelism between the arrival of the Messiah and the limit concept of State power. In the days of the Messiah, which are also "the 'state of exception' in which we live," the hidden foundation of the law comes to light, and the law itself enters into a state of perpetual suspension.

In establishing this analogy, Benjamin does nothing other than bring a genuine messianic tradition to the most extreme point of its development. The essential character of messianism may well be precisely its particular relation to the law. In Judaism as in Christianity and Shiite Islam, the messianic event above all signifies a crisis and radical transformation of the entire order of the law. The thesis I would like to advance is that the messianic kingdom is not one category among others within religious experience but is, rather, its limit concept. *The Messiah is, in other words, the figure through which religion confronts the problem of the Law, decisively reckoning with it.* And since philosophy, for its part, is constitutively involved in a confrontation with the Law, messianism represents the point of greatest proximity between religion and philosophy. This is why the three great monotheistic religions always tried in every possible way to control and reduce the essential messianic properties of religion and philosophy, without ever fully succeeding.

IV

In his essay on "The Meaning of the Torah in Jewish Mysticism,"[4] Gershom Scholem summarizes the complex relationship between messianism and law in two questions: (1) What were the form and content of the Law before the Fall? (2) What will the structure of the Torah be at the time of redemption, when man will be returned to his originary condition? The authors of the *Raya Mehemna* and the *Tikunei ha-Zohar*, two books that belong to the oldest stratum of the *Zohar*, distinguish two aspects of the Torah: the Torah of Beriah, which is the Torah in the state of creation, and the Torah of Aziluth, which is the Torah in the state of emanation. The Torah of Beriah is the law of the unredeemed world and, as such, is compared to the outer garments of the divine presence, which would have shown itself in its nudity if Adam had not sinned. The Torah of Aziluth, which is opposed to the first as redemption to exile, instead reveals the meaning of the Torah in its original fullness. The authors of these two books, moreover, establish a correspondence between the two aspects of the Torah and the two trees of Paradise, the Tree of Life and the Tree of Knowledge. The Tree of Life represents the pure and original power of the sacred, beyond all contamination by evil and death. Yet since the fall of Adam, the world has been ruled no longer by the Tree of Life but by the mystery of the second tree, which includes both good and evil. As a consequence, the world is now divided into two separate regions: the sacred and the profane, the pure and the impure, the licit and the forbidden:

> Our comprehension of revelation is currently tied to the Tree of Knowledge and presents itself as the positive law of the Torah and as the realm of the *Ha-*

lakhah. Its meaning appears to us now in what is commanded and what is prohibited and in everything which follows from this basic distinction. The power of evil, of destruction and death, has become real in the free will of man. The purpose of the law, which as it were constitutes the Torah as it can be read in the light—or shadows!—of the Tree of Knowledge, is to confine this power if not to overcome it entirely. . . . But when the world will again be subject to the Law of the Tree of Life, the face of *Halakhah* itself will change.[5]

The decisive point at which all the issues coincide is expressed in the following question: "How are we to conceive of the original structure of the Torah once the Messiah has restored its fullness?" For it is clear that the opposition between the messianic law and the law of exile cannot be an opposition between two laws of identical structure, which merely contain different commands and different prohibitions. The Messiah does not only come to bring a new Table of the Law, nor does he simply come to abolish Halakhah. His task—which Benjamin once expressed in the image of a small displacement that seems to leave everything intact—is more complex, since the original structure of the law to be restored is more complex.

V

It is in this light that we must now turn to the theories of the nature of the original Torah that, elaborated by Cabalists from the sixteenth century onward, radicalized the ideas already contained in the *Zohar* and Nachmanides. In his *Shi'ur Komah*, Moses Cordovero states:

The Torah in its innermost essence is composed of divine letters, which themselves are configurations of divine light. Only in the course of a process of materialization do these letters combine in various ways. First they form names, that is, names of God, later appellatives and predicates suggesting the divine, and still later they combine in a new way, to form words relating to earthly events and material objects.[6]

The implicit presupposition in this conception is that the original Torah was not a defined text, but rather consisted only of the totality of possible combinations of the Hebrew alphabet.

The decisive step in this progressive desemanticization of the law was accomplished by Rabbi Eliahu Cohen Itamary, of Smirne, in the eighteenth century. Confronted with the rabbinic prescription that the Torah must be written without vowels and punctuation, he offered an explanation that according to Scholem expresses the "relativization" of the Law but that, as we will see, in truth involves something different and more complicated. Rabbi Eliahu Cohen Itamary writes:

This is a reference to the state of the Torah as it existed in the sight of God, before it was transmitted to the lower spheres. *For He had before Him numerous letters that were not joined into words as is the case today, because the actual arrangement of the words would depend on the way in which this lower world conducted itself.* Because of Adam's sin, God arranged the letters before Him into the words describing death and other earthly things, such as levirate marriage. Without sin there would have been no death. The same letters would have been joined into words telling a different story. That is why the scroll of the Torah contains no vowels, no punctuation, and no accents, as an allusion to the *Torah which originally formed a heap of unarranged letters.* The divine purpose will be revealed in the Torah at the coming of the Messiah, who will engulf death forever, so that there will be no room in the Torah for anything related to death, uncleanness, and the like. For then God will annul the present combination of letters that form the words of our present Torah and will compose the letters into other words, which will form new sentences speaking of other things.[7]

A very similar formulation is attributed to the Baal Shem, the founder of Hassidism in Poland. Rabbi Pinhas, of Koretz, relates that the Baal Shem said: "It is true that the holy Torah was originally created as an *incoherent jumble of letters.* . . . All the letters of the Torah were indeed jumbled, and only when a certain event occurred in the world did the letters combine to form the words in which the event is related."[8]

The most interesting and perhaps most surprising implication of this conception is not so much the idea of the absolute mutability and plasticity of the Law (which Scholem defines, as we have mentioned, as "the relativization of the Torah") as the thesis according to which the original form of the Torah is a medley of letters without any order—that is, *without meaning.* Moshe Idel, who today, after Scholem's death, is one of the greatest scholars of the Cabala, has pointed out to me that while this last implication is logically inevitable, the Cabalists would never have stated it so crudely. To their eyes, the symmetrical implication would have been noteworthy, namely, that the original Torah contained all possible meanings. But these meanings were contained in it, to use a terminology that

was certainly familiar to the Cabalists, only potentially; in actuality, the
Torah was much more similar to the writing tablet of which Aristotle
speaks, on which nothing is written. In the sense in which we speak in
logic of "meaningful statements," the original Torah could have no meaning, insofar as it is a medley of letters without order and articulation. My
impression is that many of the contradictions and aporias of messianism
find their foundation and solution precisely in this surprising thesis, according to which the original form of law is not a signifying proposition
but, so to speak, a commandment that commands nothing. If this is true,
the crucial problem of messianism then becomes: how can the Messiah
restore a law that has no meaning?

VI

Before confronting this question, I would like to consider an interpretation of messianism that has been advanced by the scholar who, in our
century, contributed most to the study of the Cabala and whom I have
already mentioned, Gershom Scholem. According to the central thesis of
his 1959 essay "Towards an Understanding of the Messianic Idea in Judaism" (which has since been infinitely repeated by scholars and popu-
larizers), messianism is animated by two opposed tensions: the first is a
restorative tendency aiming at the *restitutio in integrum* of the origin; the
second is a utopian impulse turned instead toward the future and renewal. The contradiction that follows from these opposed forces explains
the antinomies of messianism as well as what is, according to Scholem,
messianism's essential character: "a life lived in deferral and delay," in
which nothing can be brought to fulfillment and nothing accomplished
once and for all. Messianism, Scholem writes, "possesses a tension that
never finds true release."[9] A variation of this thesis has been expressed by
Joseph Klausner and Siegmund Mowinckel, according to whom messianism is constituted by two contrasting tendencies: a political and
worldly one, and a spiritual and supernatural one. The impossible attempt to reconcile these two antagonistic tendencies marks the limits of
messianism, giving messianic time its peculiar character as an interim period between two epochs and two ages.
Despite my respect for these scholars, I would like to propose that we
overturn their claims and, along with them, the common interpretation
of messianism. The tension between two irreconcilable tendencies can-

not explain the aporias of messianism; rather, messianism's antinomical gesture is the only strategy adequate to the specific problem that messianism must master: the problem of law in its originary structure. The idea of a Torah composed only of meaningless letters is not something like a Freudian compromise between two irreconcilable elements; on the contrary, it expresses a profound philosophical intuition of the structure of law and, at the same time, constitutes the most radical attempt to confront this structure. Every interpretation of the aporetic aspects of messianism must situate them above all from this perspective.

VII

Here I will mention only some of these aspects. First of all, there is the passage of *Pesiqta Rabbati* in which a phrase of the talmudic treatise *Sanhedrin*, which reads "the Law will return to its students" (referring to the days of the Messiah), is altered so that it reads "the Law will return to its new form." Klausner has underlined the paradoxical character of this "return to the new" (an "unnatural experience,"[10] as he observes, even if it is perfectly familiar to adepts of Benjaminian gnosis). Even more paradoxical is the idea of a commandment fulfilled by being transgressed, which characterizes the most antinomical messianic communities, such as that of Shabbatai Zevi, who stated that the "violation of the Torah is its fulfillment." This formula is not only, as a common interpretation maintains, the expression of an antinomical tendency always at work in messianism; instead, it presupposes a particularly complex conception of the relationship between the Torah of Beriah and the Torah of Aziluth. What is decisive here is the concept of fulfillment, which implies that the Torah in some way still holds and has not simply been abrogated by a second Torah commanding the opposite of the first. We find the same notion in the Christian conception of the *pleroma* of the law, for example in Matthew 5:17–18 ("I am come not to destroy [*katalysai*], but to fulfill [*plērysai*]") and in the theory of the law proposed by Paul in the Epistle to the Romans (8:4: "that the righteousness of the law might be fulfilled in us"). What is at issue here are not simply antinomical tendencies but an attempt to confront the pleromatic state in which the Torah, restored to its original form, contains neither commandments nor prohibitions but only a medley of unordered letters. It is in this context that we must read the striking statement in the Tannaitic midrash *Mekhita* that "in the end, the Torah is destined to be forgotten," an opinion that could be reformulated in Sabbatean terms as "the fulfillment of the Torah is its being forgotten."

Analogous considerations could be made for the so-called "interim character" of the messianic kingdom, which, in Hering's words, seems "to oscillate between the present eon and the future eon." At first, in fact, the Messiah presented the eschatological realization of the divine kingdom, when Yahweh would appear as king, bringing salvation to his people. In rabbinic literature, however, the expression "the days of the Messiah" means only the intermediary period between the present time and the "world to come" (*olam habah*). In the *Sanhedrin* treatise (97a) we read, "the world will last six thousand years: two thousand in chaos, two thousand under the Law, two thousand during the messianic time." As we have seen, Mowinckel explains this interim character of messianic time as an attempt to reconcile the two opposed tendencies of messianism, the political and the supernatural.[11] But I would like to draw attention to the words that, in the text of the *Sanhedrin*, immediately follow the ones I just cited: "Because of our wickedness, all the time from the last period has been lost" (that is: the time under the Law is over, and yet the Messiah has not yet come). Here, just as in Benjamin's thought, where messianic time is not chronologically distinct from historical time, the days of the Messiah do not constitute a temporal period situated between historical time and the *olam habah*; rather, they are, so to speak, present in the form of a deferral and procrastination of the time under the law, that is, as a historical effect of a missing time.

One of the paradoxes of the messianic kingdom is, indeed, that another world and another time must make themselves present in this world and time. This means that historical time cannot simply be canceled and that messianic time, moreover, cannot be perfectly homogenous with history: the two times must instead accompany each other according to modalities that cannot be reduced to a dual logic (this world / the other world). In this regard Furio Jesi, the most intelligent Italian scholar of myth, once suggested that to understand the mode of Being of myth, one needs to introduce a third term into the opposition "is / is not," which he formulated as a "there is-not" [*ci non è*].[12] Here we are confronted not with a compromise between two irreconcilable impulses but with an attempt to bring to light the hidden structure of historical time itself.

VIII

If we now return to our point of departure, that is, to Benjamin's Eighth Thesis, the comparison he makes between messianic time and the state of exception shows its legitimacy and its coherence. And in this light we can also seek to clarify the structural analogy that ties law in its original state to the state of exception. Precisely this problem lies at the center of the letters that Benjamin and Scholem exchanged between July and September 1934, when Benjamin had just finished the first version of his essay on Kafka for the *Jüdische Rundschau*. The subject of the letters is the conception of law in Kafka's work.

From the moment he first reads Benjamin's essay, Scholem disagrees with his friend precisely on this point. "Here," he writes, "your exclusion of theology went too far, and you threw out the baby with the bathwater." Scholem defines the relation to the law described in Kafka's novels as "the Nothing of Revelation" (*Nichts der Offenbarung*), intending this expression to name "a stage in which revelation does not signify [*bedeutet*], yet still affirms itself by the fact that it is in force. Where the wealth of significance is gone and what appears, reduced, so to speak, to the zero point of its own content, still does not disappear (and Revelation is something that appears), there the Nothing appears."[13] According to Scholem, a law that finds itself in such a condition "is not absent, but unrealizable." "The students of whom you speak," he writes to Benjamin, "are not students who have lost the scripture . . . but students who cannot decipher it."[14]

Being in force without significance (*Geltung ohne Bedeutung*): for Scholem, this is the correct definition of the state of law in Kafka's novel. A world in which the law finds itself in this condition and where "every gesture becomes unrealizable" is a rejected, not an idyllic, world. And yet, if only through this extreme reduction, the Law maintains itself "in the zero point of its own content."

If I am not mistaken, nowhere in his later works does Scholem compare this definition of the law in Kafka's universe—"being in force without significance"—to the Cabalistic and messianic conception of the Torah as a medley of letters without order and meaning. Yet even the quickest glance shows that what is at issue here is more than a simple analogy. The formula *Geltung ohne Bedeutung* applies perfectly to the state of the Torah in the face of God, when it is in force but has not yet acquired a determinate content and meaning. But the accord also holds with respect to the state of exception and its absolutization, as suggested in the "Theses on the Philosophy of History," from which we began. I would like to propose the hypothesis that the formula "being in force without significance" defines not only the state of the Torah before God but also and above all our current relation to law—the state of exception, according to Benjamin's words, in which we live. Perhaps no other formula better expresses the conception of law that our age confronts and cannot master.

What, after all, is a state of exception, if not a law that is in force but does not signify anything? The self-suspension of law, which applies to the individual case in no longer applying, in withdrawing from it yet maintaining itself in relation to it in the ban, is an exemplary figure for *Geltung ohne Bedeutung*. Fifty years later, Benjamin's diagnosis has thus lost none of its currency. Since then, the state of emergency has become the rule in every part of our cultural tradition, from politics to philosophy and from ecology to literature. Today, everywhere, in Europe as in Asia, in industrialized countries as in those of the "Third World," we live in the ban of a tradition that is permanently in a state of exception. And all power, whether democratic or totalitarian, traditional or revolutionary, has entered into a legitimation crisis in which the state of exception, which was the hidden foundation of the system, has fully come to light. If the paradox of sovereignty once had the form of the proposition "There is nothing outside the law," it takes on a perfectly symmetrical form in our time, when the exception has become the rule: "There is nothing inside the law"; everything—every law—is outside law. The entire planet has now become the exception that law must contain in its ban. Today we live in this messianic paradox, and every aspect of our existence bears its marks.

The success of deconstruction in our time is founded precisely on its having conceived of the whole text of tradition, the whole law, as a *Geltung ohne Bedeutung*, a being in force without significance. In Scholem's terms, we could say that contemporary thought tends to reduce the law (in the widest sense of the term, which indicates all of tradition in its regulative form) to the state of a Nothing and yet, at the same time, to maintain this Nothing as the "zero point of its content." The law thus becomes ungraspable—but, for this reason, insuperable, ineradicable ("undecidable," in the terms of deconstruction). We can compare the situation of our time to that of a petrified or paralyzed messianism that, like all messianism, nullifies the law, but then maintains it as the Nothing of Revelation in a perpetual and interminable state of exception, "the 'state of exception' in which we live."

IX

Only in this context do Benjamin's theses acquire their proper meaning. In his letter of August 11, 1934, he writes to Scholem that Kafka's insistence on law "is the dead point of his work." But in a plan for the same letter, he adds that his interpretation will ultimately have to reckon with it ("if this insistence has a function, then even a reading that starts with images like mine will ultimately have to lead to it"). If we accept the equivalence between messianism and nihilism of which both Benjamin and Scholem were firmly convinced, albeit in different ways, then we will have to distinguish two forms of messianism or nihilism: a first form (which we may call imperfect nihilism) that nullifies the law but maintains the Nothing in a perpetual and infinitely deferred state of validity, and a second form, a perfect nihilism that does not even let validity survive beyond its meaning but instead, as Benjamin writes of Kafka, "succeeds in finding redemption in the overturning of the Nothing." Against Scholem's conception of a being in force without significance, a law that is valid but neither commands nor prescribes anything, Benjamin objects:

> Whether the students have lost Scripture or cannot decipher it in the end amounts to the same thing, since a Scripture without its keys is not scripture but life, the life that is lived in the village at the foot of the hill on which the castle stands. In the attempt to transform life into Scripture I see the sense of the "inversion" [*Umkehr*] toward which many of Kafka's allegories seem to tend.[15]

The Messiah's task becomes all the more difficult from this perspective. He must confront not simply a law that commands and forbids but a law that, like the original Torah, is in force without significance. But this is also the task with which we, who live in the state of exception that has become the rule, must reckon.

X

I would like to interrupt my presentation of Benjamin's conception of messianic law. I will instead try to read a story by Kafka from the perspective of this conception: "Before the Law," which is to be found in both the collection *Der Landarzt* and *The Trial*. Naturally I do not mean that Benjamin would have read the story as I will read it. Rather, I will seek indirectly to present Benjamin's conception of the messianic task in the form of an interpretation of one of Kafka's allegories. I take for granted that the reader remembers the story of the doorkeeper standing before the door of the law and the man from the country who asks if he can enter it, waiting without success only to hear the doorkeeper tell him, at the end of his life, that the door was meant for him alone. The thesis that I intend to advance is that this parable is an allegory of the state of law in the messianic age, that is, in the age of its being in force without significance. The open door through which it is impossible to enter is a cipher of this condition of the law. The two most recent interpreters of the parable, Jacques Derrida and Massimo Cacciari, both insist on this point. "The law," Derrida writes, "keeps itself [*se garde*] without keeping itself, kept [*gardée*] by a door-keeper who keeps nothing, the door remaining open and open onto nothing."[16] And Cacciari decisively underlines the fact that the power of the law lies precisely in the impossibility of entering into the already open, of reaching the place where one already is: "How can we hope to 'open' if the door is already open? How can we hope to enter-the-open [*entrare-l'aperto*]? In the open, there is, things are there, one does not enter there. . . . We can enter only there where we can open. The already-open [*il già-aperto*] immobilizes. The man from the country cannot enter, because entering into the already open is ontologically impossible."[17] It is easy to discern an analogy between the situation described in the parable and law in the state of being in force without significance, in which the law is valid precisely insofar as it commands nothing and has become unrealizable. The man from the country is consigned to the potentiality of law because law asks nothing of him, imposes on him nothing other than its ban.

If this interpretation is correct, if the open door is an image of law in the time of its messianic nullification, then who is the man from the country? In his analysis of the parable, Kurt Weinberg suggests that we are to see the "figure of a hindered Christian Messiah" in the obstinate, shy man from the country.[18] The suggestion can be taken only if we return messianism to its true context. Those who have read Sigmund Hurwitz's book, *Die Gestalt der sterbenden Messiahs*, will recall that in the Jewish tradition the figure of the Messiah is double. Since the first century B.C.E., the Messiah has been divided into Messiah ben Joseph and a Messiah ben David. The Messiah of the house of Joseph is a Messiah who dies, vanquished in the battle against the forces of evil; the Messiah of the house of David is the triumphant Messiah, who ultimately vanquishes Armilos and restores the kingdom. While Christian theologians usually try to leave this doubling of the messianic figure aside, it is clear that Christ, who died and was reborn, unites in his person both Messiahs of the Jewish tradition. It is worth underlining that Kafka, for his part, was aware of this tradition through Max Brod's book, *Heidentum, Christentum, Judentum*.

Scholem once wrote that the Messiah ben Joseph is a disconsolate figure who redeems nothing and whose destruction coincides with the destruction of history. While this diagnosis is certainly true, I am not at all sure that it can be wholly maintained if one considers the role that the Messiah ben Joseph had to play in the economy of the doubling of the messianic figure (which Kafka could have had in mind in conceiving of his country Messiah). In the Christian tradition, which knows a single Messiah, the Messiah also has a double task, since he is both redeemer and legislator; for the theologians, the dialectic between these two tasks constitutes the specific problem of messianism. (In his treatise on law, Tommaso Campanella defined the figure of the Messiah as follows, polemicizing with both Luther and Abelard on the subject of this dialectic: "Luther recognizes not the legislator, but the redeemer; Peter Abelard recognizes only the legislator, but not the redeemer. But the Catholic Church recognizes both" [*Luterus non agnoscit legislatorem, sed redemptorem, Petrus Abelardus agnoscit solum legislatorem, non autem redemptorem. Ecclesia catholica utrumque agnoscit.*])

One of the peculiar characteristics of Kafka's allegories is that at their very end they contain a possibility of an about-face that completely upsets their meaning. In the final analysis, all the interpreters of the parable read it as the apologue of the man from the country's irremediable failure or defeat before the impossible task imposed upon him by the law. Yet it is worth asking whether Kafka's text does not consent to a different reading. The interpreters seem to forget, in fact, precisely the words with which the story ends: "No one else could enter here, since this door was destined for you alone. Now I will go and close it [*ich gehe jetzt und schliesse ihn*]." If it is true that the door's very openness constituted, as we saw, the invisible power and specific "force" of the law, then it is possible to imagine that the entire behavior of the man from the country is nothing other than a complicated and patient strategy to have the door closed in order to interrupt the law's being in force. The final sense of the legend is thus not, as Derrida writes, that of an "event that succeeds in not happening" (or that happens in not happening: "an event that happens not to happen," *un événement qui arrive à ne pas arriver*),[19] but rather just the opposite: the story tells how something has really happened in seeming not to happen, and the apparent aporias of the story of the man from the country instead express the complexity of the messianic task that is allegorized in it.

It is in this light that one must read the enigmatic passage in Kafka's notebooks that says, "The Messiah will only come when he is no longer necessary, he will only come after his arrival, he will come not on the last day, but on the very last day." The particular double structure implicit in this messianic *theologumenon* corresponds to the paradigm that Benjamin probably has in mind when he speaks, in the Eighth Thesis, of "a real state of exception" as opposed to the state of exception in which we live. This paradigm is the only way in which one can conceive something like an *eskhaton*—that is, something that belongs to historical time and its law and, at the same time, puts an end to it. Although while the law is in force we are confronted only with events that happen without happening and that thus indefinitely differ from themselves, here, instead, the messianic event is considered through a bi-unitary figure. This figure probably constitutes the true sense of the division of the single Messiah (like the single Law) into two distinct figures, one of which is consumed in the consummation of history and the other of which happens, so to speak, only the day after his arrival. Only in this way can the event of the Messiah coincide with historical time yet at the same time not be identified with it, effecting in the *eskhaton* that "small adjustment" in which, according to the rabbi's saying told by Benjamin, the messianic kingdom consists.

PART THREE

Potentiality

§ 11 On Potentiality

The concept of potentiality has a long history in Western philosophy, in which it has occupied a central position at least since Aristotle. In both his metaphysics and his physics, Aristotle opposed potentiality to actuality, *dynamis* to *energeia*, and bequeathed this opposition to Western philosophy and science.

My concern here is not simply historiographical. I do not intend simply to restore currency to philosophical categories that are no longer in use. On the contrary, I think that the concept of potentiality has never ceased to function in the life and history of humanity, most notably in that part of humanity that has grown and developed its potency [*potenza*] to the point of imposing its power over the whole planet.

Following Wittgenstein's suggestion, according to which philosophical problems become clearer if they are formulated as questions concerning the meaning of words, I could state the subject of my work as an attempt to understand the meaning of the verb "can" [*potere*]. What do I mean when I say: "I can, I cannot"?

In an exergue to the collection of poems she entitled *Requiem*, Anna Akhmatova recounts how her poems were born. It was in the 1930s, and for months and months she joined the line outside the prison of Leningrad, trying to hear news of her son, who had been arrested on political grounds. There were dozens of other women in line with her. One day, one of these women recognized her and, turning to her, addressed her with the following simple question: "Can you speak of this?" Akhmatova was silent for a moment and then, without knowing how or why, found an answer to the question: "Yes," she said, "I can."

Did she perhaps mean by these words that she was such a gifted poet that she knew how to handle language skillfully enough to describe the atrocious things of which it is so difficult to write? I do not think so. This is not what she meant to say.

For everyone a moment comes in which she or he must utter this "I can," which does not refer to any certainty or specific capacity but is, nevertheless, absolutely demanding. Beyond all faculties, this "I can" does not mean anything—yet it marks what is, for each of us, perhaps the hardest and bitterest experience possible: the experience of potentiality.

What Is a Faculty?

"There is an aporia," we read in the second book of Aristotle's *De anima*,

as to why there is no sensation of the senses themselves. Why is it that, in the absence of external objects, the senses do not give any sensation, although they contain fire, earth, water, and the other elements of which there is sensation? This happens because sensibility is not actual but only potential. This is why it does not give sensation, just as the combustible does not burn by itself, without a principle of combustion; otherwise it would burn itself and would not need any actual fire.[1]

We are so accustomed to representing sensibility as a "faculty of the soul" that for us this passage of *De anima* does not seem to pose any problems. The vocabulary of potentiality has penetrated so deeply into us that we do not notice that what appears for the first time in these lines is a fundamental problem that has only rarely come to light as such in the course of Western thought. This problem—which is the originary problem of potentiality—is: what does it mean "to have a faculty"? In what way can something like a "faculty" exist?

Archaic Greece did not conceive of sensibility and intelligence as "faculties" of the soul. The very word *aisthēsis*, which means "sensation," ends in *-sis*, which means that it expresses an activity. How, then, can a sensation exist in the absence of sensation? How can an *aisthēsis* exist in the state of *anesthesia*?

These questions immediately bring us to the problem of potentiality. When we tell ourselves that human beings have the "faculty" of vision, the "faculty" of speech (or, as Hegel says, the faculty of death)—or even simply that something is or is not "in one's power"—we are already in the domain of potentiality.

What does this passage from *De anima* teach us about potentiality? What is essential is that potentiality is not simply non-Being, simple privation, but rather *the existence of non-Being*, the presence of an absence; this is what we call "faculty" or "power." "To have a faculty" means *to have* a privation. And potentiality is not a logical hypostasis but the mode of existence of this privation.

But how can an absence be present, how can a sensation *exist* as anesthesia? This is the problem that interests Aristotle.

(It is often said that philosophers are concerned with *essence*, that, confronted with a thing, they ask "What is it?" But this is not exact. Philosophers are above all concerned with *existence*, with the *mode* [or rather, the *modes*] of existence. If they consider essence, it is to exhaust it in existence, to make it exist.)

Two Potentialities

This is why Aristotle begins by distinguishing two kinds of potentiality. There is a generic potentiality, and this is the one that is meant when we say, for example, that a child has the potential to know, or that he or she can potentially become the head of State. This generic sense is not the one that interests Aristotle.

The potentiality that interests him is the one that belongs to someone who, for example, has knowledge or an ability. In this sense, we say of the architect that he or she has the *potential* to build, of the poet that he or she has the *potential* to write poems. It is clear that this *existing* potentiality differs from the *generic* potentiality of the child. The child, Aristotle says, is potential in the sense that he must suffer an alteration (a becoming other) through learning. Whoever already possesses knowledge, by contrast, is not obliged to suffer an alteration; he is instead potential, Aristotle says, thanks to a *hexis*, a "having," on the basis of which he can also *not* bring his knowledge into actuality (*mē energein*) by *not* making a work, for example. Thus the architect is potential insofar as he has the potential to not-build, the poet the potential to not-write poems.

Existence of Potentiality

Here we already discern what, for Aristotle, will be the key figure of potentiality, the mode of its *existence as potentiality*. It is a potentiality that is not simply the potential to do this or that thing but potential to not-do, potential not to pass into actuality.

This is why Aristotle criticizes the position of the Megarians, who maintain that all potentiality exists only in actuality. What Aristotle wants to posit is the existence of potentiality: that there is a presence and a face of potentiality. He literally states as much in a passage in the *Physics*: "privation [*sterēsis*] is like a face, a form [*eidos*]" (193 b 19–20).

Before passing to the determination of this "face" of potentiality that Aristotle develops in Book Theta of the *Metaphysics*, I would like to pause on a figure of potentiality that seems to me to be particularly significant and that appears in *De anima*. I refer to darkness, to shadows.

Here Aristotle is concerned with the problem of vision (418 b–419 e 1). The object of sight, he says, is color; in addition, it is something for which we have no word but which is usually translated as "transparency," *diaphanes*. *Diaphanes* refers here not to transparent bodies (such as air and water) but to a "nature," as Aristotle writes, which is in every body and is what is truly visible in every body. Aristotle does not tell us what this "nature" is; he says only "there is *diaphanes*," *esti ti diaphanes*. But he does tells us that the actuality (*energeia*) of this nature is light, and that darkness (*skotos*) is its potentiality. Light, he adds, is so to speak the color of *diaphanes* in act; darkness, we may therefore say, is in some way the color of potentiality. What is sometimes darkness and sometimes light is one in nature (*hē autē physis hote men skotos hote de phōs estin*).

A few pages later, Aristotle returns to the problem of *skotos*, "darkness." He asks himself how it can be that we feel ourselves seeing. For this to be the case it is necessary that we feel ourselves seeing either with our vision or with another sense. Aristotle's answer is that we feel ourselves seeing with vision itself. But then, he adds, an aporia arises:

> For to feel by vision can only be to see, and what is seen is color and what has color [that is, *diaphanes*]. If what we see is seeing itself, it follows that the principle of sight in turn possesses color. Therefore "to feel by vision" does not have merely one meaning, since even when we do not see we distinguish darkness from light. Hence the principle of vision must in some way possess color.[2]

In this passage, Aristotle answers the question we posed above, namely: "Why is there no sensation of the senses themselves"? Earlier we answered the question by saying that it is so "because sensation is only potential." Now we are in a position to understand what this means. When we do not see (that is, when our vision is potential), we nevertheless distinguish darkness from light; *we see darkness*. The principle of sight "in some way possesses color," and its colors are light and darkness, actuality and potentiality, presence and privation.

Potentiality for Darkness

The following essential point should be noted: if potentiality were, for example, only the potentiality for vision and if it existed only as such in the actuality of light, we could never experience darkness (nor hear silence, in the case of the potentiality to hear). But human beings can, instead, see shadows (*to skotos*), they can experience darkness: they have the *potential* not to see, the *possibility of privation*.

In his commentary on *De anima*, Themistius writes:

> If sensation did not have the potentiality both for actuality and for not-Being-actual and if it were always actual, it would never be able to perceive darkness [*skotos*], nor could it ever hear silence. In the same way, if thought were not capable both of thought and of the absence of thought [*anoia*, thoughtlessness], it would never be able to know the formless [*amorphon*], evil, the without-figure [*aneidon*]. If the intellect did not have a community [*koinonein*] with potentiality, it would not know privation.

The greatness—and also the abyss—of human potentiality is that it is first of all potential not to act, *potential for darkness*. (In Homer, *skotos* is the darkness that overcomes human beings at the moment of their death. Human beings are capable of experiencing this *skotos*.)

What is at issue here is nothing abstract. What, for example, is boredom, if not the experience of the potentiality-not-to-act? This is why it is such a terrible experience, which borders on both good and evil.

To be capable of good and evil is not simply to be capable of doing this or that good or bad action (every particular good or bad action is, in this sense, banal). Radical evil is not this or that bad deed but the potentiality for darkness. And yet this potentiality is also the potentiality for light.

All Potentiality Is Impotentiality

It is in Book Theta of the *Metaphysics* that Aristotle seeks to grasp the "face" of this privation, the figure of this original potentiality. Aristotle makes two statements that will lead our inquiry here. "Impotentiality [*adynamia*]," we read in the first, "is a privation contrary to potentiality. Thus all potentiality is impotentiality of the same and with respect to the same" (*tou autou kai kata to auto pasa dynamis adynamia*) (1046 e 25–32).

What does this sentence mean? It means that in its originary structure, *dynamis*, potentiality, maintains itself in relation to its own privation, its own *sterēsis*, its own non-Being. This relation constitutes the essence of potentiality. To be potential means: to be one's own lack, *to be in relation to one's own incapacity*. Beings that exist in the mode of potentiality *are capable of their own impotentiality*; and only in this way do they become potential. They *can be* because they are in relation to their own non-Being. In potentiality, sensation is in relation to anesthesia, knowledge to ignorance, vision to darkness.

The second statement that we will consider here reads as follows: "What is potential [*dynatos*] is capable [*endekhetai*] of not being in actuality. What is potential can both be and not be, for the same is potential both to be and not to be [*to auto ara dynaton kai einai kai mē einai*]" (1050 b 10).

In this extraordinary passage, Aristotle offers the most explicit consideration of the originary figure of potentiality, which we may now define with his own words as the *potential not to be*. What is potential is capable (*endekhetai*), Aristotle says, both of being and of not being. *Dekhomai* means "I welcome, receive, admit." The potential welcomes non-Being, and this welcoming of non-Being *is* potentiality, fundamental passivity. It is passive potentiality, but not a passive potentiality that undergoes something other than itself; rather, it undergoes and suffers its own non-Being.

If we recall that Aristotle always draws his examples of this potentiality of non-Being from the domain of the arts and human knowledge, then we may say that human beings, insofar as they know and produce, are those beings who, more than any other, exist in the mode of potentiality. Every human power is *adynamia*, impotentiality; every human potentiality is in relation to its own privation. This is the origin (and the abyss) of human power, which is so violent and limitless with respect to other living beings. *Other living beings are capable only of their specific potentiality; they can only do this or that. But human beings are the animals who are capable of their own impotentiality. The greatness of human potentiality is measured by the abyss of human impotentiality.*

Here it is possible to see how the root of freedom is to be found in the abyss of potentiality. To be free is not simply to have the power to do this or that thing, nor is it simply to have the power to refuse to do this or that thing. To be free is, in the sense we have seen, *to be capable of one's own impotentiality*, to be in relation to one's own privation. This is why freedom is freedom for both good and evil.

The Act of Impotentiality

But what is the relation between impotentiality and potentiality, between the potentiality to not-be and the potentiality to be? And how can there be potentiality, if all potentiality is always already impotentiality? *How is it possible to consider the actuality of the potentiality to not-be?* The actuality of the potentiality to play the piano is the performance of a piece for the piano; but what is the actuality of the potentiality to not-play? The actuality of the potentiality to think is the thinking of this or that thought; but what is the actuality of the potentiality to not-think?

The answer Aristotle gives to this question is contained in two lines that, in their brevity, constitute an extraordinary testament to Aristotle's genius. In the philosophical tradition, however, Aristotle's statement has gone almost entirely unnoticed. Aristotle writes: "A thing is said to be potential if, when the act of which it is said to be potential is realized, there will be nothing impotential" (*esti de dynaton touto, hoi ean hyparxei hē energeia ou legetai ekhein tēn dynamēn, ouden estai adynaton*) (*Metaphysics*, 1047 a 24–26). Usually this sentence is interpreted as if Aristotle had wanted to say, "What is possible (or potential) is that with respect to which nothing is impossible (or impotential). If there is no impossibility, then there is possibility." Aristotle would then have uttered a banality or a tautology.

Let us instead seek to understand the text in all its difficulty. What is the potentiality of which, in the moment of actuality, there will be nothing impotential? It can be nothing other than *adynamia*, which, as we have seen, belongs to all *dynamis*: the potentiality to not-be. What Aristotle then says is: *if a potentiality to not-be originally belongs to all potentiality, then there is truly potentiality only where the potentiality to not-be does not lag behind actuality but passes fully into it as such.* This does not mean that it disappears in actuality; on the contrary, it *preserves itself* as such in actuality. What is truly potential is thus what has exhausted all its impotentiality in bringing it wholly into the act as such.

Salvation and Gift

We may now conclude with a passage of *De anima* that is truly one of the vertices of Aristotle's thought and that fully authorizes the medieval image of a mystical Aristotle. "To suffer is not a simple term," Aristotle writes.

> In one sense it is a certain destruction through the opposite principle, and in another sense the preservation [*sōtēria*, salvation] of what is in potentiality by what is in actuality and what is similar to it. . . . For he who possesses science [in potentiality] becomes someone who contemplates in actuality, and either this is not an alteration—since here there is the gift of the self to itself and to actuality [*epidosis eis auto*]—or this is an alteration of a different kind.[3]

Contrary to the traditional idea of potentiality that is annulled in actuality, here we are confronted with a potentiality that conserves itself and saves itself in actuality. Here potentiality, so to speak, survives actuality and, in this way, *gives itself to itself*.

§ 12 The Passion of Facticity

The Absent "Mood" (*Stimmung*)

It has often been observed that the problem of love is absent from Heidegger's thought. In *Being and Time*, which contains ample treatments of fear, anxiety, and *Stimmungen* in general, love is mentioned only once, in a note referring to Pascal and Augustine. Thus W. Koepps,[1] in 1928, and Ludwig Binswanger,[2] in 1942, reproached Heidegger for not having included love in his analytic of Dasein, which is founded solely on "care" (*Sorge*); and in a *Notiz* that is undoubtedly hostile, Karl Jaspers wrote that Heidegger's philosophy is "without love, hence also unworthy of love in its style."[3]

Such critiques, as Karl Löwith has remarked,[4] remain fruitless as long as they do not succeed in replacing Heidegger's analytic with an analytic centered on love. Nevertheless, Heidegger's silence—or apparent silence—on love remains problematic. We know that between 1923 and 1926, while Heidegger was preparing his greatest work, he was involved in a passionate relationship with Hannah Arendt, who was at this time his student in Marburg. Even if the letters and poems in the Deutsches Literaturarchiv in Marbach that bear witness to this relationship are not yet accessible, we know from Hannah Arendt herself that, twenty years after the end of their relationship, Heidegger stated that it had been "the passion of his life" (*dies nun einmal die Passion des Lebens gewesen sei*) and that *Being and Time* had thus been composed under the sign of love.[5]

How, then, is it possible to explain the absence of love from the analytic of Dasein? It is all the more perplexing if one considers that on

Hannah Arendt's part, the relationship produced precisely a book on love. I am referring to her *Doktordissertation* (published in 1929), *The Concept of Love in St. Augustine*, in which it is not difficult to discern Heidegger's influence. Why does *Being and Time* remain so obstinately silent on the subject of love?

Let us closely examine the note on love in *Being and Time*. It is to be found in §29, which is dedicated to the analysis of "state-of-mind" (*Befindlichkeit*) and "moods" (*Stimmungen*). The note does not contain even one word by Heidegger; it is composed solely of two citations. The first is from Pascal: "And thence it comes about that in the case where we are speaking of human things, it is said to be necessary to know them before we love them, and this has become a proverb; but the saints, on the contrary, when they speak of divine things, say that we must love them before we know them, and that we enter into truth only by charity; they have made of this one of their most useful maxims." The second is from Augustine: "One does not enter into truth except though charity" (*Non intramur in veritatem, nisi per charitatem*).[6] The two citations suggest a kind of ontological primacy of love as access to truth.

Thanks to the publication of Heidegger's last Marburg lectures from the summer semester of 1928, we know that the reference to this fundamental role of love originated in conversations with Max Scheler on the problem of intentionality. "Scheler first made it clear," Heidegger writes, "especially in the essay 'Liebe und Erkenntnis,' that intentional relations are quite diverse, and that even, for example, love and hatred ground knowing [*Lieben und Haß das Erkennen fundieren*]. Here Scheler picks up a theme of Pascal and Augustine."[7] In both the essay cited by Heidegger and a text of the same time published posthumously under the title *Ordo amoris*, Scheler repeatedly insists on the preeminent status of love. "Before he is an *ens cogitans* or an *ens volans*," we read in *Ordo amoris*, "man is an *ens amans*." Heidegger was thus perfectly conscious of the fundamental importance of love, in the sense that it conditions precisely the possibility of knowledge and the access to truth.

On the other hand, in the lectures of the 1928 summer course, love is referred to in the context of a discussion of the problem of intentionality in which Heidegger criticizes the established notion of intentionality as a cognitive relation between a subject and object. This text is precious since it demonstrates how Heidegger, through a critique that does not spare his teacher, Husserl, overcame the notion of intentionality and arrived at the structure of transcendence that *Being and Time* calls Being-in-the-world.

For Heidegger, what remains unexplained in the conception of intentionality as a relation between a subject and an object is precisely what is in need of explanation, that is, the relation itself:

> The vagueness of the relation falls back on the vagueness of that which stands in relation. . . . The most recent attempts conceive the subject-object relation as a "being relation" [*Seinsbeziehung*]. . . . Nothing is gained by the phrase "being relation," as long as it is not stated what sort of being is meant, and as long as there is vagueness about the sort of being [*Seinsart*] of the beings between which this relation is supposed to obtain. . . . Being, even with Nicolai Hartmann and Max Scheler, is taken to mean being-on-hand [*Vorhandensein*]. This relation is not nothing, but it is still not being as something on hand. . . . One of the main preparatory tasks of *Being and Time* is to bring this "relation" radically to light in its primordial essence and to do so with full intent.[8]

For Heidegger, the subject-object relation is less original than the self-transcendence of Being-in-the-world by which Dasein opens itself to the world before all knowledge and subjectivity. Before the constitution of anything like a subject or an object, Dasein—according to one of the central theses of *Being and Time*—is already open to the world: "knowing is grounded beforehand in a Being-already-alongside-the-world [*Schon-Sein-bei-der-Welt*]."[9] And only on the basis of this original transcendence can something like intentionality be understood in its own mode of Being.

If Heidegger therefore does not thematically treat the problem of love, although recognizing its fundamental status, it is precisely because the mode of Being of an opening that is more original than all knowledge (and that takes place, according to Scheler and Augustine, in love) is, in a certain sense, the central problem of *Being and Time*. On the other hand, if it is to be understood on the basis of this opening, love can no longer be conceived as it is commonly represented, that is, as a relation between a subject and an object or as a relation between two subjects. It must, instead, find its place and proper articulation in the Being-already-in-the-world that characterizes Dasein's transcendence.

But what is the mode of Being of this Being-already-in-the-world? In what sense is Dasein always already in the world and surrounded by things before even knowing them? How is it possible for Dasein to open itself to something without thereby making it into the objective correlate of a knowing subject? And how can the intentional relation itself be brought to light in its specific mode of Being and its primacy with respect to subject and object?

It is in this context that Heidegger introduces his notion of "facticity" (*Faktizität*).

Facticity and Dasein

The most important contribution made by the publication (which has barely begun) of Heidegger's lecture courses from the early 1920s consists in decisively showing the centrality of the notions of facticity and factical life (*faktisches Leben*) in the development of Heidegger's thought. The abandonment of the notion of intentionality (and of the concept of subject that was its correlate) was made possible by the establishment of this category. The path taken here was the following: intentionality-facticity-Dasein. One of the future tasks of Heideggerian philology will no doubt be to make this passage explicit and to determine its genealogy (as well as to explain the progressive eclipse of the concept of facticity in Heidegger's later thought). The observations that follow are only a first contribution in this direction.

First of all, it must be said that Heidegger's first students and friends long ago emphasized the importance of the concept of facticity in the formation of Heidegger's thought. As early as 1927, in a work that appeared as the second half of the *Jahrbuch für Philosophie und Phänomenologische Forschung* in which the first edition of *Being and Time* was published, the mathematician and philosopher Oskar Becker wrote, "Heidegger gives the name of ontology to the hermeneutics of facticity, that is, the interpretation of human Dasein."[10] Becker is referring here to the title of Heidegger's 1923 summer-semester course held in Freiburg, "Ontology, or Hermeneutics of Facticity."[11] What does this title mean? In what sense is ontology, the doctrine of Being, a doctrine of facticity?

The references to Husserl and Sartre that one finds in philosophical dictionaries under the heading "Facticity" are misleading here, for Heidegger's use of the term is fundamentally different from theirs. Heidegger distinguishes Dasein's *Faktizität* from *Tatsächlichkeit*, the simple factuality of intraworldly beings. At the start of his *Ideas*, Husserl defines the *Tatsächlichkeit* of the objects of experience. These objects, Husserl writes, appear as things found at determinate points in space and time that possess a certain content of reality but that, considered in their essence, could also be elsewhere and otherwise. Husserl thus insists on contingency (*Zufälligkeit*) as an essential characteristic of factuality. For Heidegger, by contrast, the proper trait of facticity is not *Zufälligkeit* but *Verfallenheit*. Everything is complicated, in Heidegger, by the fact that Dasein is not simply, as in Sartre, thrown into the "there" of a given contingency; instead, Dasein must rather itself be its "there," be the "there" (*Da*) of Being. Once again, the difference in modes of Being is decisive here.

The origin of the Heideggerian use of the term "facticity" is most likely to be found not in Husserl but in Augustine, who writes that *facticia est anima*,[12] "the human soul is *facticia*," in the sense that it was "made" by God. In Latin, *facticius* is opposed to *nativus*; it means *qui non sponte fit*, what is not natural, what did not come into Being by itself ("what is made by hand and not by nature," as one finds in the dictionaries). The term must be understood in all its force, for it is the same adjective that Augustine uses to designate pagan idols, in a sense that seems to correspond perfectly to our term "fetish": *genus facticiorum deorum*, the nature of "factical" gods.

If one wants to understand the development of the concept of facticity in Heidegger's thought, one should not forget this origin of the word, which ties it to the semantic sphere of non-originarity and making. What is important here is that for Heidegger, this experience of facticity, of a constitutive non-originarity, is precisely the original experience of philosophy, the only legitimate point of departure for thinking.

One of the first appearances of this meaning of the term *faktisch* is to be found (as far as one can judge from the present state of Heidegger's *Gesamtausgabe*) in the 1921 summer course on Augustine and Neoplatonism, which Otto Pöggeler and Oskar Becker have summarized.[13] Here Heidegger seeks to show that primitive Christian faith (as opposed to Neoplatonic metaphysics, which conceives of Being as a *stets Vorhandenes* and considers *fruitio dei*,[14] consequently, to be the rapture of an eternal presence) was an experience of life in its facticity and essential restlessness (*Unruhe*). As an example of this "factical experience of life" (*faktische Lebenserfahrung*), Heidegger analyzes a passage from chapter 23 of Book 10 of the *Confessions*, where Augustine questions man's relation to truth:

> I have known many men who wished to deceive, but none who wished to be deceived. . . . Because they hate to be deceived themselves, but are glad if they can deceive others, they love the truth when it reveals itself but hate it when

it reveals them [*cum se ipsa indicat . . . cum eos ipsos indicat*]. They reap their just reward, for those who do not wish to stand condemned by the truth find themselves unmasked against their will and also find that truth is veiled for them. This is precisely the behaviour of the human heart. In its blind inertia, in its abject shame, it loves to lie concealed, yet it wishes that nothing should be concealed from it [*latere vult se autem ut lateat aliquid non vult*]. Its reward is just the opposite of its desire, for it cannot conceal itself from the truth, but truth remains hidden in it [*ipse non lateat veritatem, ipsum autem veritas lateat*].[15]

What interests Heidegger here as a mark of factical experience is this dialectic of concealment and unconcealment, this double movement by which whoever wants to know everything while remaining concealed in knowledge is known by a knowledge that is concealed from him. Facticity is the condition of what remains concealed in its opening, of what is exposed by its very retreat. From the beginning, facticity is thus characterized by the same cobelonging of concealment and unconcealment that, for Heidegger, marks the experience of the truth of Being.

The same movement, the same restlessness of facticity was at the center of Heidegger's lectures for the Freiburg winter course of 1921–22, which bore the title "Phenomenological Interpretations of Aristotle." This course was to a large degree dedicated to the analysis of what Heidegger later called "factical life" (*das faktische Leben*), which still later would become Dasein. In the lectures Heidegger begins by describing the original and irreducible character of facticity for thought:

> [The determinations of factical life] are not indifferent qualities that can be harmlessly established, as when I say, "this thing is red." They are alive in facticity, that is, they enclose factical possibilities of which they can never be freed—never, thank God [*God sei Dank nie*]. As a consequence, to the degree that it is authentic, a philosophical interpretation directed toward what is most important [*die Hauptsache*] in philosophy, facticity, is itself factical; and it is factical in such a way that, as philosophico-factical, it radically gives itself possibilities of decision and thus itself. But it can do so only if it exists, in the guise of its Dasein [*wenn sie da ist—in der Weise ihres Daseins*].[16]

Far from signifying the immobility of a factual situation (as in Sartre or Husserl), facticity designates the "character of Being" (*Seinscharakter*) and "e-motion" (*Bewegtheit*) proper to life. The analysis Heidegger sketches here constitutes a kind of prehistory of the analytic of Dasein[17] and the self-transcendence of Being-in-the-world, whose fundamental determinations are all to be found here under different names. For factical life is never in the world as a simple object: "the e-motion [of factical life] is such that, as movement, it gives itself, in itself, to itself; it is the e-motion of factical life that constitutes factical life, such that factical life, insofar as it lives in the world, does not properly speaking produce its movement but, rather, lives in the world as the in-which [*worin*], the of-which [*worauf*] and the for-which [*wofür*] of life."[18]

Heidegger calls the "fundamental movement" (*Grundbewegung*) of facticity *Ruinanz* (from the Latin *ruina*, "tumbling," "fall"). This is the first appearance of the concept that will become *die Verfallenheit*, "falling," in *Being and Time*. *Ruinanz* presents the same intertwining of the proper and the improper, the *spontaneous* and the *facticious*, as the "thrownness" (*Geworfenheit*) of Dasein: "a movement that produces itself and that, nevertheless, does not produce itself, producing the emptiness in which it moves; for its emptiness is the possibility of movement."[19] And Heidegger likens facticity, insofar as it expresses the fundamental structure of life, to Aristotle's concept of *kinēsis*.[20]

What had not yet found definite expression in the courses at the start of the 1920s takes on, in *Being and Time*, the theoretical form that has become familiar to us today. Heidegger introduces the concept of facticity as early as §12, when he defines the "basic constitution" (*Grundverfassung*) of Dasein. To situate this concept correctly, one must, above all, place it in the context of a distinction between modes of Being. Being-in-the-world, Heidegger says, is not the property of a "present-at-hand" being (*ein Vorhandenes*) such as, for example, a corporeal thing (*Körperding*) that is in another thing of the same mode, like water in a glass or clothes in a wardrobe. Instead, Being-in-the-world expresses the very structure of Dasein; it concerns an "existential" and not a "categorial." Two worldless (*weltlose*) beings can certainly be beside each other (one thus says, for example, that the chair is near the wall), and we can even say that one touches the other. But to speak of touching in the proper sense of the word, for the chair to be truly near the wall (in the sense of Being-already-alongside-the-world), the chair would have to be able to encounter the wall.

How do matters stand with Dasein, who is not "worldless"? It is important to grasp the conceptual difficulty at issue here. It goes without saying that if Dasein were simply an intraworldly being, it could encounter neither the being it is nor other beings. On the other hand, however, if Dasein were deprived of all factuality, how could it encounter anything? To be near beings, to have a world, Dasein must so to speak be a "fact" (*Faktum*) without being factual (*Vorhandenes*); it must both be a "fact" (*Faktum*) and have a world. It is here that Heidegger introduces the notion of facticity:

> Dasein itself . . . [is] present-at-hand "in" the world, or, more exactly, *can* with some right and within certain limits be *taken* as merely present-at-hand. To do this, one must completely disregard or just not see the existential state of Being-in [*In-Sein*]. This latter kind of presence-at-hand becomes accessible not by disregarding Dasein's specific structures but only by understanding them in advance. Dasein understands its ownmost Being in the sense of a certain "factual Being-present-at-hand" [*tatsächlichen Vorhandenseins*]. And yet the factuality [*Tatsächlichkeit*] of the fact [*Tatsache*] of one's own Dasein is at bottom quite different ontologically from the factual occurrence of some kind of mineral, for example. Whenever Dasein is, it is as a Fact; and the factuality of such a Fact is what we shall call Dasein's *facticity*. This is a definite way of Being [*Seinsbestimmtheit*], and it has a complicated structure which cannot even be grasped *as a problem* until Dasein's basic existential states have been worked out. The concept of "facticity" implies that an entity "within-the-world" has Being-in-the-world in such a way that it can understand itself as bound up in its "destiny" with the Being of those entities which it encounters within its own world.[21]

As far as form is concerned, facticity presents us with the paradox of an existential that is also a categorial and a "fact" (*Faktum*) that is not factual. Neither "present-at-hand" (*vorhanden*) nor "ready-to-hand" (*zuhanden*), neither pure presence nor object of use, facticity is a specific mode of Being, one whose conceptualization marks Heidegger's reformulation of the question of Being in an essential manner. It should not be forgotten that this reformulation is above all a new articulation of the modes of Being.

The clearest presentation of the characteristics of facticity is to be found in §29 of *Being and Time*, which is devoted to the analysis of "state-of-mind" (*Befindlichkeit*) and "moods" (*Stimmungen*). An opening that precedes all knowledge and all lived experience (*Erlebnis*) takes place in the "state-of-mind": *die primäre Entdeckung der Welt*, "the original disclosure of the world." But what characterizes this disclosure is not the full light of the origin but precisely irreducible facticity and opacity. Through its "moods," Dasein is brought before other beings and, above all, before what it itself is; but since it does not bring itself there by itself, it is irremediably delivered over to what already confronts it and gazes upon it as an inexorable enigma:

> In having a mood, Dasein is always disclosed moodwise as that entity to which it has been delivered over in its Being; and in this way it has been delivered over to the Being which, in existing, it has to be. "To be disclosed" does not mean "to be known as this sort of thing." . . . The pure "that it is" shows itself, but the "whence" and the "whither" remain in darkness. . . . This characteristic of Dasein's Being—this "that it is"—is veiled in its "whence" and "whither," yet disclosed in itself all the more unveiledly; we call it the "thrownness" of this entity into its "there." The expression "thrownness" is meant to suggest the *facticity of its being delivered over*. . . . *Facticity is not the factuality of the* factum brutum *of something present-at-hand, but a characteristic of Dasein's Being—one which has been taken up into existence, even if proximally it has been thrust aside [abgedrängt].*[22]

Let us pause to consider the traits of this facticity, this factical being-thrown (we have seen that Heidegger leads "thrownness" back to facticity). Its origin and characteristic structure as a category organizing the analytic of Dasein have rarely been considered.

The first trait of facticity is *die ausweichende Abkehr*, "evasive turning-away." Dasein's openness delivers it over to something that it cannot escape but that nevertheless eludes it and remains inaccessible to it in its constant distraction: "the first essential characteristic of states-of-mind [is] that *they disclose Dasein in its thrownness, and—proximally and for the most part—in the manner of an evasive turning-away.*"[23]

A kind of original repression thus belongs to this character of Dasein's Being. The term Heidegger uses, "repressed" (*abgedrängt*), designates something that has been displaced, pushed back, but not completely effaced, something that remains present in the form of its retreat, as in Freudian "repression" (*Verdrängung*).[24] But Heidegger expresses the most essential trait of facticity, the trait from which all others derive, in a form that has many variations, even thought it remains constant in its conceptual core: "Dasein is delivered over to the being that it is and must be," "Dasein is and must be its own 'there,'" "Dasein is each time its possibility," "Dasein is the being whose Being is at issue for it in its very Being." What do these formulas mean as expressions of facticity?

Heidegger's 1928 Marburg summer-semester lectures (which often contain invaluable commentaries on certain crucial passages in *Being and Time*) explain the matter in absolutely unambiguous terms: "By it [the term 'Dasein'] we designate the being for which its own proper mode of Being in a definite sense is not indifferent," [*Dasein*] *bedeutet das Seiende, dem seine eigene Weise zu sein in einem bestimmten Sinne ungleichgültig ist.*[25]

Dasein must be its way of Being, its manner, its "guise," we could say, using a word that corresponds etymologically and semantically to the German *Weise*.[26] We must reflect on this paradoxical formulation, which for Heidegger marks the original experience of Being, without which both the repetition of the "question of Being" (*Seinsfrage*) and the relation between essence and existence sketched in §9 of *Being and Time* remain absolutely unintelligible. Here the two fundamental determinations of classical ontology—*existentia* and *essentia*, *quod est* and *quid est*, *Daß-sein* and *Wassein*—are abbreviated into a constellation charged with tension. For Dasein (insofar as it is and must be its own "there"), existence and essence, "Being" and "Being such," *on* and *poion* are as inseparable as they are for the soul in Plato's Seventh Letter (343 b–c).

> The *"essence"* of Dasein lies in its existence. The characteristics that can be exhibited in this entity are not, therefore, present-at-hand "properties" of some present-at-hand entity with particular properties; they are in each case possible ways for it to be, and no more than that. All the Being-as-it-is [*So-sein*] which this entity possesses is primarily Being.[27]

"All the Being-as-it-is [*So-sein*] which this entity possesses is primarily Being": one must think here not so much of the definition of the ontological status of God (*Deus est suum esse*, "God is his Being")[28] as of Schelling's positive philosophy and his concept of *das Seyende-Sein*, "being Being," where the verb "to be" also has a transitive sense; Dasein must be its being-such, it must "existentiate" its essence and "essentialize" its existence.[29]

As a "character of Being" (*Seinscharakter*), facticity thus expresses Dasein's original ontological character. If Heidegger can simultaneously pose the question of the meaning of Being anew and distance himself from ontology, it is because the Being at issue in *Being and Time* has the character of facticity from the beginning. This is why for Dasein, quality, *Sosein*, is not a "property" but solely a "possible guise" (*mögliche Weise*) to be (a formula that must be heard in accordance with the same ontological contraction that is expressed in Nicholas of Cusa's *possest*). Original opening is produced in this factical movement, in which Dasein must be its *Weise*, its fashion of Being, and in which Being and its guise are both distinguishable and the same. The term "fashion" must he heard here in its etymological sense (from *factio*, *facere*) and in the sense that the word has in Old French: "face," like the English "face." Dasein is factical, since it must be its face, its fashion, its manner—at once what reveals it and that into which it is irreparably thrown.

It is here that one must see the root of *ausweichende Abkehr*, "evasive turning-away," and of the impropriety constitutive of Dasein. It is because it must be its guise that Dasein remains disguised—hidden away in what opens it, concealed in what exposes it, and darkened by its own light. Such is the factical dimension of this "lighting" (*Lichtung*), which is truly something like a *lucus a non lucendo*.[30]

Here it is possible to see the full sense in which Heidegger's ontology is a hermeneutics of facticity. Facticity is not added to Dasein; it is inscribed in its very structure of Being. Here we are in the presence of something that could be defined, with an oxymoron, as "original facticity" or *Urfaktizität*. And it is precisely such an "original facticity" that the 1928 summer lectures call *transzendentale Zerstreuung*, "transcendental distraction, dispersion, or dissemination," or *ursprüngliche Streuung*, "original dispersion." I do not want to dwell on these passages, which have already been analyzed by Jacques Derrida.[31] It suffices to recall that here Heidegger sketches the figure of an original facticity that constitutes *die innere Möglichkeit für die faktische Zerstreuung in die Leiblichkeit und damit in die Geschlechtlichkeit*, "the intrinsic possibility for being factically dispersed into bodiliness and thus into sexuality."[32]

Facticity and Fetishism

How are we to understand this original facticity? Is *Weise* something like a mask that Dasein must assume? Is it here that a Heideggerian ethics finds its proper place?

Here the terms "factical" and "facticity" show their pertinence. The German adjective *faktisch*, like the French *factice*, appeared relatively late in the European lexicon: the German in the second half of the eighteenth century, the French a little earlier. But both terms are, in fact, erudite forms, based on the Latin, which hark back to ancient linguistic history. Thirteenth-century French, in accordance with its phonological laws, thus formed a number of terms on the basis of the Latin *faticius*, such as the adjective *faitis* (or *faitiche*, *fetiz*) and the noun *faitisseté*. At the same time, German, perhaps by borrowing the French term, formed the adjective *feit*. *Faitis*, like its German counterpart, *feit*, simply means "beautiful, pretty." In particular, it is used in conformity with its etymological origin to designate that which, in a human body, seems made by design, fashioned with skill, made-for, and which thereby attracts desire and love.[33] It is as if the Being-such of a being, its guise or manner, were separated from it in a kind of paradoxical self-transcendence. It is in the context of this semantic history that one must situate the appearance of the term "fetish" (in German, *Fetisch*). Dictionaries inform us that the term entered into European languages in the late seventeenth century by means of the Portuguese *feitiço*. But the word is in fact morphologically identical to the French *faitis*, which, through the borrowing from the Portuguese, is thus in some way resurrected.

An analysis of the term's meaning in its Freudian and Marxian senses is particularly instructive from this point of view. Let us recall that for Marx, the fetish character of the commodity, what makes it inappropriable, consists not in its artificial character but rather in the fact that in it a product of human labor is given both a use value and an exchange value. In the same way, for Freud, the fetish is not an inauthentic object. Instead, it is both the presence of something and the sign of its absence; it is and is not an object. And it is as such that it irresistibly attracts desire without ever being able to satisfy it.

One could say that in this sense the structure of Dasein is marked by a kind of original fetishism, *Urfetischismus*[34] or *Urfaktizität*, on account of which Dasein cannot ever appropriate the being it is, the being to which it is irreparably consigned. Neither something "present-at-hand" (*Vorhandenes*) nor something "ready-to-hand" (*Zuhandenes*), neither exchange value nor use value, Being—which must be its manners of Being—exists in facticity. But for this very reason, its "guises" (*Weisen*) are not simulacra that it could, as a free subject, assume or not assume. From the beginning, they belong to its existence and originally constitute its *ēthos*.[35]

The Proper and the Improper

This is the perspective from which we must read the unresolved dialectic of *eigentlich* and *uneigentlich*, the proper and the improper, to which Heidegger devotes some of the most beautiful pages of *Being and Time*. We know that Heidegger always specified that the words *eigentlich* and *uneigentlich* are to be heard in the etymological sense of "proper" and "improper." On account of its facticity, Dasein's opening is marked by an original impropriety; it is constitutively divided into "propriety" (*Eigentlichkeit*) and "impropriety" (*Uneigentlichkeit*). Heidegger often emphasizes that the dimension of impropriety and everydayness of the "They" (*das Man*) is not something derivative into which Dasein would fall by accident; on the contrary, impropriety is as originary as propriety. Heidegger obstinately reaffirms the original character of this cobelonging: "*Because Dasein is essentially falling, its state of Being is such that it is in 'untruth.'*"[36]

At times, Heidegger seems to retreat from the radicality of this thesis, fighting against himself to maintain a primacy of the proper and the true. But an attentive analysis shows not only that the co-originarity of the proper and the improper is never disavowed, but even that several passages could be said to imply a primacy of the improper. Whenever *Being and Time* seeks to seize hold of the experience of the proper (as, for example, in proper Being-toward-death), it does so solely by means of an analysis of impropriety (for example, factical Being-toward-death). The factical link between these two dimensions of Dasein is so intimate and original that Heidegger writes, "*authentic* existence is not something which floats above falling everydayness; existentially, it is only a modified way in which such everydayness is seized upon."[37] And on the subject of proper decision, he states, "resoluteness appropriates untruth authentically."[38]

Authentic existence has no content other than inauthentic existence; the proper is nothing other than the apprehension of the improper. We must reflect on the inevitable character of the improper that is implied in these formulations. Even in proper Being-toward-death and proper decision, Dasein seizes hold of its impropriety alone, mastering an alienation and becoming attentive to a distraction. Such is the originary status of facticity. But what does it mean to seize hold of impropriety? How is it possible to appropriate untruth properly? If one does not reflect on these questions and merely attributes to Heidegger a simple primacy of the proper, one will not only fail to understand the deepest intention of the analytic of Dasein; one will equally bar access to the thought of the *Ereignis*, which constitutes the key word of Heidegger's later thought and which has its "original history" (*Urgeschichte*), in Benjamin's sense of the term, in the dialectic of the proper and the improper.

Theory of Passions

Let us now return, after this long detour, to the problem of love that was our point of departure. An attentive analysis shows that the statement that Heidegger's thought is "without love" (*ohne Liebe*) is not only inexact from a philosophical point of view but also imprecise on the philological level. Several texts could be invoked here. I would like to pause to consider the two that strike me as the most important.

Almost ten years after the end of his relationship with Hannah Arendt, in the 1936 lecture course on Nietzsche entitled "The Will to Power as Art," Heidegger thematically treated the problem of love in several very dense pages in which he sketched an altogether singular theory of the passions. He begins by withdrawing passions from the domain of psychology by defining them as "the basic modes that constitute Dasein . . . the ways man confronts the *Da*, the openness and concealment of beings, in which he stands."[39] Immediately afterward, he clearly distinguishes love and hate from other feelings, positing them as passions (*Leidenschaften*) as opposed to simple affects (*Affekte*). While affects such as anger and joy are born and die away in us spontaneously, love and hate, as passions, are always already present and traverse our Being from the beginning. This is why we speak of "nurturing hatred" but not of "nurturing anger" (*ein Zorn wird genährt*).[40] We must cite at least the decisive passage on passion:

> Because hate traverses [*durchzieht*] our Being more originally, it has a cohesive power; like love, hate brings an original closure [*eine ursprüngliche Geschlossenheit*] and perdurance to our essential Being. . . . But the persistent closure that comes to Dasein through hate does not close it off and bind it. Rather, it grants vision and premeditation. The angry man loses the power of reflection. He who hates intensifies reflection and rumination to the point of "hardboiled" malice. Hate is never blind; it is perspicacious. Only anger is blind. Love is never blind: it is perspicacious. Only infatuation [*Verliebtheit*] is blind, fickle, and susceptible—an affect, not a passion [*ein Affekt, keine Leidenschaft*]. To passion belongs a reaching out and opening up of oneself [*das weit Ausgreifende, sich Öffnende*]. Such reaching out occurs even in hate, since the hated one is pursued everywhere relentlessly. But such reaching out [*Aus-*

griff] in passion does not simply lift us up and away beyond ourselves. It gathers our essential Being to its proper ground [*auf seinem eigentlichen Grund*], it exposes our ground for the first time in so gathering, so that the passion is that through which and in which we take hold of ourselves [*in uns selbst Fuß fassen*] and achieve lucid mastery of the beings around us and within us [*hellsichtig des Seiende um uns und in uns mächtig werden*].[41]

Hatred and love are thus the two *Grundweisen*, the two fundamental guises or manners, through which Dasein experiences the *Da*, the opening and retreat of the being that it is and must be. In love and hate, as opposed to affects (which are blind to the very thing they reveal and which, like *Stimmungen*, are only uncovered in distraction), man establishes himself more deeply in that into which he is thrown, appropriating his very facticity and thus gathering together and opening his own ground. It is therefore not an accident that hatred, with its "original closure," is given a primordial rank alongside love (like evil in Heidegger's course on Schelling and fury [*das Grimmige*] in his "Letter on Humanism"): the dimension at issue here is the original opening of Dasein, in which "there come[s] from Being itself the assignment [*Zuweisung*] of those directions [*Weisungen*] that must become law and rule for man."[42]

Potentia Passiva

This original status of love (more precisely, of passion) is reaffirmed in a passage in the "Letter on Humanism" whose importance here cannot be overestimated. In this text, "to love" (*lieben*) is likened to *mögen* (which means both "to want" and "to be able"), and *mögen* is identified with Being in a context in which the category of potentiality-possibility is considered in an entirely new fashion:

> To embrace a "thing" or a "person" in its essence means to love it [*sie lieben*], to favor it [*sie mögen*]. Thought in a more originary way, such favoring [*mögen*] means to bestow essence as a gift. Such favoring is the proper essence of enabling [*Vermögen*], which not only can achieve this or that but also can let something essentially unfold [*wesen*] in its provenance, that is, let it be. It is on the "strength" [*kraft*] of such enabling by favoring that something is properly able to be. This enabling is what is properly "possible" [*das eigentlich "Mögliche"*], that whose essence resides in favoring. . . . Being is the enabling-favoring, the "may be." As the element, Being is the "quiet power" of the favoring-enabling, that is, of the possible. Of course, our words *möglich* and

Möglichkeit, under the dominance of "logic" and "metaphysics," are thought solely in contrast to "actuality"; that is, they are thought on the basis of a definite—the metaphysical—interpretation of Being as *actus* and *potentia*, a distinction identified with the one between *existentia* and *potentia*. When I speak of the "quiet power of the possible" I do not mean the *possibile* of a merely represented *possibilitas*, nor *potentia* as the *essentia* of an *actus* of *existentia*; rather, I mean Being itself.[43]

To understand the thematic unity evoked here, it must be considered with respect to the problem of freedom as it is presented in the last pages of "On the Essence of Reasons." Once again, the dimension of facticity (better: of original or transcendental facticity) is essential: "For Dasein, to exist means to behave toward being [*Seiendes*] while situated in the midst of being [*Seiendes*]. It means to behave toward being that is not like Dasein, toward itself and toward being like itself, so that what is at issue in its situated behaving is the capacity to be [*Seinskönnen*] of Dasein itself. The project of world outstrips the possible; the Why arises in this outstripping."[44]

Freedom thus reveals Dasein in its essence to be "capable of being, with possibilities that gape open before its finite choice, that is, in its destiny."[45] Insofar as it exists factically (that is, insofar as it must be its manners of Being), Dasein always exists in the mode of the possible: in the excess of possibilities with respect to beings and, at the same time, in a lack of possibilities with respect to them, since its possibilities appear as radical incapacities in the face of the very being to which it is always already consigned.

This cobelonging of capacity and incapacity is analyzed in a passage in the 1928 summer lecture course, which anticipates the themes of "On the Essence of Reasons" in urging the superiority of the category of the possible over the category of the real:

Insofar . . . as freedom (taken transcendentally) constitutes the essence of Dasein, Dasein, as existing, is always, in essence, necessarily "further" than any given factical being. On the basis of this upswing, Dasein is, in each case, beyond beings, as we say, but it is beyond in such a way that it, first of all, experiences beings in their resistance, against which transcending Dasein is powerless. The powerlessness is metaphysical, i.e., to be understood as essential; it cannot be removed by reference to the conquest of nature, to technology, which rages about in the "world" today like an unshackled beast; for this domination of nature is the real proof for the metaphysical powerlessness of

Dasein, which can only attain freedom in its history. . . . Only because, in our factical intentional comportment toward beings of every sort, we, outstripping in advance, return to and arrive at beings from possibilities, only for this reason can we let beings themselves be what and how they are. And the converse is true. Because Dasein, as factically existing, transcending already, in each case, encounters beings and because, with transcendence and world-entry, the powerlessness, understood metaphysically, is manifest, for this reason Dasein, which can be powerless (metaphysically) only as free, must hold itself to the condition of the possibility of powerlessness, to the freedom to ground. And it is for this reason that we essentially place every being, as being, into question regarding its ground. We inquire into the why in our comportment toward beings of every sort, because in ourselves possibility is higher than actuality, because with Dasein itself this being-higher becomes existent.[46]

The passage on *mögen* (and its relation to love) in the "Letter on Humanism" must be read in close relation to this primacy of possibility. The *potentia* at issue here is essentially *potentia passiva*, the *dynamis tou paskhein* whose secret solidarity with active potentiality (*dynamis tou poiein*) Heidegger emphasized in his 1931 lecture course on Aristotle's *Metaphysics*. All potentiality (*dynamis*), Heidegger writes in his interpretation of Aristotle, is impotentiality (*adynamia*), and all capacity (*dynamis*) is essentially passivity (*dekhesthai*).[47] But this impotentiality is the place of an original event (*Urgeschehen*) that determines Dasein's Being and opens the abyss of its freedom: "What does not stand within the power of freedom is *that* Dasein is a self by virtue of its possibility—a factical self because it is free—and *that* transcendence comes about as a primordial happening. This sort of powerlessness (thrownness) is not due to the fact that being infects Dasein; rather, it defines the very Being of Dasein as such."[48]

Passion, *potentia passiva*, is therefore the most radical experience of possibility at issue in Dasein: a capacity that is capable not only of *potentiality* (the manners of Being that are in fact possible) but also, and above all, of *impotentiality*. This is why for Dasein, the experience of freedom coincides with the experience of impotentiality, which is situated at the level of the original facticity or "original dispersion" (*ursprüngliche Streuung*), which, according to the 1928 summer course, constitutes the "inner possibility" of Dasein's factical dispersion.

As passive potentiality and *Mögen*, passion is capable of its own impotentiality; it lets be not only the possible but also the impossible, thus gathering together Dasein in its ground, to open it and, possibly, to allow it to master what exists in it and around it. In this sense, the "immobile force of the possible" is essentially passion, passive potentiality: *mögen* (to be able) is *lieben* (to love).

But how can such mastery take place if it appropriates not a thing but simply impotentiality and impropriety? How is it possible to be capable not of possibility and potentiality but of an impossibility and impotentiality? What is freedom that is above all passion?

The Passion of Facticity

Here the problem of love, as passion, shows its proximity to that of the *Ereignis*, which constitutes the central motif of Heidegger's thought from the 1940s onward. Love, as passion of facticity, may be what makes it possible to cast light on the concept of the *Ereignis*. We know that Heidegger explains the word *Ereignis* on the basis of the term *eigen* and understands it as "appropriation," situating it with respect to *Being and Time*'s dialectic of *eigentlich* and *uneigentlich*. But here it is a matter of an appropriation in which what is appropriated is neither something foreign that must become proper nor something dark that must be illuminated. What is appropriated here and brought not to light but to "lighting" (*Lichtung*) is solely an expropriation, an occultation as such. "Appropriation is in itself *expropriation*. This word contains in a manner commensurate with Appropriation the early Greek *lēthē* in the sense of concealing" (*Das Ereignis ist in ihm selbst Enteignis, in welches Wort die frühgriechische* lêthê *im Sinne des Verbergens ereignishaft aufgenommen ist*).[49] The thought of the *Ereignis* is thus "not an extinguishing of the oblivion of Being, but placing oneself in it and standing within it. Thus the awakening [*erwachen*] from the oblivion of Being to the oblivion of Being is the unawakening [*entwachen*] into Appropriation."[50] What now takes place is that concealment no longer conceals itself but becomes "the attention of thinking" (*die Verbergung sich nicht verbirgt, ihr gilt vielmehr das Aufmerksam des Denkens*).[51]

What do these enigmatic sentences mean? If what human beings must appropriate here is not a hidden thing but the very fact of hiddenness, Dasein's very impropriety and facticity, then "to appropriate it" can only be *to be properly improper*, to abandon oneself to the inappropriable. Withdrawal, *lēthē*, must come to thinking as such; facticity must show itself in its concealment and opacity.

The thought of the *Ereignis*, insofar as it is the end of the history of Being, is therefore in a certain sense also a repetition and completion of the thought of facticity that, in the early Heidegger, marked the reformulation of the "question of Being" (*Seinsfrage*). Here it is an issue not simply of the many manners (*Weisen*) of Dasein's factical existence but of the original facticity (or transcendental dispersion) that constitutes its "inner possibility" (*innere Möglichkeit*). The *Mögen* of this *Möglichkeit* is neither potentiality nor actuality, neither essence nor existence; it is, rather, an impotentiality whose passion, in freedom, opens the ground of Dasein. In the *Ereignis*, original facticity no longer retreats, either in distracted dispersion or historical destiny, but is instead appropriated in its very distraction and borne in its *lēthē*.

The dialectic of the proper and the improper thus reaches its end. Dasein no longer has to be its own *Da* and no longer has to be its own *Weisen*: by now, it definitively inhabits them in the mode of the "dwelling" (*Wohnen*) that in §12 of *Being and Time* characterized Dasein's Being-in (*In-Sein*).

In the word *Ereignis*, we should therefore hear the Latin *assuescere*, "accustoming," on the condition of thinking the "*suus*" in this term, the "self" (*se*) that constitutes its core. And if one remembers that the origin of Dasein's destinal character was (according to §9 of *Being and Time*) its "having to be," it is also possible to understand why the *Ereignis* is without destiny, *geschickslos*. Here Being (the possible) has truly exhausted its historical possibilities, and Dasein, who is capable of its own incapacity, attains its own extreme manner: the *immobile* force of the possible.

This does not mean that all facticity is abolished and that all e-motion is effaced. "The lack of destiny of Appropriation does not mean that it has no 'e-motion' [*Bewegtheit*]. Rather, it means that the manner of movement most proper to Appropriation, turning toward us in withdrawal [*Zuwendung in Entzug*], first shows itself as what is to be thought."[52] This is the sense of the *Gelassenheit*, the "abandonment," that a late text defines as *die Offenheit für das Geheimnis*, "the openness to the mystery":[53] *Gelassenheit* is the e-motion of the *Ereignis*, the eternally nonepochal opening to the "ancient something [*Uralte*] which conceals itself in the word *a-lētheia*."[54]

We may now approach a provisional definition of love. What man introduces into the world, his "proper," is not simply the light and opening of knowledge but above all the opening to concealment and opacity. *Alētheia*, truth, is the safeguard of *lēthē*, nontruth; memory, the safeguard of oblivion; light, the safeguard of darkness. It is only in the insistence of this abandonment, in this safeguarding, which is forgetful of everything, that something like knowledge and attention can become possible.

Love suffers all of this (in the etymological sense of the word passion, *pati, paskhein*). Love is the *passion of facticity* in which man bears this nonbelonging and darkness, appropriating (*adsuefacit*) them while guarding them as such. Love is thus not, as the dialectic of desire suggests, the affirmation of the self in the negation of the loved object; it is, instead, the passion and exposition of facticity itself and of the irreducible impropriety of beings. *In love, the lover and the beloved come to light in their concealment, in an eternal facticity beyond Being.* (This is perhaps what Hannah Arendt means when, in a text written with her first husband in 1930, she cites Rilke, saying that love "is the possibility for each to veil his destiny to the other.")

Just as in *Ereignis*, the appropriation of the improper signifies the end both of the history of Being and of the history of epochal sendings, so in love the dialectic of the proper and the improper reaches its end. This, finally, is why there is no sense in distinguishing between authentic love and inauthentic love, heavenly love and *pandemios* love, the love of God and self-love. Lovers bear the impropriety of love to the end so that the proper can emerge as the appropriation of the free incapacity that passion brings to its end. Lovers go to the limit of the improper in a mad and demonic promiscuity; they dwell in carnality and amorous discourse, in forever-new regions of impropriety and facticity, to the point of revealing their essential abyss. Human beings do not originally dwell in the proper; yet they do not (according to the facile suggestion of contemporary nihilism) inhabit the improper and the ungrounded. Rather, *human beings are those who fall properly in love with the improper, who—unique among living beings—are capable of their own incapacity.*

This is why if it is true that, according to Jean-Luc Nancy's beautiful phrase, love is that of which we are not masters, that which we never reach but which is always happening to us, it is also true that man can appropriate this incapacity and that, to cite Hölderlin's words to Casimir Ulrich Böhlendorff, *der freie Gebrauch des Eigenen das Schwerste ist*, the free use of the proper is the most difficult task.

§ 13 *Pardes*: The Writing of Potentiality

Pardes

The second chapter of the talmudic treatise *Hagigah* (literally, "Offering") considers those matters that it is permitted to study and those that must not in any case become objects of investigation. The Mishnah with which the chapter opens reads as follows:

> Forbidden relationships must not be explained in the presence of three [people]; the work of creation must not be explained in the presence of two [people]; the Chariot [*merkebah*, the chariot of Ezekiel's vision, which is the symbol of mystical knowledge] must not be explained in the presence of one, unless he is a sage who already knows it on his own. It is better never to have been born than to be someone who investigates into the four things. The four things are: what is above; what is below; what is first; and what is after [that is, the object of mystical knowledge, but also metaphysical knowledge, which claims to study the supernatural origin of things].

At 14 b we find the following story, which marks the beginning of a brief cycle of aggadoth concerning Elisha ben Abuya, who is called "Aher" (literally, the "Other") after having sinned:

> Four rabbis entered *Pardes*: Ben Azzai, Ben Zoma, Aher, and Rabbi Akiba. Rabbi Akiba said, "When you reach the stones of pure marble, do not say: 'Water! Water!' For it has been said that *he who says what is false will not be placed before My eyes*." Ben Azzai cast a glance and died. Of him Scripture says: *precious to the eyes of the Lord is the death of his saints*. Ben Zoma looked and went mad. Of him Scripture says: *have you found honey? Eat as much as you can, otherwise you will be full and you will vomit*. Aher cut the branches. Rabbi Akiba left unharmed.

According to rabbinical tradition, *Pardes* ("garden," "Paradise") signifies supreme knowledge. In the Cabala, the Shechinah, the presence of God, is thus called *Pardes ha-torah*, the Paradise of the Torah, that is, its fullness, its fulfilled revelation. This gnostic interpretation of the term "Paradise" is common to many heretical movements, both Christian and Jewish. Almeric of Bène, whose followers were burnt at the stake on November 12, 1210, stated that Paradise is "the knowledge of truth, and we should await no other."

The entry of the four rabbis into *Pardes* is therefore a figure for access to supreme knowledge, and the aggadah contains a parable on the mortal risks inherent in this access. What, from this perspective, is the significance of the "cutting of the branches" attributed to Aher in the context of Ben Azzai's death and Ben Zoma's madness? We do not know for certain, but the Cabala identifies the "cutting of the branches" with the gravest sin that can be committed on the road to knowledge. This sin is defined as "isolation of the Shechinah" and consists in the separation of the Shechinah from the other Sefiroth and in the comprehension of it as an autonomous power. For the Cabalists, the Shechinah is the last of the ten Sefiroth, that is, attributes or words of God, and it is the one that expresses the divine presence itself, God's manifestation or dwelling on earth. In cutting the branches (that is, the other Sefiroth), Aher separates the knowledge and revelation of God from the other aspects of divinity.

It is therefore not an accident if, in other texts, the cutting of branches is identified with the sin of Adam, who, instead of contemplating the totality of the Sefiroth, preferred to contemplate only the last one, which seemed in itself to represent all the others. In this way, he separated the tree of knowledge from the tree of life. The Aher-Adam analogy is significant; like Adam, Aher, the "Other," represents humanity insofar as he isolates knowledge, which is nothing other than the fulfilled form of divine manifestation, from the other Sefiroth in which divinity shows itself, making knowledge into his own destiny and specific power. In this condition of "exile," the Shechinah loses its powers and becomes maleficent (with a striking image, the Cabalists say that it "sucks the milk of evil").

Exile

Moses of Leon, the author of the *Zohar*, offers us a different interpretation of the story of the four rabbis. According to his reading, the aggadah is in truth a parable on the exegesis of the sacred text and, more precisely, on the four senses of Scripture. Each of the four consonants of the word *Pardes* refers to one of the senses: P stands for *peshat*, the literal sense; R stands for *ramez*, the allegorical sense; D stands for *derasha*, talmudic interpretation; and S stands for *sod*, the mystical sense. Correspondingly, in the *Tikunei ha-Zohar*, each of the four rabbis incarnates one level of interpretation: Ben Azzai, who enters and dies, is the literal sense; Ben Zoma is the talmudic sense; Aher is the allegorical sense; and Akiba, who enters and leaves unharmed, is the mystical sense. How, from this perspective, is one to understand Aher's sin? In the cutting of the branches and the isolation of the Shechinah we can see a moral risk implicit in every act of interpretation, in every confrontation with a text or discourse, whether human or divine. This risk is that speech, which is nothing other than the manifestation and the unconcealment of something, may be separated from what it reveals and acquire an autonomous consistency. It is significant that the *Zohar* elsewhere defines the isolation of the Shechinah as a separation of the word from the voice (the Sefira *Tipheret*). The cutting of the branches is, therefore, an *experimentum linguae*, an experience of language that consists in separating speech both from the voice and pronunciation and from its reference. A pure word isolated in itself, with neither voice nor referent, with its semantic value indefinitely suspended: this is the dwelling of Aher, the "Other," in Paradise. This is why he can neither perish in Paradise by adhering to meaning, like Ben Zoma and Ben Azzai, nor leave unharmed, like Rabbi Akiba. He fully experiences the exile of the Shechinah, that is, human language. Of him, the Talmud says: "he will not be judged, nor will he enter into the world to come."

Terminus

Benjamin once wrote that terminology is the proper element of thought and that, for every philosopher, the *terminus* in itself encloses the nucleus of his system. In Latin, *terminus* means "limit, border." It was originally the name of a divinity who was still represented in the classical age as an anthropomorphous figure whose body gradually faded away into a dot firmly planted on the ground. In medieval logic, which transmitted the word's current sense to modern languages, a "term" was a word that did not signify itself (*suppositio materialis*) but instead stood for the thing it signified, referring to something (*terminus supponit pro re, supposito personalis*). According to this conception, a thought without terms—a thought unfamiliar with a point at which thought ceases to refer to itself and is firmly grounded on the soil of reference—is not a philosophical thought. Ockham, the head of the school of philosophers usually defined as "terminists," therefore excluded from terms in the strict sense conjunctions, adverbs, and other syncategorematic expressions. In the terminology of modern philosophy, it is no longer possible to maintain either the clear opposition between self-reference and reference or the exclusion of syncategorematic terms (if, that is, one admits that it ever was). It was already impossible to say whether certain fundamental terms of Kantian thought (such as the transcendental object and the thing in itself) were referential or self-referential. Since Kant, moreover, the terminological relevance of syncategorematic expressions has been steadily growing. M. Puder thus noted the importance of the adverb *gleichwohl* in the articulation of Kantian philosophy. And in his Marburg lectures of summer 1927, Heidegger called attention to the frequency of the adverb *schon* and this word's relevance for the proper determination of the problem of temporality. Even a simple punctuation mark can acquire a terminological character. The strategic importance of hyphens in *Being and Time* (as in the expression "Being-in-the-world") thus did not escape an observer as attentive as Karl Löwith.

If it is true that, as has been efficiently stated, terminology is the poetry of thought, this displacement and transformation of the properly *poetic* moment of thought undoubtedly characterizes contemporary philosophy. But this does not mean that philosophical terms have lost their specific sense and that, abandoning its name-giving gesture, philosophy has therefore become indistinguishable from literature and has been returned to the "conversation" of humanity, as some have argued. Philosophical terms remain names, but their referential character can no longer be understood simply according to the traditional scheme of signification; it now implies a different and decisive experience of language. Terms, indeed, become the place of a genuine *experimentum linguae*.

This crisis (in the etymological sense) of terminology is the proper situation of thought today, and Jacques Derrida is the philosopher who has perhaps most radically taken this situation into account. His thought interrogates and calls into question precisely the terminological moment (hence the properly poetic moment) of thinking, exposing its *crisis*. This explains the success of deconstruction in contemporary philosophy, as well as the polemics that surround it. Deconstruction suspends the terminological character of philosophical vocabulary; rendered inde-terminate, terms seem to float interminably in the ocean of sense. This is not, of course, an operation accomplished by deconstruction out of capriciousness or unnatural violence; on the contrary, precisely this calling into question of philosophical terminology constitutes deconstruction's insuperable contemporaneity.

Nevertheless, it would be the worst misunderstanding of Derrida's gesture to think that it could be exhausted in a deconstructive use of philosophical terms that would simply consign them to an infinite wandering or interpretation. Although he calls into question the poetico-terminological moment of thinking, Derrida does not abdicate its naming power; he still "calls" by names (as when Spinoza says, "by *causa sui* I understand . . . ," or when Leibniz writes, "the Monad, of which we will speak here . . ."). For Derrida, there is certainly a philosophical terminology; but the status of this terminology has wholly changed, or more exactly, has revealed the abyss on which it always rested. Like Aher, Derrida enters into the Paradise of language, where terms touch their limits. And, like Aher, he "cuts the branches"; he experiences the exile of terminology, its paradoxical subsistence in the isolation of all univocal reference.

But what is at issue in the terms of Derrida's thought? What is named by a philosophical terminology that no longer wants to refer to something and yet, at the same time, above all experiences the fact that there are names? What can be the meaning of a *terminus interminatus*? And if all thought defines itself above all through a certain experience of language, what is the *experimentum linguae* of Derrida's terminology?

Nomen Innomabile

Derrida himself has often defined the status of his own terminology. In the three passages that follow, this status is determined as *nonname*, as undecidable and as trace:

> For us, *différance* remains a metaphysical name, and all the names that it receives in our language are still, as names, metaphysical. . . . "Older" than Being itself, such a *différance* has no name in our language. But we "already know" that if it is unnamable, it is provisionally so, not because our language has not yet found or received this *name*, or because we would have to seek it

in another language. . . . It is rather because there is no *name* for it at all, not even the name of essence or of Being, not even that of "*différance*," which is not a name, which is not a pure nominal unity, and unceasingly dislocates itself in a chain of differing and deferring substitutions. . . . This unnamable is not an ineffable Being which no name could approach: God, for example. This unnamable is the play which makes possible nominal effects, the relatively unitary and atomic structures that are called names, the chains of substitutions of names in which, for example, the nominal effect *différance* is itself *enmeshed*, carried off, reinscribed.[1]

Henceforth, in order better to mark this interval . . . it has been necessary to analyze, to set to work, *within* the text of the history of philosophy, as well as *within* the so-called literary text . . . certain marks . . . that *by analogy* . . . I have called undecidables, that is, unities of simulacrum, "false" verbal properties (nominal or semantic) that can no longer be included within philosophical (binary) opposition, but which, however, inhabit philosophical opposition, resisting and disorganizing it, *without ever* constituting a third term. . . . It is a question of re-marking a nerve, a fold, an angle that interrupts totalization: in a certain place, a place of well-determined form, no series of semantic valences can any longer be closed or reassembled. Not that it opens onto an inexhaustible wealth of meaning or the transcendence of a semantic excess. By means of this angle, this fold, this doubled fold of an undecidable, a mark marks both the marked and the mark, the re-marked site of the mark. The writing which, at this moment, re-marks itself (something completely other than a representation of itself) can no longer be counted on the list of themes (it is not a theme, and can in no case become one); it must be subtracted from (hollow) and added to (relief) the list.[2]

The relationship between the two texts, between presence in general . . . and that which exceeds it . . . —such a relationship can never offer itself in order to be read in the form of presence, supposing that anything ever can offer itself in order to be *read* in such a form. And yet, that which gives us to think beyond the closure cannot be simply absent. Absent, either it would give us nothing to think or it still would be a negative mode of presence. Therefore the sign of this excess must be absolutely excessive as concerns all possible presence-absence, all possible production or disappearance of beings in general, and yet, *in some manner* it must still signify, in a manner unthinkable by metaphysics as such. In order to exceed metaphysics it is necessary that a trace be inscribed within the text of metaphysics, a trace that continues to signal not in the direction of another presence, or another form of presence, but in the direction of an entirely other text. . . . The mode of inscription of such a trace in the text of metaphysics is so unthinkable that it must be described as an erasure of the trace itself. The trace is produced as its own erasure. And it belongs to the trace to erase itself, to elude that which might maintain it in presence. The trace is neither perceptible nor imperceptible. . . . Presence, then, far from being, as is commonly thought, *what* the sign signifies, what a trace refers to, presence, then, is the trace of the trace, the trace of the erasure of the trace.[3]

Paradoxes

What status is ascribed to the term in these three dense passages? First of all, the nonname *différance* (like Derrida's other terms) does not refer to something unnamable or ineffable, a *quid* beyond language for which names would be lacking. What is unnamable is *that there are names* ("the play which makes possible nominal effects"); what is nameless yet in some way signified is the name itself. This is why the point from which every interpretation of Derrida's terminology must depart (its "literal sense," to take up the Cabalistic exegesis of the aggadah of Aher) is its self-referential structure: "the sign of this excess must be absolutely excessive as concerns all possible presence-absence, all possible production or disappearance of beings in general, and yet, *in some manner* it must still signify," "by means of this angle, this fold, this doubled fold of an undecidable, a mark marks both the marked and the mark."

Deprived of its referential power and its univocal reference to an object, the term still *in some manner* signifies itself; it is self-referential. In this sense, even Derrida's undecidables (even if they are such only "by analogy") are inscribed in the domain of the paradoxes of self-reference that have marked the crisis of the logic of our time. Here it is possible to observe the insufficiency of the manner in which both philosophical and linguistic reflection have generally understood the problem of self-reference. This manner owes much to the medieval distinction between *intentio prima* and *intentio secunda*. In medieval logic, an *intentio prima* is a sign that signifies not another sign or an *intentio* but an object; it is a referential term (*signum natum supponere pro suo significato*). An *intentio secunda* is, instead, a sign that signifies an *intentio prima*. But what does it mean to signify a sign, to intend an *intentio*? How is it possible to intend an *intentio* without turning it into an object, an *intentum*? Are the two modes (first and second) of *intentio* truly homogeneous? Do they differ only with regard to their object?

The insufficiency here consists in the fact that *intentio secunda* (the intention of a sign) is thought according to the scheme of *intentio prima* (reference to an object). Self-reference is thus referred to the acoustic or graphic consistency of the word, that is, to the identity of the term as an object (the *suppositio materialis* of medieval logicians). There is thus, properly speaking, no self-reference, since the term signifies a segment of the world and not intentionality itself. What is understood is not truly an *intentio* but a thing, an *intentum*.

Only if one abandons this first level of self-referentiality (or rather, pseudo-self-referentiality) does one reach the heart of the problem. But everything, for that very reason, is then complicated. For there to be the signification of an intentionality and not of an object, it is necessary that the term signify itself, but *signify itself only insofar as it signifies*. It is thus necessary that the *intentio* neither be a referent nor, for that matter, simply refer to an object. In the semiotic scheme by which *aliquid stat pro aliquo*, A stands for B, the *intentio* cannot indicate the first *aliquid* or the second; it must, rather, above all refer to the "standing for" itself. The aporia of Derrida's terminology is that in it, one *standing for* stands for another *standing for*, without anything like an objective referent constituting itself in its presence. But, accordingly, the very notion of sense (of "standing for") then enters into a state of crisis. This is the root of the particular terseness of Derrida's terminology.

For an intention to refer to itself and not to an object, it must exhaust itself neither in the pure presence of an *intentum* nor in its absence. But the status of Derrida's terminology therefore follows coherently from the notion of trace as it is elaborated in *Speech and Phenomena* and *Of Grammatology*. In its inaugural gesture, the grammatological project appeared above all as a "destruction of the concept of the 'sign'" and as a "liberation of semiotics" in which "the self-identity of the signified retreats and is infinitely dislocated." In Derrida, the irreducible character of signification implies the impossibility of the "extinction of the signifier in the voice" grounding the Western conception of truth. "Trace" names precisely this inextinguishable instance of *repraesentamen* in every presence, this excess of signification in all sense. To return to the terms of medieval logic, there can be neither an *intentio prima* nor an *intentio secunda*; every intention is always *secundo-prima* or *primo-secunda*, such that in it intentionality always exceeds intent and signification always anticipates and survives the signified. This is why

> the trace is not only the disappearance of the origin . . . it means that the origin did not even disappear, that it was never constituted except reciprocally by a nonorigin, the trace, which thus becomes the origin of the origin. From

then on, to wrench the concept of the trace from the classical scheme, which would derive it from a presence or from an originary nontrace and which would make of it an empirical mark, one must indeed speak of an originary trace or arche-trace. Yet we know that that concept destroys its name and that, if all begins with the trace, there is above all no originary trace.[4]

The concept "trace" is not a concept (just as "the name '*différance*' is not a name"): this is the paradoxical thesis that is already implicit in the grammatological project and that defines the proper status of Derrida's terminology. Grammatology was forced to become deconstruction in order to avoid this paradox (or, more precisely, to seek to dwell in it correctly); this is why it renounced any attempt to proceed by decisions about meaning. But in its original intention, grammatology is not a theory of polysemy or a doctrine of the transcendence of meaning; it has as its object not an equally inexhaustible, infinite hermeneutics of signification but a radicalization of the problem of self-reference that calls into question and transforms the very concept of meaning grounding Western logic.

From this perspective, the central paradox of grammatology ("The concept 'trace' is not a concept") strikingly recalls the paradox that Frege, in 1892, stated in "Object and Concept," and which was the first sign of the crisis that a few years later shook the edifice of formal logic: "the concept 'horse' is not a concept." Frege's paradox (as defined by Philippe de Rouilhan in a recent book) consists in the fact that every time we *name* a concept (instead of using it as a predicate in a proposition), it ceases to function as a concept and appears as an object. We think we mean an object (*ein Begriff gemeint ist*) but, instead, we are naming an object (*ein Gegenstand genannt ist*); we intend an *intentio* but we find ourselves before an *intentum*.[5]

Frege's paradox is thus the consequence of a more general principle that can be stated in the following fashion: *a term cannot refer to something and, at the same time, refer to the fact that it refers to it.* Or, taking up the White Knight's line in *Through the Looking-Glass*: "the name of the name is not the name." It is worth noting that this "White Knight's theorem" lies at the basis both of Wittgenstein's thesis according to which "*we* cannot express through language what expresses *itself* in language" and Milner's linguistic axiom, "the linguistic term has no proper name."[6] In each case, what is essential is that if I want to say an *intentio*, to name the name, I will no longer be able to distinguish between word and thing, concept and object, the term and its reference.

As Reach showed for Carnap's attempt to name the name through quotation marks and as is implicit in Gödel's theorem, the logicians' expedients to avoid the consequences of this radical anonymity of the name are destined to fail. It does not suffice, however, to underline (on the basis of Gödel's theorem) the necessary relation between a determinate axiomatics and undecidable propositions: what is decisive is solely how one conceives this relation. It is possible to consider an undecidable as a purely negative *limit* (Kant's *Schranke*), such that one then invokes strategies (Bertrand Russell's theory of types or Alfred Tarski's metalanguage) to avoid running up against it. Or one can consider it as a *threshold* (Kant's *Grenze*), which opens onto an exteriority and transforms and dislocates all the elements of the system.

This is why the notion of "trace" constitutes the specific achievement of Derrida's thought. He does not limit himself to reformulating logical paradoxes; rather, like Heidegger—who in *On the Way to Language* wrote, "there is no word for the word," and proposed an experience of language in which language itself came to language—Derrida makes these paradoxes into the place of an experiment in which the very notion of sense must be transformed and must give way to the concept of trace. But why does the attempt to name the name now take the form of "a writing without presence and without absence, without history, without cause, without *archē*, without *telos*, absolutely dislocating all dialectics, all theology, all teleology, all ontology"? What is the nature of Derrida's *experimentum linguae*, if it must have the form of writing?

Scribe

The late Byzantine lexicon that goes under the name of *Suda* contains, in the entry "Aristotle," the following definition: *Aristotelēs tēs physeōs grammateus ēn ton kalamon apobrekhōn eis noun*, "Aristotle was the scribe of nature who dipped his pen in thought." In a slightly altered form, this definition had already appeared in Cassiodorus (and was then passed on to Bede and Isidore of Seville), where it characterized not the "scribe of nature" but, instead, Aristotle the logician: *Aristoteles, quando perihermeneias scriptabat, calamum in mente tingebat*, "When he wrote *De interpretatione*, Aristotle dipped his pen in thought." According to this tradition, the work grounding the Western conception of linguistic signification and its link to thought was written "by dipping a pen in thought." Thought was able to write about the relation between language and thought and between thought and the world only by referring purely to itself, filling its pen with the ink of its own opacity.

What is the origin of this striking metaphor? What in Aristotle's text could have authorized the image of a "writing of thought"? And what would such a writing be?

A comparison between thought and the act of writing is contained in the famous passage of *De anima* (430 a 1) in which Aristotle likens the potential intellect to a writing tablet (*grammateion*) on which nothing is written: "the mind [nous] is like a writing tablet on which nothing is actually written." This famous image of a *tabula rasa* (or rather, as Alexander of Aphrodisias suggests, of a *rasum tabulae*, that is, of the light stratum of wax on which the pen inscribed characters) is contained in the section of *De anima* devoted to the potential or passive intellect (*nous pathetikos*). The nature of the intellect is such that it is pure potentiality (429 a 21–22: "It [*nous*] has no other nature other than that of being potential, and before thinking it is absolutely nothing"). *Nous* is thus a potentiality that exists as such, and the metaphor of the writing tablet on which nothing is written expresses the way in which a pure potentiality exists. All potential to be or do something is, for Aristotle, always also potential not to be or not to do (*dynamis mē einai, dynamis mē energein*), without which potentiality would always already have passed into act and be indistinguishable from it (this is the thesis held by the Megarians, whom Aristotle explicitly refutes in Book Theta of the *Metaphysics*). This *potential not to* is the cardinal secret of the Aristotelian doctrine of potentiality, which transforms every potentiality in itself into an impotentiality (*pasa dynamis adynamia* [*Metaphysics*, 1046 a 32]). Just as the geometer is a geometer because he is capable of not doing geometry, and just as the kithara player is a kithara player because he is capable of not playing the kithara, so thought exists as a potential not to think (the potential intellect of the medievals), as a writing tablet on which nothing is written. The pure potentiality of thought is a potentiality that is capable of not thinking, that is capable of not passing into actuality. But this pure potentiality (the *rasum tabulae*) is itself intelligible; it can itself be thought: "it [the intellect] is intelligible like other intelligibles" (*De anima*, 430 a 2).

It is in the light of this conception of potentiality that we must read the passage of *De anima* in which Aristotle repeats the argument of Book Lambda of the *Metaphysics* concerning thinking that thinks itself: "When the mind [the potential intellect] has actually become all [of the intelligibles], as the learned man when active is said to do (and this happens when he can exercise his function by himself), even then the mind is in a sense potential . . . and is then capable of thinking itself" (429 b 6–10).[7] The thinking of thinking is first of all a potential to think (and *not to think*) that is turned back upon itself, *potentia potentiae*. Only on this basis is it possible to comprehend fully the doctrine of Book Lambda on *noēsis noēseōs*, the "thinking of thinking"; pure actuality, that is, the actuality of an act, is pure potentiality, that is, the potentiality of a potentiality.

The apothegm on the scribe of nature who dips his pen in thought thus acquires its proper sense as the image of a *writing of potentiality*. Aristotle could write his logical works (that is, those that treat the pure potentiality of thought and language) only by dipping his pen in *nous*, that is, in pure potentiality. Potentiality, which turns back on itself, is an absolute writing that no one writes: a potential to be written, which is written by its own potential not to be written, a *tabula rasa* that suffers its own receptivity and can therefore *not not-write itself*. According to Albert the Great's felicitous intuition in his commentary on *De anima*: *hoc simile est, sicut diceremus, quod litterae scribent se ipsas in tabula*, it is as if "the letters wrote themselves on the tablet."

Matter

It is in the context of this writing of the potentiality that no one writes that we must situate Derrida's concept of the trace and its aporias. The trace is nothing other than the most rigorous attempt to reconsider—against the primacy of actuality and form—the Aristotelian paradox of potentiality, the gesture of the scribe who dips his pen in thought and writes solely with his potentiality (not to write). The trace, writing "without presence or absence, without history, without cause, without *arkhē*, without *telos*," is not a form, nor is it the passage from potentiality to actuality; rather, it is a potentiality that is *capable* and that experiences itself, a writing tablet that suffers not the impression of a form but the imprint of its own passivity, its own formlessness.

But everything is then once again complicated. For what can it mean to think neither a thing nor a thought, but a pure potential to think, to name neither objects nor referential terms, but the pure *dynamis* of

speech, to write neither texts nor letters, but the pure potential to write?
What does it mean to experience a potentiality, to experience a passivity,
if the words "experience" and "passion" still have meaning here? Does the
aporia of self-reference, which the writing of potentiality aimed to resolve,
not then return once again?

A passage from Plotinus's treatise "On the Two Matters" poses precisely
these questions. How, Plotinus asks, is it possible to conceive of a non-
form (*amorphon*) and an indetermination (*aoristia*)? How is it possible to
grasp what has neither size nor form? Only through an indetermination
will it be possible to conceive of an indetermination:

> What, then, is this indetermination in the Soul? Does it amount to an utter
> absence of Knowledge [*agnoia*], as if the Soul or Mind had withdrawn? No:
> the indeterminate has some footing in the sphere of affirmation. The eye is
> aware of darkness as a base capable of receiving any colour not yet seen
> against it: so the Mind, putting aside all attributes perceptible to sense—all
> that corresponds to light—comes upon a residuum which it cannot bring un-
> der determination: it is thus in the state of the eye which, when directed to-
> wards darkness, has become in some way identical with the object of its spu-
> rious vision. There is vision, then, in this approach of the Mind toward
> Matter? Some vision, yes; of shapelessness, of colourlessness, of the unlit, and
> therefore of the sizeless. More than this would mean that the Soul is already
> bestowing Form. But is not such a void precisely what the Soul experiences
> [*pathos*] when it has no intellection whatever? No: in that case it affirms noth-
> ing, or rather has no experience: but in knowing Matter, it has an experience,
> what may be described as the impact of the shapeless [*paskhei pathos hoion ty-
> pon tou amorphou*].[8]

In the dark, the eye does not see anything but is, as it were, affected by
its own incapacity to see; in the same way, perception here is not the experience of something—a formless being—but rather perception of its
own formlessness, the self-affection of potentiality. Between the experience of something and the experience of nothing there lies the experience
of one's own passivity. The trace (*typos, ikhnos*) is from the beginning the
name of this self-affection, and what is experienced in this self-affection is
the event of matter. The aporias of self-reference thus do not find their
solution here; rather, they are dislocated and (according to the Platonic
suggestion) transformed into *euporias*. The name can be named and language can be brought to speech, because self-reference is displaced onto

the level of potentiality; what is intended is neither the word as object nor
the word insofar as it *actually* denotes a thing but, rather, a pure potential to signify (and not to signify), the writing tablet on which nothing is
written. But this is no longer meaning's self-reference, a sign's signification of itself; instead, it is the materialization of a potentiality, the materialization of its own possibility. Matter is not a formless *quid aliud* whose
potentiality suffers an impression; rather, it can exist as such because it is
the materialization of a potentiality through the passion (*typos, ikhnos*) of
its own impotentiality. The potential to think, experiencing itself and being capable of itself as potential not to think, makes itself into the trace
of its own formlessness, a trace that no one has traced—pure matter. In
this sense, the trace is the passion of thought and matter; far from being
the inert substratum of a form, it is, on the contrary, the result of a
process of materialization.

   In the *Timaeus*, Plato gives us the model of such an experience of matter. *Khōra*, place (or rather nonplace), which is the name he gives to matter, is situated between what cannot be perceived (the Idea, the *anais-
thēton*) and what can be perceived (the sensible, perceptible as *aisthēsis*).
Neither perceptible nor imperceptible, matter is perceptible *met' anais-
thēsias* (a paradoxical formulation that must be translated as "*with* the absence of perception"). *Khōra* is thus the perception of an imperception,
the sensation of an *anaisthēsis*, a pure taking-place (in which truly nothing
takes place other than place).

   This is why Aristotle develops his theory of matter as potentiality on
the basis of Timaeus's *khōra*. Like the eye when it is confronted with darkness, the faculty of sensation, we read in *De anima*, can sense its own lack
of sensation, its own potentiality. Potential thought (the Neoplatonists
speak of two matters, one sensible and one intelligible), the writing tablet
on which nothing is written, can thus think itself. It thinks its own potentiality and, in this way, makes itself into the trace of its own formlessness, writes its own unwrittenness while letting itself take place in separating itself (*ho de nous khōristos*, 429 b 5).

   Derrida's trace, "neither perceptible nor imperceptible," the "re-marked
place of a mark," pure taking-place, is therefore truly something like the
experience of an intelligible matter. The *experimentum linguae* that is at
issue in grammatological terminology does not (as a common misunderstanding insists) authorize an interpretative practice directed toward the

infinite deconstruction of a text, nor does it inaugurate a new formalism. Rather, it marks the decisive event of matter, and in doing so it opens onto an ethics. Whoever experiences this ethics and, in the end, finds his matter can then dwell—without being imprisoned—in the paradoxes of self-reference, being capable of not not-writing. Thanks to Aher's obstinate dwelling in the exile of the Shechinah, Rabbi Akiba can enter the Paradise of language and leave unharmed.

§ 14 Absolute Immanence

Life

By virtue of a striking coincidence, the last texts published by Michel Foucault and Gilles Deleuze before their deaths have at their center the concept of life. The meaning of this testamentary coincidence (for what is at issue in both cases is something like a will) goes beyond the secret solidarity between two friends. It implies the statement of a legacy that clearly concerns the coming philosophy, which, to make this inheritance its own, will have to take its point of departure in the concept of life toward which the last works of both philosophers gesture. (Such, at least, is the hypothesis guiding this inquiry.)

Foucault's text is entitled "Life: Experience and Science," and was published in the January–March 1985 issue of *Revue de Métaphysique et de Morale* (it was submitted to the journal in April 1984 and therefore constitutes the last text to which the author could have given his *imprimatur*, even if it takes up and modifies a text of 1978).[1] What characterizes these pages, which Foucault conceived as a great homage to his teacher, Georges Canguilhem, is a curious inversion of what had been Foucault's earlier understanding of the idea of life. It is as if Foucault, who, with *The Birth of the Clinic*, had begun under the inspiration of Xavier Bichat's new vitalism and definition of life as "the set of functions that resist death," ended by considering life instead as the proper domain of error. "At the limit," Foucault writes, "life . . . is what is capable of error. . . . With man, life reaches a living being who is never altogether in his place, a living being who is fated 'to err' and 'to be mistaken.'"[2] This displacement can be seen as further documentation of the crisis that Foucault, according to Deleuze, experienced after the first volume of *The History of Sexuality*. But what is at issue here is surely something more than disappointment or pessimism; it is something like a new experience that necessitates a general reformulation of the relations between truth and the subject and that, nevertheless, concerns the specific area of Foucault's research. Tearing the subject from the terrain of the *cogito* and consciousness, this experience roots it in life. But insofar as this life is essentially errancy, it exceeds the lived experiences and intentionality of phenomenology: "Does not the entire theory of the subject have to be reformulated once knowledge, instead of opening onto the truth of the world, is rooted in the 'errors' of life?"[3]

What is the nature of a knowledge that has as its correlate no longer the opening to a world and to truth, but only life and its errancy? Alain Badiou, who is certainly one of the most interesting philosophers of the generation immediately following Foucault and Deleuze, still conceives of the subject on the basis of a contingent encounter with truth, leaving aside the living being as "the animal of the human species," as a mere support for this encounter. It is clear that what is at issue in Foucault is not simply an epistemological adjustment but, rather, another dislocation of the theory of knowledge, one that opens onto entirely unexplored terrain. And it is precisely this terrain, which coincides with the field of biopolitics, that could have furnished Foucault with the "third axis, distinct from both knowledge and power," which Deleuze suggests he needed, and which the essay on Canguilhem defines *in limine* as "a different way of approaching the notion of life."

Philosophy of Punctuation

Deleuze's text, which will be our sole subject of study for the rest of this chapter, bears the title "Immanence: A Life ... " ("Immanence: Une vie ... ") and appeared in the journal *Philosophie* two months before the philosopher's death. Unlike Foucault's essay, it is a brief piece that has the cursory *ductus* of a summary note. Even its title, despite its vague and almost suspended appearance, must have been carefully considered. The two key concepts are neither united in a syntagma nor tied by the particle "and" (which is so characteristic of Deleuze's titles); instead, each term is followed by a punctuation mark (first a colon, then ellipsis dots). The choice of this absolutely nonsyntactical articulation (which is neither hy-potactic nor paratactic but, so to speak, atactic) of the two terms is surely not accidental.

Elements for a philosophy of punctuation are, with the exception of the brief indications in Adorno's essay, almost entirely lacking.[4] It has been observed that in philosophical texts, not only nouns but also adverbs can acquire the dignity of genuine terms (Puder and Löwith have noted the special function of the adverbs *gleichwohl* and *schon* in, respectively, Kant and Heidegger). It is less well known that even punctuation marks (for example, the hyphen in expressions such as Being-in-the-world) can take on a technical function (the hyphen is, in this sense, the most di-alectical of punctuation marks, since it unites only to the degree that it distinguishes and distinguishes only to the degree that it unites). Deleuze himself has suggested that punctuation has a strategic importance in his works. In *Dialogues*, after developing his theory of the special meaning of the conjunction "and," he adds, "It is too bad, for that matter, that many writers do away with punctuation, which in French also holds for AND."[5] If one keeps in mind the simultaneously destructive and creative charac-ter that this theory attributes to the particle at issue ("and" [*et*] takes the place of "is" [*est*] and disarticulates ontology, yet "and" also "makes lan-guage spin," introducing *agencement* and stuttering), this implies that in the title "Immanence: A Life ... ," the use of the colon between "Imma-nence" and "A Life" as well as of the final ellipsis dots carries out a deci-sive intention.

The Colon: Immanation

In treatises on punctuation, the function of the colon is generally defined in terms of an intersection of two parameters: a pause value (stronger than the semicolon and less than the period) and a semantic value, which marks the indissoluble relation between two meanings, each of which is in itself partially complete. In the series that goes from the equals sign (identity of meaning) to the hyphen (the dialectic of unity and separation), the colon thus occupies an intermediary function. Deleuze could have written "Immanence Is a Life," or "Immanence and a Life" (in the sense in which "and" takes the place of "is" to create an *agencement*) and, furthermore (according to the principle underlined by J. H. Masmejan[6] that only a comma can take the place of a colon): "Immanence, A Life." Deleuze instead used a colon, clearly because he had in mind neither a simple identity nor a simple logical connection. (When Deleuze writes in the text, "one can say of pure immanence that it is A LIFE, and nothing else," it suffices to recall the title's colon to exclude the possibility that he intends an identity between "immanence" and "a life.") The colon introduces something more than an *agencement* between immanence and a life; it introduces an *agencement* of a special kind, something like an absolute *agencement* that also includes "nonrelation," or the relation derived from nonrelation of which Deleuze speaks in his discussion of the relationship to the Outside in his book on Foucault. If we take up Adorno's metaphor of the colon as a green light in the traffic of language—the aptness of which is verified by punctuation treatises, which classify the colon among "opening" marks—we can then say that between immanence and a life there is a kind of crossing with neither distance nor identification, something like a passage without spatial movement. In this sense, the colon represents the dislocation of immanence in itself, the opening to an alterity that nevertheless remains absolutely immanent: that is, the movement that Deleuze, playing on Neoplatonic emanation, calls *immanation*.

Ellipsis Dots: Virtuality

Analogous remarks could be made for the ellipsis dots that close (and that at the same time leave open) the title. One could even say that the value of the ellipsis dots as a technical term is nowhere as apparent as in the very title "Immanence: A Life ... " Elsewhere, Deleuze observes how Céline's use of ellipsis dots deposes the power of syntactical ties: "*Guignol's Band* achieves the ultimate aim: exclamatory sentences and suspensions that do away with all syntax in favor of a pure dance of words."[7] The fact that an asyntactical and, more generally, asemantic element is present in punctuation is implicit in the constant relation between punctuation and breathing that appears from the very first treatises on punctuation and that takes the form of a necessary interruption of meaning ("the middle dot," one reads in Dionysius Thrax's *Grammar*, "indicates where one is to breathe"). But here the ellipsis dots function not so much to suspend meaning and make words dance outside all syntactic hierarchy as to transform the very status of the word "life," from which the ellipsis dots become inseparable. If terminology, as Deleuze once said, is the poetry of philosophy, here the rank of *terminus technicus* falls neither to the concept *life* nor to the syntagma *a life*, but solely to the nonsyntagma *a life* . . . . Here the incompleteness that is traditionally thought to characterize ellipsis dots does not refer to a final, yet lacking, meaning (Claudel: "a period is everything; an ellipsis is not everything"); rather, it indicates an indefinition of a specific kind, which brings the indefinite meaning of the particle "a" to its limit. "The indefinite as such," Deleuze writes, "does not mark an empirical indetermination, but a determination of immanence or a transcendental determinability. The indefinite article cannot be the indetermination of the person without being the determination of the singular."[8]

The technical term *a life* ... expresses this transcendental determinability of immanence as singular life, its absolutely virtual nature and its definition through this virtuality alone. "A life," Deleuze writes, "contains only virtual entities. It is composed of virtualities, events, singularities. What one calls virtual is not something lacking in reality."[9] Suspending all syntactic ties, the ellipsis dots nevertheless maintain the term "life" in relation to its pure determinability and, while carrying it into this virtual field, exclude the possibility that the indefinite article "a" might (as in Neoplatonism) transcend the Being that follows it.

Beyond the *Cogito*

Considered as a simultaneously asyntagmatic and indivisible block, the title "Immanence: A Life ... " is therefore something like a diagram condensing the thought of the late Deleuze. At first glance, it already articulates the fundamental character of Deleuzian immanence, that is, its "not referring to an object" and its "not belonging to a subject"—in other words, its being immanent only to itself and, nevertheless, in movement. It is in this sense that Deleuze evokes immanence at the beginning of the text, under the name of "transcendental field." Here "transcendental" is opposed to "transcendent," since it does not imply a consciousness but is solely defined as what "escapes all transcendence, both of the subject and of the object."[10] The genesis of the notion of transcendental field can be found in Deleuze's *Logic of Sense*, with reference to Sartre's 1937 essay "La transcendence de l'ego." In this text (which Deleuze judges to be "decisive"), Sartre posits, according to Deleuze, "an impersonal transcendental field, not having the form of a synthetic personal consciousness of a subjective identity."[11] Here Deleuze makes use of this concept—which Sartre does not succeed in fully liberating from the plane of consciousness—to reach a pre-individual and absolutely impersonal zone beyond (or before) every idea of consciousness. It is impossible to understand Deleuze's concept of transcendental field or its strict correlate, the concept of singularity, if one does not register the irrevocable step they take beyond the tradition of consciousness in modern philosophy. Not only is it impossible, according to Deleuze, to understand the transcendental, as Kant does, "in the personal form of an I"; it is also impossible (here Deleuze's polemical target is Husserlian phenomenology) "to preserve for it the form of consciousness, even if we define this impersonal consciousness by means of pure intentionalities and retentions, which still presuppose centers of individuation. The error of all efforts to determine the transcendental as consciousness is that they think of the transcendental in the image of, and in resemblance to, that which it is supposed to ground."[12] From Descartes to Husserl, the *cogito* made the transcendental possible as a field of consciousness. But if it thus appears in Kant as a pure consciousness without any experience, in Deleuze, by contrast, the transcendental is resolutely separated from every idea of consciousness, appearing as an experience without either consciousness or subject: a transcendental empiricism, in Deleuze's truly paradoxical formula.

Thus liquidating the values of consciousness, Deleuze carries out the gesture of a philosopher who, despite Deleuze's lack of fondness for him, is certainly closer to Deleuze than is any other representative of phenomenology in the twentieth century: Heidegger, the "pataphysical" Heidegger of the wonderful article on Alfred Jarry, the Heidegger with whom Deleuze, through this incomparable Ubuesque caricature, can finally reconcile himself.[13] For Dasein, with its Being-in-the-world, is certainly not to be understood as an indissoluble relation between a subject—a consciousness—and its world; and *alētheia*, whose center is ruled by darkness and *lēthē*, is the opposite of an intentional object or a world of pure ideas. An abyss separates Heidegger's concepts from the Husserlian intentionality from which they derive, and it is this abyss that, in displacing these concepts along the line that goes from Nietzsche to Deleuze, makes them into the first figures of the new postconscious and postsubjective, impersonal and non-individual transcendental field that Deleuze's thought leaves as a legacy to "his" century.

The Principle of Immanence

A genealogy of the idea of immanence in Deleuze must begin with the third and eleventh chapters of Deleuze's great monograph on Spinoza. Here the idea of immanence has its origin in Spinoza's affirmation of the univocity of Being in contrast to the Scholastic thesis of *analogia entis*, according to which Being is not said of God and finite creatures in the same way. "For Spinoza, on the other hand," Deleuze writes,

> the concept of univocal Being is perfectly determinate, as what is predicated in one and the same sense of substance in itself, and of modes that are in something else. . . . Thus it is the idea of immanent cause that takes over, in Spinoza, from univocity, freeing it from the indifference and neutrality to which it had been confined by the theory of a divine creation. And it is in immanence that univocity finds its distinctly Spinozist formulation: God is said to be the cause of all things *in the very sense* (*eo sensu*) that he is said to be cause of himself.[14]

The principle of immanence, therefore, is nothing other than a generalization of the ontology of univocity, which excludes any transcendence of Being. Yet through Spinoza's idea of an immanent cause in which agent and patient coincide, Being is freed from the risk of inertia and immobility with which the absolutization of univocity threatened it by making Being equal to itself in its every point. Spinoza's immanent cause produces by remaining in itself, just like the emanational cause of the Neoplatonists. But the effects of Spinoza's immanent cause do not leave it, unlike those of the emanational cause. With a striking etymological figure that displaces the origin of the term "immanence" from *manere* ("to remain") to *manare* ("to flow out"), Deleuze returns mobility and life to immanence: "A cause is immanent . . . when its effect is 'immanate' in the cause, rather than emanating from it."[15]

Immanence flows forth; it always, so to speak, carries a colon with it. Yet this springing forth, far from leaving itself, remains incessantly and vertiginously within itself. This is why Deleuze can state—with an expression that shows his full awareness of the decisive position that immanence would later assume his thought—that "immanence is the very vertigo of philosophy."[16]

What Is Philosophy? gives what one could call the theory of this vertigo. The extreme consequences of the concept of "immanation" are drawn out in the idea that the plane of immanence, like the transcendental field of which it is the final figure, has no subject. It is immanent not to something, but only to itself: "Immanence is immanent only to itself and consequently captures everything, absorbs All-One, and leaves nothing remaining to which it could be immanent. In any case, whenever immanence is interpreted as immanent *to* Something, we can be sure that this Something reintroduces the transcendent."[17] The risk here is that the plane of immanence, which in itself exhausts Being and thought, will instead be referred "to something that would be like a dative." The third "example" of chapter 2 presents the entire history of philosophy, from Plato to Husserl, as the history of this risk. Deleuze thus strategically makes use of the absolutization of the principle of immanence ("immanence is immanent only to itself") to trace a line of immanence within the history of philosophy (one that culminates in Spinoza, who is therefore defined as the "prince of philosophers") and, in particular, to specify his own position with respect to the tradition of twentieth-century phenomenology. Starting with Husserl, immanence becomes immanent to a transcendental subjectivity, and the cipher of transcendence thus reappears at its center:

> This is what happens in Husserl and many of his successors who discover in the Other or in the Flesh, the mole of the transcendent within immanence itself. . . . In this modern moment we are no longer satisfied with thinking immanence as immanent to a transcendent; *we want to think transcendence within the immanent, and it is from immanence that a breach is expected. . . .* The Judeo-Christian word replaces the Greek logos: no longer satisfied with ascribing immanence to something, immanence itself is made to disgorge the transcendent everywhere."[18]

(The allusion to Maurice Merleau-Ponty and Emmanuel Levinas—two philosophers whom Deleuze, in fact, considers with great interest—is clear.)

But immanence is not merely threatened by this illusion of transcendence, in which it is made to leave itself and to give birth to the transcendent. This illusion is, rather, something like a necessary illusion in Kant's sense, which immanence itself produces on its own and to which every philosopher falls prey even as he tries to adhere as closely as possible to the plane of immanence. The task that thought cannot renounce is also the most difficult one, the task in which the philosopher constantly risks going astray. Insofar as immanence is the "movement of the infinite"[19] beyond which there is nothing, immanence has neither a fixed point nor a horizon that can orient thought; the "movement has engulfed everything," and the only possible point of orientation is the vertigo in which outside and inside, immanence and transcendence, are absolutely indistinguishable. That Deleuze encounters something like a limit point here is shown by the passage in which the plane of immanence appears as both what must be thought and as what cannot be thought: "Perhaps this is the supreme act of philosophy: not so much to think THE plane of immanence as to show that it is there, unthought in every plane, and to think it in this way as the outside and inside of thought, as the not-external outside and the not-internal inside."[20]

A Life

In this light, the indication contained in Deleuze's "testament" acquires particular urgency. The philosopher's supreme gesture is to consign immanence to the title "Immanence: A Life ... ," that is, to consider immanence as "a life ... ." But what does it mean for absolute immanence to appear as life? And in what sense does Deleuze's title express his most extreme thought?

Deleuze begins by specifying what we could have imagined, namely, that to say that immanence is "a life ... " is in no way to attribute immanence to life as to a subject. On the contrary, "a life ... " designates precisely the being immanent to itself of immanence, the philosophical vertigo that is by now familiar to us: "one can say of pure immanence that it is A LIFE, and nothing else. It is not immanence to life; rather, immanence that is in nothing is in itself a life. A life is the immanence of immanence, absolute immanence ... ."[21] At this point, Deleuze gives a succinct genealogical sketch by means of references to passages in Fichte and Maine de Biran. Immediately afterward, as if realizing the insufficiency of his references and fearing that his final thought might remain obscure, he has recourse to a literary example:

> No one told better than Dickens what a life is, taking account of the indefinite article as an index of the transcendental. At the last minute, a scoundrel, a bad subject despised by all, is saved as he is dying, and at once all the people taking care of him show a kind of attention, respect, and love for the dying man's smallest signs of life. Everyone tries to save him, to the point that

in the deepest moment of his coma, the villainous man feels that something sweet is reaching him. But the more he comes back to life, the more his saviors become cold, and he rediscovers his coarseness, his meanness. Between his life and his death there is a moment that is nothing other than that of *a* life playing with death. The life of the individual gives way to an impersonal yet singular life, a life that gives rise to a pure event, freed from the accidents of internal and external life, that is, of the subjectivity and objectivity of what happens. "Homo tantum," for whom everyone feels and who attains a kind of beatitude.[22]

Deleuze's reference is to the episode in *Our Mutual Friend* in which Riderhood nearly drowns. It suffices to skim these pages to realize what could have so forcefully attracted Deleuze's attention. First of all, Dickens clearly distinguishes Riderhood the individual and the "spark of life within him" from the scoundrel in which he lives: "No one has the least regard for the man: with them all, he has been an object of avoidance, suspicion and aversion; but the spark of life within him is curiously separable from himself now, and they have a deep interest in it, probably because it *is* life, and they are living and must die."[23] The place of this separable life is neither in this world nor in the next, but between the two, in a kind of happy netherworld that it seems to leave only reluctantly:

> See! A token of life! An indubitable token of life! The spark may smoulder and go out, or it may glow and expand, but see! The four rough fellows seeing, shed tears. Neither Riderhood in this world, nor Riderhood in the other, could draw tears from them; but a striking human soul between the two can do it easily. He is struggling to come back. Now he is almost here, now he is far away again. Now he is struggling harder to get back. And yet—like us all, when we swoon—like us all, every day of our life, when we wake—he is instinctively unwilling to be restored to the consciousness of this existence, and would be left dormant, if he could.[24]

What makes Riderhood's "spark of life" interesting is precisely this state of suspension, which cannot be attributed to any subject. It is significant that Dickens refers to this state as "abeyance," using a word that originates in legal parlance and that indicates the suspension of rules or rights between validity and abrogation ("the spark of life was deeply interesting while it was in abeyance, but now that it got established in Mr. Riderhood, there appears to be a general desire that circumstances had admitted of its being developed in anybody else, rather than in the gentleman").[25] This is why Deleuze can speak of an "impersonal life" situated on a threshold beyond good and evil, "since only the subject who incarnated it in the middle of things made it good or bad."[26] And it is in relation to this impersonal life that Deleuze's brief reference to Maine de Biran becomes fully comprehensible. Starting with *Mémoire sur la décomposition de la pensée*, Maine de Biran's entire work is motivated by the indefatigable attempt to grasp, prior to the I and the will and in close dialogue with the physiology of his time, a "mode of existence that is so to speak impersonal."[27] Maine de Biran calls this mode of existence "affectibility" (*affectibilité*) and defines it as a simple organic capacity of affection without personality that, like Condillac's statue, becomes all its modifications and yet, at the same time, constitutes "a manner of existing that is positive and complete in its kind."[28]

Not even Dickens's text, however, seems to satisfy Deleuze. The fact is that the bare life that it presents seems to come to light only in the moment of its struggle with death ("a life should not be contained in the simple moment in which individual life confronts universal death").[29] But even the next example, which is meant to show impersonal life insofar as it coexists with the life of the individual without becoming identical to it, bears on a special case, one that lies in the vicinity not of death but of birth. "The smallest infants," Deleuze writes, "all resemble each other and have no individuality; but they have singularities, a smile, a gesture, a grimace, events that are not subjective characters. The smallest infants are traversed by an immanent life that is pure potentiality [*pure puissance*], even beatitude through suffering and weaknesses."[30]

One could say that the difficult attempt to clarify the vertigo of immanence by means of "a life" leads us instead into an area that is even more uncertain, in which the child and the dying man present us with the enigmatic cipher of bare biological life as such.

The Animal on the Inside

In the history of Western philosophy, bare life as such is identified at a decisive moment. It is the moment in which Aristotle, in *De anima*, isolates the most general and separable meaning of "living being" (*zōon*) among the many ways in which the term is said. "It is by living," Aristotle observes,

> that the animal is distinguished from the inanimate. But life is said in many ways, and we say that a thing lives if any one of the following is present in

it—thought, sensation, movement or rest in a place, besides the movement implied in nutrition and decay or growth. This is why all plants seem to us to live. It is clear that they have in themselves a principle and a capacity by means of which they grow and decay in opposite directions. . . . This principle may be separated from others, but the others cannot exist apart from it in mortal beings. This is evident in the case of plants; for they have no other capacity of the soul. This, then, is the principle through which all living things have life. . . . By "nutritive faculty" [*threptikon*] I mean that part of the soul that even the plants share.[31]

It is important to observe that Aristotle does not at all define what life is. He merely divides it up in isolating the nutritive function and then orders it into a series of distinct and correlated faculties (nutrition, sensation, thought). What is clearly at work here is the exemplary principle of Aristotle's thought, the principle of the ground. This principle consists in reformulating all questions that have the form of "what is it?" as questions that have the form of "through what thing (*dia ti*) does something belong to something else?" "The *dia ti*," the "through-what," or "why," we read in *Metaphysics*, 1041 a 11, "is always to be sought in the following fashion: through what thing does something belong to something else?" To ask why (*dia ti*) a thing is said to be a living being is to seek the ground through which life belongs to this thing. The undifferentiated ground on whose presupposition individual living beings are said to be alive is nutritive life (or vegetative life, as it was called by ancient commentators, referring to the particular status of plants in Aristotle as obscurely and absolutely separated from *logos*).

In the history of Western science, the isolation of this bare life constitutes an event that is in every sense fundamental. When Bichat, in his *Recherches physiologiques sur la vie et la mort*, distinguishes "animal life," which is defined by its relation to an external world, from "organic life," which is nothing other than a "habitual succession of assimilation and excretion," it is still Aristotle's nutritive life that constitutes the background against which the life of superior animals is separated and on which the "animal living on the outside" is opposed to the "animal on the inside." And when, at the end of the eighteenth century, as Foucault has shown, the State started to assume the care of life and the population as one of its essential tasks and politics became biopolitics, it carried out its new vocation above all through a progressive generalization and redefinition of the concept of vegetative or organic life (which coincides with the bi-

ological heritage of the nation). And today, in discussions of *ex lege* definitions of new criteria for death, it is a further identification of this bare
life—which is now severed from all cerebral activity and subjects—that
still decides if a particular body will be considered alive or, instead, abandoned to the extreme vicissitudes of transplantation.

But what, then, separates this pure vegetative life from the "spark of
life" in Riderhood and the "impersonal life" of which Deleuze speaks?

Unattributable Life

Deleuze is aware that he enters a dangerous territory in displacing immanence into the domain of life. Riderhood's dying life and the infant's
nascent life seem to border on the dark area once inhabited by Aristotle's
nutritive life and Bichat's "animal on the inside." Like Foucault, Deleuze
is perfectly conscious of the fact that any thought that considers life shares
its object with power and must incessantly confront power's strategies.
Foucault's diagnosis of the transformation of power into biopower leaves
no doubts on the matter: "Against this power that was still new in the
nineteenth century," Foucault writes, "the forces that resisted relied for
support on the very thing it invested, that is, on life and man as a living
being. . . . Life as a political object was in a sense taken at face value and
turned back against the system that was bent on controlling it."[32] And
Deleuze remarks: "Life becomes resistance to power when power takes life
as its object. Here again, the two operations belong to the same horizon."[33] The concept of resistance here must be understood not merely as
a political metaphor but as an echo of Bichat's definition of life as "the set
of functions that resist death." Yet one may legitimately ask if this concept truly suffices to master the ambivalence of today's biopolitical conflict, in which the freedom and happiness of human beings is played out
on the very terrain—bare life—that marks their subjection to power.

If a clear definition of "life" seems to be lacking in both Foucault and
Deleuze, the task of grasping the sense of "life" in Deleuze's last work is
all the more urgent. What is decisive here is that its role seems exactly opposed to the one played by nutritive life in Aristotle. While nutritive life
functions as the principle allowing for the attribution of life to a subject
("This, then, is the principle through which all living things have life"),
a life ... , as the figure of absolute immanence, is precisely what can never
be attributed to a subject, being instead the matrix of infinite desubjecti-

fication. *In Deleuze, the principle of immanence thus functions antithetically to Aristotle's principle of the ground.* But there is more. While the specific aim of the isolation of bare life is to mark a division in the living being, such that a plurality of functions and a series of oppositions can be articulated (vegetative life / relational life; animal on the inside / animal on the outside; plant/man; and at the limit, *zoē / bios*, bare life and politically qualified life), *a life ...* marks the radical impossibility of establishing hierarchies and separations. The plane of immanence thus functions as a principle of virtual indetermination, in which the vegetative and the animal, the inside and the outside and even the organic and the inorganic, in passing through one another, cannot be told apart:

> A life is everywhere, in all the moments that traverse this or that living subject and that measure lived objects—immanent life carrying events or singularities that effect nothing but their own actualization in subjects and objects. This undefined life does not itself have moments, however close to one another they might be; it has only inter-times [*entre-temps*], inter-moments [*entre-moments*]. It neither follows nor succeeds, but rather presents the immensity of empty time, where one sees the event that is to come and that has already happened in the absolute of an immediate consciousness.[34]

At the end of *What Is Philosophy?*, in one of the most important passages of Deleuze's late philosophy, life as absolute immediacy is defined as "pure contemplation without knowledge." Here Deleuze distinguishes two possible modes of understanding vitalism, the first as act without essence, the second as potentiality without action:

> Vitalism has always had two possible interpretations: that of an Idea that acts but is not—that acts therefore only from the point of view of an external cerebral knowledge (from Kant to Claude Bernard); or that of a force that is but does not act—that is therefore a pure intentional Awareness (from Leibniz to Ruyer). If the second interpretation seems to us to be imperative, it is because the contraction that preserves is always in a state of detachment in relation to action or even to movement and appears as a pure contemplation without knowledge.[35]

Deleuze's two examples of this "contemplation without knowledge," this force that preserves without acting, are sensation ("sensation is pure contemplation") and habit ("even when one is a rat, it is through contemplation that one 'contracts' a habit").[36] What is important is that this contemplation without knowledge, which at times recalls the Greek conception of theory as not knowledge but touching (*thigein*), here functions to define life. As absolute immanence, *a life* ... is pure contemplation beyond every subject and object of knowledge; it is pure potentiality that preserves without acting. Brought to the limit of this new concept of contemplative life—or, rather, living contemplation—we cannot then fail to examine the other characteristic that, in Deleuze's last text, defines life. In what sense can Deleuze state that *a life* ... is "potentiality, complete beatitude"?[37] To answer this question we will, however, first have to further deepen the meaning of the "vertigo" of immanence.

Pasearse

Among the works of Spinoza that have been preserved, there is only one passage in which he makes use of the mother tongue of Sephardi Jews, Ladino. It is a passage in the *Compendium grammatices linguae hebraeae*[38] in which the philosopher explains the meaning of the reflexive active verb as an expression of an immanent cause, that is, of an action in which agent and patient are one and the same person. *Se visitare*, "to visit oneself," the first Latin equivalent that Spinoza gives to clarify the meaning of this verbal form (which in Hebrew is formed by adding a prefix not to the normal form but to the intensive form, which in itself already has a transitive meaning), is clearly insufficient; yet Spinoza immediately qualifies it by means of the singular expression *se visitantem constituere*, "to constitute oneself visiting." Two more examples follow, whose Latin equivalents (*se sistere, se ambulation dare*) strike Spinoza as so insufficient that he must resort to the mother tongue of his people. In Ladino (that is, in the archaic Spanish spoken by Sephardim at the time of their expulsion from Spain), "to stroll" or "to take a walk" is expressed by the verb *pasearse* ("to walk-oneself," which in modern Spanish is instead expressed as *pasear* or *dar un paseo*). As an equivalent for an immanent cause, which is to say, an action that is referred to the agent himself, the Ladino term is particularly felicitous. It presents an action in which agent and patient enter a threshold of absolute indistinction: a walk as walking-oneself.

In chapter 12, Spinoza poses the same problem with reference to the corresponding form of the infinitive noun (in Hebrew, the infinitive is declined as a noun):

> Since it often happens that the agent and the patient are one and the same person, the Jews found it necessary to form a new and seventh kind of in-

finitive with which to express an action referred to both the agent and the patient, an action that thus has the form of both an activity and a passivity. . . . It was therefore necessary to invent another kind of infinitive, which expressed an action referred to the agent as immanent cause . . . , which, as we have seen, means "to visit oneself," or "to constitute oneself as visiting" or, finally, "to show oneself as visiting" [*constituere se visitantem, vel denique praebere se visitantem*].[39]

The immanent cause thus involves a semantic constellation that the philosopher-grammarian grasps, not without difficulty, by means of a number of examples ("to constitute oneself as visiting," "to show oneself as visiting," *pasearse*) and whose importance for the understanding of the problem of immanence cannot be underestimated. *Pasearse* is an action in which it is impossible to distinguish the agent from the patient (who walks what?) and in which the grammatical categories of active and passive, subject and object, transitive and intransitive therefore lose their meaning. *Pasearse* is, furthermore, an action in which means and end, potentiality and actuality, faculty and use enter a zone of absolute indistinction. This is why Spinoza employs expressions such as "to constitute oneself as visiting," "to show oneself as visiting," in which potentiality coincides with actuality and inoperativeness with work. The vertigo of immanence is that it describes the infinite movement of the self-constitution and self-manifestation of Being: Being as *pasearse*.

It is not an accident that the Stoics used precisely the image of the walk to show that modes and events are immanent to substance (Cleanthus and Chrysippus, indeed, ask themselves: who walks, the body moved by the hegemonic part of the soul or the hegemonic part itself?). As Epictetus says, with an extraordinary invention, the modes of Being "do Being's gymnastics" (*gymnasai*, in which one should also etymologically hear the adjective *gymnos*, "bare").[40]

Beatitude

In this light, Deleuze's notes on Foucault, published by François Ewald under the title "Desire and Pleasure," contain an important definition. Life, Deleuze, says, is not at all nature; it is, rather, "desire's variable field of immanence." Given what we know of Deleuzian immanence, this means that the term "life" designates nothing more and nothing less than *the immanence of desire to itself*. It is clear that for Deleuze, desire implies neither alterity nor a lack. But how is it possible to conceive of a desire that as such remains immanent to itself? Or in other words, how is it possible to conceive of absolute immanence in the form of desire? To phrase the question in the terms of Spinoza's *Compendium*: how is it possible to conceive of a movement of desire that does not leave itself, that is, simply as immanent cause, as *pasearse*, as desire's self-constitution as desiring?

Spinoza's theory of "striving" (*conatus*) as the desire to persevere in one's own Being, whose importance Deleuze often underlines, contains a possible answer to these questions. Whatever the ancient and medieval sources of Spinoza's idea (Harry A. Wolfson lists a number of them, from the Stoics to Dante), it is certain that in each case, its paradoxical formulation perfectly expresses the idea of an immanent movement, a striving that obstinately remains in itself. All beings not only persevere in their own Being (*vis inertiae*) but *desire* to do so (*vis immanentiae*). The movement of *conatus* thus coincides with that of Spinoza's immanent cause, in which agent and patient cannot be told apart. And since *conatus* is identical to the Being of the thing, to desire to persevere in one's own Being is to desire one's own desire, to constitute oneself as desiring. *In* conatus, *desire and Being thus coincide without residue.*

In his *Cogitatia metaphysica*, Spinoza defines life as *conatus* ("life is the force by which a thing perseveres in its own Being"). When Deleuze writes that life is desire's variable field of immanence, he therefore offers a rigorously Spinozian definition of life. But to what degree can life, thus defined in terms of *conatus* and desire, be distinguished from the nutritive potentiality of which Aristotle speaks and, in general, from the vegetative life of the medical tradition? It is worth noting that when Aristotle defines the characteristic functions of the nutritive soul (*threptikē psychē*) in *De anima*, he makes use of an expression that closely recalls Spinoza's determination of *conatus sese conservandi*. Aristotle writes: "It [*trophē*, nutritivity] preserves its substance. . . . This principle of the soul is a potentiality capable of preserving whoever possesses it as such [*dynamis estin hoia sōzein to echon autēn hēi toiouton*].[41] The most essential character of nutritive life, therefore, is not simply growth but above all self-preservation. This means that whereas the medico-philosophical tradition seeks carefully to distinguish the various faculties of the soul and to regulate human life according to the high canon of the life of the mind, Deleuze (like Spinoza) brings the paradigm of the soul back to the lower scheme of nutritive life. While decisively rejecting the function of nutritive life in Aris-

totle as the ground of the attribution of a subjectivity, Deleuze nevertheless does not want to abandon the terrain of life, which he identifies with
the plane of immanence.[42]

But what does it then mean to "nourish"? In an important essay, Émile
Benveniste seeks to determine a unity for the many, often discordant
meanings of the Greek word *trephein* (to nourish, to grow, and to coagu-
late). "In reality," he writes,

> the translation of *trephō* by "nourish" in the use that is actually the most com-
> mon does not suit all the examples and is itself only an acceptation of both a
> broader and a more precise sense. In order to account for the ensemble of se-
> mantic connections of *trephō*, we have to define it as: "to encourage (by ap-
> propriate measures) the development of that which is subject to growth." . . .
> It is here that a peculiar and "technical" development is inserted, and it is pre-
> cisely the sense of "curdle." The Greek expression is *trephein gala* (*Od.* 9. 246),
> which must now be literally interpreted as "to encourage the natural growth
> of milk, to let it attain the state toward which it is tending."[43]

If the original meaning of *trephō* is "to let a being reach the state toward
which it strives," "to let be," then the potentiality that constitutes life in
the original sense (self-nourishment) coincides with the very desire to preserve one's own Being that, in Spinoza and Deleuze, defines the potentiality of life as absolute immanence.

It is, then, possible to comprehend why Deleuze writes that a life is
"potentiality, complete beatitude." Life is "composed of virtuality";[44] it is
pure potentiality that coincides with Being, as in Spinoza, and potentiality,
insofar as it "lacks nothing" and insofar as it is desire's self-constitution
as desiring, is immediately blessed. All nourishment, all letting be is
blessed and rejoices in itself.

In Spinoza, the idea of beatitude coincides with the experience of the
self as an immanent cause, which he calls *acquiescentia in se ipso*, "being
at rest in oneself," and defines precisely as *laetitia, concomitante idea sui
tamquam causa*, "rejoicing accompanied by the idea of the self as cause."
Wolfson has observed that in Spinoza, the reference of the term *acquiescentia* to *mens* or *anima* may reflect Uriel Acosta's use of *alma* and *espirito*
with *descansada*.[45] But it is far more important that the expression *acquiescentia in se ipso* is an invention of Spinoza's, which is not registered in
any Latin lexicon. Spinoza must have had in mind a concept that, as an
expression of an immanent cause, corresponded to the Hebrew reflexive

verb; but he was forced to confront the fact that in Latin, both the verb *quiesco*, "to rest," and its compound *acquiesco*, "to be at rest," are intransitive and therefore do not allow a form such as *quiescere* (or *acquiescere*) *se*, "resting oneself" (whereas Ladino, by contrast, furnished him with the form *pasearse*, in which agent and patient are identical, and could in this case perhaps have offered the reflexive *descansarse*). This is why he forms the expression *acquiescentia*, constructing it with the preposition *in* followed by the reflexive pronoun *se*. The syntagma *acquiescentia in se ipso*, which names the highest beatitude attainable by human beings, is a Hebrewism (or a Ladinoism) formed to express the apex of the movement of an immanent cause.[46]

It is precisely in this sense that Deleuze uses the term "beatitude" as the essential character of "a life ... ." *Beatitudo* is the movement of absolute immanence.

Perspectives

It is now possible to clarify the sense in which we were able to state at the beginning of this chapter that the concept of "life," as the legacy of the thought of both Foucault and Deleuze, must constitute the subject of the coming philosophy. First of all, it will be necessary to read Foucault's last thoughts on biopower, which seem so obscure, together with Deleuze's final reflections, which seem so serene, on "a life ... " as absolute immanence and beatitude. To read together, in this sense, is not to flatten out and to simplify; on the contrary, such a conjunction shows that each text constitutes a corrective and a stumbling block for the other. Only through this final complication is it possible for the texts of the two philosophers to reach what they seek: for Foucault, the "different way of approaching the notion of life," and for Deleuze, a life that does not consist only in its confrontation with death and an immanence that does not once again produce transcendence. We will thus have to discern the matrix of desubjectification itself in every principle that allows for the attribution of a subjectivity; we will have to see the element that marks subjection to biopower in the very paradigm of possible beatitude.

This is the wealth and, at the same time, the ambiguity contained in the title "Immanence: A Life ... ." To assume this legacy as a philosophical task, it will be necessary to reconstruct a genealogy that will clearly distinguish in modern philosophy—which is, in a new sense, a philosophy of life—between a line of immanence and a line of transcendence, approximately according to the following diagram:

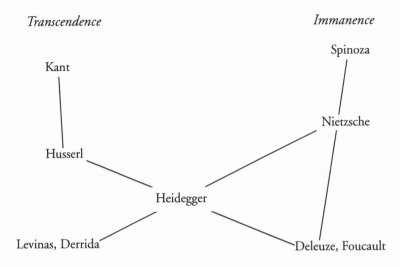

It will be necessary, moreover, to embark on a genealogical inquiry into the term "life." This inquiry, we may already state, will demonstrate that "life" is not a medical and scientific notion but a philosophical, political, and theological concept, and that many of the categories of our philosophical tradition must therefore be rethought accordingly. In this dimension, there will be little sense in distinguishing between organic life and animal life or even between biological life and contemplative life and between bare life and the life of the mind. Life as contemplation without knowledge will have a precise correlate in thought that has freed itself of all cognition and intentionality. *Theōria* and the contemplative life, which the philosophical tradition has identified as its highest goal for centuries, will have to be dislocated onto a new plane of immanence. It is not certain that, in the process, political philosophy and epistemology will be able to maintain their present physiognomy and difference with respect to ontology. Today, blessed life lies on the same terrain as the biological body of the West.

PART FOUR

Contingency

§ 15 Bartleby, or On Contingency

> At the same time that he created his throne, God created a writing
> table so big that a man could walk on it for a thousand years. The
> table was made of the whitest pearl; its extremities were made of ru-
> bies, and its center was made of emerald. Everything that was written
> on it was of the purest light. God looked upon this table a hundred
> times a day, and every time he looked upon it he constructed and de-
> stroyed, creating and killing. . . . At the same time that he created this
> table, God also created a pen of light, which was so long and wide that
> a man could run along either its length or its width for five hundred
> years. After having created his pen, God ordered it to write. "What
> shall I write?," said the pen. "You will write my wisdom and all my
> creatures," God answered, "from the world's beginning to its end."
>
> —*The Book of the Ladder*, chapter 20

The Scribe, or On Creation

*As a scrivener, Bartleby belongs to a literary constellation. Its polar star is
Akaky Akakievich ("for him, the whole world was in some sense contained in
his copies . . . he had his favorite letters, and when he got to them he truly lost
his wits"); its center is formed by the twin stars, Bouvard and Pécuchet ("the
good idea that both secretly nourished—copying"); and its other extremity is
lit by the white lights of Simon Tanner ("I am a scribe" is the only identity
he claims for himself) and Prince Myshkin, who can effortlessly reproduce any
handwriting. A little further on lies the asteroid belt of Kafka's courtroom
clerks. But Bartleby also belongs to a philosophical constellation, and it may
be that it alone contains the figure merely traced by the literary constellation
to which Bartleby belongs.*

1. The late Byzantine lexicon that goes under the name of *Suda* contains the following definition in the entry "Aristotle": *Aristotelēs tēs physeōs
grammateus ēn ton kalamon apobrekhōn eis noun*, "Aristotle was the scribe
of nature who dipped his pen in thought." In the "Notes" to his translation of Sophocles, Hölderlin cites this passage for no apparent reason,
subverting it by means of a minimal correction. Aristotle, he says, was the
scribe of nature who dipped his benevolent pen (*eunoun* instead of *eis
noun*). Isidore of Seville's *Etymologies* records a different version of the

same phrase, which originates in Cassiodorus: *Aristoteles, quando peri-hermeneias scriptebat, calamum in mente tingebat,* "When he wrote *De interpretatione*," one of the fundamental logical works of the *Organon*, "Aristotle dipped his pen in thought." In each case, what is decisive is not so much the image of the scribe of nature (which is also to be found in Atticus) as the fact that *nous*, thought or mind, is compared to an ink pot in which the philosopher dips his pen. The ink, the drop of darkness with which the pen writes, is thought itself.

What is the origin of this definition, which presents the fundamental figure of the philosophical tradition in the humble garb of a scribe, likening thought to an act of writing, albeit of a special kind? There is only one text in the entire Aristotelian *corpus* that contains a similar image, which may have furnished Cassiodorus or an unknown writer with the basis for his metaphor. This passage belongs not to the logical *Organon* but to Aristotle's treatise on the soul. It is the passage in book 3, in which Aristotle compares *nous*, the intellect or potential thought, to a writing tablet on which nothing is written: "the *nous* is like a writing tablet [*grammateion*]," we read, "on which nothing is actually written" (*De anima*, 430 a 1).

In Greece in the fourth century B.C., ink and papyrus were not the only means of writing. It was much more common, especially for private use, to write by engraving a stylus in a writing tablet covered with a thin layer of wax. Having reached a crucial point in his treatise, the point at which he considers the nature of the potential intellect and the mode of its passage to the act of intellection, Aristotle refers to an object of this kind, which was probably the very same writing tablet on which he was recording his thoughts at that moment. Much later, once writing with pen and ink had become the dominant practice and Aristotle's image risked appearing antiquated, someone modernized it in the sense later recorded by *Suda*.

2. The image had great fortune in the tradition of Western philosophy. The Latin translator who rendered *grammateion* by *tabula rasa* consigned it to a history that led to Locke's "white sheet" ("let us suppose that, in the beginning, the mind is what is called a white sheet, without any characters, without any 'ideas'"), and also to the incongruous expression, which still exists in Italian, of "making a clean sweep" (*far tabula rasa*). The image was ambiguous, and this ambiguity certainly contributed to

its success. Alexander of Aphrodisius noted that the philosopher should have spoken not of a *grammateion* but, more precisely, of its *epitedeiotes*, that is, the light layer of wax covering it, on which the stylus inscribes letters (in the terms of the Latin translators, not a *tabula rasa* but a *rasura tabulae*). The observation, which Alexander had special reasons to insist on, was, however, exact. The difficulty that Aristotle seeks to avoid through the image of the writing tablet is that of the pure potentiality of thought and how it is possible to conceive of its passage to actuality. For, if thought in itself had a determinate form, if it were always already something (as a writing tablet is a thing), it would necessarily appear in the intelligible object and thus hinder intellection. This is why Aristotle takes care to specify that *nous* "has no other nature than that of being potential, and before thinking it is absolutely nothing" (*De anima*, 429 a 21–22).

The mind is therefore not a thing but a being of pure potentiality, and the image of the writing tablet on which nothing is written functions precisely to represent the mode in which pure potentiality exists. For Aristotle, all potential to be or to do something is always also potential not to be or not to do (*dynamis mē einai, mē energein*), without which potentiality would always already have passed into actuality and would be indistinguishable from it (according to the Megarians' thesis, which Aristotle explicitly refutes in Book Theta of the *Metaphysics*). The "potential not to" is the cardinal secret of the Aristotelian doctrine of potentiality, which transforms every potentiality in itself into an impotentiality (*tou autou kai kata to auto pasa dynamis adynamia*) (*Metaphysics*, 1046 a 32). Just as the architect retains his potential to build even when he does not actualize it and just as the kithara player is a kithara player because he can also not play the kithara, so thought exists as a potential to think and not to think, as a wax writing tablet on which nothing is written (the potential intellect of medieval philosophers). And just as the layer of sensitive wax is suddenly grazed by the scribe's stylus, so the potentiality of thought, which in itself is nothing, allows for the act of intelligence to take place.

3. In Messina, between 1280 and 1290, Abraham Abulafia composed the Cabalistic treatises that remained in European libraries in manuscript form for centuries and that were brought to the attention of nonspecialists only in the twentieth century (thanks to Gershom Scholem and

Moshe Idel). In these works, divine creation is conceived as an act of writing in which letters can be said to represent the material vehicle through which the creative word of God, which is likened to a scribe moving his pen, incarnates itself in created things:

> The secret at the origin of all creatures is the letter of the alphabet and every letter is a sign that refers to creation. Just as the scribe holds his pen in his hand and uses it to draw several drops of ink, picturing in his mind the form that he wants to give to matter, so similar acts are performed in the higher and lower realms of creation (in all these gestures, the scribe's hand is the living organ moving the inanimate pen used as an instrument to make ink flow onto the pergamen, which represents the body, the subject of matter and form). This can be understood by anyone with intelligence, for to say more is prohibited.

Abulafia was a reader of Aristotle and, like every cultured Jew of his age, was acquainted with the philosopher through Arabic translations and commentaries. The problem of the passive intellect and its relation to the active or poetic intellect (which Aristotle, in *De anima*, liquidates with a few enigmatic sentences) was treated with exceptional subtlety by the *falasifa* (as the disciples of Aristotle in Islam were called). The prince of the *falasifa* himself, Avicenna, conceived of the creation of the world as an act in which the divine intelligence thinks itself. The creation of the sublunary world (which, in the emanationist process that Avicenna had in mind, is the work of the last angel-intelligence, who is none other than Aristotle's agent intellect) was therefore also understood according to the model of thought thinking itself and in this way letting the multiplicity of creatures be. Every act of creation (as was well known by the thirteenth-century love poets, who transformed Avicenna's angels into ladies) is an act of intelligence; and inversely, every act of intelligence is an act of creation that lets something be. But precisely in *De anima*, Aristotle represented the potential intellect as a writing tablet on which nothing is written. As a consequence, in the marvelous treatise on the soul that the medievals knew as *Liber VI naturalium*, Avicenna uses the image of writing to illustrate the various kinds or levels of the potential intellect. There is a potentiality (which he calls material) that resembles the condition of a child who may certainly one day learn to write but does not yet know anything about writing. Then there is a potentiality (which he calls possible) that belongs to the child who has begun to write with pen and ink and knows how to form the first letters. And there is, finally, a complete or perfect potentiality that belongs to the scribe who is in full possession of the art of writing in the moment in which he does not write (*potentia scriptoris perfecti in arte sua, cum non scripserit*). Later, in the Arabic tradition, creation was thus likened to an act of writing; the agent or poetic intellect, which illuminates the passive intellect and allows it to pass into actuality, is therefore identified with an angel, whose name is "Pen" (*Qalam*).

When, in the holy city, the great Andalusian Sufi Ibn Arabi drew up a plan of the work to which he would devote his last years, *The Illuminations of Mecca*, it was therefore not an accident that he decided to dedicate its second chapter to the science of letters (*'ilm al-hurûf*), which concerned the hierarchical levels of vowels and consonants as well as their correspondences with the divine names. In the process of acquiring knowledge, the science of letters marks the transition from the inexpressible to the expressible; in the process of creation, it indicates the passage from potentiality to actuality. Ibn Arabi defines existence, pure Being, which for the Scholastics is simply ineffable, as "a letter of which you are the meaning." He graphically represents the passage of creation from potentiality to actuality as a *ductus* that ties the three letters *alif-lâm-mîm* together in a single gesture:

The first part of this grapheme, the letter *alif*

signifies the descent of potential Being toward the attribute. The second part, *lâm*

indicates the extension of the attribute toward actuality. And the third part, *mîm*

marks the descent of actuality toward manifestation.

Here, the equation of writing and the process of creation is absolute. The scribe who does not write (of whom Bartleby is the last, exhausted figure) is perfect potentiality, which a Nothing alone now separates from the act of creation.

4. Who moves the scribe's hand so that it will pass into the actuality of writing? According to what laws does the transition from the possible to the real take place? And if there is something like possibility or potentiality, what—in it or outside it—causes it to exist? In Islam, these questions constituted the subject of the rupture between the *motekallemim*, that is, the Sunnite theologians, and the *falasifa*. Fixing their gaze upon Aristotle's writing tablet, the *falasifa* inquired into the principles and laws by which the possible, which exists in the mind of God or the artificer, does or does not take place in the creative act. Against them, the Asharites, who represent the dominant current of Sunnite orthodoxy, hold an opinion that not only destroys the very concepts of cause, law, and principle but also invalidates all discourse on the possible and the necessary, thus undermining the very basis of the *falasifa*'s research. The Asharites conceive of the act of creation as an incessant and instantaneous production of miraculous accidents that cannot influence each other and that are, therefore, independent of all laws and causal relations. When the dyer soaks the white cloth in the indigo barrel or when the blacksmith hardens the blade in the fire, the dye does not penetrate the cloth to color it and the heat of the fire does not render the blade incandescent. Rather, it is God himself who establishes a coincidence, one that is habitual but in itself purely miraculous, by which color is produced in the cloth the moment it is immersed in the indigo barrel and incandescence appears in the blade every time it is placed in the fire.

> When the scribe moves his pen, it is thus not he who moves it; this movement is only an accident that God creates in the scribe's hand. God has established, as habit, that the movement of the hand coincides with that of the pen and that the movement of the pen coincides with the production of writing; but the hand has no causal influence whatsoever in the process, since an accident cannot act upon another accident. . . . For the movement of the pen, God thus created four accidents that do not in any way cause each other but merely coexist together. The first accident is my will to move my pen; the second is my potential to move it; the third is the very movement of my hand; the fourth, finally, is the movement of my pen. When man wants something and does it, this therefore means that, first, his will was created for him, then his faculty of acting, and, last of all, the action itself.

This is not simply a conception of the creative act that differs from the one offered by the philosophers. What the theologians want is to break Aristotle's writing tablet forever, to drive all experience of possibility from the world. But no sooner is the problem of potentiality expelled from the domain of human beings than it reappears in God. This is why Ghazali, who as a brilliant professor in the *madrasa* of Baghdad had tenaciously maintained the position of the Asharites in a book called *The Self-Destruction of the Philosophers*, was forced to reckon once again with the figure of the scribe subsequently, during his wanderings from the mosque of the Rock in Jerusalem to the minarets of Damascus. In his *Revival of the Religious Sciences*, Ghazali thus composes an apologue on divine potentiality that begins as follows:

A man enlightened by the light of God saw a sheet of paper dipped in black ink, and asked it, "How is it that you, who were once stunningly white, are now covered with black marks? Why did your face turn black?" "You are unjust with me," the sheet answered, "for I was not the one who blackened my face. Ask the ink, who for no reason moved out of the pot, to spill onto me." So the man turned to the ink, looking for explanations; but the ink answered by referring him to the pen, which had torn it from its tranquil dwelling place and exiled it onto the sheet of paper. When the man questioned the pen, the pen told him to turn to the hand who, after seizing it and cruelly breaking its tip, dipped it into the ink pot. The hand, who claimed to be nothing more than miserable flesh and bones, then suggested that the man turn to the Potentiality that moved it. But this Potentiality referred the man to the Will, and the Will referred him to Science, until, moving from cause to cause, the enlightened one finally reached the impenetrable veils of divine Potentiality, from which a terrible voice thundered, "One does not ask God for reasons for what he does; but reasons for your actions will be demanded."

Islamic fatalism (which is the origin of the darkest name for the concentration-camp inhabitant, the *Muselmann*) is thus grounded not in an attitude of resignation but, on the contrary, in a limpid faith in the incessant operation of divine miracles. Yet it is certain that in the world of the *motekallemim*, the category of possibility was wholly destroyed; human potentiality was groundless. There was only the inexplicable movement of the divine hand, which could not be foreseen and which the writing tablet had no reason to expect. In opposition to this absolute demodalization of the world, the *falasifa* remained faithful to Aristotle's legacy. In its deepest intention, philosophy is a firm assertion of potentiality, the construction of an experience of the possible as such. Not thought but the potential to think, not writing but the white sheet is what philosophy refuses at all costs to forget.

5. Potentiality, however, is the hardest thing to consider. For if potentiality were always only the potential to do or to be something, we would never experience it as such; it would exist only in the actuality in which it is realized, as the Megarians maintained. An experience of potentiality as such is possible only if potentiality is always also potential not to (do or think something), if the writing tablet is capable of not being written on. But precisely here everything becomes far more complicated. How is it possible to think a potential not to think? What does it mean for a potential not to think to pass into actuality? And if the nature of thought is to be potential, then what will it think?

In Book Lambda of the *Metaphysics* (1074 b 15–35), at the point where he discusses the divine mind, Aristotle confronts precisely these aporias:

> The question of thought implies certain aporias. For it seems to be the most divine of phenomena, but its mode of Being appears problematic. If thought thought nothing [if, that is, it kept to its potential not to think], why would it be venerable? It would be like a man who slept. And if thought actually thought something, it would be subordinate to this thing, since its Being would be not actuality but potentiality [it would be determined by something other than its own essence, which is to be potential]. And in either case, whether its nature is potential thought [*nous*] or actual thought [*noēsis*], what does it think? Either itself or something other than itself. If it thought something other than itself, it would either always think of the same thing or sometimes of one thing and sometimes of another. But does it make any difference whether it is thinking of that which is noble rather than something accidental? Would it not be absurd to be thinking of certain things? Clearly, then, it thinks that which is most divine, most honorable, and does not change. . . . And if thought were not thinking but a potential to think, it would follow that the continuity of its thinking would tire it. Moreover, it is clear that in this case, there would be something more honorable than thought, namely, the object of thought; indeed, thinking and actual thought belong even to that which thinks the worst objects. If this is to be avoided (for there are things which it is better not to see than to see), actual thought cannot be the best of things. Therefore thought thinks itself, if it is the most excellent of all things, and thought is the thinking of thinking.[1]

The aporia here is that the highest thought can neither think nothing nor think something, neither remain potential nor become actual, neither write nor not write. And it is to escape from this aporia that Aristotle formulates his famous idea of thought thinking itself, which is a kind of

mean between thinking nothing and thinking something, between potentiality and actuality. Thought that thinks itself neither thinks an object nor thinks nothing. It thinks a pure potentiality (to think and not to
think); and what thinks its own potentiality is what is most divine and
blessed.

But the aporia returns as soon as it is dissolved. What does it mean for
a potential to think to think itself? How is it possible, in actuality, to
think a pure potentiality? How can a writing tablet on which nothing is
written turn back upon itself, *impress itself*?

Reflecting on the enigma of thought thinking itself and the *tabula rasa*
in his commentary on *De anima*, Albert the Great pauses to consider precisely these questions. Albert declares himself to be "in complete agreement" with Averroes, who had given the greatest privilege to the potential intellect, making it into a single entity common to all human beings;
yet Averroes had treated this decisive point quite hastily. Aristotle's statement that the intellect itself is intelligible could not be understood in the
same sense in which one says that any object whatsoever is intelligible.
The potential intellect is not a thing. It is nothing other than the *intentio*
through which a thing is understood; it is not a known object but simply
a pure knowability and receptivity (*pura receptibilitas*). Anticipating
Wittgenstein's thesis on the impossibility of metalanguage, Albert sees
clearly that to say that an intelligibility grasps itself cannot be to reify it
by dividing it into a meta-intelligence and an object-intelligence. The
writing of thought is not the writing of a foreign hand, which moves a
stylus to graze the soft wax; rather, at the point at which the potentiality
of thought turns back on itself and pure receptivity so to speak feels its
own feeling, precisely then, Albert writes, it is as if the letters, on their
own, wrote themselves on the writing tablet (*et hoc simile est, sicut si
diceremus quod litterae scriberent seipsas in tabula*).

6. It is a commonplace that the three great monotheistic religions are
in accord on the creation of the world from nothing. Christian theologians thus oppose creation, which is an *operari ex nihilo*, to the art of the
artificer, which is instead always a *facere de materia*. An equally decisive
argument is to be found in the polemic of the rabbis and the *motekallemim* against the view, which is attributed to the philosophers, that it is
impossible for God to have created the world from nothing, since *nihil
ex nihilo fit*. In each case, what is essential is the refutation of the very idea

that something such as matter (that is, potential Being) could preexist God. But what does it mean "to create from nothing"? As soon as one examines the problem closely, everything is complicated; more and more, the Nothing begins to resemble something, albeit something of a special kind.

Maimonides, who argued for the truth of creation from nothing in his *Guide for the Perplexed*, was nevertheless familiar with a passage of the authoritative midrash known as *Pirke Rabbi Eliezer* "that strongly shakes the faith of the theologian and the man of science" by suggesting the existence of something like a matter of creation. "Of what," one reads in this text, "were the heavens created? God took the light from his garments and spread it out like a sheet. Thus the heavens were made, as it is written: 'He wraps himself in light as in a garment, and spreads the heavens as a rug.'" Moreover, according to the Sufis the verse in the Koran in which God addresses the creature, saying "We created you when you were nothing (were a nonthing)," proved that this nonthing was not a pure Nothing, since God had already turned to the Nothing in the act of creation, saying "Be!"

The fact is that by the time Jewish, Islamic, and Christian theologians formulated the idea of creation from nothing, Neoplatonism had already conceived of its highest principle as a Nothing from which all things proceed. Just as the Neoplatonists had distinguished two Nothings, one that, so to speak, transcends beings from above and one that exceeds them from below, so they distinguished two matters, one corporeal and the other incorporeal, the dark and eternal background of intelligible beings. Cabalists and mystics brought this thesis to its limit and, with their characteristic radicality, clearly stated that the Nothing from which all creation proceeds is God himself. Divine Being (or rather hyper-Being) is the Nothing of beings, and only by, so to speak, sinking into this Nothing was God able to create the world. In his *De divisione naturae*, commenting on the verse "and the earth was without form and void; and darkness was upon the face of the deep" (*terra autem erat inanis et vacua et tenebrae erant super faciem abyssi*), John Scotus Eriugena refers the biblical text to the primordial ideas or causes of beings that are eternally made in the mind of God. Only in descending into this darkness and this abyss did God create the world and, at the same time, himself (*descendens vero in principiis rerum ac velut se ipsam creans in aliquo inchoat esse*).

The problem that is at issue here is, in truth, that of the existence in God of possibility or potentiality. Since Aristotle stated that all potentiality is also potentiality not (to be or do), the theologians were forced to strip God of all potential to be and to will at the same time that they affirmed his omnipotence. If God had the potential to be, he could also not be, which would contradict his eternity. On the other hand, if God were capable of not wanting what he wants, he would be capable of wanting non-Being and evil, which is equivalent to introducing a principle of nihilism into God. The theologians thus conclude that, while he contains unlimited potentiality in himself, God is nevertheless bound to his will and cannot do or want anything other than what he has willed. God's will, like his Being, is absolutely without potentiality.

According to the mystics and Cabalists, by contrast, the obscure matter that creation presupposes is nothing other than divine potentiality. The act of creation is God's descent into an abyss that is simply his own potentiality and impotentiality, his capacity to and capacity not to. In David of Dinant's radical formulation, which was condemned as heretical in 1210, God, thought, and matter are thus one and the same, and this undifferentiated abyss is the Nothing from which the world proceeds and on which it eternally rests. In this context, "abyss" is not a metaphor. As Jakob Böhme clearly states, it is the life of darkness in God, the divine root of Hell in which the Nothing is eternally produced. Only when we succeed in sinking into this Tartarus and experiencing our own impotentiality do we become capable of creating, truly becoming poets. And the hardest thing in this experience is not the Nothing or its darkness, in which many nevertheless remain imprisoned; the hardest thing is being capable of annihilating this Nothing and letting something, from Nothing, be. "Praise is due to God," Ibn Arabi writes at the beginning of his *Illuminations*, "for He has made things exist from the Nothing, annihilating it."

The Formula, or On Potentiality

1. This is the philosophical constellation to which Bartleby the scrivener belongs. As a scribe who has stopped writing, Bartleby is the extreme figure of the Nothing from which all creation derives; and at the same time, he constitutes the most implacable vindication of this Noth-

ing as pure, absolute potentiality. The scrivener has become the writing tablet; he is now nothing other than his white sheet. It is not surprising, therefore, that he dwells so obstinately in the abyss of potentiality and does not seem to have the slightest intention of leaving it. Our ethical tradition has often sought to avoid the problem of potentiality by reducing it to the terms of will and necessity. Not what you *can* do, but what you *want* to do or *must* do is its dominant theme. This is what the man of the law repeats to Bartleby. When he asks him to go to the post office ("just step around to the Post Office, won't you?"), and Bartleby opposes him with his usual "I would prefer not to," the man of the law hastily translates Bartleby's answer into "You *will* not?" But Bartleby, with his soft but firm voice, specifies, "I *prefer* not" ("I *prefer* not," which appears three times, is the only variation of Bartleby's usual phrase; and if Bartleby then renounces the conditional, this is only because doing so allows him to eliminate all traces of the verb "will," even in its modal use).[2] When the man of the law honestly tries, in his own way, to understand the scrivener, the readings to which he dedicates himself leave no doubts as to the categories he intends to use: "'Edwards on the Will,' and 'Priestly on Necessity.'"[3] But potentiality is not will, and impotentiality is not necessity; despite the salutary impression that the books give him, the categories of the man of the law have no power over Bartleby. To believe that will has power over potentiality, that the passage to actuality is the result of a decision that puts an end to the ambiguity of potentiality (which is always potentiality to do and not to do)—this is the perpetual illusion of morality.

Medieval theologians distinguish between *potentia absoluta*, an "absolute potentiality" by which God can do anything (according to some, even evil, even acting such that the world never existed, or restoring a girl's lost virginity), and *potentia ordinata*, an "ordered potentiality," by which God can do only what is in accord with his will. Will is the principle that makes it possible to order the undifferentiated chaos of potentiality. If it is true that God could have lied, broken his oaths, incarnated himself in a woman or an animal instead of in the Son, he thus did not want to do so and he could not have wanted to do so; and a potentiality without will is altogether unrealizable and cannot pass into actuality.

Bartleby calls into question precisely this supremacy of the will over potentiality. If God (at least *de potentia ordinata*) is truly capable only of what he wants, Bartleby is capable only without wanting; he is capable only *de potentia absoluta*. But his potentiality is not, therefore, unrealized; it does not remain unactualized on account of a lack of will. On the contrary, it exceeds will (his own and that of others) at every point. Inverting Karl Valentin's witticism "I wanted to want it, but I didn't feel able to want it," one could say of Bartleby that he succeeds in being able (and not being able) absolutely without wanting it. Hence the irreducibility of his "I would prefer not to." It is not that he does not *want* to copy or that he does not *want* to leave the office; he simply would prefer not to. The formula that he so obstinately repeats destroys all possibility of constructing a relation between being able and willing, between *potentia absoluta* and *potentia ordinata*. It is the formula of potentiality.

2. Gilles Deleuze has analyzed the particular structure of Bartleby's formula, likening it to expressions that linguists define as agrammatical, such as Cummings's "he danced his did" or "j'en ai un de pas assez." Deleuze argues that the destructive force of Bartleby's formula consists in its secret agrammaticality: "the formula 'disconnects' words and things, words and actions, but also speech acts and words—it severs language from all reference, in accordance with Bartleby's absolute vocation, *to be a man without references*, someone who appears suddenly and then disappears, without reference to himself or anything else."[4] Philippe Jaworski, for his part, has observed that Bartleby's formula is neither affirmative nor negative and that Bartleby neither accepts nor refuses, stepping forward and stepping backward at the same time. As Deleuze suggests, the formula thus opens a zone of indistinction between yes and no, the preferable and the nonpreferable. But also—in the context that interests us—between the potential to be (or do) and the potential not to be (or do). The final "to" that ends Bartleby's phrase has an anaphoric character, for it does not refer directly to a segment of reality but, rather, to a preceding term from which it draws its only meaning. But here it is as if this anaphora were absolutized to the point of losing all reference, now turning, so to speak, back toward the phrase itself—an absolute anaphora, spinning on itself, no longer referring either to a real object or to an anaphorized term: *I would prefer not to prefer not to.* . . .

What is the origin of this formula? Critics have cited one of Melville's letters to Hawthorne, in which he praises "no" over "yes" as a possible precursor to Bartleby's phrase ("For all men who say yes, lie; and all men who say no—why, they are in the happy condition of judicious, unencumbered travelers in Europe; they cross the frontiers into Eternity with nothing but a carpetbag—that is to say, the Ego"). The reference could not be more out of place. Bartleby does not consent, but neither does he simply refuse to do what is asked of him; nothing is farther from him than the heroic pathos of negation. In the history of Western culture, there is only one formula that hovers so decidedly between affirmation and negation, acceptance and rejection, giving and taking. The formula, which is morphologically and semantically similar to the scrivener's litany, is recorded, among other places, in a text that was familiar to every cultured man of the nineteenth century: Diogenes Laertius's *Lives of Eminent Philosophers*. We are referring to the expression *ou mallon*, "no more than," the technical term with which the Skeptics denoted their most characteristic experience: *epokhē*, suspension.

"The Skeptics," Diogenes writes in his life of Pyrrho, "use this expression neither positively [*thetikōs*] nor negatively [*anairetikōs*], as when they refute an argument by saying: 'Scylla exists no more than [*ou mallon*] a chimera.'"[5] The term, however, is nevertheless not to be understood as indicating a genuine comparison: "But the Skeptics refute even the 'no more than.' For just as providence exists no more than it does not exist, so the 'no more than' is no more than it is not." Sextus Empiricus reaffirms the self-referential status of *ou mallon* just as decisively: "Even as the proposition 'every discourse is false' says that it too, like all propositions, is false, so the formula 'no more than' says that it itself is no more than it is not. . . . And even if this expression appears as an affirmation or a negation, still this is not the sense in which we use it but rather an indifferent [*adiaforōs*] and illegitimate sense [*katakrēstikōs*]."

The way in which the scrivener makes use of his obstinate formula could not be characterized more precisely. But the analogy can also be followed up in another direction. In his *Outlines of Pyrrhonism*, having commented on the meaning of the expression *ou mallon*, Sextus adds: "the most important thing is that, in uttering this expression, the Skeptic says the phenomenon and announces the affect without any opinion [*apaggellei to pathos adoxastōs*]." Although it is not usually recorded as such, this last expression (*pathos apaggellein*) is also a technical term of the Skeptics' lexis. We find it once again, in the same sense, in another passage of Sextus's *Outlines*: "When we say 'everything is incomprehensible,' we do not mean to state that what the dogmatics seek is by nature incomprehensible; we limit ourselves to announcing the passion [or affect: *to heautou pathos apaggellontos*]."

Aggellō and *apaggellō* are verbs that express the function of the *aggelos*, the messenger, who simply carries a message without adding anything, or who performatively announces an event (*polemon apaggellein* means "to declare war"). The Skeptic does not simply oppose aphasia to *phasis*, silence to discourse; rather, he displaces language from the register of the proposition, which predicates something of something (*legein ti kata tinos*), to that of the announcement, which predicates nothing of nothing. Maintaining itself in the *epokhē* of the "no more than," language is transformed into the angel of the phenomenon, the pure announcement of its passion. As the adverb *adoxastōs* specifies, "passion" here indicates nothing subjective; *pathos* is purified of all *doxa*, all subjective appearance, and becomes the pure announcement of appearance, the intimation of Being without any predicate.

In this light, Bartleby's formula shows its full sense. It inscribes whomever utters it in the line of *aggeloi*, messengers. One of these messengers is Kafka's Barnaby, who, we read, "was perhaps simply a messenger, one who knew nothing of the content of the letters entrusted to him," one whose "gaze, smile, and walk seemed to be those of a messenger, although he himself was not aware of it." As a messenger, Bartleby was sent "for some mysterious purpose of an all-wise Providence, which it was not for a simple mortal . . . to fathom."[6] But if the formula he repeats hovers so obstinately between acceptance and refusal, negation and position, if it predicates nothing and, in the end, even refutes itself, what is the message he has come to tell us, what does his formula announce?

3. "The Skeptics understand potentiality-possibility [*dynamis*] as any opposition between sensibles and intelligibles. By virtue of the equivalence found in the opposition between words and things, we thus reach the *epokhē*, the suspension, which is a condition in which we can neither posit nor negate, accept nor refuse." According to this striking text of Sextus, the Skeptics viewed suspension not simply as indifference but as an experience of possibility or potentiality. What shows itself on the threshold between Being and non-Being, between sensible and intelligible, between word and thing, is not the colorless abyss of the Nothing but the luminous spiral of the possible. To be able is *neither to posit nor to negate*. But in what way does what is-no-more-than-it-is-not still preserve in itself something like potentiality?

Leibniz once expressed the originary potentiality of Being in the form of a principle usually defined as the "principle of sufficient reason." This principle has the following form: *ratio est cur aliquid sit potius quam non sit*, "there is a reason for which something does rather than does not exist." Insofar as it cannot be reduced either to the pole of Being or to the pole of the Nothing, Bartleby's formula (like its Skeptic archetype) calls into question the "strongest of all principles," appealing precisely to the *potius*, the "rather" that articulates its scansion. Forcibly tearing it from its context, the formula emancipates potentiality (*potius*, from *potis*, which means "more powerful") from both its connection to a "reason" (*ratio*) and its subordination to Being.

Commenting on the principle of sufficient reason, which his teacher Leibniz had left unproven, Christian Wolff explains that our reason is disgusted by the idea of something taking place without a reason. If one takes away this principle, he writes, "the true world becomes a fairy-tale world, in which the will of men takes the place of reasons for what happens" (*mundus verus abit in mundum fabulosum, in quo voluntas hominis stat pro ratione eorum, quae fiunt*). The *mundus fabulosus* at issue here is that of

> the absurd fairy tale told by old women and that, in our vernacular, is called *Schlarrafenland*, the Land of Plenty. . . . You would like a cherry—and, at your command, there appears a cherry tree full of ripe fruit. According to your wish, the fruit flies toward your mouth and, if you so will it, divides in half in mid air, letting the pit and the bad parts fall to the ground so that you do not have to spit them out. Pigeons roasted on a spit fall from the sky and spontaneously enter the mouths of whoever is hungry.

What is truly disgusting to the philosopher's eyes, however, is not that will and caprice take the place of reason in the domain of things but that *ratio* is thus also extinguished in the domain of will and potentiality. "Not only are there now no principles of possibility and no principles of actuality external to man; what is more, not even the will has a principle for its willing, but instead indifferently wills anything. Hence it does not even want what it desires [*ideo nimirum vult, quia libet*]; there is no reason for it to want one thing rather than another." It is not true, therefore, that once the principle of reason is removed, human will takes the place of *ratio*, transforming the true world into a fable. Precisely the contrary is true, namely, that once *ratio* is removed, the will is ruined together with it.

In the ascetic *Schlarrafenland* in which Bartleby is at home, there is only a "rather" fully freed of all *ratio*, a preference and a potentiality that no longer function to assure the supremacy of Being over Nothing but exist, without reason, in the indifference between Being and Nothing. The indifference of Being and Nothing is not, however, an equivalence between two opposite principles; rather, it is the mode of Being of potentiality that is purified of all reason. Leibniz did not allow the possible to have any autonomous "potential to make itself exist" (*puissance pour se faire exister*), which he argued was to be found outside the possible, in God, insofar as he is a necessary being, that is, "existentifying" (*Est ergo causa cur existentia praevaleat non-existentiae, seu ens necessarium est existentificans*). Now wholly subverted, the Leibnizian principle instead takes on the Bartleby-like form of the following statement: "the fact that there is no reason for something to exist rather than not to exist is the existence of something no more than nothing." In the place of the Prince of Denmark's *boutade*, which reduces every problem to the opposition between to be and not to be, Being and non-Being, the scrivener's formula suggests a third term that transcends both: the "rather" (or the "no more than"). This is the one lesson to which Bartleby always holds. And, as the man of the law seems to intuit at a certain point, the scrivener's trial is the most extreme trial a creature can undergo. For to hold to the Nothing, non-Being, is certainly difficult; but it is the characteristic experience of the ungrateful guest—nihilism—with whom we are all too familiar today. And to hold simply to Being and its necessary positivity is also difficult; but is this not precisely the sense of the complicated Western onto-theo-logical ceremony whose morality is in secret solidarity with the guest it would like to drive away? To be capable, in pure potentiality, to bear the "no more than" beyond Being and Nothing, fully experiencing the impotent possibility that exceeds both—this is the trial that Bartleby announces. The green screen that isolates his desk traces the borders of an experimental laboratory in which potentiality, three decades before Nietzsche and in a sense that is altogether different from his, frees itself of the principle of reason. Emancipating itself from Being and non-Being alike, potentiality thus creates its own ontology.

The Experiment, or On Decreation

1. In a work on Robert Walser, Walter Lüssi invented the concept of an experiment without truth, that is, an experience characterized by the dis-

appearance of all relation to truth. Walser's writing is "pure poetry" (*reine Dichtung*) because it "refuses, in the widest sense, to recognize the Being of something as something." This concept should be transformed into a paradigm for literary writing. Not only science but also poetry and thinking conduct experiments. These experiments do not simply concern the truth or falsity of hypotheses, the occurrence or nonoccurrence of something, as in scientific experiments; rather, they call into question Being itself, before or beyond its determination as true or false. These experiments are without truth, for truth is what is at issue in them.

When Avicenna, proposing the experience of the flying man, imagines a dismembered and disorganized human body, showing that, thus fragmented and suspended in the air, man can still say "I am," and that the pure entity is the experience of a body without either parts or organs; when Cavalcanti describes the poetic experience as the transformation of the living body into a mechanical automaton ("I walk like a man outside life / who seems, to those who see him, a man / made of branches or rocks or wood / who is led along by artifice");[7] when Condillac introduces his marble statue to the sense of smell, such that the statue "is no more than the scent of a rose"; when Dante desubjectifies the "I" of the poet into a third person (*I' mi son un*), a generic, homonymous being who functions only as a scribe in the dictation of love; when Rimbaud says "I is another"; when Kleist evokes the perfect body of the marionette as a paradigm of the absolute; and when Heidegger replaces the physical "I" with an empty and inessential being that is only its own ways of Being and has possibility only in the impossible—each time we must consider these "experiments without truth" with the greatest seriousness. Whoever submits himself to these experiments jeopardizes not so much the truth of his own statements as the very mode of his existence; he undergoes an anthropological change that is just as decisive in the context of the individual's natural history as the liberation of the hand by the erect position was for the primate or as was, for the reptile, the transformation of limbs that changed it into a bird.

The experiment that Melville entrusts to Bartleby is of this kind. If what is at issue in a scientific experiment can be defined by the question "Under what conditions can something occur or not occur, be true or be false?" what is at issue in Melville's story can instead be formulated in a question of the following form: "Under what conditions can something occur *and* (that is, at the same time) not occur, be true *no more than not be true?*" Only inside an experience that has thus retreated from all relation to truth, to the subsistence or nonsubsistence of things, does Bartleby's "I would prefer not to" acquire its full sense (or, alternatively, its nonsense). The formula cannot but bring to mind the propositions with which Wittgenstein, in his lecture on ethics, expresses his ethical experience par excellence: "I marvel at the sky because it exists," and "I am safe, whatever happens." The experience of a tautology—that is, a proposition that is impenetrable to truth conditions on account of always being true ("The sky is blue or the sky is not blue")—has its correlate in Bartleby in the experience of a thing's *capacity* to be true and, at the same time, not to be true. If no one dreams of verifying the scrivener's formula, this is because experiments without truth concern not the actual existence or nonexistence of a thing but exclusively its potentiality. And potentiality, insofar as it can be or not be, is by definition withdrawn from both truth conditions and, prior to the action of "the strongest of all principles," the principle of contradiction.

In first philosophy, a being that can both be and not be is said to be contingent. The experiment with which Bartleby threatens us is an experiment *de contingentia absoluta*.

2. In his "Elements" of natural right Leibniz summarizes the figures of modality as follows:

possibile (possible)		*potest* (can)	
impossibile (impossible)	*est quicquid* (is something that)	*non potest* (cannot)	*fieri (seu verum esse)* (do [or be true])
necessarium (necessary)		*non potest non* (cannot not)	
contingens (contingent)		*potest non* (can not)	

The fourth figure, the contingent, which can be or not be and which coincides with the domain of human freedom in its opposition to necessity, has given rise to the greatest number of difficulties. If Being at all times and places preserved its potential not to be, the past itself could in some sense be called into question, and moreover, no possibility would ever pass into actuality or remain in actuality. The aporias of contingency are, as a result, traditionally tempered by two principles.

The first, which could be defined as the *principle of the irrevocability of the past* (or of the unrealizability of potentiality in the past) is attributed by Aristotle to the tragic poet Agathon: "There is no will with regard to the past. This is why no one wants Troy to have been sacked, since no one decides what happened but only what will be and is possible; what has happened cannot not have been. This is why Agathon is right in saying: 'This only is denied even to God, / The power to undo what has been done.'"[8] This is the principle that the Latins expressed in the formula *factum infectum fieri nequit*, and that Aristotle, in *De coelo*, restates in terms of an impossibility of realizing the potentiality of the past: "there is no potentiality of what was, but only of Being and Becoming."

The second principle, which is closely tied to the first, is that of *conditioned necessity*, which limits the force of contingency with respect to actuality. Aristotle expresses it as follows: "what is is necessary as long as it is, and what is not is necessary as long as it is not" (*De interpretatione*, 19 a 22). Wolff, who summarizes it in the formula *quodlibet, dum est, necessario est*, defines this principle as a *canon tritissimus in philosophia* and founds it, not without reason, on the principle of noncontradiction ("It is impossible that A is and, at the same time, is not"). The logical strength of this second principle with respect to potentiality, however, is far from certain. Aristotle himself seems to belie it, for he writes in the *Metaphysics* that "all potentiality is, at the same time [*hama*], potentiality for the opposite" and reaches the conclusion that "he who walks has the potential not to walk, and he who does not walk has the potential to walk" (1047 a).

As Duns Scotus makes clear, the fact is that if there is a contradiction between two actual opposed realities (being P and not-being P), nothing keeps a thing from being actual and, at the same time, maintaining its potential not to be or to be otherwise. "By contingent," he writes, "I mean not something that is not necessary or eternal, but something whose opposite could have happened in the very moment in which it happened." At the same instant, I can thus act in one way and be able to act otherwise (or not to act at all). Scotus gives the name "will" not to decision but to the experience of the constitutive and irreducible co-belonging of capacity to and capacity not to, the will to and the will not to. According to the lapidary formula with which he expresses the only possible meaning of human freedom, "he who wills experiences his capacity not to will" (*experitur qui vult se posse non velle*). The will (like the Freudian unconscious, with its constitutive ambivalence) is the only domain that is with-drawn from the principle of noncontradiction; "only the will is indiffer-ent to contraries" (*voluntas sola habet indifferentiam ad contraria*), since "with respect to the same object, it is capable both of willing and not will-ing, which are nevertheless contraries." Without retreating before the consequences of this thesis, Scotus extends the contingent character of willing even into divine will and the act of creation:

> In the same act of will, God wills contraries; he does not will that they exist together (since this is impossible), but he nevertheless wills them at the same time. In the same way, it is through a single intuition or a single science that he knows that contraries do not exist together and that, nevertheless, they are known together in the same cognitive act, which is one single act.

And, with ferocious irony, Scotus proposes that those who doubt con-tingency be submitted to the experiment already suggested by Avicenna: "those who deny contingency should be tortured until they admit that they could also have not been tortured."

3. Contingency is threatened by another objection, namely, that the necessary occurrence or nonoccurrence of a future event retroactively in-fluences the moment of its prediction, canceling its contingency. This is the problem of "future contingents," which Leibniz summarizes in the *Theodicy* once again under the sign of writing: "It was true a hundred years ago that I would write today, just as three hundred years from now it will be true that I wrote today." Let us suppose that someone says that tomorrow there will be or will not be a battle at sea. If the battle occurs tomorrow, then it was already true the day before that it would take place, which means that it could not not take place; if, inversely, the battle does not occur, then it was always already true to say that it would not take place, which means that it was impossible for it to take place. In both cases, contingency is replaced by necessity and impossibility.

In medieval theology, the problem of future contingents is dramatically linked to that of divine prescience, which either calls into question the freedom of human will or destroys the very possibility of the revelation of divine will. On the one hand, once the future is necessary, the most rigid necessity deprives decision of all meaning; on the other hand, con-tingency and absolute uncertainty involve the angels and Christ himself. Richard Fitzralph, professor at Oxford at the beginning of the fourteenth century, thus argues *ad absurdum* in his *quaestio biblica* that "sweating blood at Gethesmene, Christ foresaw his death no more than the continuation of his life, and the angels in the heavens did not foresee their eternal beatitude more than they imagined their eternal misery, since they knew that, if God wanted it, they could be forever miserable."

How can one impede the argument *de praesenti ad praeteritum* that ruins the contingency of the future, without thereby depriving statements about the future of all certainty? Aristotle's solution to the problem is elegant: "it is necessary," he writes in *De interpretatione*, "that every thing be or not be, as well as that it will be or will not be; but it is not at all the case that one then says that one thing or the other, once isolated, is necessary. For example, I say that tomorrow there will or will not be a battle at sea; and yet it is not necessary for a battle at sea to occur, nor is it necessary for it not to occur" (19 a 28–32).

Necessity thus concerns not the occurrence or nonoccurrence of the particular event but rather the alternative "it-will-occur-or-it-will-not-occur" as a whole. In other words, only the tautology (in Wittgenstein's sense) "tomorrow there will or will not be a battle at sea" is necessarily always true, whereas each of the two members of the alternative is returned to contingency, its possibility to be or not to be.

In this context, it is all the more crucial to uphold the principle of conditioned necessity. This is why Aristotle must define the possible-potential (*dynaton*) in the following terms: "A thing is said to be potential if, when the act of which it is said to be potential is realized, there will be nothing impotential" (*esti de dynaton touto, hōi ean hyparxei hē energeia ou legetai ekhein tēn dynamēn, ouden estai adynaton*) (*Metaphysics*, 1047 a 24–26). The last three words of the definition (*ouden estai adynaton*) do not mean, as the usual and completely trivializing reading maintains, "there will be nothing impossible" (that is, what is not impossible is possible). They specify, rather, the condition in which potentiality—which can both be and not be—can realize itself (this is also shown by the analogous definition of the contingent in the *Prior Analytics*, 32 a 28–20, where Aristotle's text must be translated as follows: "I say that the contingent can also occur and that once it exists, given that it is not necessary, there will be no potential in it not to be"). What is potential can pass over into actuality only at the point at which it sets aside its own potential not to be (its *adynamia*), when nothing in it is potential not to be and it when it can, therefore, not not-be.

Yet how is one to understand this nullification of the potential not to be? And once the possible is realized, what happens to what was capable of not being?

4. In the *Theodicy*, in an apologue that is as grandiose as it is terrible, Leibniz justified the right of what was against what could have been but was not. Continuing the story told by Lorenzo Valla in his dialogue, *De libero arbitrio*, Leibniz imagines that Sextus Tarquinius travels to the temple of Jove at Dodona, unsatisfied with the response given to him by the oracle of Apollo at Delphi, who predicted ill fortune if he wanted to be king in Rome. Sextus accuses Jove of having condemned him to a miserable life and asks Jove to change his fate or, at least, admit his wrong. Sextus abandons himself to his destiny when Jove refuses his request, once again telling him he must renounce the kingship of Rome. But Theodorus, Jove's priest, who is present at the scene, wants to know more. Following Jove's advice, he visits the temple of Pallas in Athens, where he falls into a deep sleep and dreams that he has traveled to an unknown country. There, the goddess shows him the Palace of Destinies, an immense pyramid that shines at its peak, extending infinitely downwards. Each of the innumerable apartments that compose the palace represents one of Sextus's possible destinies, to which there corresponds a possible world that was never realized. In one of these apartments, Theodorus sees Sextus leaving Dodona's temple persuaded by the god; he travels to Corinth, where he buys a small garden, discovers a treasure while cultivating it, and lives happily to a ripe old age, loved and respected by all. In another chamber, Sextus is in Thrace, where he marries the daughter of the king and inherits the throne, becoming the happy sovereign of a people that venerates him. In another, he leads a life that is mediocre but painless. And so it continues, from apartment to apartment, from possible destiny to possible destiny:

> The halls rose in a pyramid, becoming even more beautiful as one mounted towards the apex, and representing more beautiful worlds. They finally reached the highest one, which completed the pyramid and was the most beautiful of all. For the pyramid had a beginning, but one could not see its end; it had an apex, but no base, since it went on to infinity. This is so, the goddess explained, because among an endless number of possible worlds there is the best of all; otherwise God would not have determined to create it. But there is not one that does not also have less perfect worlds beneath it; this is why the pyramid goes on descending to infinity. Theodorus, entering this highest hall, became entranced in ecstasy. . . . "We are in the real true world,"

said the goddess, "and you are at the source of happiness. Behold what Jupiter makes ready for you, if you continue to serve him faithfully. Here is Sextus as he is, and as he will be in reality. He leaves the temple in a rage, scorning the counsel of the Gods. You see him going to Rome, bringing confusion everywhere, violating the wife of his friend. There he is driven out with his father, beaten, unhappy. If Jupiter had placed here a Sextus happy at Corinth or King in Thrace, it would be no longer this world. And nevertheless he could not have failed to choose this world, which surpasses in perfection all the others, and which forms the apex of the pyramid."[9]

The pyramid of possible worlds represents the divine intellect, whose ideas, Leibniz writes, "contain possibilities for all eternity." God's mind is the Piranesi-like prison or, rather, the Egyptian mausoleum that, until the end of time, guards the image of what was not, but could have been. And God, Leibniz says, who has chosen the best of all possible worlds (that is, the world that is most possible, for it contains the greatest number of compossible events), sometimes visits this immense mausoleum "to enjoy the pleasure of recapitulating things and of renewing his own choice, which cannot fail to please him." It is difficult to imagine something more pharisaic than this demiurge, who contemplates all uncreated possible worlds to take delight in his own single choice. For to do so, he must close his own ears to the incessant lamentation that, throughout the infinite chambers of this Baroque inferno of potentiality, arises from everything that could have been but was not, from everything that could have been otherwise but had to be sacrificed for the present world to be as it is. The best of all possible worlds projects an infinite shadow downward, which sinks lower and lower to the extreme universe—which even celestial beings cannot comprehend—in which nothing is compossible with anything else and nothing can take place.

5. It is in the "Egyptian architecture" of this Palace of Destinies that Bartleby conducts his experiment. He holds strictly to the Aristotelian statement that the tautology "it-will-occur-or-it-will-not-occur" is necessarily true as a whole, beyond the taking place of either of the two possibilities. Bartleby's experiment concerns precisely the place of this truth; it has to do exclusively with the occurrence of a potentiality as such, that is, something that can both be and not be. But such an experiment is possible only by calling into question the principle of the irrevocability of the past, or rather, by contesting the retroactive unrealizability of potentiality. Overturning the sense of the argument *de praesenti ad praeteritum*,

Bartleby inaugurates an absolutely novel *quaestio disputata*, that of "past contingents." The necessary truth of the tautology "Sextus-will-go-to-Rome-or-will-not-go-to-Rome" retroactively acts on the past not to make it necessary but, rather, to return it to its potential not to be.

Benjamin once expressed the task of redemption that he assigned to memory in the form of a theological experience of the past: "What research has established can be modified by remembrance. Remembrance can make the incomplete (happiness) complete, and the complete (pain) incomplete. This is theology—but the experience of remembrance forbids us to conceive of history in a fundamentally atheological manner, even as we are not allowed to write history directly in theological concepts." Remembrance restores possibility to the past, making what happened incomplete and completing what never was. Remembrance is neither what happened nor what did not happen but, rather, their potentialization, their becoming possible once again. It is in this sense that Bartleby calls the past into question, re-calling it—not simply to redeem what was, to make it exist again but, more precisely, to consign it once again to potentiality, to the indifferent truth of the tautology. "I would prefer not to" is the *restitutio in integrum* of possibility, which keeps possibility suspended between occurrence and nonoccurrence, between the capacity to be and the capacity not to be.

Potentiality can be turned back toward the past in two ways. The first is the one Nietzsche assigns to the eternal return. For him, precisely the repugnance, the "counterwill" (*Widerwille*), of will toward the past and its "thus it was" is the origin of the spirit of revenge, the worst punishment devised by men: "'It was'—that is the name of the will's gnashing of teeth and most secret melancholy. Powerless against what has been done, he is an angry spectator of all that is past. The will cannot will backwards . . . its fury is that time cannot go backwards. 'What was'—this is the stone the will cannot turn over."[10]

The impossibility of "wanting Troy to have been sacked," of which Aristotle speaks in the *Nichomachean Ethics*, is what torments the will, transforming it into resentment. This is why Zarathustra is the one who teaches the will to "will backwards" (*zurückwollen*) and to transform every "thus it was" into a "thus I willed it": "this alone is liberation." Solely concerned with repressing the spirit of revenge, Nietzsche completely forgets the laments of what was not or could have been otherwise. An echo of this lament is still audible in Blanqui, when, in a prison cell in the Fort du Taureau, evoking the eternal return ten years before Nietzsche, he bitterly grants actual existence to all the possible worlds of the Palace of Destinies:

> The number of our doubles is infinite in time and space. One can hardly demand more from the mind. These doubles are flesh and blood, even in pants, in crinolone and chignon. They are not ghosts but eternity made real. And yet this is a great defect; there is no progress. Alas, these are vulgar new editions, repeats. Such are the exemplars of past worlds, of worlds to come. Let us not forget that *everything that could have happened here has happened somewhere else.*

In Zarathustra, this echo is completely muffled. In the end, Nietzsche's eternal return is only an atheistic variation of Leibniz's *Theodicy*. Each of the pyramid's apartments now hosts the eternal repetition of what happened, thereby canceling the difference between the actual world and the possible world and returning potentiality to what was. And it is not an accident that Leibniz was the first to formulate—in almost the same terms—Nietzsche's decisive experience:

> If the human species lasted long enough in its present state, a time would necessarily come in which even the lives of individuals would return in the same circumstances, down to the smallest details. I myself would return, to live once again in the city called Hannover, on the banks of the Leine river, once again busy studying the history of Brunswick and writing the same letters to the same friends.

Bartleby holds fast to this solution until he decides to give up copying. Benjamin discerns the inner correspondence between copying and the eternal return when he compares Nietzsche's concept to *die Strafe des Nachsitzens*, that is, the punishment assigned by the teacher to negligent schoolchildren that consists in copying out the same text countless times. ("The eternal return is copying projected onto the cosmos. Humanity must copy out its texts in innumerable repetitions.") The infinite repetition of what was abandons all its potential not to be. In its obstinate copying, as in Aristotle's contingency, there is no potential not to be. The will to power is, in truth, the will to will, an eternally repeated action; only as such is it potentialized. This is why the scrivener must stop copying, why he must give up his work.

6. At the end of Melville's story, the man of the law discretely proposes an interpretation of Bartleby on the basis of a piece of gossip. This "re-

port" is that Bartleby "had been a subordinate clerk in the Dead Letter Office at Washington, from which he had been suddenly removed by a change in the administration."[11] As elsewhere in the story, the man of the law furnishes the reader with correct information; but as always, the explanation he draws from it is off the mark. He insinuates that having worked in that office pushed the scrivener's innate temperament to "a pallid hopelessness." Bartleby's deplorable behavior and his mad formula, he suggests, can be clarified as the final stage of a preexistent pathological disposition precipitated by unfortunate circumstances. This explanation is trivial not so much because, like all psychological explanations, it ends by presupposing itself, as because it entirely fails to question the particular link between dead letters and Bartleby's formula. Why does a pallid hopelessness express itself in precisely this way and not another?

Yet it is the man of the law, once again, who allows us to answer the question. "Sometimes," he says,

> from out of the folded paper the pale clerk takes a ring—the finger it was meant for, perhaps, moulders in the grave; a bank-note sent in swiftest charity—he whom it would relieve, nor eats nor hungers any more; pardon for those who died despairing; hope for those who died unhoping; good tidings for those who died stifled by unrelieved calamities. On errands of life, these letters speed to death.[12]

There could be no clearer way to suggest that undelivered letters are the cipher of joyous events that could have been, but never took place. What took place was, instead, the opposite possibility. On the writing tablet of the celestial scribe, the letter, the act of writing, marks the passage from potentiality to actuality, the occurrence of a contingency. But precisely for this reason, every letter also marks the nonoccurrence of something; every letter is always in this sense a "dead letter." This is the intolerable truth that Bartleby learned in the Washington office, and this is the meaning of the singular formula, "on errands of life, those letters speed to death."

Until now, it has not been noted that this formula is, in fact, a barely disguised citation from Romans 7:10, *euretē moi hē entolē hē eis zōēn, autē eis thanaton*, which, in the translation Melville would have known, reads as follows: "And the commandment, which was ordained to life, I found to be unto death" (*entolē* is a "mandate," what is sent for a reason—hence *epistolē*, "letter"—and is more correctly rendered by "errand" than by "commandment"). In Paul's text, the mandate, the *entolē*, is that of the

Law from which the Christian has been freed. The mandate is referred to
the "oldness of the letter" to which the apostle has just opposed the "newness of spirit": "But now we are delivered from the Law, that being dead
where we were held; that we should serve in newness of spirit, not in the
oldness of the letter" (Rom. 7:6, but see also 2 Cor. 3:6, "the letter killeth,
but the spirit giveth life"). In this light, not only the relationship between
Bartleby and the man of the law but even that between Bartleby and writing acquires a new sense. Bartleby is a "law-copyist," a scribe in the evan-
gelical sense of the term, and his renunciation of copying is also a reference to the Law, a liberation from the "oldness of the letter." Critics have
viewed Bartleby, like Joseph K., as a Christ figure (Deleuze calls him "a
new Christ") who comes to abolish the old Law and to inaugurate a new
mandate (ironically, it is the lawyer himself who recalls this to him: "A
new commandment give I unto you that ye love one another"). But if
Bartleby is a new Messiah, he comes not, like Jesus, to redeem what was,
but to save what was not. The Tartarus into which Bartleby, the new sav-
ior, descends is the deepest level of the Palace of Destinies, that whose
sight Leibniz cannot tolerate, the world in which nothing is compossible
with anything else, where "nothing exists rather than something." And
Bartleby comes not to bring a new table of the Law but, as in the Cabalistic speculations on the messianic kingdom, to fulfill the Torah by destroying it from top to bottom. Scripture is the law of the first creation
(which the Cabalists call the "Torah of Beriah"), in which God created
the world on the basis of its potential to be, keeping it separate from its
potential not to be. Every letter of this Torah is, therefore, turned both
toward life and toward death; it signifies both the ring and the finger intended for it, which disintegrates in the grave, both what was and what
could not be.

The interruption of writing marks the passage to the second creation,
in which God summons all his potential not to be, creating on the basis
of a point of indifference between potentiality and impotentiality. The
creation that is now fulfilled is neither a re-creation nor an eternal repetition; it is, rather, a decreation in which what happened and what did not
happen are returned to their originary unity in the mind of God, while
what could have not been but was becomes indistinguishable from what
could have been but was not.

A Persian Neoplatonist once expressed the shadow that contingency
casts on every creature in the image of the dark wing of the archangel
Gabriel:

Know that Gabriel has two wings. The first, the one on the right, is pure light. This wing is the sole and pure relation of Gabriel's Being with God. Then there is the left wing. This wing is grazed with a dark figure resembling the crimson color of the moon at dawn or the peacock's claw. This shadowy figure is Gabriel's capacity to be, which has one side turned toward non-Being (since it is, as such, also a capacity not to be). If you consider Gabriel in his act of Being through God's Being, then his Being is said to be necessary, since under this aspect it cannot not be. But if you consider him in his right to existence in itself, this right is immediately to the same degree a right not to be, since such is the right of a being that does not have its capacity to be in itself (and that is, therefore, a capacity not to be).

Decreation is the immobile flight sustained by the black wing alone. At this wing's every beating, the actual world is led back to its right not to be; all possible worlds are led back to their right to existence. Sextus the ill-fated tyrant of Rome and Sextus the happy peasant of Corinth blend together and can no longer be told apart. Gabriel's dark wing is the eternal scale keeping the best of all possible worlds carefully balanced against the counterweight of all impossible worlds. Decreation takes place at the point where Bartleby stands, "in the heart of the eternal pyramid" of the Palace of Destinies, which, in this ironic and inverted theodicy, is also called the Halls of Justice. His word is not Justice, which gives a reward or a perpetual punishment to what was, but instead Palingenesis, *apokatastasis pantōn*, in which the new creature—for the new creature is what is at issue here—reaches the indemonstrable center of its "occurrence-or-nonoccurrence." This is the irrevocable end of the letter's journey, which, on errands of life, sped toward death. And it is here that the creature is finally at home, saved in being irredeemable. This is why in the end, the walled courtyard is not a sad place. There is sky and there is grass. And the creature knows perfectly well "where it is."

Reference Matter

Notes

Editor's Introduction

1. Walter Benjamin, *Gesammelte Schriften*, ed. Rolf Tiedemann and Hermann Schweppenhäuser (Frankfurt am Main: Suhrkamp, 1974–89), vol. 1, pt. 3, p. 1238. The German text reads as follows: "Die historische Methode ist eine philologische, der das Buch des Lebens zugrunde liegt. 'Was nie geschrieben wurde, lesen' heißt es bei Hofmannsthal. Der Leser, an den hier zu denken ist, ist der wahre Historiker." Cf. the passage in "Über das mimetische Vermögen" where Benjamin cites the same phrase of Hofmannsthal, in *Gesammelte Schriften*, vol. 2, pt. 1, p. 213.

2. Aristotle, *De interpretatione*, 17 a 25; see also Aristotle, *De anima*, 430 b 26. In "Tradition of the Immemorial," Agamben also notes that the Aristotelian definition of the proposition is already implicit in Plato, *Sophist*, 262 e 6–7.

3. Varro, *De lingua latina*, VIII, 5–6. See Agamben, "Language and History," Chapter 3 in the present volume. See also Chapter 4, "Philosophy and Linguistics."

4. Jean-Claude Milner, *Introduction à une science du langage* (Paris: Seuil, 1990), p. 409. Cf. Agamben's "Philosophy and Linguistics," Chapter 4 in the present volume.

5. *The Wittgenstein Reader*, ed. Anthony Kenny (London: Blackwell, 1994), p. 12; the original is in Ludwig Wittgenstein, *Tractatus logico-philosophicus*, prop. 4.026, in his *Werkausgabe*, vol. 1 (Frankfurt am Main: Suhrkamp, 1984), pp. 28–29. See Agamben, "Language and History," Chapter 3 in the present volume.

6. *Wittgenstein Reader*, p. 8; original in Wittgenstein, *Tractatus*, prop. 3.221, p. 19.

7. Agamben comments on this passage in chapters 3 and 4 of the present volume: "Tradition of the Immemorial" and "Philosophy and Linguistics."

8. See Lewis Carroll, *Alice in Wonderland*, ed. Donald J. Gray (New York: W. W. Norton, 1992), pp. 186–87.

9. K. Reach, "The Name Relation and the Logical Antinomies," *Journal of Symbolic Logic* 3 (1938): 97–111; Agamben refers to this essay in "Philosophy and Linguistics," Chapter 4 in the present volume.

10. Agamben refers here to the work of Philippe de Rouilhan, *Frege: Les paradoxes de la représentation* (Paris: Minuit, 1988).

11. *Wittgenstein Reader*, p. 14; original in Wittgenstein, *Tractatus*, prop. 4.121, p. 33. Agamben cites this passage in "Pardes," Chapter 13 in the present volume.

12. Milner, *Introduction*, p. 332. Cf. Agamben, "Philosophy and Linguistics," Chapter 4 in the present volume.

13. Martin Heidegger, *On the Way to Language*, trans. Peter D. Hertz (New York: Harper and Row, 1971), p. 86; the original is in Martin Heidegger, *Gesamtausgabe*, vol. 12: *Unterwegs zur Sprache* (Frankfurt am Main: Klostermann, 1985), p. 181.

14. Paul Celan, *Gesammelte Werke*, ed. Beda Allemann and Stefan Reichard with Rolf Bücher (Frankfurt am Main: Suhrkamp, 1983), 3: 181.

15. Walter Benjamin, "Aus einer kleinen Rede über Proust, an meinem vierzigsten Geburtstag gehalten," in his *Gesammelte Schriften*, vol. 2, pt. 3, pp. 1064–65.

16. Plato, Epistle VII, 341 a 7–d 5, in *Plato, with an English Translation*, vol. 7: *Timaeus, Critias, Celitophon, Menexenus, Epistles*, trans. R. G. Bury (Cambridge, Mass.: Harvard University Press, 1952), pp. 529–31.

17. Ibid., 344 d 3, p. 541.

18. Ibid., 342 a–b, p. 533.

19. Plato, *Phaedo*, 99 e 4–6: "It seemed to me necessary to seek refuge in the *logoi*, to find the truth of beings in them." This passage is cited by Agamben in "The Thing Itself," Chapter 1 in this volume.

20. Plato, Epistle VII, 342 d–e, in *Plato, with an English Translation*, 7: 535.

21. Agamben's reading is based on the texts of *Parisinus graecus* 1807 and *Vaticanus graecus* 1. As he indicates in "The Thing Itself," Marsilio Ficino's translation of the passage still respects the original Platonic formulation: *quintum vero oportet ipsum ponere quo quid est cognoscibile, id est quod agnosci potest, atque vere existit.*

22. Giorgio Agamben, *The Coming Community*, trans. Michael Hardt (Minneapolis: University of Minnesota Press, 1993), p. 76; the original is in Giorgio Agamben, *La comunità che viene* (Turin: Einaudi, 1991), p. 51.

23. Plato, *Republic*, 511 b 3–c 2. See Agamben, "The Thing Itself," Chapter 1 in this volume.

24. Aristotle, *De interpretatione*, 16 a 3–7. The Greek text is in *Aristotle in Twenty-Three Volumes*, vol. 1: *The Categories, On Interpretation, and Prior*

Analytics, trans. Hugh Tredennick (Cambridge, Mass.: Harvard University Press, 1983), p. 114. My translation.

25. Plato, Epistle VII, 342 c 6, in *Plato, with an English Translation,* 7: 535.

26. See Augustine, *De dialectica,* sec. 5. On the Stoic roots of Augustine's philosophy of language, see Karl Barwick, *Probleme der stoischen Sprachlehre und Rhetorik* (Berlin: Akademie, 1957), esp. pp. 8–29, "Augustins Dialektik und ihr Verhältnis zu Varros Schriften *De dialectica* und *De lingua latina.*" Barwick shows very clearly that Augustine's definitions of both "speech" and "articulation" (*loqui est articolata voce signum dare; articulatam dico quae comprendi litteris potest*) are reformulations of Stoic principles (see *Stoicorum veterum fragmenta,* ed. Jacob von Arnim [Leipzig: 1903], vol. 2, frag. 167; vol. 3, frag. 213, 26).

27. In addition to this discussion in "The Thing Itself," see Agamben's fullest consideration of status of the *gramma* in *De interpretatione,* in the third "Excursus" of Giorgio Agamben, *Linguaggio e la morte, Un seminario sul luogo della negatività* (Turin: Einaudi, 1982), pp. 52–54; translated as *Language and Death: The Place of Negativity,* trans. Karen E. Pinkus with Michael Hardt (Minneapolis: University of Minnesota Press, 1991), pp. 38–40. This passage also takes the form of a critique of Derrida's "grammatology."

28. Émile Bréhier, *La théorie des incorporels dans l'ancien stoïcisme* (Paris: Vrin, 1997), pp. 14–15.

29. Ammonius, *Commentarius in Aristotelis de Interpretatione,* ed. Adolf Busse (Berlin: Reimer, 1897), p. 17; cited in Bréhier, *La théorie des incorporels,* p. 15.

30. On the status of the incorporeal in Stoic philosophy, the best work remains Bréhier's *La théorie des incorporels.*

31. Seneca, Epistle 117, in L. Annæi Senecæ, *Pars prima sive Opera Philosophica,* ed. M. N. Bouillet, vol. 4 (1827; reprint, Brescia: Paideia Editore, 1977), pp. 287–300. The importance of this text for medieval logic has been repeatedly underlined. Among others, see Jan Pinborg, *Logik und Semantik im Mittelalter, Ein Überblick* (Stuttgart: Frommann-Holzboog, 1972), p. 57.

32. Seneca, Epistle 117, p. 292.

33. In his edition of the *Stoicorum veterum fragmenta,* von Arnim lists the Stoics' texts on logic under the heading *Peri sēmainomenon ē lekton* ("On the Signified or the Expressible"), suggesting an identity between "signified" and "expressible" in the doctrine of the Stoa. The relation of *sēmainomenon* and *lekton* is certainly one of the most difficult and obscure points of Stoic logic, and there is little agreement among scholars on the subject. Bréhier writes, "If the 'signified' is an 'expressible,' it is certainly not the case that every expressible is a signified" (*La théorie des incorporels,* p. 15). Benson Mates, by contrast, treats the two terms as essentially equivalent and consequently argues that what is said in this passage of the *sēmainomenon* holds for the *lekton* as such. See Benson Mates,

"Signs, Sense and Denotation," in his *Stoic Logic* (Berkeley: University of California Press, 1973), pp. 11–26. Also see the recent extended study by Andreas Schubert, *Untersuchungen zur stoischen Bedeutungslehre* (Göttingen: Vandenhoeck and Ruprecht, 1994).

34. Sextus Empiricus, *Adversus Mathematicos*, VIII, 12.

35. It is worth noting that in Diogenes Laertius's definition of the Stoic proposition, *pragma* and *lekton* appear to have the same denotation: *pragma autoteles hoson eph' heautōi* (*Vitae*, VII, 65). Scholars have often indicated the close relation between *pragma* and *lekton* in Stoic terminology: see Mates, *Stoic Logic*, p. 28; Pierre Hadot, *Études de philosophie ancienne* (Paris: Les Belles Lettres, 1988), pp. 67–69; and Schubert, *Untersuchungen zur stoischen Bedeutungslehre*, pp. 17–22.

36. In addition to Seneca's Epistle 117 (see note 31 above), Varro, Aulus Gellius, and a number of Christian texts also transmitted the doctrine of the *lekton* to the Middle Ages. Of particular importance is Augustine's *De magistro*, sec. 5, in which the Stoic *lekton* appears as *dicibile*: "Quod dixi dicibile, verbum est, nec tamen verbum, sed quod in verbo intelligitur et animo continetur, significat." In Isidore of Seville's *Etymologiarum sive originum*, II, 22, 2, we read: "nam lekton dictio dicitur." See also John of Salisbury, *Metalogicon*, II, 4. Much useful information on the history of the doctrine of the proposition is to be found in Gabriel Nuchelmans, *Theories of the Proposition: Ancient and Medieval Conceptions of the Bearers of Truth and Falsity* (Amsterdam-London: North-Holland, 1973). A precise philosophical and historical study of the concept of the "expressible," however, remains to be written.

37. *Dictum*, *dicibile*, and *enuntiabile* are *termini technici* that appear throughout the logical tracts of the early terminists. The fullest development of the problem appears in the so-called *Ars meliduna*. See E. M. de Rijk, "*Ars Meliduna*: The Theory of the *Enuntiabile*," in *The Origin and Development of the Theory of the Supposition*, vol. 2, pt. 1 of his *Logica modernorum: A Contribution to the History of Early Terminist Logic* (Assen: Van Gorcum, 1967), pp. 357–90.

38. On the origin and dating of the *Ars disputandi Burana*, see ibid., pp. 397–98. The text of the *Ars* is printed in de Rijk, *Logica modernorum*, vol. 2, pt. 2: *Texts and Indices*, pp. 175–213.

39. In De Rijk, *Logica modernorum*, vol. 2, pt. 2, p. 208. My translation.

40. Jean Jolivet, *Arts du langage et théologie chez Abélard* (Paris: Vrin, 1969), pp. 77–85, esp. 82n.

41. See Hubert Elie, *Le complexe significabile* (Paris: Vrin, 1937), esp. pp. 17–41. It is worth noting that according to Elie (p. 19), the classical passage that "in some way constitutes the central point of all discussions of the *Complexe significabile*" is to be found in the other treatise that, alongside *De interpretatione*,

formed Aristotle's logical *Organon*. See Aristotle, *Categories*, 12 b 6–15, in which the term "thing" seems to occupy a position similar to that of Plato's "thing itself": "What is affirmed in a statement [*logos*] is not of itself affirmation, nor is what is denied a denial. An affirmation is an affirmative statement, a denial is a negative statement. But what is affirmed or denied in a statement is a thing [*pragma*], not a statement." The paradox of "empty reference" constitutes a further point of proximity between medieval logic and Meinong's thought. See Alain de Libera, "Roger Bacon et la référence vide, Sur quelques antécédents médiévaux du paradoxe de Meinong," in *Lectionum Varietates, Hommage à Paul Vignaux*, ed. J. Jolivet, Z. Kaluza, and A. de Libera (Paris: Vrin, 1991), pp. 85–120.

42. Alexius von Meinong, "Über Gegenstände höherer Ordnung und deren Verhältnis zur inneren Wahrnehmung," in his *Gesammelte Abhandlungen*, vol. 2: *Zur Erkenntnistheorie und Gegenstandstheorie* (Leipzig: J. A. Barth, 1914), p. 384. As Meinong himself informs us, the distinction between content and object in modern epistemology has its origin in Twardowski's work on the subject, *Zur Lehre von Inhalt und Gegenstand der Vorstellungen* (1894). The fundamental importance, for twentieth-century philosophy as a whole, of the problem of "psychologism" and, in particular, the question of the "content" of representations and judgments—from Frege's "thought" (*Gedanke*) to Husserl's "expression" and his classical analyses of the nonreality of the "noema"—has yet to be fully considered.

43. Bertrand Russell, "Meinong's Theory of Complexes and Assumptions," *Mind* 13 (1904): 204–19, 336–54, 509–24.

44. See J. N. Finlay, *Meinong's Theory of Objects and Values* (Oxford: Oxford University Press, 1963), pp. 44–58.

45. Gilles Deleuze, *Logique du sens* (Paris: Minuit, 1969), p. 34.

46. Proclus, *In Platonem Tim.*, 271 d. Cited in Victor Goldschmidt, *Le système stoïcien et l'idée du temps* (Paris: Vrin, 1969), p. 12; also cited in Schubert, *Untersuchungen zur stoischen Bedeutungslehre*, p. 22.

47. See Walter Benjamin, "Über die Sprache überhaupt und die Sprache des Menschen," in his *Gesammelte Schriften*, vol. 2, pt. 1, pp. 140–57. Benjamin himself (p. 142) italicizes the last three letters of the word *mitteilbar*.

48. Aristotle, *De anima*, 417 a 2–5. The Greek text is in *Aristotle in Twenty-Three Volumes*, vol. 8: *On the Soul, Parva Naturalia, On Breath*, trans. W. S. Hett (Cambridge, Mass.: Harvard University Press, 1986), p. 94. My translation.

49. Giorgio Agamben, *Homo Sacer: Sovereign Power and Bare Life*, trans. Daniel Heller-Roazen (Stanford, Calif.: Stanford University Press, 1998), p. 46.

50. Aristotle, *De anima*, 417 b 2–16. The Greek text is in *Aristotle in Twenty-Three Volumes*, 8: 98. My translation.

51. Agamben, *Homo Sacer*, p. 47.

52. Martin Heidegger, *Basic Writings*, ed. David Farrel Krell (New York: Harper San Francisco, 1977), p. 238; the original is in Martin Heidegger, *Gesamtausgabe*, vol. 9: *Wegmarken* (Frankfurt am Main: Klostermann, 1976), p. 317.

53. Philippe Jaworski, cited in Gilles Deleuze, "Bartleby, or the Formula," in Deleuze's *Essays Critical and Clinical*, trans. Daniel W. Smith and Michael A. Greco (Minneapolis: University of Minnesota Press, 1997), p. 70; the original of Deleuze's essay is "Bartleby ou la formule," in his *Critique et clinique* (Paris: Éditions du Minuit, 1993), p. 92. In its Italian edition, Agamben's "Bartleby, or On Contingency" was published together with Deleuze's essay under the title *Bartleby: La formula della creazione* (Macerata: Quodlibet, 1993).

54. Deleuze, *Essays Critical and Clinical*, p. 71; original in Deleuze, *Critique et clinique*, p. 92.

55. Diogenes Laertius, *Lives of Eminent Philosophers*, trans. R. D. Hicks, vol. 2 (Cambridge, Mass.: Harvard University Press, 1955), p. 488.

56. Sextus Empiricus, *Pyrrōneiōn hypotypōseōn*, I, 7, 15.

57. Émile Benveniste, "La nature des pronoms," in *Problèmes de linguistique générale*, vol. 1 (Paris: Gallimard, 1966), p. 255. On the performative and Benveniste's notion of the "instance of discourse," see "La nature des pronoms," pp. 251–57, and two other essays by Benveniste in the same volume: "Structures de relations de personne dans le verbe," pp. 225–36, and "Les verbes délocutifs," pp. 277–85.

58. See Roman Jakobson, "Shifters, Verbal Categories, and the Russian Verb," in *Selected Writings*, vol. 2 (The Hague: Mouton, 1971). Agamben's *Language and Death* takes as one of its subjects the particular metaphysical and logical status of these parts of discourse.

59. Walter Benjamin, *The Origin of the German Tragic Drama*, trans. John Osborne (London: Verso, 1977), p. 46; the original is in Benjamin, *Gesammelte Schriften*, vol. 1, pt. 1, p. 227.

60. Ibid., English p. 36; original p. 216.

61. Ibid., English p. 36; original p. 217.

62. It should be noted that in this definition of "gesture," Agamben also implicitly draws on Benjamin's concept of gesture, in particular insofar as he formulates it in his texts on Kafka and Brecht. The only other contemporary philosopher to have noted the significance of Benjamin's reflections on gesture is Werner Hamacher, a thinker whose proximity to Agamben is apparent in his lapidary definition of "gesture" as "what remains of language after meaning is withdrawn from it." See Werner Hamacher, "The Gesture in the Name: On Benjamin and Kafka," in *Premises: Essays on Philosophy and Literature from Kant to Celan*, trans. Peter Fenves (Cambridge, Mass.: Harvard University Press, 1997), pp. 294–336; the original is Werner Hamacher, "Die Geste im Namen: Benjamin und Kafka," in *Entferntes Verstehen: Studien zu Philosophie und Liter-*

atur von Kant bis Celan (Frankfurt am Main: Suhrkamp, 1998), pp. 280–323.

63. Benjamin, *Origin*, p. 182; original in Benjamin, *Gesammelte Schriften*, vol. I, pt. I, p. 357.

64. Giorgio Agamben, *Mezzi senza fini* (Turin: Bollati Boringhieri, 1996), p. 92.

§1 *The Thing Itself*

1. Plato, Epistle VII, 340 b 3–7, in *Plato, with an English Translation*, vol. 7: *Timaeus, Critias, Celitophon, Menexenus, Epistles*, trans. R. G. Bury (Cambridge, Mass.: Harvard University Press, 1952), p. 527. All page citations included in the text of this chapter refer to this edition. Some of the translations have been modified.

2. Among modern scholars, only Andreae restored the text to its earlier form; see his study on the Platonic Letters in *Philologus* 78 (1923): 34ff.

3. Plato, Epistle II, 314 c 3–4, in *Plato, with an English Translation*, 7: 417.

4. *Republic*, 511 b 3–c 2, in *Plato, The Republic*, trans. Paul Shorey (Cambridge, Mass.: Harvard University Press, 1956), 2: 113–15.

5. Aristotle, *De interpretatione*, 16 a 3–7. The Greek text is in *Aristotle in Twenty-Three Volumes*, vol. 1: *The Categories, On Interpretation, and Prior Analytics*, trans. Hugh Tredennick (Cambridge, Mass.: Harvard University Press, 1983), p. 114.

§3 *Language and History*

1. Walter Benjamin, *Gesammelte Schriften*, ed. Rolf Tiedemann and Hermann Schweppenhäuser (Frankfurt am Main: Suhrkamp, 1974–89), vol. 1, pt. 3, p. 1239.

2. Ibid., p. 1235.

3. Isidore of Seville, *Etymologiarum sive originum*, I, XLI.

4. Augustine, *De ordine*, 2, 12, 37.

5. Varro, *De lingua latina*, VIII, 5–6.

6. *The Wittgenstein Reader*, ed. Anthony Kenny (London: Blackwell, 1994), p. 12; the original is in Ludwig Wittgenstein, *Tractatus logico-philosophicus*, prop. 4.026, in his *Werkausgabe*, vol. 1 (Frankfurt am Main: Suhrkamp, 1984), pp. 28–29.

7. Dante, *Il Convivio*, II, XIII, 8–10; in *Dante's "Il Convivio" (The Banquet)*, trans. Richard H. Lansing (New York: Garland, 1990), p. 69.

8. Ibid.

9. Benjamin, *Gesammelte Schriften*, vol. 2, pt. 1, p. 139.

10. Ibid., p. 138.

11. Walter Benjamin, *Reflections: Essays, Aphorisms, Autobiographical Writings*, ed. Peter Demetz, trans. Edmund Jephcott (New York: Schocken, 1978), p. 318; the original is in Benjamin, *Gesammelte Schriften*, vol. 2, pt. 1, p. 144.

12. Ibid., English p. 320; original pp. 145, 146.

13. Ibid., English p. 328; original p. 153.

14. [Here "to mean" renders the Italian *voler dire*, which (like the corresponding French expression, *vouloir dire*) signifies both "to want to say" and "to signify."—Ed.]

15. Walter Benjamin, *Illuminations*, ed. Hannah Arendt, trans. Harry Zohn (New York: Schocken, 1968), p. 74; the original is in Benjamin, *Gesammelte Schriften*, vol. 4, pt. 1, p. 13.

16. Ibid., English p. 75; original p. 14.

17. Ibid., English p. 80; original p. 19.

18. Ibid., English p. 74; original p. 13.

19. Ibid., English p. 75; original p. 14.

20. Ibid., English and original.

21 Benjamin, *Gesammelte Schriften*, vol. 1, pt. 3, p. 1235.

22. Hans-Georg Gadamer, *Truth and Method*, trans. Joel Winsheimer and Donald G. Marshall (New York: Continuum, 1993), p. 458; the original is in *Warheit und Methode* (Tübingen: J. C. B. Mohr [Paul Siebeck], 1960), pp. 523–34.

23. Benjamin, *Gesammelte Schriften*, vol. 1, pt. 3, p. 1231.

24. Gershom Scholem, "The Name of God and the Linguistic Theory of the Kabbalah (Part 2)," *Diogenes* 79 (1973): 194; the original is in Gershom Scholem, *Judaica*, vol. 3 (Frankfurt am Main: Suhrkamp, 1973), p. 69.

25. Walter Benjamin, *The Origin of the German Tragic Drama*, trans. John Osborne (London: Verso, 1977), p. 36; the original is in Benjamin, *Gesammelte Schriften*, vol. 1, pt. 1, pp. 216–17.

26. Ibid., English p. 47; original p. 226.

27. Ibid., English p. 47; original p. 228.

28. Walter Benjamin, *One-Way Street and Other Writings*, trans. Edmund Jephcott and Kingsley Shorter (London: Verso, 1979), p. 361; the original is in *Gesammelte Schriften*, vol. 2, pt. 2, p. 478.

§4 *Philosophy and Linguistics*

1. Jean-Claude Milner, *Introduction à une science du langage* (Paris: Seuil, 1990), p. 10. All page citations included in the text of this chapter refer to this edition.

2. Ibid., pp. 109–26. See also Milner's article "L'exemple et la fiction," in *Transparence et opacité*, ed. T. Papp and P. Pica (Paris: Le Cerf, 1988), pp. 145–81.

3. K. Reach, "The Name Relation and the Logical Antinomies," *Journal of Symbolic Logic* 3 (1938): 97–111.

4. See Milner, *Introduction*, pp. 216–36.

5. Jean-Claude Milner, "Lacan et la science," lecture given in May 1990, on the occasion of the conference "Lacan et la Philosophie."

§5 *Kommerell, or On Gesture*

1. Max Kommerell, *Gedanken über Gedichte* (Frankfurt am Main: Klostermann, 1956), p. 36.

2. Max Kommerell, *Dichterische Welterfahrungen* (Frankfurt am Main: Klostermann, 1952), pp. 153, 155.

3. Max Kommerell, *Jean Paul* (Frankfurt am Main: Klostermann, 1933), p. 42.

4. Max Kommerell, *Geist und Buchstabe der Dichtung* (Frankfurt am Main: Klostermann, 1962), p. 317.

5. Kommerell, *Jean Paul*, p. 48.

6. Ibid., pp. 44–45.

7. Ibid., p. 47.

8. Kommerell, *Geist und Buchstabe der Dichtung*, p. 316.

9. Walter Benjamin, *Illuminations*, ed. Hannah Arendt, trans. Harry Zohn (New York: Schocken, 1968), p. 120; the original is in Walter Benjamin, *Gesammelte Schriften*, ed. Rolf Tiedemann and Hermann Schweppenhäuser (Frankfurt am Main: Suhrkamp, 1974–89), vol. 2, pt. 2, p. 418.

10. *The Correspondence of Walter Benjamin, 1910–1940*, ed. Gershom Scholem and Theodor W. Adorno, trans. Manfred R. Jacobson and Evelyn M. Jacobson (Chicago: The University of Chicago Press, 1994), p. 335; the original is in Walter Benjamin, *Briefe*, ed. Gershom Scholem and Theodor W. Adorno (Frankfurt am Main: Suhrkamp, 1966), 2: 499–500.

11. *Kein ding sei wo das wort gebricht.* This is the last verse of the poem "Das Wort," from Stefan George, *Das Neue Reich.*

12. Stefan George, *Werke* (Düsseldorf: H. Küpper, 1958), 1: 490.

13. Benjamin, *Gesammelte Schriften*, 3: 259.

14. Max Kommerell, *Briefe und Aufzeichnungen*, ed. Inge Jens (Olten and Freiburg: Walter-Verlag, 1967), p. 197.

15. Benjamin, *Gesammelte Schriften*, 3: 259.

16. Kommerell, *Jean Paul*, p. 418.

17. See G. Mattenklott, "Max Kommerell, Versuch eines Portraits," *Merkur* 40 (1986): 541–54.

18. Max Kommerell, *Essays, Notizen, Poetische Fragmente*, ed. Inge Jens (Olten and Freiburg: Walter-Verlag, 1969), pp. 82–85.

19. Max Kommerell, *Der Dichter als Führer in der deutschen Klassik* (Frankfurt am Main: Klostermann, 1982), p. 7.

§6 *Warburg and the Nameless Science*

1. Robert Klein is the author of the *boutade* on Warburg as the creator of a discipline "that, in contrast to many others, exists but has no name." Robert Klein, *La forme et l'intelligible* (Paris: Gallimard, 1970), p. 224.

2. With the rise to power of Nazism in 1933, the Warburg Institute moved to London, where it was incorporated into the University of London in 1944. See Fritz Saxl, "The History of Warburg's Library," in Ernst H. Gombrich, *Aby Warburg: An Intellectual Biography* (London: The Warburg Institute and University of London, 1970), pp. 325ff.

3. The lovely "intellectual biography" of Warburg published by the present director of the Warburg Institute, Ernst H. Gombrich (*Aby Warburg*), only partially fills this gap. For now it constitutes the only source of information about Warburg's unpublished works.

4. As reported by Saxl, "History of Warburg's Library," p. 326.

5. *Ästhetisierende Kunstgeschichte.* The term can be found in, among other writings, an unpublished text of 1923. See Gombrich, *Aby Warburg*, p. 88.

6. The lecture was published in English in 1939: Aby Warburg, "A Lecture on the Serpent Ritual," *Journal of the Warburg Institute* 2 (1939): 277–92.

7. Giorgio Pasquali, "Aby Warburg," *Pegaso*, April 1930; reprinted in Giorgio Pasquali, *Pagine stravaganti* (Florence: Sansoni, 1968), 1: 44.

8. Tito Vignoli, *Myth and Science* (New York: Appleton, 1882).

9. Warburg was occupied with the construction of his library for his whole life, and it may well have been the work to which he dedicated the most time and effort. A prophetic childhood experience lies at its origin. At the age of thirteen, Aby, who was the first-born son of a family of bankers, offered to give his right of primogeniture to his younger brother Max in exchange for the promise that his brother would buy him all the books he wanted. Max accepted, surely without realizing that his brother's childhood joke would one day become reality.

Warburg ordered his books not by the alphabetical or arithmetical criteria used in large libraries, but rather according to his interests and his system of thought, to the point of rearranging the order of his books whenever his methods of research changed. The law guiding the library was that of the "good neighbor," which states that the solution of one's own problem is contained not in the book one is looking for but in the one beside it. Warburg thus transformed the library into a kind of labyrinthine image of himself, one whose power of attraction was enormous. Saxl recounts that when Ernst Cassirer first entered the library, he declared that he had either to flee immediately or to remain inside it for years. Like a true maze, the library led the reader to his goal by leading him astray, from one "good neighbor" to another, in a series of detours at the end of which he fatally encountered the Minotaur that had been waiting for him from the beginning, who was, in a certain sense, Warburg himself. Whoever has worked in the library knows how true this is even today, despite the concessions that have been made over the years to the demands of contemporary organizational principles.

10. See Gombrich, *Aby Warburg*, p. 222.

11. Ibid., p. 89.

12. Aby Warburg, "Italian Art and International Astrology in the Palazzo Schifanoia in Ferrara," in *German Essays on Art History*, ed. Gert Schiff (New York: Continuum, 1988), pp. 252–53. The original is in Aby M. Warburg, *Ausgewählte Schriften und Würdigungen*, ed. Dieter Wuttke with Carl Georg Heise (Baden-Baden: Valenti Koerner, 1979), p. 185.

13. For Spitzer, see in particular Leo Spitzer, *Essays in Historical Semantics* (New York: S. F. Vanni, 1948). For an assessment of Ludwig Traube's work, see Giorgio Pasquali's remarks in "Paleografia quale scienza dello spirito," *Nuova Antologia* 1 (June, 1931); reprinted in Pasquali, *Pagine stravaganti*, p. 115.

14. The German term used by Warburg, *Nachleben*, does not literally mean "renaissance," as it has sometimes been rendered, nor does it mean "survival." It implies the idea of the continuity of the pagan inheritance that was essential for Warburg.

15. In a letter to his friend Mesnil, Warburg formulated his concern in a traditional fashion: "What did antiquity represent for the men of the Renaissance?" Elsewhere, Warburg specified that "later, in the course of the years, [the problem] was extended to the attempts to understand the meaning of the survival of paganism for the whole of European civilization ... " Quoted in Gombrich, *Aby Warburg*, p. 307.

16. On the opposition between "cold" societies, which are societies without history, and "warm" societies, which contain numerous historical factors, see Claude Lévi-Strauss, *La pensée sauvage* (Paris: Plon, 1962), pp. 309–10.

17. Gombrich, *Aby Warburg*, p. 242.

18. "The dynamograms of ancient art are handed down in a state of maximal tension but unpolarized with regard to the passive or active energy charge to the responding, imitating, or remembering artists. It is only the contact with the new age that results in polarization. This polarization can lead to a radical reversal (inversion) of the meaning they held for classical antiquity. . . . The essence of thiasotic engrams as balanced charges in a Leydan bottle before their contact with the selective will of the age." Warburg, quoted in Gombrich, *Aby Warburg*, pp. 248–49.

19. Warburg's interpretation of Dürer's *Melancholy* as a work of "humanistic comfort against the fear of Saturn," which transforms the image of the planetary demon into the plastic incarnation of a thinking man, largely determines Erwin Panofsky and Fritz Saxl's conclusions in their *Dürers Melencolia I, Eine quellen- und typengeschichtliche Untersuchung* (Leipzig: B. G. Teubner, 1923).

20. The pages in which Warburg develops this interpretation, which focuses

specifically on the figures of Nietzsche and Burckhardt, are among the most beautiful he ever wrote: "We must learn to see Burckhardt and Nietzsche as the receivers of mnemic waves and realise that the consciousness of the world affects the two in a very different way. . . . Both of them are very sensitive seismographs whose foundations tremble when they must receive and transmit the waves. But there is one important difference: Burckhardt received the waves from the regions of the past, he sensed the dangerous tremors and he saw to it that the foundations of his seismograph were strengthened. . . . He felt how dangerous his profession was, and that he really should simply break down, but he did not succumb to romanticism. . . . Burckhardt was a necromancer, with his eyes open. Thus he conjured up spectres which quite seriously threatened him. He evaded them by erecting his observation tower. He is a seer such as Lynkeus (in Goethe's *Faust*); he sits in his tower and speaks . . . he was and remained a champion of enlightenment but one who never desired to be anything but a simple teacher. . . . What type of seer is Nietzsche? He is the type of a Nabi, the ancient prophet who runs out into the street, tears his clothes, cries woe and perhaps carries the people with him. His gesture is derived from that of the leader with the thyrsus who compels everyone to follow him. Hence his observations about the dance. In the figures of Jacob Burckhardt and Nietzsche two ancient types of prophets are contrasted in that region where the Latin and the German tradition meet. The question is which type of seer can bear the traumas of his vocation. The one attempts to transpose them into a call. The lack of response constantly saps his foundations; after all he is really a teacher. Two sons of clergymen who react so differently to the feeling of God's presence in the world." Quoted in Gombrich, *Aby Warburg*, pp. 254–57.

21. Ibid., p. 253.

22. Ibid., p. 223. Warburg's conception of symbols and their life in social memory may recall Jung's idea of the archetype. Jung's name, however, never appears in Warburg's notes. In any case, it should not be forgotten that for Warburg, images are not ahistorical entities but historical realties inserted in a process of cultural transmission.

23. On Giulio Camillo and his theater, see Frances Yates, *The Art of Memory* (Chicago: The University of Chicago Press, 1966), chap. 6, "Renaissance Memory: The Memory Theatre of Giulio Camillo," pp. 129–59.

24. On the hermeneutic circle, see Spitzer's magisterial observations in the first chapter of Leo Spitzer, *Linguistics and Literary History* (New York: Russell and Russell, 1962), pp. 1–29.

25. I take this observation from Martin Heidegger, who philosophically grounded the hermeneutic circle in *Sein und Zeit* (Tübingen: Niemeyer, 1928), pp. 151–53; translated as Martin Heidegger, *Being and Time*, trans. John Macquarrie and Edward Robinson (New York: Harper and Row, 1962), pp. 192–95.

26. Aby Warburg, *Sandro Botticellis "Geburt der Venus" und "Frühling"* (Hamburg: Von Leopold Voss, 1893), p. 47; reprinted in Warburg, *Ausgewählte Schriften und Würdigungen*, p. 61.

27. Quoted in Gombrich, *Aby Warburg*, p. 303.

28. Aby Warburg, "Orientalisierende Astrologie," *Zeitschrift der Deutschen Morgenländischen Gesellschaft* 6 (1927). Since it is always necessary to save reason from rationalists, it is worth noting that the categories that Warburg uses in his diagnosis are infinitely more subtle than the contemporary opposition between rationalism and irrationalism. Warburg interprets this conflict in terms of polarity and not dichotomy. One of Warburg's greatest contributions to the science of culture is his rediscovery of Goethe's notion of polarity for a global comprehension of culture. This is particularly important if one considers that the opposition of rationalism and irrationalism has often distorted interpretations of the cultural tradition of the West.

29. Erwin Panofsky, *Meaning in the Visual Arts* (Chicago: University of Chicago Press, 1955), p. 31.

30. Erwin Panofsky, *Studies in Iconology: Humanistic Themes in the Art of the Renaissance* (Oxford: Oxford University Press, 1939), p. 178.

31. Neither Panofsky nor the scholars who were closer to Warburg and who, after Warburg's death, assured the continuity of the institute—from Fritz Saxl to Gertrud Bing and Edgar Wind (the present director, Ernst Gombrich, became part of the Institute after Warburg's death)—ever claimed to be Warburg's successors in his research in a nameless science beyond the borders of art history. Each of them deepened Warburg's legacy within art history (often with impressive results), but without thematically embarking upon a global approach to the cultural phenomena. And it is likely that this fact has its counterpart in the objectively vital organizational needs of the institute, whose activity has nevertheless marked an incomparable renewal in the study of art history. It remains true that, as far as the "nameless science" is concerned, Warburg's *Nachleben* still awaits its polarizing encounter with the selective will of the epoch. On the personality of the scholars associated with the Warburg Institute, see Carlo Ginzburg, "Da A. Warburg a E. H. Gombrich," *Studi Medievali* 7, no. 2 (1966).

32. See Claude Lévi-Strauss, "Histoire et ethnologie," *Revue de Métaphysique et morale* 3–4 (1949), reprinted in Claude Lévi-Strauss, *Anthropologie structurale* (Paris: Plon, 1973–74), 1: 24–25.

33. Valéry's statement (in *Regards sur le monde actuel* [Paris: Stock, 1944]) is not to be understood here in a merely geographical sense.

34. "Der Eintritt des antikisierenden Idealstils in die Malerei der Frührenaissance," in *Kunstchronik*, May 8, 1914.

§7 *Tradition of the Immemorial*

1. Plato, Epistle II, 312 d 5–313 e 7; the Greek text is in *Plato, with an English Translation*, vol. 7: *Timaeus, Critias, Cleitophon, Menexenus, Epistles*, trans. R. G. Bury (Cambridge, Mass.: Harvard University Press, 1952), p. 410.

2. Martin Heidegger, "On the Essence of Truth," in *Basic Writings*, ed. David Farrel Krell (New York: Harper San Francisco, 1977), p. 138; the original is in Martin Heidegger, *Gesamtausgabe*, vol. 9: *Wegmarken* (Frankfurt am Main: Klostermann, 1976), p. 94.

3. Plato, Epistle VII, 343 b 9–c 3; the Greek text is in *Plato, with an English Translation*, 7: 536.

4. Plotinus, *Ennead* II, 4, 5; the Greek text is in *Plotinus, with an English Translation*, vol. 2: *Ennead II, 1–9*, trans. A. H. Armstrong (Cambridge, Mass.: Harvard University Press, 1961), pp. 112–14.

5. Plato, *Theatetus*, 201 e–202 b, in *Plato, with an English Translation*, vol. 2, trans. Harold North Fowler (Cambridge, Mass.: Harvard University Press, 1962), pp. 222–24.

6. *The Wittgenstein Reader*, ed. Anthony Kenny (London: Blackwell, 1994), p. 8; the original is in Ludwig Wittgenstein, *Tractatus logico-philosophicus*, prop. 3.221, in his *Werkausgabe*, vol. 1 (Frankfurt am Main: Suhrkamp, 1984), p. 19.

7. Aristotle, *De anima*, 430 b 26–29; the Greek text is in *Aristotle in Twenty-Three Volumes*, vol. 8: *On the Soul, Parva Naturalia, On Breath*, trans. W. S. Hett (Cambridge, Mass.: Harvard University Press, 1986), p. 174.

8. Aristotle, *Physics*, 189 a 30–31; the Greek text is in *Aristotle: The Physics*, trans. Francis M. Cornford (Cambridge, Mass.: Harvard University Press, 1967), p. 62.

9. Dante Alighieri, *De monarchia*, I, 2, in *Monarchy and Three Political Letters*, trans. Donald Nicholl (London: Weidenfeld and Nicolson, 1954), pp. 4–5.

10. Nicholas Cusanus, "Trialogus de possest," in *Philosophisch-theologische Schriften*, ed. Leo Gabriel, trans. Wilhelm Dupré (Vienna: Herder, 1966), 2: 324–28.

11. Proclus, *The Elements of Theology: A Revised Text*, trans. E. R. Dodds (Oxford: Clarendon, 1963), prop. 23, pp. 27–29.

12. Damascius, *Aporiai kai lyseis*, I, 5, in *Traité des premiers principes*, vol. 1: *De l'ineffable et de l'un*, ed. Leendert Gerrit Westernink, trans. Joseph Combès (Paris: Les Belles Lettres, 1986), pp. 10–11. [My translation from the Greek.—Ed.]

13. Friedrich Hölderlin, "Patmos," strophe 10, in *Hölderlin: Selected Verse*, ed. and trans. Michael Hamburger (London: Anvil, 1986), p. 199.

14. Jean-Luc Nancy, *Le discours de la syncope* (Paris: Aubier-Flammarion, 1976), pp. 1–7.

15. Friedrich Hölderlin, *Essays and Letters on Theory*, trans. and ed. Thomas Pfau (Albany: State University of New York Press, 1988), p. 37.

16. Ibid., p. 38.

17. Isaak von Sinclair, *Philosophical Notes*, published in Hannelore Hegel, *Isaak von Sinclair zwischen Fichte, Hölderlin und Hegel* (Frankfurt am Main: Klostermann, 1971), pp. 268–69.

18. Ibid., pp. 273–74.

19. Hölderlin, *Essays and Letters on Theory*, p. 101.

20. Paul Celan, *Gesammelte Werke*, ed. Beda Allemann and Stefan Reichard with Rolf Bücher (Frankfurt am Main: Suhrkamp, 1983), 3: 181.

§8 *Se

1. Georg Wilhelm Friedrich Hegel, *Hegel's Science of Logic*, trans. A. V. Miller (New York: Humanities Press, 1976), p. 777; the original is G. W. F. Hegel, *Wissenschaft der Logik*, in *Werke in zwanzig Bänden* (Frankfurt am Main: Suhrkamp, 1970), 6: 490.

2. Georg Wilhelm Friedrich Hegel, *The Difference Between Fichte's and Schelling's System of Philosophy*, trans. H. S. Harris (Albany: State University of New York, 1977), p. 89; the original is in G. W. F. Hegel, *Die Differenz des Fichte'schen und Schelling'schen Systems der Philosophie*, in *Werke in zwanzig Bänden*, 2: 30.

3. Georg Wilhelm Friedrich Hegel, *Phenomenology of Spirit*, trans. A. V. Miller (Oxford: Oxford University Press, 1977), p. 488; the original is G. W. F. Hegel, *Die Phänomenologie des Geistes*, in *Werke in zwanzig Bänden*, 3: 585.

4. Hegel, *Difference Between Fichte's and Schelling's System*, pp. 106–7; original in Hegel, *Die Differenz des Fichte'schen und Schelling'schen Systems*, p. 25.

5. Hegel, *Phenomenology of Spirit*, pp. 487–88; original in Hegel, *Die Phänomenologie des Geistes*, pp. 524–25.

6. Georg Wilhelm Friedrich Hegel, *Jensener Logik, Metaphysik und Naturphilosophie*, ed. Georg Lasson (Leipzig: Felix Meiner, 1923), pp. 204–6.

7. Hegel, *Phenomenology of Spirit*, p. 490; original in Hegel, *Die Phänomenologie des Geistes*, p. 588.

8. Ibid., English p. 492; original p. 590.

9. *Hegel's Science of Logic*, p. 842; original in Hegel, *Wissenschaft der Logik*, p. 571.

10. Hegel, *Phenomenology of Spirit*, p. 492; original in Hegel, *Die Phänomenologie des Geistes*, p. 590.

11. Ibid., English and original.

12. *Hegel's Science of Logic*, p. 825; original in Hegel, *Wissenschaft der Logik*, p. 550.

13. Ibid., English p. 843; original p. 573.

14. Martin Heidegger, *On Time and Being*, trans. Joan Stambaugh (New York: Harper and Row, 1972), p. 49; the original is in Martin Heidegger, *Zur Sache des Denkens* (Tübingen: Niemeyer, 1969), p. 53.

15. Martin Heidegger, *On the Way to Language*, trans. Peter D. Hertz (New York: Harper and Row, 1971), p. 54; the original is in Martin Heidegger, *Gesamtausgabe*, vol. 12: *Unterwegs zur Sprache* (Frankfurt am Main: Klostermann, 1985), p. 146.

16. Heidegger, *On Time and Being*, p. 19; original in Heidegger, *Zur Sache des Denkens*, p. 20.

17. Martin Heidegger, *Identity and Difference*, trans. Joan Stambaugh (New York: Harper and Row, 1969), p. 37; the original is in Martin Heidegger, *Identität und Differenz* (Pfullingen: Neske, 1957), p. 26.

18. Heidegger, *On Time and Being*, p. 54; original in Heidegger, *Zur Sache des Denkens*, p. 58.

19. Ibid., English pp. 40–41; original p. 44.

20. Ibid., English p. 54; original p. 58.

21. Heidegger, *Identity and Difference*, p. 37; original in Heidegger, *Identität und Differenz*, p. 26.

22. [The Italian word *assuefazione*, like the corresponding English word "assuefaction," contains the pronoun *suo*, which derives from the reflexive **se*. Agamben's division of the word by hyphens is meant to emphasize this derivation.—Ed.]

23. Martin Heidegger, *Hegel's Phenomenology of Spirit*, trans. Parvis Emad and Kenneth Maly (Bloomington: Indiana University Press, 1988), p. 149; the original is in Martin Heidegger, *Gesamtausgabe*, vol. 32: *Hegels Phänomenologie des Geistes* (Frankfurt am Main: Klostermann, 1980), p. 216.

24. Heidegger, *On the Way to Language*, p. 130; original in Heidegger, *Unterwegs zur Sprache*, p. 249.

25. Heidegger, *Identity and Difference*, p. 47; original in Heidegger, *Identität und Differenz*, p. 37.

26. Martin Heidegger, *Basic Writings*, ed. David Farrell Krell (New York: Harper Collins, 1977), p. 199; the original is in *Gesamtausgabe*, vol. 9: *Wegmarken* (Frankfurt am Main: Klostermann, 1976), p. 319.

27. Heidegger, *On the Way to Language*, p. 133; original in Heidegger, *Unterwegs zur Sprache*, p. 253.

28. Hegel, *Phenomenology of Spirit*, p. 491; original in Hegel, *Die Phänomenologie des Geistes*, p. 588.

29. Martin Heidegger, *Being and Time*, trans. John Macquarrie and Edward Robinson (New York: Harper and Row, 1962), pp. 41–49; the original is in *Sein und Zeit* (Tübingen: Niemeyer, 1986), pp. 19–26.

30. Hegel, *Phenomenology of Spirit*, p. 490; original in Hegel, *Die Phänomenologie des Geistes*, p. 589.

§9 Benjamin and the Demonic

1. Walter Benjamin, "Agesilaus Santander," in Gershom Scholem, *On Jews and Judaism in Crisis: Selected Essays*, ed. Werner J. Dannhauser (New York: Schocken, 1976), p. 208. Benjamin's text appears in English in Scholem's chapter "Walter Benjamin and His Angel." All page citations in the body of my chapter refer to this edition of Benjamin's and Scholem's works.

2. Walter Benjamin, *Gesammelte Schriften*, ed. Rolf Tiedemann and Hermann Schweppenhäuser (Frankfurt am Main: Suhrkamp, 1974–89), vol. 2, pt. 1, p. 313.

3. *The Correspondence of Walter Benjamin, 1910–1940*, ed. Gershom Scholem and Theodor W. Adorno, trans. Manfred R. Jacobson and Evelyn M. Jacobson (Chicago: The University of Chicago Press, 1994), p. 612; the original is in Walter Benjamin, *Briefe*, ed. Gershom Scholem and Theodor W. Adorno (Frankfurt am Main: Suhrkamp, 1966), 2: 825.

4. I considered the prehistory of this iconographical type in Giorgio Agamben, *Stanze: La parola e il fantasma nella cultura occidentale* (Turin: Einaudi, 1977), pp. 142–44; translated as *Stanzas: Word and Phantasm in Western Culture*, trans. Ronald Martinez (Minneapolis: University of Minnesota Press, 1993), pp. 119–21.

5. Walter Benjamin, *The Origin of the German Tragic Drama*, trans. John Osborne (London: Verso, 1977), p. 226; the original is in Benjamin, *Gesammelte Schriften*, vol. 1, pt. 1, p. 399.

6. Benjamin, *Gesammelte Schriften*, vol. 2, pt. 3, p. 1112.

7. Walter Benjamin, *Reflections: Essays, Aphorisms, Autobiographical Writings*, ed. Peter Demetz, trans. Edmund Jephcott (New York: Schocken, 1978), pp. 272–73; the original is in Benjamin, *Gesammelte Schriften*, vol. 2, pt. 1, p. 367.

8. Moses of Leon, *Zohar*, quoted in Gershom Scholem, *On the Mystical Shape of the Godhead: Basic Concepts in the Kabbalah*, trans. Joachim Neugroschel (New York: Schocken, 1991), p. 186.

9. From this perspective, it is possible to discern the full meaning of the fact that Benjamin had a "secret name," "Benedix Schönflies," as Werner Fuld notes in his *Walter Benjamin zwischen den Stühlen: Eine Biographie* (Frankfurt am Main: Fischer, 1979). The two parts of the secret name would correspond precisely to the two faces and to the two names of the saving Shechinah angel. I do not know if it has been noted that the name Schönflies (which was Benjamin's mother's last name) is evoked by Benjamin as a name of one of the oceanids, Calliroe, in a passage of his essay on Goethe's *Elective Affinities* concerning Ottilie's beauty. See Benjamin, *Gesammelte Schriften*, vol. 1, pt. 1, p. 183.

10. Cf. Gershom Scholem, "*Shekhina*: The Feminine Element in Divinity," in *On the Mystical Shape of the Godhead*, pp. 140–96.

11. Benjamin, *Reflections*, pp. 312–13; original in Benjamin, *Gesammelte Schriften*, vol. 2, pt. 1, p. 204.

12. *Zohar*, quoted in Scholem, *On the Mystical Shape of the Godhead*, pp. 251–73.

13. Ibid., p. 263.

14. *Shushan Sodoth*, quoted in Scholem, *On the Mystical Shape of the Godhead*, p. 253.

15. Isaac Cohen, quoted ibid., p. 259.

16. Texts quoted in Henri Corbin, *En Islam iranien* (Paris: Gallimard, 1971), 2: 294–322.

17. Ibid., p. 322.

18. Benjamin, *Reflections*, p. 307; original in Benjamin, *Gesammelte Schriften*, vol. 2, pt. 1, p. 174.

19. Ibid., English p. 254; original p. 349.

20. Ibid., English p. 255; original p. 350.

21. Benjamin, *Gesammelte Schriften*, vol. 2, pt. 3, p. 1100.

22. Gershom Scholem, *On the Kabbalah and Its Symbolism*, trans. Ralph Manheim (New York: Schocken, 1996), p. 155.

23. Benjamin, *Reflections*, p. 250; original in Benjamin, *Gesammelte Schriften*, vol. 2, pt. 1, p. 345.

24. Ibid., English p. 259; original p. 354.

25. Ibid., English p. 273; original p. 367.

26. Benjamin, *Gesammelte Schriften*, vol. 2, pt. 3, p. 1107.

27. Benjamin, *Reflections*, p. 272; original in Benjamin, *Gesammelte Schriften*, vol. 2, pt. 1, p. 366.

28. Walter Benjamin, *Illuminations*, ed. Hannah Arendt, trans. Harry Zohn (New York: Schocken, 1968), pp. 253–54; the original is in Benjamin, *Gesammelte Schriften*, vol. 1, pt. 2, pp. 693–94.

29. Ibid., English p. 254; original p. 694.

30. Benjamin, *Gesammelte Schriften*, vol. 1, 3, p. 1246.

31. Benjamin, *Illuminations*, p. 262; original in Benjamin, *Gesammelte Schriften*, vol. 1, pt. 2, p. 702.

32. Benjamin, *Gesammelte Schriften*, vol. 1, pt. 3, p. 1242.

33. Benjamin, *Gesammelte Schriften*, vol. 2, pt. 3, p. 1230.

34. Walter Benjamin, *One-Way Street and Other Writings*, trans. Edmund Jephcott and Kingsley Shorter (London: Verso, 1979), p. 361; the original is in *Gesammelte Schriften*, vol. 2, pt. 2, p. 478.

35. *Correspondence of Walter Benjamin, 1910–1940*, p. 565; original in Benjamin, *Briefe*, 2: 763.

36. Ibid., English and original.

37. Benjamin, *Illuminations*, p. 140; original in Benjamin, *Gesammelte Schriften*, vol. 2, pt. 2, p. 438.

38. Benjamin, *Reflections*, pp. 312–13; original in Benjamin, *Gesammelte Schriften*, vol. 2, pt. 1, p. 204.

39. Benjamin, *Gesammelte Schriften*, vol. 1, pt. 3, p. 1153.

40. Ibid., p. 1152.

41. *Correspondence of Walter Benjamin, 1910–1940*, p. 549; original in Benjamin, *Briefe*, 2: 742.

42. Benjamin, *Origin*, p. 45; original in Benjamin, *Gesammelte Schriften*, vol. 1, pt. 1, p. 226.

43. Ibid., English p. 47; original p. 228.

44. Ibid., English p. 46; original p. 227.

45. Benjamin, *Gesammelte Schriften*, vol. 1, pt. 3, p. 1245.

46. Ibid., p. 1233.

47. Benjamin, *Illuminations*, p. 255; original in Benjamin, *Gesammelte Schriften*, vol. 1, pt. 2, p. 682.

48. Ibid., original p. 682.

49. Benjamin, *Gesammelte Schriften*, vol. 1, pt. 3, p. 1238.

50. Benjamin, *Gesammelte Schriften*, vol. 2, pt. 3, p. 1064.

51. Benjamin, *Gesammelte Schriften*, vol. 4, pt. 1, p. 438.

§10 *The Messiah and the Sovereign*

1. Walter Benjamin, *Illuminations*, ed. Hannah Arendt, trans. Harry Zohn (New York: Schocken, 1968), p. 257; the original is in Walter Benjamin, *Gesammelte Schriften*, ed. Rolf Tiedemann and Hermann Schweppenhäuser (Frankfurt am Main: Suhrkamp, 1974–89), vol. 1, pt. 2, p. 697.

2. Benjamin, *Gesammelte Schriften*, vol. 1, pt. 3, p. 1245.

3. Carl Schmitt, *Political Theology: Four Chapters on the Concept of Sovereignty*, trans. George Schwab (Cambridge, Mass.: MIT Press, 1985), p. 15; the original is in Carl Schmitt, *Politische Theologie, Vier Kapiteln zur Lehre von der Souveränität* (Munich-Leipzig: Duncker and Humbolt, 1922), p. 22.

4. Georges Vajda's French translation of this essay was first published as "La signification de la Loi dans la mystique juive" in *Diogène* 14–15 (1956); this version now appears in Gershom Scholem, *Le nom et les symboles de Dieu dans la mystique juive* (Paris: Cerf, 1988). It subsequently appeared in German, with certain changes, as the second chapter of Scholem's *Über die Kabbalah und ihre Symbolik* (Zurich: Rhein Verlag, 1960). An English translation of this text can be found in Gershom Scholem, *On the Kabbalah and Its Symbolism*, trans. Ralph Manheim (New York: Schocken, 1996), pp. 32–86.

5. Gershom Scholem, "Towards an Understanding of the Messianic Idea in Judaism," in *The Messianic Idea in Judaism and Other Essays on Jewish Spirituality* (New York: Schocken, 1971), pp. 23–24; the original is in Gershom Scholem, "Zur Verständnis der messianischen Idee im Judentum," in *Judaica I* (Frankfurt am Main: Suhrkamp, 1963), pp. 47–50.

6. Moses Cordovero, *Shi'ur Komah*, quoted in Scholem, *On the Kabbalah and Its Symbolism*, p. 71.

7. Rabbi Eliahu Cohen Itamary, quoted ibid., p. 74.

8. Rabbi Pinhas, quoted ibid., p. 76.

9. Scholem, "Messianic Idea in Judaism," p. 35; original in Scholem, "Messianischen Idee im Judentum," pp. 73–74.

10. Joseph Klausner, *The Messianic Idea in Israel, from Its Beginnings to the Completion of the Mishnah*, ed. and trans. W. F. Stinespring (London: Allen and Unwin, 1956), pp. 445–46.

11. Siegmund Mowinckel, *He That Cometh: The Messianic Concept in the Old Testament and Later Judaism*, trans. G. W. Anderson (New York: Abingdon, 1956), p. 277.

12. Furio Jesi, *Lettura del "Bateau ivre" di Rimbaud* (Macerata: Quodlibet, 1996), p. 29.

13. *The Correspondence of Walter Benjamin and Gershom Scholem, 1932–1940*, ed. Gershom Scholem, trans. Gary Smith and Andre Lefevre (Cambridge, Mass.: Harvard University Press, 1992), p. 142; the original is in Walter Benjamin and Gershom Scholem, *Briefwechsel 1933–1940*, ed. Gershom Scholem (Frankfurt am Main: Suhrkamp, 1985), p. 175.

14. Ibid., English p. 147; original p. 180.

15. Ibid., English p. 135; original p. 167.

16. Jacques Derrida, "Before the Law," in *Acts of Literature*, ed. Derek Attridge (London: Routledge, 1992), p. 206; the original is Jacques Derrida, "Préjugés," in *Spiegel und Gleichnis, Festschrift für Jacob Taubes*, ed. N. W. Bolz and W. Hübner (Würzburg: Königshausen und Neumann, 1983), p. 356.

17. Massimo Cacciari, *Icone della legge* (Milan: Adelphi, 1985), p. 69.

18. Kurt Weinberg, *Kafkas Dichtungen: Die Travestien des Mythos* (Bern: Francke, 1963), pp. 130–31.

19. Derrida, "Before the Law," p. 210; original in Derrida, "Préjugés," p. 359.

§11 *On Potentiality*

1. Aristotle, *De anima*, 417 a 2–5; the Greek text is in *Aristotle in Twenty-Three Volumes*, vol. 8: *On the Soul, Parva Naturalia, On Breath*, trans. W. S. Hett (Cambridge, Mass.: Harvard University Press, 1986), p. 94.

2. Ibid., 425 b 15–25; p. 146.

3. Ibid., 417 b 2–16; p. 98.

§12 *The Passion of Facticity*

1. W. Koepps, *Merimna und Agape, Seeberg Festschrift* (1929).

2. Ludwig Binswanger, *Grundformen und Erkenntnis menschlichen Daseins* (Zurich: M. Niehans, 1942).

3. Karl Jaspers, *Notizen zu Martin Heidegger* (Munich: Piper, 1978), p. 34.

4. Karl Löwith, "Phänomenologische Ontologie und protestantische Theologie," in Otto Pöggeler, ed., *Heidegger: Perspektiven zur Deutung seines Werkes* (Köln: Kiepenheuer and Witsch, 1970), p. 76.

5. See Elisabeth Young-Bruehl, *Hannah Arendt: For the Love of the World* (New Haven, Conn.: Yale University Press, 1984), p. 247.

6. Martin Heidegger, *Being and Time*, trans. John Macquarrie and Edward Robinson (New York: Harper and Row, 1962), p. 492; the original is in Martin Heidegger, *Sein und Zeit* (Tübingen: Niemeyer, 1928), p. 139.

7. Martin Heidegger, *The Metaphysical Foundations of Logic*, trans. Michael Heim (Bloomington: Indiana University Press, 1984), p. 134; the original is in Martin Heidegger, *Gesamtausgabe*, vol. 26: *Metaphysische Anfangsgründe der Logik im Ausgang von Leibniz* (Frankfurt am Main: Klostermann, 1978), p. 169.

8. Ibid., English pp. 130–31; original pp. 163–64.

9. Heidegger, *Being and Time*, p. 88; original in Heidegger, *Sein und Zeit*, p. 61.

10. Oskar Becker, "Mathematische Existenz, Untersuchung zur Logik und Ontologie mathematischer Phänomene," *Jahrbuch für Philosophie und Phänomenologische Forschung* 7 (1927): 621.

11. In Heidegger's *Gesamtausgabe* (vol. 62), the title of the course appears as "Ontologie: Phänomenologische Hermeneutik der Faktizität." According to the note on p. 72 of *Sein und Zeit* (*Being and Time*, p. 490), Heidegger was already concerned with "the hermeneutics of facticity" in his 1919–20 winter semester lectures.

12. See the entry under *facticius* in the *Thesaurus linguae latinae* and the entry under *factio* in Ernout-Meillet's etymological dictionary.

13. Otto Pöggeler, *Der Denkweg Martin Heideggers* (Pfullingen: Neske, 1963), pp. 36–45. See also Oskar Becker, *Dasein und Dawesen* (Pfullingen: Neske, 1963), and K. Lehmann, "Christliche Geschichtserfahrung und ontologische Frage beim jungen Heidegger," in Pöggeler, ed., *Heidegger: Perspektiven*, pp. 140–68. [Since the first publication of the present essay, Heidegger's 1921 lecture course has been published in Heidegger, *Gesamtausgabe*, vol. 60: *Phänomenologie des religiösen Lebens* (Frankfurt am Main: Klostermann, 1995), pp. 160–299, under the title "Augustinus und der Neuplatonismus."—Ed.]

14. The Augustinian opposition between *uti* (using something with a view to other ends) and *frui* (enjoying something for itself) is important for the prehistory of the distinction between *Vorhandenheit*, "present-at-handness," and

Zuhandenheit, "ready-to-handness," in Heidegger's *Being and Time.* As we will see, Dasein's facticity is opposed both to *Vorhandenheit* and to *Zuhandenheit* and therefore cannot properly speaking be the object of either a *frui* or an *uti.*

15. Saint Augustine, *Confessions,* trans. R. S. Pine-Coffin (London: Penguin Books, 1961), pp. 229–30.

16. Martin Heidegger, *Gesamtausgabe,* vol. 61: *Phänomenologische Interpretationen zu Aristoteles: Einführung in die phänomenologische Forschung* (Frankfurt am Main: Klostermann, 1985), p. 99.

17. See the observations in H. Tietjen, "Philosophie und Faktizität," *Heidegger Studies* 2 (1986).

18. Heidegger, *Phänomenologische Interpretationen zu Aristoteles,* p. 130.

19. Ibid., p. 131.

20. Heidegger, "Problem der Faktizität—'kinesis'-Problem" (Problem of facticity, *kinesis*-problem), ibid., p. 117. If one recalls the fundamental role that *kinesis,* according to Heidegger, played in Aristotle's thought (in his seminars at Le Thor, Heidegger still spoke of *kinesis* as the fundamental experience of Aristotle's thought), one can also evaluate the central place of facticity in the thought of the early Heidegger.

21. Heidegger, *Being and Time,* p. 82; original in Heidegger, *Sein und Zeit,* pp. 55–56.

22. Ibid., English p. 174; original pp. 134–46.

23. Ibid., English p. 175; original p. 136.

24. The analogy is, of course, purely formal. But the fact that Heideggerian ontology coincides with the territory of psychology is important for its position in the history of the "question of Being" (*Seinsfrage*).

25. Heidegger, *Metaphysical Foundations of Logic,* p. 136; original in Heidegger, *Metaphysische Anfangsgründe der Logik,* p. 171.

26. The word *Weise* (which derives from the same root as the German *wissen* and the Latin *videre*) must be considered as a *terminus technicus* of Heidegger's thought. In his 1921–22 winter lectures, Heidegger plays on all the possible meanings of the verb *weisen* and its derivations: "Leben bekommt jeweils eine Grundweisung und es wächst in eine solche hinein. . . . Bezugssinn je in einer Weise ist in sich ein Weisen und hat in sich eine Weisung, die das Leben sich gibt, die es erfährt: Unterweisung." Heidegger, *Phänomenologische Interpretationen zu Aristoteles,* p. 98.

27. Heidegger, *Being and Time,* p. 67; original in Heidegger, *Sein und Zeit,* p. 42.

28. In the "Letter on Humanism," Heidegger explicitly refutes this interpretation of the *essentia / existentia* relation: "It would be the ultimate error if one wished to explain the sentence about man's ek-sistent essence as if it were the secularized transference to human beings of a thought that Christian theology

expresses about God (*Deus est suum esse*); for ek-sistence is not the realization of an essence nor does ek-sistence itself even effect and posit what is essential" (in Martin Heidegger, *Basic Writings*, ed. David Farrell Krell [New York: Harper San Francisco, 1977], p. 207; the original is in Martin Heidegger, *Gesamtausgabe*, vol. 9: *Wegmarken* [Frankfurt am Main: Klostermann, 1976], pp. 158–59). Another passage in the same text shows that the relation between existence and essence remained a fundamental question in Heidegger's thought even after *Being and Time*. "In *Being and Time* no statement about the relation of *essentia* and *existentia* can yet be expressed since there it is still a question of preparing something precursory" (*Basic Writings*, p. 209; original in *Wegmarken*, p. 329).

29. A genealogy of the contraction of *essentia* and *existentia* effected by Heidegger would show that this relation has often been conceived in the history of philosophy as something far more complex than a simple opposition. Without discussing Plato (who in the Seventh Letter explicitly states that *on* and *poion* are indissociable), we may consider Aristotle's *ti en einai* from the same perspective. Moreover, the notion of Stoic substance, *idios poion*, implies precisely the paradox of a "being-such" (*poion*) that would be proper. Victor Goldschmidt thus shows that the "manners of Being" (*pos ekhein*) do not constitute an extrinsic determination of substance but instead reveal substance and exemplify it (they "do its gymnastics," according to Epictetus's beautiful image). The relation between Spinoza's definition of *causa sui* (*cuius essentia involvit existentiam*) and Heidegger's determination of Dasein (*das Wesen des Daseins liegt in seiner Existenz*) remains to be considered.

30. The observation is L. Amoroso's; see his "La *Lichtung* di Heidegger come lucus a non lucendo," in *Il pensiero debole*, ed. Gianni Vattimo and Pier Aldo Rovatti (Milan: Feltrinelli, 1983), pp. 137–63.

31. See Jacques Derrida, "Geschlecht," in *Martin Heidegger: Cahiers de l'Herne* (Paris: Éditions de l'Herne, 1983), pp. 571–96.

32. Heidegger, *Metaphysical Foundations of Logic*, p. 137; original in Heidegger, *Metaphysische Anfangsgründe der Logik*, p. 173. In the same text, Heidegger relates Dasein's facticity to its spatiality (*Räumlichkeit*). If one considers that the word *Streuung* derives from the same root as the Latin *sternere* (*stratum*), which refers to extension and horizontality, it is possible to see in this *ursprüngliche Streuung* one of the reasons for the irreducibility of Dasein's spatiality to its temporality, which is affirmed at the end of "Zeit und Sein" ("On Time and Being").

33. One thus reads "Faitisse estoit et avenante / je ne sais femme plus plaisante," in the *Romance of the Rose*; "voiz comme elles se chaucent bien et faitissement," in Jean de Meun; "votre gens corps votre beauté faictisse," in Baudes; "ils ont doubz regard et beaulté / et jeunesse et faitischeté," in Gaces. But the true meaning of the word *faitis* can best be seen in Villon's text, in which

he writes, "Hanches charnues, / eslevées, propres, faictisses / à tenir amoureuses lisses."

34. The word *Urfetischismus* is obviously to be taken in an ontological, and not a psychological, sense. It is because facticity originally belongs to Dasein that it can encounter something like a fetish in the strict sense of the term. On the status of the fetish in §17 of *Being and Time*, see Werner Hamacher's important observations in "Peut-être la question," in *Les fins de l'homme: A partir du travail de Jacques Derrida* (Paris: Galilée, 1981), pp. 353–54.

35. "Dasein exists factically. We shall inquire whether existentiality and facticity have an ontological unity, or whether facticity belongs essentially to existentiality" (Heidegger, *Being and Time*, p. 225); "Das Dasein existiert faktisch. Gefragt wird nach der ontologischen Einheit von Existentialität und Faktizität, bzw. der wesenhaften Zugehörigkeit dieser zu jener" (Heidegger, *Sein und Zeit*, p. 181).

36. Ibid., English p. 264; original p. 222.

37. Ibid., English p. 224; original p. 179.

38. Ibid., English p. 345; original p. 299.

39. Martin Heidegger, *Nietzsche: The Will to Power as Art*, trans. David Farrell Krell, p. 45; the original is in Martin Heidegger, *Nietzsche*, vol. 1 (Pfullingen: Neske, 1961), p. 55.

40. Ibid., English p. 47; original p. 58.

41. Ibid., English pp. 47–48; original pp. 58–59.

42. Heidegger, *Basic Writings*, p. 238; original in *Wegmarken*, pp. 360–61.

43. Ibid., English p. 196; original pp. 316–17.

44. Martin Heidegger, *The Essence of Reasons* (Evanston, Ill.: Northwestern University Press, 1969), p. 115; original in *Wegmarken*, pp. 168–69.

45. Ibid., English p. 129; original p. 174.

46. Heidegger, *Metaphysical Foundations of Logic*, pp. 215–16; original in Heidegger, *Metaphysische Anfangsgründe der Logik*, pp. 279–80.

47. Martin Heidegger, *Aristotle's Metaphysics Omega 1–3*, trans. Walter Brogan and Peter Warnek (Bloomington: Indiana University Press, 1995), p. 94; the original is in Martin Heidegger, *Gesamtausgabe*, vol. 33: *Aristoteles; Metaphysik Theta 1–3: Vom Wesen und Wirklichkeit der Kraft* (Frankfurt am Main: Klostermann, 1981), p. 114.

48. Heidegger, *Essence of Reasons*, pp. 129–31; original in Heidegger, *Wegmarken*, p. 175.

49. Martin Heidegger, *On Time and Being*, trans. Joan Stambaugh (New York: Harper and Row, 1972), p. 41; the original is in Martin Heidegger, *Zur Sache des Denkens* (Tübingen: Niemeyer, 1969), p. 44.

50. Ibid., English p. 30; original p. 32. The thought expressed here is so disconcerting that the English, French, and Italian translators did not want to admit what is, nevertheless, clear: namely, that the word *entwachen* in this context

cannot mean the same thing as *erwachen*. In this passage, Heidegger establishes an opposition that is perfectly symmetrical with that between *Enteignis* and *Ereignis*.

51. Ibid., English p. 41; original p. 44.

52. Ibid.

53. Martin Heidegger, *Discourse on Thinking*, trans. John N. Anderson and E. Hans Freund (New York: Harper and Row, 1966), p. 56; the original is in Martin Heidegger, *Gelassenheit* (Pfullingen: Neske, 1959), p. 24.

54. Heidegger, *On Time and Being*, p. 24; original in Heidegger, *Zur Sache des Denkens*, p. 25.

§13 *Pardes*

1. Jacques Derrida, *Margins of Philosophy*, trans. Alan Bass (Chicago: University of Chicago Press, 1982), pp. 26–27; the original is in Jacques Derrida, *Marges de la philosophie* (Paris: Éditions de Minuit, 1972), p. 28.

2. Jacques Derrida, *Positions*, trans. Alan Bass (Chicago: University of Chicago Press, 1981), pp. 42–43, 46; the original is in Jacques Derrida, *Positions* (Paris: Éditions de Minuit, 1972), pp. 58–72.

3. Derrida, *Margins of Philosophy*, pp. 65–66; original in Derrida, *Marges de la philosophie*, pp. 75–77.

4. Jacques Derrida, *Of Grammatology*, trans. Gayatri Chakravorti Spivak (Baltimore: Johns Hopkins University Press, 1976), p. 61; the original is in Jacques Derrida, *De la grammatologie* (Paris: Minuit, 1967), p. 90.

5. Philippe de Rouilhan, *Frege: Les paradoxes de la représentation* (Paris: Minuit, 1988).

6. *The Wittgenstein Reader*, ed. Anthony Kenny (London: Blackwell, 1994), p. 14; the original is in Ludwig Wittgenstein, *Tractatus logico-philosophicus*, prop. 4.121, in his *Werkausgabe*, vol. 1 (Frankfurt am Main: Suhrkamp, 1984), p. 33; and Jean-Claude Milner, *Introduction à une science du langage* (Paris: Seuil, 1990), p. 332.

7. *Aristotle in Twenty-Three Volumes*, vol. 8: *On the Soul, Parva Naturalia, On Breath*, trans. W. S. Hett (Cambridge, Mass.: Harvard University Press, 1986), pp. 166–67.

8. Plotinus, *The Enneads*, trans. Stephen MacKenna (London: Penguin Books, 1991), pp. 99–100.

§14 *Absolute Immanence*

1. This text has been reprinted in Michel Foucault, *Dits et écrits* (Paris: Gallimard, 1994), 4: 763.

2. Ibid., p. 774.

3. Ibid., p. 776.

4. Theodor Wiesengrund Adorno, "Satzzeichen," *Akzente* 6 (1956).

5. Gilles Deleuze and Claire Parnet, *Dialogues* (Paris: Flammarion, 1977), p. 73.

6. J. H. Masmejan, *Traité de la ponctuation* (Paris, 1781).

7. Gilles Deleuze, *Essays Critical and Clinical,* trans. Daniel W. Smith and Michael A. Greco (Minneapolis: University of Minnesota Press, 1997), p. 112; the original is in Gilles Deleuze, *Critique et Clinique* (Paris: Éditions de Minuit, 1993), p. 141.

8. Gilles Deleuze, "Immanence: Une vie ... ," *Philosophie* 47 (1995): 6.

9. Ibid.

10. Ibid., p. 4.

11. Gilles Deleuze, *The Logic of Sense*, trans. Mark Lester with Charles Stivale, ed. Constantin V. Boundas (New York: Columbia University Press, 1990), p. 98; the original is in Gilles Deleuze, *Logique du sens* (Paris: Minuit, 1973), p. 132.

12. Ibid., English p. 105; original p. 143.

13. The history of the relations between Heidegger and Deleuze—through Blanchot, for example, and the often unacknowledged Heideggerian dimension of contemporary French philosophy—remains to be written. In any case, however, it is certain that the Heidegger of Deleuze is altogether different from the Heidegger of Lévinas and Derrida.

14. Gilles Deleuze, *Expressionism in Philosophy*, trans. Martin Joughin (New York: Zone Books, 1990), p. 67; the original is in Gilles Deleuze, *Spinoza et le problème de l'expression* (Paris: Éditions de Minuit, 1986), p. 58.

15. Ibid., English p. 172; original p. 156.

16. Ibid., English p. 180; original p. 164.

17. Gilles Deleuze and Félix Guattari, *What Is Philosophy?* trans. Hugh Tomlinson and Graham Burchell (New York: Columbia University Press, 1994), p. 45; the original is in Gilles Deleuze and Félix Guattari, *Qu' est-ce-que la philosophie?* (Paris: Minuit, 1991), p. 47.

18. Ibid., English p. 46–47; original pp. 48–49.

19. Ibid., English p. 40; original p. 40.

20. Ibid., English pp. 59–60; original p. 59.

21. Deleuze, "Immanence: Une vie ... ," p. 4.

22. Ibid., p. 5.

23. Charles Dickens, *Our Mutual Friend* (Oxford: Oxford University Press, 1989), p. 443.

24. Ibid., pp. 444–45.

25. Ibid., pp. 446–47.

26. Deleuze, "Immanence: Une vie ... ," p. 5.

27. Pierre Maine de Biran, *Mémoire sur la décomposition de la pensée*, in *Œuvres*, vol. 3 (Paris: Vrin, 1988), p. 388.

28. Ibid., p. 370.

29. Deleuze, "Immanence: Une vie ... ," p. 5.

30. Ibid., p. 6.

31. Aristotle, *De anima*, 413 a 20–b 10, in *Aristotle in Twenty-Three Volumes*, vol. 8: *On the Soul, Parva Naturalia, On Breath*, trans. W. S. Hett (Cambridge, Mass.: Harvard University Press, 1986), pp. 74–75.

32. Michel Foucault, *The History of Sexuality, Volume I: An Introduction*, trans. Robert Hurley (New York: Random House, 1978), p. 144–45; the original is in *La volonté de savoir* (Paris: Gallimard, 1976), pp. 190–91.

33. Gilles Deleuze, *Foucault*, trans. Séan Hand (Minneapolis: University of Minnesota Press, 1988), p. 92; the original is in Gilles Deleuze, *Foucault* (Paris: Éditions de Minuit, 1986), p. 95.

34. Deleuze, "Immanence: Une vie ... ," p. 5.

35. Deleuze and Guattari, *What Is Philosophy?* p. 213; original in Deleuze and Guattari, *Qu' est-ce-que la philosophie?* p. 201.

36. Ibid., English p. 342; original p. 342.

37. Deleuze, "Immanence: Une vie ... ," p. 4.

38. Spinoza, *Opera*, ed. Carl Gebhardt (Heidelberg: C. Winter, 1925), 3: 361.

39. Ibid.

40. See Victor Goldschmidt, *Le système stoïcien et l'idée du temps* (Paris: Vrin, 1969), pp. 22–23. Deleuze cites this passage in *Logic of Sense*, p. 147; original in his *Logique du sens*, p. 198.

41. Aristotle, *De anima*, 416 b 12–20. The Greek text is in *Aristotle in Twenty-Three Volumes*, 8: 92.

42. When Aristotle defines the intellect (*nous*) by its capacity to think itself, it is important to remember that he has already considered a self-referential paradigm, as we have seen, in his discussion of nutritive life and its power of self-preservation. In a certain sense, thought's thinking itself has its archetype in nutritive life's self-preservation.

43. Émile Benveniste, *Problems in General Linguistics*, trans. Mary Elizabeth Meek (Coral Gables, Fla.: University of Miami Press, 1971), p. 252; the original is in Émile Benveniste, *Problèmes de linguistique générale*, vol. 1 (Paris: Gallimard, 1966), pp. 292–93.

44. Deleuze, "Immanence: Une vie ... ," p. 6.

45. Harry A. Wolfson, *The Philosophy of Spinoza* (Cambridge, Mass.: Harvard University Press, 1958), p. 325.

46. The term *acquiescentia* is registered in the *Thesaurus* of neither Estienne nor Teubner. As to the ablative construction of *acquiescere* with *in* (in the sense, Estienne specifies, of *acquiescere in re aliqua, aut in aliquo homine, cum quadam*

animi voluptate, quieteque consistere et oblectari in re aliqua, in qua prius in dubio aut solicitudine anima fuisset), it is never used with the reflexive pronoun.

§15 *Bartleby, or On Contingency*

1. A different translation of this passage can be found in *Aristotle's Metaphysics*, trans. Hippocrates G. Apostle (Grinnell, Iowa: The Peripatetic Press, 1979), p. 209.

2. Herman Melville, "Bartleby the Scrivener," in *Billy Budd, Sailor and Other Stories*, ed. Harold Beaver (London: Penguin Books, 1985), p. 73.

3. Ibid., pp. 88–89.

4. Gilles Deleuze, *Essays Critical and Clinical*, trans. Daniel W. Smith and Michael A. Greco (Minneapolis: University of Minnesota Press, 1997), pp. 73–74; the original is in Gilles Deleuze, *Critique et clinique* (Paris: Éditions de Minuit, 1993), p. 95.

5. Diogenes Laertius, *Lives of Eminent Philosophers*, trans. R. D. Hicks, vol. 2 (Cambridge, Mass.: Harvard University Press, 1955), p. 488.

6. Melville, "Bartleby the Scrivener," p. 89.

7. "I' vo come colui ch' è fuor di vita / che pare, a chi lo sguarda, ch' omo / sia fatto di rame o di pietra o di legno / che si conduca solo per maestria."

8. *Aristotle in Twenty-Three Volumes*, vol. 19: *The Nichomachean Ethics*, trans. H. Rackham (Cambridge, Mass.: Harvard University Press, 1982), 1139 b 6–10 (p. 331).

9. Gottfried Wilhelm Leibniz, *Theodicy: Essays on the Goodness of God, the Freedom of Man, and the Origin of Evil*, trans. E. M. Huggard (London: Routledge and Kegan Paul, 1951), p. 372.

10. Friedrich Nietzsche, *Thus Spoke Zarathustra*, trans. Walter Kaufmann (London: Penguin, 1954), p. 139.

11. Melville, "Bartleby the Scrivener," p. 99.

12. Ibid.

Index of Names

MERIDIAN

Crossing Aesthetics

Werner Hamacher, *pleroma—Reading in Hegel*

Serge Leclaire, *Psychoanalyzing*

Serge Leclaire, *A Child Is Being Killed*

Sigmund Freud, *Writings on Art and Literature*

Cornelius Castoriadis, *World in Fragments: Writings on Politics, Society, Psychoanalysis, and the Imagination*

Thomas Keenan, *Fables of Responsibility: Aberrations and Predicaments in Ethics and Politics*

Emmanuel Levinas, *Proper Names*

Alexander García Düttmann, *At Odds with AIDS: Thinking and Talking About a Virus*

Maurice Blanchot, *Friendship*

Jean-Luc Nancy, *The Muses*

Massimo Cacciari, *Posthumous People: Vienna at the Turning Point*

David E. Wellbery, *The Specular Moment: Goethe's Early Lyric and the Beginnings of Romanticism*

Edmond Jabès, *The Little Book of Unsuspected Subversion*

Hans-Jost Frey, *Studies in Poetic Discourse: Mallarmé, Baudelaire, Rimbaud, Hölderlin*

Pierre Bourdieu, *The Rules of Art: Genesis and Structure of the Literary Field*

Nicolas Abraham, *Rhythms: On the Work, Translation, and Psychoanalysis*

Jacques Derrida, *On the Name*

David Wills, *Prosthesis*

Maurice Blanchot, *The Work of Fire*

Jacques Derrida, *Points...: Interviews, 1974–1994*

J. Hillis Miller, *Topographies*

Philippe Lacoue-Labarthe, *Musica Ficta (Figures of Wagner)*

Jacques Derrida, *Aporias*

Emmanuel Levinas, *Outside the Subject*

Jean-François Lyotard, *Lessons on the Analytic Sublime*

Peter Fenves, *"Chatter": Language and History in Kierkegaard*

Jean-Luc Nancy, *The Experience of Freedom*

Jean-Joseph Goux, *Oedipus, Philosopher*

Haun Saussy, *The Problem of a Chinese Aesthetic*

Jean-Luc Nancy, *The Birth to Presence*

Library of Congress Cataloging-in-Publication Data

Agamben, Giorgio, 1942–
    Potentialities : collected essays in philosophy / Giorgio Agamben ; edited and
translated with an introduction by Daniel Heller-Roazen
    p.   cm. — (Meridian: crossing aesthetics)
Includes bibliographical references and index.
ISBN 0-8047-3277-9 (cloth : alk. paper) — ISBN 0-8047-3278-7 (pbk. : alk. paper)
    1. Aesthetics, Modern—20th century. 2. Language and languages—Philosophy. 3.
History—Philosophy. I. Heller-Roazen, Daniel. II. Title. III. Meridian (Stanford,
Calif.)

BH201.A395 1999
195—dc21   99-039449

⊛ This book is printed on acid-free, archival-quality paper.

Original printing 1999
Last figure below indicates year of this printing:
08   07   06   05   04   03   02

Typeset by Robert C. Ehle in 9/11 Adobe Garamond